FLEMING COUNTY, KENTUCKY

BIRTH RECORDS

1852–1853, 1855–1859, 1874–1875, 1878

Frances T. Ingmire

Heritage Books
2025

HERITAGE BOOKS

AN IMPRINT OF HERITAGE BOOKS, INC.

Books, CDs, and more—Worldwide

For our listing of thousands of titles see our website
at
www.HeritageBooks.com

A Facsimile Reprint
Published 2025 by
HERITAGE BOOKS, INC.
Publishing Division
5810 Ruatan Street
Berwyn Heights, MD 20740

— Publisher's Notice —
In reprints such as this, it is often not possible to remove
blemishes from the original. We feel the contents of this
book warrant its reissue despite these blemishes and

International Standard Book Number
Paperbound: 978-0-7884-7760-7

COUNTY Fleming

S Sex
C condition A-alive D-dead

DATE	NAME OF CHILD	S	C	NAME OF FATHER	NAME OF MOTHER	CO.	RESIDENCE
12/28/1852	Henry	M	A	William Crain	Charity	B	All residents Fleming Co.
8/31/1852	Martha Darnall	F	A	Wm. H. Darnall	Evaline Weare	W	near Elizaville
8/28/1852	Jane	F	A	Wm. H. Darnall	Maria	B	near Ellizaville
12/28/1852	Charles	M	A	Sarah Markwell	Martha	M	near Ellizaville
8/26/1852	Dorsey	F	A	W. W. Hitt	Angeline	B	Fleming Co.
12/ 8/1852	Martha Ann Meyers	F	A	Wm. Meyers	Elizabeth --	W	
10/24/1852	Margarett C. Graves	F	A	Charles A. Graves	Mary Jane Benley	W	
11/ 1/1852	Ann	F	A	A. D. Morehead	Lucinda	B	
12/ /1852	Emily	F	A	A. D. Morehead	Judy	B	
12/28/1852	N. Cary H. Turner b. Mount Gilead, Ky.	F	A	Jno. H. Turner	Margaret C. Ross	W	
12/21/1852	John S. Cox b. Flemingsburg, Ky.	M	A	L. B. Cox	Ellen T. Bollen	W	
12/18/1852	Amelia Wirelkeld b. near Elizaville, Ky.	F	A	James Wirelkeld	Ann Meop (Moss ?)	W	
3/25/1852	Jno. Thomas Kincade	M	A	Wm. Kincade	B. W. Hill	W	
12/ /1852	Lukins b. Flemingsburg, Ky.	M	A	Geo. W. Taylor	Mary	M	Flemingsburg,
/ /1852	Mary b. Mount Carmel, Ky.	F	A	S. Robertson	Lucinda	M	
/ /1852	Charlotte b. Mount Carmel, Ky.	F	A	S. Robertson	Mary	B	
6/15/1852	John Johnson b. near Elizaville, Ky.	M	A	Jas. T. Johnson	Eleanor Wilson	W	
9/ 3/1852	Joseph Jackson	M	A	Joseph Jackson	Eliza Swain	W	
1/18/1853	Milton Re. Weakly.	M	A	Charles Bell	Hannah	B	
4/27/1852	Charlotte Mary Huff b. Fairview, Ky.	F	A	Wm. Huff	Elizabeth Stickrod	W	
11/14/1852	Martha E. J. McCarty b. Fairview, Ky.	F	A	David McCarty	- - Cora	W	
11/ 1/1852	Ann b. Mount Carmel, Ky.	F	A	A. D. Morehead	Lucinda	B	
3/17/1852	Lucy Grace Quaintance	F	A	Wm. Quaintance	Patsy Darnatt	W	
1/ /1852	Not named	F	A	A. K, Marshall	Lana	B	
6/ /1852	William	M	A	A. K. Marshall	Hannah	B	

1

COUNTY Fleming

S Sex
C Condition A-Alive D-Dead

DATE	NAME OF CHILD	S	C	NAME OF FATHER	NAME OF MOTHER	CO.	RESIDENCE
11/12/1852	Len P. Faris	F	A	John Faris	Margaret Tolan	W	All residents
3/ 3/1852	Inetta & Allice Re. Twins	F	A	George F. Barnes	Fanny	B	Fleming Co., Ky.
11/ 4/1852	Not named	M	A	Eli Wilson	Mary Bell	W	b. Martha Mills
1/ 6/1852	Not named b. Martha Mills, Ky.	M	A	Leri T. Hicks	Ruth Beam	W	
11/ /1852	Not Named	M	A	John T. Walker	Sarah	B	
8/16/1852	Not named	F	A	Eli Browning	Priscilla Ann Porter	W	
5/ 1/1852	Henry W. Rice b. Pin Hook, Ky.	M	A	Henry A. Rice	Margaret Mears	W	
9/ /1852	Lucy Ellen Rhoden	F	A	Thomas Rhoden	Mary Ann McCall	W	
12/24/1852	John Newman	M	A	Alex Newman	Sarah I. Williams	W	
3/ 9/1852	Margaret J. A. McCall	F	A	Jackson McCall	Dolly Hzsong	W	
5/ /1852	Emily Bett	F	A	Hickison Bett	Martha Ann Tant	W	
9/ 5/1852	George W. Henderson b. Flemingsburg, Ky.	M	A	Wm. Henderson	Eliza Ann McIntire	W	
10/11/1852	Eliza Susan McIntire b. near Flemingsburg, Ky.	F	A	Jas. B. McIntire	Mary Turner	W	
9/20/1852	Albert Thomas Hull b. Pin Hook, Ky.	M	A	Wm. R. Hull	Ann Havens	W	
12/26/1852	No Name b. Sherburne, Ky. (near)	M	A	Edward Moxen	Roda Powel	W	
8/ 6/1852	Manchester Watson b. near Sherburne, Ky.	M	A	Henry Watson	Levina Harmon	W	
4/13/1852	Michael Rigdon b. near Sherburne, Ky.	M	A	Wm. Rigden	Mahida Newman	W	
7/15/1852	Lucinda Williams b. near Sherburne, Ky.	F	A	Alfred Williams	O. Ann Marizey	W	
5/ 2/1852	Benjamin T. Simmers b. Elizaville, Ky.	M	A	Jesse Simmers	Elbert Watton	W	
5/22/1852	William O. Saunders b. near Sherburne, Ky.	M	A	Samuel Sanders	Nancy Buckley	W	
5/ 6/1852	George A. Sanders b. near Sherburne, Ky.	M	A	Jas. A. Sanders	Mary Arnold	W	
4/14/1852	Hester Jane Wilson b. near Sherburne, Ky.	F	A	Daniel Wilson	Martha P. Powel	W	
2/ /1852	Henry Thomas Littleton b. near Sherburne, Ky.	M	A	Geo. W. Littleton	Rhoda Sanders		

COUNTY Fleming

S Sex
C Condition A-Alive D-Dead

DATE	NAME OF CHILD	S	C	NAME OF FATHER	NAME OF MOTHER	CO.	RESIDENCE
7/ 5/1852	No name b. near Sherburne, Ky., Re. Weakly.	F	A	Andrew Poter	Martha A. Wilson	W	All residents Fleming Co., Ky.
11/ 2/1852	Fleming E. Holland b. near Sherburne, Ky.	F	A	Benson Holland	Eliz.(?) Wilson	W	
9/ 9/1852	Wm. Jno. Tally b. near Sherburne, Ky.	M	A	William J. Tally	Elizth. Keel	W	
9/15/1852	John Wm. Rice b. near Sherburne, Ky.	M	A	John Rice	Elizth. Rigdon	W	
12/ 5/1852	No name b. near Sherburne, Ky.	F	A	John B. Johnson	Elizth. Johnson	W	
12/ 6/1852	Nancy Courtney b. Centerville, Ky.	F	A	Wm. F. Courtney	Mary Reeves	W	
10/ 3/1852	Franklin Stickton b. Flemingsburg, Ky.	M	A	Richd. L. Stockton	Isabella Pepper	W	
10/10/1852	John W. Ross b. Flemingsburg, Ky.	M	A	Geo. W. Ross	Nancy Powers	W	
12/20/1852	Susan b. Flemingsburg, Ky.	F	A	Isaac Darnall	Betsy	B	
12/27/1852	John Summers b. Flemingsburg, Ky. (near)	M	A	George Summers	Mary N. Ticklen	W	
2/21/1852	George W. Horton b. near Mt. Gilead	M	A	Geo. W. Horton	Tolitha M. Foxworthy	W	
6/15/1852	Dinah b. near Flemingsburg, Ky.	F	A	Wm. M. Walker	Dinah	B	
12/ 5/1852	Lewis & Frank b. near Flemingsburg, Ky.	M	A	Harriet Trimble	Charlotte	B	
4/ 9/1852	Charles M. Jones b. Elizaville, Ky.	M	A	Jas. M. Jones	Elizabeth Chrisinson	W	
8/ 6/1852	Henry W. Williams b. Blue Lick	M	A	John W. Williams	Eleanor F. Jones	W	
3/ /1852	No name b. near Mouth Fleming, bad health.	F	A	James Stamfield	Sally Stamfield	W	
1/ 9/1852	Susan b. Elizaville, Ky.	F	A	S. B. Allen	Lucy	M	
1/ 3/1852	Lucinda J. Blake b. Mouth of Fleming.	F	A	James Blake	Mary Dolly	W	
12/25/1852	James A. Mitchie b. Mouth of Fleming	M	A	Alfred Mitchel	Amanda Faris	W	

S Sex
C Condition A-Alive D-Dead

COUNTY Fleming

DATE	NAME OF CHILD	S	C	NAME OF FATHER	NAME OF MOTHER	CO.	RESIDENCE
1/ 7/1852	Thos. Fleming Fanow b. Bishops Mills	M	A	John J. Fanow	Joannah Parks	W	All residents Fleming Co., Ky.
5/20/1852	Martha Ann Taylor	F	A	A. R. Taylor	Margaret Stuart	W	
11/ 7/1852	Minerva Ellen Mitchel	F	A	James Mitchel	Rachel M. Jolly	W	
10/ 7/1852	Elvira Bruce b. South Carolina	F	A	James Bruce	Martha A. Johnson	W	
5/ 3/1852	Frances b. Johnsons Creek	F	A	James Bruce	Charity	M	
7/10/1852	Elizabeth b. Johnsons Creek	F	A	Henry Bruce Sr.	Hager	B	
9/18/1852	Henry b. near Elizaville, Ky.	M	A	John J. Rogers	Ellen	B	
7/18/1852	Joseph Samuel Morrison b. near Flemingsburg, Ky.	M	A	John B. Morrison	Mary Littlepohn	W	
8/13/1852	Joshua Givens b. Mt. Carmel	M	A	Moses Givens	Mary B. Rogers	W	
3/10/1852	Harry b. Farrows Creek	M	A	Richd. Soward	Milly	M	
1/13/1852	Harrison b. Farrows Creek	M	A	R. Soward	Mary	B	
4/ 5/1852	Rachel b. Farrows Creek	F	A	R. Soward	Ann	B	
5/ 2/1852	Edmund b. Farrow Creek	M	A	James Ross	Prissilla	B	
8/12/1852	Charles b. Farrows Creek	M	A	Wm. Wallingsford	Marcy	B	
8/12/1852	Eliza Turner b. near Mount Carmel	F	A	Robt. C. Turner	Lydia Magowen	W	
12/ 1/1852	No name b. near Martha Mills.	M	A	M. T. Howe	Nancy	B	
11/ /1852	Julian Weir b. near Flemingsburg, Ky.	F	A	N. H. Weir	Elizth. T. Thompson	W	
10/ /1852	Amanda b. Flemingsburg, Ky.	F	A	James Dudley	Maria	M	
2/14/1852	Juelda James Deaning b. Pine Hook	F	A	Jas. T. Deaning	Elizabeth Jane Thompson	W	
10/ /1852	Margaret b. near Elizaville	F	A	John H. Purdum	Dulonida	B	

4

COUNTY Fleming

S Sex
C Condition A-Alive D-Dead

DATE	NAME OF CHILD	S	C	NAME OF FATHER	NAME OF MOTHER	CO.	RESIDENCE
4/26/1852	Simpson Taylor Berry b. Elizaville	M	A	Wm. H. Berry	Elvira Taylor	W	All residents Fleming Co., Ky.
5/ 8/1852	Mary E. Biddle b. Fleming Creek	F	A	Stephen Biddle	Elizabeth Shockey	W	
1/ 3/1852	Rebecca Randall b. Johnson Creek	F	A	A. J. Randall	Mary A. Summers	W	
6/16/1852	No name b. Poorhouse Fleming Co., Illegitimate	M	A		Nelly Humphries	W	
6/ 5/1852	Austin Berry b. Elizaville, Ky.	M	A	Arthur Berry	Achsah Ficklin Late Anderson	W	
3/13/1852	Frank b. Elizaville, Ky.	M	A	Wm. F. Morgan	Mary	M	
1/ 6/1852	John D. Williams b. Fleming Creek	M	A	Harrison Williams	Frances Dudley	W	
8/25/1852	Martha Hysong	F	A	John Hysong	Ann Payne	W	
5/23/1852	Jennet Maxwell b. Johnson Creek	F	A	James Maxwell	Jennet Mothwen	W	
3/21/1852	Ann Bell Patton b. Elizaville, Ky.	F	A	A. M. Patton	L. Gallaher Ash Ber?	W	
2/20/1852	Demida Thomas b. Elizaville, Ky.	F	A	D. J. Eckman	Elizabeth Thomas	W	
3/12/1852	No name b. Johnsons Creek	F	A	Dennis Burns	Mary Wilson	W	
1/ /1852	Isaac P. Armstrong b. near P. Plains	M	A	Robt. Armstrong	Sarah A. Darnall	W	near Poplar Plains
1/ /1852	b. near Mt. Carmel, Re. slave	M	A	Martin P. Marshall		B	near Mt. Carmel
1/ 7/1852	Mary E. Williams b. on Northfork	F	A	Marcus Williams	Juliann Redenour	W	on North Fork
1/ 8/1852	William J. Phelps b. on Triplett	M	A	Z. R. Phelps	Martha Kissick	W	on Triplett
1/ 7/1852	Mahala E. Crain b. near Hillsboro	F	A	Marshall Crain	Louisa E. Hopkins	W	near Hillsboro
1/10/1852	John Stags b. Blue Bank	M	A	Thos. Staggs	Polly A. Jordan	W	Blue Bank
1/13/1852	Jesse Mason Pearce b. Fox	M	A	Wm. Pearce	Mary Ann --	W	Fox

COUNTY Fleming

S Sex
C Condition A-Alive D-Dead

DATE	NAME OF CHILD	S	C	NAME OF FATHER	NAME OF MOTHER	CO.	RESIDENCE
1/15/1852	b. Triplett		A	Wm. Hamilton	Mary Smoot	W	Triplett
1/22/1852	Mary Ellen Hunt b. Triplett	F	A	Cal Hunt	wid. Debora Davis	W	
1/26/1852	Aaron H. Vangant b. Flemingsburg	M	A	John Vangant	Nancy Markwell	W	near Flemings-burg
1/29/1852	Ann Maria Teagle b. Fox	F	A	Abram Teagle	Elizth. Ann Fourray	W	Fox
2/ /1852	Catharine b. near Flemingsburg, Re. slave	F	A	Osburn Belt		B	near Flemings-burg
2/ 3/1852	Maranda R. Stone b. Flemingsburg, Ky.	F	A	Francis M. Stone	Caroline L. Carter	W	Flemingsburg
2/ 5/1852	b. Poplar Plains	F	A	E. Logan	Eliza Jane Pearce	W	Poplar Plains
2/ 6/1852	b. near Hillsboro	F	A	Wm. Houst	Susan Evans	W	near Hillsboro
2/ 8/1852	Lucy Ann b. Hillsboro, Re. slave	F	A	John Gray		B	near Hillsboro
2/ 8/1852	Alex Humphries b. Triplett	M	A	Danl. Humphries	Susannah Stanforg	W	Triplett
2/10/1852	Mary Alice Denton b. near Hillsboro	F	A	James Denton	Sulbria Watson	W	near Hillsboro
2/12/1852	George M. Norris b. Triplett	M	A	Wm. H. Norris	Lucy Ann Logan	W	Licking
2/13/1852	Barbary A. Utterbakc b. Morgan County	F	A	Daird Utterback	Nancy Clark	W	Triplett
2/14/1852	Virginia Humphries	F	A				
2/14/1852	Milton H. Humphries b. Fox, Twins (mother died March)	F	A	William Humphries	Elizabeth Williams	W	Fox
2/14/1852	b. Fox	F	A	Andrew McKee		W	Fox
2/17/1852	Jonathan M. Cassity b. Red Brush	M	A	Franklin Cassity	Mary T. Kissick	W	Fox
2/19/1852	Irena Wacker b. Fox	F	A	Saml. Walker	Polly Ann Dale	W	Fox
2/20/1852	Lewyllen Story b. near Hillsboro	F	A	Alfred Story	Harrit Ann Vanlandingham	W	near Hillsboro

COUNTY Fleming

DATE	NAME OF CHILD	S	C	NAME OF FATHER	NAME OF MOTHER	CO.	RESIDENCE
2/27/1852	Robt. Simeon Ingram b. Mt. Carmel	M	A	Wm. H. Ingrain	Virginia Evans	W	Mt. Carmel
3/ /1852	Nancy E. Swim b. Triplett	F	A	Wm. L. Swim	Sarah Ann Sanders	W	Triplett
3/ /1852	James Hickerson b. Fleming	M	A	James Hickison	Polly Lewman	W	Fleming
3/ 1/1852	b. Licking, slave	M	A	Fielding Green Sr.		B	Licking
3/ 1/1852	Leroyller b. near P. Plains, slave	F	A	Jas. M. Triplett		B	
3/ 4/1852	Mary J. Robinson b. Flemingsburg, Ky.	F	A	Wm. P. Robinson	Rachel Sims	W	near Phelps Mills
3/ 6/1852	M. E. Glass b. near Martha Mills	F	A	Andrew Glass	Eliza Ann Sutton	W	near Martha Mills
3/ 7/1852	Marshall P. Swim b. Triplett	M	A	Asahel L. Swim	Elizabeth Robbins	W	Triplett
3/ 8/1852	Samuel P. Shepard b. near Pin Hook	M	A	Robt. Shepard	Lydia Pickeel	W	near Pin Hook
3/ 9/1852	James Harvy b. Fox, Illegitimate	M	A		Mary Perdew	W	Upper Fox
3/11/1852	Henry S. Hawkins b. Fox	M	A	Jas. A. Hawkins	Susan Logan	W	Fox
3/13/1852	Hiram Gardner b. Fox	M	A	Parker G. Gardner	Elizth. Daris	W	Fox
3/14/1852	Verriller Hopkins b. Bath. Ky.	M	A	Herod Hopkins	Emily J. Hopkins	W	South Lick
3/16/1852	Thomas M. Beaucamp b. Poplar Plains	M	A	Wm. Beaucamp	Nancy J. Hinton	W	Poplar Plains
3/17/1852	Lucy Quaintance b. near P. Plains	F	A	Wm. Quaintance	Martha Darnall	W	near Flemingsburg
3/20/1852	Elizabeth M. Porter b. Grant Co.	F	A	George M. Porter	Margaret Toring	W	Triplett
3/23/1852	James W. Thompson b. Fox	M	A	Benjamin Thompson	Jane Markmell	W	Fox
3/25/1952	Mary Agnes Harmon b. South Lick	F	A	William Harmon	Elizabeth Dillon	W	South Lick

KENTUCKY COUNTIES VITAL STATISTICS

COUNTY __Fleming__

S Sex
C Condition A-Alive D-Dead

DATE	NAME OF CHILD	S	C	NAME OF FATHER	NAME OF MOTHER	CO.	RESIDENCE
3/26/1852	Mary Ferrin b. North Fork	F	A	Benjm. Ferrin	Milly Jane Miller	W	North Fork
3/26/1852	Lucinda F. Dearing b. near P. Plains	F	A	Burgess Dearing	Amanda Eunnors	W	near Poplar Plains
3/31/1852	James Sampson b. Poplar Plains, Free Negro	M	A	James Sampson Sr.	Maria	M	Poplar Plains
4/ /1852	John R. Johnson b. Triplett	M	A	John R. Johnson	Manerva Yeazle	W	Triplett
4/ /1852	Emily Ramey b. Fleming Co.	F	A	Harrison Ramey	Mahala Jones	W	Triplett
4/ /1852	Emily Haveres b. near Mouth of Fox	F	A	Alfred Haveres	Maria Lloyd	W	Fox
4/ /1852	William C. Newman b. Mouth of Fox	M	A	James Newman	Mary Ann Havere	W	Fox
4/ /1852	b. near Hillsboro	M	A	John Nealis	Matilda R. Wory	W	near Hillsboro
4/ 1/1852	Eliza b. near P. Plains, Re. slave	F	A	Mrs. Amanda Houie	Nancy	B	near Poplar Plains
4/ 2/1852	Sarah Crawford b. near Hillsboro	F	A	John Crawford	Martha J. Payne	W	near Hillsboro
4/ 2/1852	Lewis Cap Heflin b. Fox	M	A	William Heflin	Polly Ann Royce	W	Fox
4/ 4/1852	Claybourne Hurst b. near Poplar Plains	M	A	Miles Hurst	Mary Doyle	W	near Poplar Plains
4/ 8/1852	Dewps Plummer b. near Mt. Carmel	M	A	George Plummer	Matilda	W	near Mt. Carmel
4/10/1852	America E. Purkins b. Hillsboro	F	A	Edwing Purkins	Eliza J. Day	W	Hillsboro
4/10/1852	Newell G. Roberts b. Northfork	M	A	William H. Roberts	Julia Burriss	W	North Fork
4/13/1852	Catharine Crotty b. Mt. Carmel Gate	F	A	Patrick Crotty	Margaret Roney	W	Mt. Carmel Gate House
4/16/1852	Lewis H. Rigdon b. Fox	M	A	Eli T. Rigdon	Dicy Hurst	W	near Morgans
4/15/1852	Asa Thomas b. Northfork	M	A	Nathanel Thomas	America Holland	W	North Fork
4/16/1852	Louisa McKee b. Fox	F	A	Benjm. T. McKee	Cynthia Williams	W	Fox

COUNTY __Fleming__

S Sex
C Condition A-Alive D-Dead

DATE	NAME OF CHILD	S	C	NAME OF FATHER	NAME OF MOTHER	CO.	RESIDENCE
4/17/1852	b. Triplett	F	A	Jeremiah Ham	Sarah ---	W	Triplett
4/16/1852	b. Fox, premature.	-	-	Zacharias Bramel	- - -	W	Fox
4/18/1852	Francis D. Johnson b. Triplett	M	A	Z. R. Johnson	Amanda Ann Sanders	W	Triplett
4/18/1852	James M. Estill b. near State	M	A	Silvester Estill	Elizabeth McKinney	W	Licking
4/18/1852	Walter Scott Fleming b. Poplar Plains	M	A	William Fleming	Eliza Power	W	Poplar Plains
4/20/1852	Alice Johnson b. Fox	F	A	Adjutant Johnson	Caroline Atckison	W	Fox
4/21/1852	Lewyllon Babbs b. Flemingsburg	F	A	James Babbs	Mary Heflin	W	Fox
4/22/1852	Francis Leonia Rawlings b. near P. Plains	F	A	Northroll Rawlings	Alice Lewis	W	Lewis Co.
4/22/1852	Johns T. Lewman b. near Flemingsburg	M	A	M. S. Lewman	Louisa Harn	W	near Flemingsburg
4/23/1852	Elizbh. T. Harmon b. near Sherburne	M	A	Elijah T. Harmon	Susannah White	W	Licking
4/25/1852	James M. Wright b. Triplett	M	A	Jackson Wright	Biddy Ann Swim	W	Triplett
4/26/1852	Sarah E. Cooper b. Triplett	F	A	George Cooper	Mary Likes	W	Triplett
4/29/1852	Elias D. Humphries b. Fox	M	A	Alfred Humphries	Rebecca Humphries	W	Fox
4/30/1852	George B. Vansanett b. Fox	M	A	G. M. Vansanett	Isabella Ann Cooper	W	Fox
4/30/1852	Dorsey b. near P. Plains, slave	M	A	Jas. M. Triplett		B	
5/ /1852	b. Mason Co.			Josiah Browning	Sarah Mattingly	W	near Mt. Carmel
5/ /1852	Robert Hamm b. Triplett	M	A	Christopher Ham	Rebecca Reed	W	Triplett
5/ 1/1852	Betsey b. near Poplar Plains, slave	F	A	E. E. Pearce		M	
5/ 1/1852	b. near Poplar Plains		A	William Staggs	Terresa Estill	W	

S Sex
C Condition A-Alive D-Dead

COUNTY __Fleming__

DATE	NAME OF CHILD	S	C	NAME OF FATHER	NAME OF MOTHER	CO.	RESICENCE
5/ 2/1852	Henry B. Williams b. Triplett	M	A	William Williams	Rebecca Maeuchy	W	Triplett
5/ 6/1852	Robt. H. Muse b. Fox	M	A	George Muse	Eliza Kirk	W	Fox
5/ 5/1852	Shelton H. Bradley b. Bath Co.	M	A	Herman Bradley	Amanda E. Filson	W	Fox
5/ /1852	b. Fox	F	A	William O. Philips ?	Mystilla C. A. Filson	W	Poplar Plains
5/ 9/1852	George Whitecraft b. Hillsboro	M	A	Dr. Jno. E. Whitecraft	Mary Robinson	W	Hillsboro
5/11/1852	b. near Poplar Plains, slave	M	A	Fleming Peed		B	
5/12/1852	William Doyle b. near Poplar Plains	M	A	William Doyle	Rebecca Heepheustins	W	Fox
5/13/1852	Leander Arnold b. Poplar Plains	M	A	John Arnold	Matilda Jourdan	W	Poplar Plains
5/14/1852	George W. Christy b. Fox	M	A	William E. Christy	Olivia Gray	W	Fox
5/14/1852	Etkelbert Muse b. Fox	M	A	Hiram B. Muse	Martha Eliott	W	Fox
5/16/1852	b. Poplar Plains	F	A	T. N. Hutchison	-- Morgan	W	Poplar Plains
5/16/1852	Daniel M. Hamm b. Triplett	M	A	Robt. Hamm	Sarah Reed	W	Triplett
5/19/1852	b. Triplett	F	A	D. S. Hamm	Rebecca M. Roberts	W	Triplett
5/20/1852	Susan Levina Ross b. Fox	F	A	Richd. Ross	Elizabeth Doyle	W	near Poplar Plains
5/22/1852	Mary Owings McKee b. Fox	F	A	Jno. A. McKee	Eliza Jane Branas	W	Fox
5/25/1852	Henry M. Humphries b. Fox	M	A	Saml. Humphries	Crilla Jane Calvert	W	Fox
5/26/1852	William Dudley Jourdan b. Blue Bank	M	A	Greenup Jordan	Minerva Dougherty	W	near Poplar Plains
6/ /1852	b. near Hillsboro		A	Warrick Hurst	Selener Johnson	W	Fox
6/ /1852	John b. Flemingsburg, Re. slave	M	A	John A. Cavan		M	Flemingsburg

COUNTY __Fleming__

S Sex
C Condition A-Alive D-Dead

DATE	NAME OF CHILD	S	C	NAME OF FATHER	NAME OF MOTHER	CO.	RESIDENCE
6/ /1852		F	A	William Fleming	Ann	B	Poplar Plains
	b. Poplar Plains, Re. slave						
6/ 1/1852	John E. Webster	M	A	John A. Webster	Angeline	W	near Plummers Mill
	b. Fox						
6/ 1/1852	- - - -	F	A	- - - -	- - - -	B	Fleming Co.
	b. Fleming Co.						
6/ 3/1852	Chas Newton Jones	M	A	Wm. F. Jones	Rachel Hinton	W	Fox
	b. near Poplar Plains						
6/ 4/1852	Josephine B. Evans	F	A	Magners Evans	Harriet Parker	W	Wilsons Run
	b. near Flemingsburg						
6/ 9/1852	Jas. C. Northcott	M	A	Joseph B. Northcott	Louisa Emmons	W	near Hillsboro
	b. near Hillsboro						
6/10/1852	Eliza Jane Evans	F	A	Robt. T. Evans	Lucinda Emmons	W	Poplar Plains
	b. Poplar Plains						
6/11/1852	Edward W. Lamar	M	A	Wm. Lamar	Mahala Collins	W	North Fork
6/11/1852	- - - -	-	D	Wm. Lamar	Mahala Collins	W	North Fork
	b. near Mt. Carmel, twins, 1 stillborn.						
6/13/1852	Wm. E. Deaning	M	A	Allan Deaning	Mary J. Downey	W	near Hillsboro
	b. near Hillsboro						
6/13/1852	Wm. P. Fleming	M	A	Chas. M. Fleming	Emily M. Marshall	W	near Flemingsburg
	b. near Flemingsburg						
6/13/1852	Mary Bell Shanklin	F	A	Jos. A. Shanklin	Sophia Lewman	W	Wilsons Run
	b. Beach Woods						
6/13/1852	- - - -	-	-	Jas. D. Ringo	Emily Pleakruatrluer	W	Licking
	b. Burgis Mill						
6/15/1852	Jas. Frederick McGregor	M	A	Jas. McGregor	Margaret Hines	W	Fox
	b. Fox						
6/19/1852	Archimidese P. Hurst	M	A	Alfred Hurst	Susannah Swim	W	Triplett
	b. Triplett						
6/20/1852	Robt. Fountain	M	A	Andrew Fountain	Louisa A. Piobb	W	Fox
	b. Fox Springs						
6/21/1852	Emily Kidmell	F	A	M. Kidmell	Nancy DeBell	W	Wilsons Run
	b. Wilsons Run						
6/22/1852	Thos. Wm. Ham	M	A	Wm. B. Ham	Messa Estill	W	Triplett
6/22/1852	- - - -	F	D	Wm. B. Ham	Messa Estill	W	Triplett
	b. Triplett, twins, 1 stillborn						

COUNTY   Fleming

S Sex
C Condition A-Alive D-Dead

DATE	NAME OF CHILD	S	C	NAME OF FATHER	NAME OF MOTHER	CO.	RESIDENCE
6/25/1852	Nathan F. White b. Licking	M	A	Nathanel White	Mary O. Click	W	Licking
6/25/1852	John M. Hawkins b. Triplett	M	A	Richd. Hawkins	Sarah A. Gray	W	Triplett
6/27/1852	Levi F. McKee b. Fox	M	A	Wm. McKee	Emily McKee	W	Fox
6/27/1852	Elizabeth A. Hiner b. near Poplar Plains	F	A	Saml. Hiner	Prissilla D. Jones	W	Fox
6/27/1852	Harvey Kendall b. near Poplar Plains	M	A	H. O. Kendall	Elizth. McCann	W	near P. Plains
6/28/1852	Ann Elizth. Triplett b. Wilsons run	F	A	Greenbury Triplett	Mary D. Mills	W	Wilsons Run
7/ /1852	Lewis McRoberts b. Triplett	M	A	Wm. S. McRoberts	Susannah Cooper	W	Triplett
7/ /1852	Henry b. near P. Plains, Re. slave.	M	A	Robert Cowser		B	
7/ /1852	b. Fox, Stillborn		D	Alfred C. Jones	Eliza Kissick	W	Fox
7/ /1852	Jacob M. Rash b. near Pin Hook	M	A	Morris Rash	E. Powers	W	near Pin Hook
7/ 1/1852	Sarah E. Lytte b. near Pin Hook	F	A	Saml. Lytte	Elizth. Todd	W	near Pin Hook
7/ 1/1852	Robt. Humphries b. Fox	M	A	Wm. M. Humphries	Mariah L. Walker	W	Fox
7/ 2/1852	Wesley W. Lee b. Triplett	M	A	Jackson Lee	Nancy Ferguson	W	Triplett
7/ 3/1852	Diana R. Day b. Sanders & Day Mill	F	A	S. A. Day	Marcinda Jones	W	Licking
7/ 4/1852	Louisa Sutton b. near Flemingsburg	F	A	Thos. P. Sutton	Celia Goading	W	near Flemingsburg
7/ 6/1852	Wm. St. Clair Emmons b. near P. Plains	M	A	Rufus Emmons	Louisa Hendria	W	near P. Plains
7/ 7/1852	b. near P. Plains	M	A	James Smith	Angeline J. Thompson	W	near P. Plains
7/ 9/1852	James Wm. Gray b. Fox	M	A	James M. Gray	Mary A. Lewis	W	Fox
7/11/1852	Sally Jane b. near P. Plains, Re. slave.	F	A	Isiah Vansaudt		B	

12

S Sex
C Condition A-Alive D-Dead

COUNTY Fleming

DATE	NAME OF CHILD	S	C	NAME OF FATHER	NAME OF MOTHER	CO.	RESIDENCE
7/11/1852	Emma Ann Swim b. Triplett	F	A	John H. Swim	Hannah Wright	W	Triplett
7/13/1852	Wm. A. Heflin b. near Pin Hook	M	A	Wm. Heflin	Matilda R. Story	W	near Pin Hook
7/14/1852	Rolby Trully Arnold b. Beech Woods	M	A	Henry Arnold	Fanny Muse	W	Beech Woods
7/17/1852	Sarah Matilda Ross b. Blue Bank	F	A	William Ross	Asa P. Dale	W	Bluebank
7/19/1852	America Ross b. near Hillsboro	F	A	Silas Ross	America Dunkins	W	Fox
7/19/1852	Wm. J. Markwell b. Fox	M	A	Thos. P. Markwell	Sarah J. Griffish	W	Fox
7/20/1852	Mary E. Leforges b. near Hillsboro	F	A	Lewis Leforge	Esther Ann Ledford	W	near Hillsboro
7/21/1852	Davis R.E.McRoberts b. Triplett, Illegitimate	M	A	Saml. McRoberts	Maranda Danis	W	Triplett
7/21/1852	William Moore b. Triplett	M	A		Elizabeth S. Moore	W	Triplett
7/23/1852	Matilda Carpenter b. Fox	F	A	Elijah L. Carpenter	Mahala Jordan	W	Fox
7/24/1852	b. near Hillsboro	M	A	John Watson	Louesa Freeman	W	near Hillsboro
7/24/1852	Wm. B. Jones b. Fox	M	A	Saml. B.H. Jones	Martha M. Plummer	W	Fox
7/25/1852	Perry F. Martin b. Bath	M	A	Robt. Martin	Ann Moore	W	Poplar Plains Gate
7/25/1852	Walter M. Condiff b. near Hillsboro	M	A	-- Condiff	Martha Fawns	W	near Hillsboro
7/26/1852	- - - - b. Wilsons Run, Illegitimate & distroyed at birth.	-	-	-- --	Ann Mariah Sanders	W	Wilsons Run
7/27/1852	Charlotte Gardner b. Blue Bank	F	A	Aaron Gardner	Elizabeth Hurst	W	Blue Bank
7/27/1852	Calvin L. Robertson b. near Flemingsburg	M	A	Thos. Robertson	Maranda Asbany	W	near Flemingsburg
7/28/1852	Mary C. Royse b. Fox	F	A	William Royze	Rebecca Royse	W	Fox
8/ /1852	James W. Hamilton b. Fox	M	A	Danl. Hamilton	Emily Boyd	W	Fox

S Sex
C Condition A-Alive D-Dead

COUNTY __Fleming__

DATE	NAME OF CHILD	S	C	NAME OF FATHER	NAME OF MOTHER	CO.	RESIDENCE
8/ /1852	Kitty	F	A	Martin P. Marshall		B	
	b. near Mt. Carmel, Re. slave.						
8/ /1852	- - - -	-	A	Jacob Lawson		B	
	b. near Sherburne, Re. slave.						
8/ 2/1852	- - - -	-	A	Jefferson Rice	Drucilla Fuqua	W	near Mouth Locust
	b. near Licking						
8/ 3/1852	Luther Burgess Crawford	M	A	M. L. Crawford	Elizabeth Sanders	W	Fox
	b. near Philps Mill						
8/ 5/1852	Odd Biggetoff Summitt	M	A	Jas. Summitt	Nancy P. Scott	W	Locust
	b. Locust						
8/ 8/1852	Richard Jones	M	A	Wm. E. Jones	Elizth. Reeves	W	Fox
	b. Fox						
8/ 9/1852	Poington Williams	M	A	Jas. Williams	Harriet Sanders	W	Triplett
	b. Triplett						
8/ 9/1852	Wm. W. Hedges	M	A	John Hedger	Louisa Lee	W	Triplett
	b. Triplett						
8/ 9/1852	Alkaner Y. Tibbs	M	A	Willoughby Tibbs	Tabatha O. Bannon	W	near Mt. Carmel
	b. near Mt. Carmel						
8/16/1852	Sanford McClerg	M	A	John McCling	Nancy Evans	W	Triplett
	b. Triplett						
8/16/1852	John D. Gooding	M	A	Lenox Gooding	Martha A. Callahan	W	Fox
	b. near Poplar Plains						
8/20/1852	- - - -	M	D	Stephen Sybold	Nancy Daris	W	near Mt. Carmel
	b. near Mt. Carmel, Stillborn.						
8/23/1852	William Ann Denton	F	A	F. G. Denton	Frances Rawlings	W	Licking
	b. Licking						
8/24/1852	Josephine Likes	F	A	Thos. M. Likes	Charity Lathrum	W	near Mouth Fox
	b. near Licking						
8/28/1852	Parthena D. Rawlings	F	A	Middleton Rawlings	Cyntha Smost	W	Fox
	b. near Phelps Mill						
8/30/1852		F	A	John Bell	Martha Hendrix	W	near P. Plains
	b. near P. Plains						
8/31/1852	Amos Riggs	M	A	Caleb Riggs	Isabella Soroff	W	near Hillsboro
	b. near Hillsboro						
Summer	Michael Hines	M	A	Thos. Hynes	Nancy --	W	Flemingsburg
	b. Flemingsburg						
Summer	Elizabeth Summitt	F	A	George Summitt	Eleanor Crain	W	near Hillsboro
	b. near Hillsboro						

DATE	NAME OF CHILD	S	C	NAME OF FATHER	NAME OF MOTHER	CO.	RESIDENCE
Fall/1852			A	Smith Hamm	Martha Hamms	W	Triplett
	b. Triplett						
Fall/1852	Lucy Ann Frances Hurst	F	A	Laudon Hurst	Nancy Daris	W	Fox
	b. Fox						
9/ /1852	Roland	F	A	Wm. H. Hendria		B	near P. Plains
	b. near P. Plains, Re. slave						
9/ /1852	Abigail E. Howse	F	A	Samuel Howse	Wd. Sarah Cooper	W	Triplett
	b. Triplett						
9/ /1852	Molton	F	A	Elijah Hart		B	near Poplar Plains
	b. near P. Plains, Re. slave.						
9/ /1852	Mary Elizabeth	F	A	Joseph D. Farrow		B	near Flemingsburg
	b. near Flemingsburg, Re. slave						
9/ /1852	Laura	F	A	Martin L Marshall		B	near Mt. Carmel
	b. near Mt. Carmel, Re. slave.						
9/ /1852	- - - -	-	D	Robt. Graham		W	near Hillsboro
	b. Locust, Stillborn						
9/ 2/1852	Mary E. Carpenter	F	A	James E. Carpenter	Devinda Johnson	W	Fox
	b. Fox						
9/ 6/1852	Author	-	A	Andrew Howe		B	
	b. near Poplar Plains, Re. slave.						
9/ 8/1852	James Ross	M	A	Ben Ross	Celia Holland	W	near P. Plains
	b. near Poplar Plains						
9/ 8/1852	Lucinda Arnold	F	A	Chas. B. Arnold	Mary R. Carpenter	W	Beech Woods
	b. Beech Woods						
9/ 9/1852	Lucy Ann Oaley	F	A		Celia Ann Aoley	W	Triplett
	b. Triplett						
9/10/1852	Mary R. Smith	F	A	Edwin T. Smith	Margaret A. Cooper	W	near P. Plains
	b. near P. Plains						
9/11/1852	Thos. M. Pearce	M	A	E. B. Pearce	Eliza Cochran	W	Poplar Plains
	b. Poplar Plains						
9/12/1852	John D. Doyle	M	A	John W. Doyle	Elizabeth House	W	near P. Plains
	b. near P. Plains						
9/15/1852	Fidelia Ann Browning	F	A	Dr. W. G. Browning	Mary P. Cochrell	W	Mt. Carmel
	b. Mt. Carmel						
9/20/1852	Elias Hurst	M	A	Nelson Hurst	Martha Hurst	W	near P. Plains
	b. near P. Plains						
9/23/1852	James Henry West	M	A	James West	Rebecca Hamilton	W	near P. Plains
	b. near P. Plains						

COUNTY Fleming   C Condition A-Alive D-Dead

DATE	NAME OF CHILD	S	C	NAME OF FATHER	NAME OF MOTHER	CO.	RESIDENCE
9/24/1852	Norris Sampson b. Flemingsburg	M	A	Henry J. Sampson	Maranda Clark	W	Flemingsburg
9/25/1852	Simpson Miner Story b. near Hillsboro	M	A	Nelson Story	Rosannah Story	W	near Hillsboro
9/25/1852	Spencer b. Licking, Re. slave.	M	A	Fielding Green		B	Licking
9/27/1852	Mota Ellen b. Bald Hill, Re. slave.	F	A	Mrs. Kitty Boyse		B	Bald Hill
9/29/1852	Henry Hewitt b. Locust	M	A	Henry Hewitt	Elizabeth Millburn	W	Locust
10/ /1852	Mary H. Markwell b. Triplett	F	A	Joel Markwell	Esther Royse	W	Triplett
10/ /1852	Josephine b. near Flemingsburg, Re. slave.	F	A	H. T. Darnall		B	near Flemings-burg
10/ /1852	Melvena Denton b. Licking	F	A	Abram Denton	Betsey BAker	W	Licking
10/ 2/1852	John L. Markwell b. b. near Mouth State.	M	A	Elias W. Markwell	Sarah Ann Whitney	W	Licking
10/ 5/1852	David P. May b. Triplett	M	A	John May	Elizth. T. Cochran	W	Triplett
10/ 5/1852	Noble W. B. Johnson b. near Mouth State	M	A	Thomas J. Johnson	Malinda J. Allender	W	Licking
10/ 5/1852	- - - - b. near Mouth State	-	A	Abram Burk	Polly Allender	W	Licking
10/ 8/1852	Matilda C. Dabyinple b. South Lick	F	A	Danl. Dabyinple	Amanda J. Newman	W	South Lick
10/10/1852	John Robt. Gully b. near Pin Hook	M	A	Lewis Gally	Elizth. Overby	W	near Pin Hook
10/13/1852	- - - - b. Allison, Re. slave.	M	A	Wm. H. Smith	Tillis	B	Allison
10/13/1852	Ann E. Clary b. near Mt. Carmel	F	A	Warner Clary	Mary W. Gulick	W	near Mt. Carmel
10/15/1852	- - - - b. near Hillsboro	F	A	Joseph Story	Jane Graham	W	Locust
10/16/1852	Mary E. Johsnon b. Triplett	F	A	Benjm. Johnson	Rutha Moore	W	B.F. Triplett
10/20/1852	Paul Avory Emmons b. near Phelps Mill	M	A	William Emmons	Susan Reeves	W	Fox

DATE	NAME OF CHILD	S	C	NAME OF FATHER	NAME OF MOTHER	CO.	RESIDENCE
10/20/1852	Almeda Farris b. near Pin Hook	F	A	Ambrose Faris	Louisa M. Caner	W	near Pin Hook
10/22/1852	Henry Augustine Zimmerman b. Hillsboro	M	A	R. T. D. Zimmerman	Lucinda Atchison	W	Triplett
10/27/1852	- - - - b. near Hillsboro	F	A	Jas. C. Reeves	Eveline Emmons	W	near Hillsboro
10/31/1852	Nancy S. Perry b. near Mt. Carmel	F	A	Perry	Elmiretta Silvey	W	near Mt. Carmel
10/31/1852	- - - - b. Licking	F	A	James Mills (Wills?)	Martha Ann Nealis	W	Licking
11/ /1852	Martha Stamper b. Licking	F	A	Richard Stamper	Polly Ann Mayers	W	Licking
11/ /1852	- - - - b. Red Brush	-		Chas. Lynum	Jane Vernattin	W	Red Brush
11/ 1/1852	Franklin P. Plummer b. Crain Creek	M	A	Simpson H. Plummer	Nancy Ann Seuer	W	
11/ 4/1852	- - - - b. near Flemingsburg, Re. slave.	M	A	Jerry Hall	Lucretia	B	
11/ 4/1852	Joseph A. Jones b. Fox	M	A	Joseph T. Jones	Cyntha Ann Gooding	W	near Morgans
11/ 5/1852	Mary P. Colbert b. Triplett	F	A	Jas. M. Colbert	Jerietta Razor	W	Triplett
11/10/1852	Amanda Enise McClerg b. Triplett	F	A	Joseph McClerg	Hanna Euise	W	Triplett
11/13/1852	William Reuben Grannis b. near Poplar Plains	M	A	Wm. Grannis	Norcissa Hurst	W	Bourbon
11/17/1852	Martha L. Markwell b. near Poplar Plains	F	A	F. M. Markwell	Hanna Harmon	W	near P. Plains
11/18/1852	Hamilton S. Newman b. Triplett	M	A	Thomas Newman	Margaret Watson	W	Triplett
11/18/1852	- - - - b. Locust	M	A	John Story	Rebecca Day	W	near Hillsboro
11/19/1852	George Carpenter b. Fox	M	A	Harvey Carpenter	Eliza Jourdan	W	Fox
11/28/1852	Adaline b. near Flemingsburg, Re. slave.	F	A	Abram Gooding		B	
12/ /1852	Joicy A. Lee b. Bath	F	A	Matthias Lee	Margaret Hawkins	W	Licking

COUNTY Fleming

S Sex
C Condition A-Alive D-Dead

DATE	NAME OF CHILD	S	C	NAME OF FATHER	NAME OF MOTHER	CO.	RESIDENCE
12/ /1852	- - - - b. near Mouth State	F	A	Greenup Pickrell	Mary Pierce	W	near Mouth State
12/ /1852	John F. Comady b. near D. Morgans	M	A	Peter Comady	Charlotte Jordan	W	near Morgans
12/ /1852	- - - - b. near Mouth State	M	A	John McNesby	Sarah Atchison	W	Mouth of State
12/ 3/1852	Lucinda J. Cline b. Fox	F	A	Saml. F. Cline	Elizabeth Ann Harget	W	Fox
12/ 5/1852	Wm. S. Montgomery b. near Hillsboro	M	A	Alex Montgomery	Elastine Bateman	W	near Hillsboro
12/ 5/1852	Mary b. near P. Plains	F	A	Jonthn. Clinkimbeard		B	Fleming
12/15/1852	William Roe b. Fox	M	A	R. G. Leuis	Minnie	M	Fox
12/17/1852	Green F. Rankins b. South Lick	M	A	James Raukins	Kesia Harman	W	Texas
12/21/1852	- - - - b. Triplett, Re. Premature & died in a few hours.	M	A	E. M. Porter	Cyntha Story	W	Triplett
12/22/1852	Franklin P. Chander b. Mt. Carmel	M	A	T. B. Chandler	Mary Mirder	W	Mt. Carmel
12/22/1852	 b. near P. Plains	M	A	Thos. Buttar	Paulina R. Shannon	W	near P. Plains
12/22/1852	Sarah Allice b. Mt. Carmel	F	A	Alex Foxworthy	Sarah Goddard	W	Mt. Carmel
12/23/1852	America J. Ham b. Triplett	F	A	Fielding Ham	Sibba Thompson	W	Triplett
12/24/1852	Columbus R. Hedrick b. Bath	M	A	Roland Hedrick	Elizabeth Roe	W	Triplett
12/27/1852	Margaret Dearing b. near Flemingsburg	F	A	Jas. Thos. Dearing	Mary Bateman	W	Fleming
12/28/1852	Francis D. Boyd b. near Phelps Mill	M	A	Jas. Boyd	Louisa Dairs	W	Fox
12/28/1852	- - - - b. Fox, Stillborn, Re. slave.	-	D	R. G. Lewis		M	
12/30/1852	- - - - b. near Poplar Plains, Re. slave	M	A	Mrs. Rosanna Bradly	Betty	B	
12/31/1852	Bruce T. Lyons b. near Hillsboro	M	A	S. B. Lyons	Martha Day	W	near Hillsboro

KENTUCKY COUNTIES VITAL STATISTICS

S Sex
C Condition A-Alive D-Dead

COUNTY Fleming

DATE	NAME OF CHILD	S	C	NAME OF FATHER	NAME OF MOTHER	CO.	RESIDENCE
5/ 2/1852	- - - - b. near Secrest	M	A	Daniel Hargate	-- Rozse	W	Fox
3/14/1852	- - - - b. Bells Springs	M	A	Aletha Bell	- - - -	B	Fox
3/17/1852	- - - - b. Poplar Plains, Re. The father a slave, the mother free.	F	A	Joshua Marshall	Fanny Hackley	B	Poplar Plains
3/23/1852	- - - -	F	A	Hiram Manchester	- - - -	W	Fox
3/23/1852	- - - - b. Fox, Re. Twins.	M	A	Hiram Manchester	- - - -	W	Fox
3/25/1852	- - - - b. near Secrest	M	A	John Faris	Emily Secrest	W	between Plains & F. Burg
2/25/1852	- - - - b. P. Plains	F	A	John Silory	Amanda Bridges	W	Sherburn
4/ 5/1852	- - - - b. Fox	F	A	Moses Hurst	-- Hurst	W	Missouri
2/15/1852	- - - - b. Pin Hook	F	A	Jas. T. Dearing	Betsy Jane Thompson	W	Pin Hook
2/14/1852	- - - - b. Poplar Plains	F	A	David Arnold	Jane Crain	W	Poplar Plains
/ /1852	Cassmara A. Lee b. Triplett	F	A	Hiram Lee	Elizabeth Logan	W	Triplett
/ /1852	Martin P. Marshall Bell b. b. near Mt. Carmel	M	A	Edward Bell	Sarah Johnson	W	near Mt. Carmel
/ /1852	- - - - b. Triplett	-	-	Rebecca Wilson	- - - -	B	Triplett
/ /1852	- - - - b. Triplett	-	-	Rebecca Wilson	- - - -	B	Triplett

State of Kentucky, Fleming County Sct.
   I, William T. Dudley, Clerk of the court for the County aforesaid, certify that the foregoing 7 pages contain a true list of Births returned by the Commissioner of Tax for Fleming County for the year 1853. June 9th 1853.
                              W. T. Dudley CFCC

| 7/19/1853 | Elizabeth Shields b. near Hillsboro | F | A | Alexander Shields | Lucinda Crain | W | near Hillsboro |

19

COUNTY Fleming

S Sex
C Condition A-Alive D-dead

DATE	NAME OF CHILD	S	C	NAME OF FATHER	NAME OF MOTHER	CO.	RESIDENCE
3/ 4/1853	Susan E. Walton b. near Hillsboro	F	A	Parker Walton	Evaline Williams	W	all Residents near Hillsboro
10/ 5/1853	Mary b. near Hillsboro, Re. slave.	F	A	Danil Barksdale		B	
12/12/1852	Jane Whitecraft b. near Hillsboro	F	A	Dr. John E. Whitecraft	Mary Robertson	W	
5/ 8/1853	b. near Hillsboro	F	A	W. W. Turney	Mary Cochran	W	
4/26/1853	Mary Bell Nalis b. near Hillsboro	F	A	Charles Nalis	Martha Harrison	W	
8/17/1853	Robt. G. Nalis b. near Hillsboro	M	A	David Nalis	Sally A. Nalis	W	
3/22/1853	b. near Hillsboro	M	A	Samuel Stahorn	Martha Hunt	W	
7/ 2/1853	b. near Hillsboro	M	A	Ezekiel Cloyd		W	
9/17/1853	b. near Hillsboro	F	A	Benjamin Ross	Ethania Filson	W	
11/20/1853	b. near Hillsboro	F	A	James Denton	-- Walton	W	
1/ 9/1853	Rebecca Todd b. near Hillsboro	F	A	Thomas Todd	Sophronia Browning	W	
12/ 6/1853	Simpson Denton b. near Hillsboro	M	A	Abram Denton	Emerine Jones	W	
10/ 6/1853	Samuel F. L. Shields b. near Hillsboro	M	A	E. G. Shields	Rebecca Robertson	W	
11/ 4/1853	James M. Shield b. near Hillsboro	M	A	Samuel Shields	Elizabeth Nalis	W	
9/19/1853	Lucinda Robison b. near Hillsboro	F	A	William R. Robison	Rachael Sims	W	
10/ 3/1853	b. near Hillsboro	F	A	Samuel Ross	-- Proctor	W	
12/ 4/1853	b. near Hillsboro	F	A	Johnson Phelps	Nancy Saumders	W	
11/27/1853	b. near Hillsboro	F	A	James Nalis	Sarah Nalis	W	
5/13/1852	Jonathan	M	A	William Hyatt	Lavina Hedges	W	(twins)

COUNTY Fleming

S Sex
C Condition A-Alive D-Dead

DATE	NAME OF CHILD	S	C	NAME OF FATHER	NAME OF MOTHER	CO.	RESIDENCE
5/13/1853	Sarah Hyatt	F	A	William Hyatt	Lavina Hedges	w	near Hillsboro
	b. near Hillsboro, Re. Twins.						
12/30/1853			A	Samuel Lytle	Elizabeth Todd	W	near Pin Hook
	b. near Tilton						
10/31/1853	Alex H. Lee	M	A	W. P. Lee	Margaret Todd	W	near Pin Hook
	b. near Tilton						
10/27/1853		M	A	Hiram McGlothin	Kesiah Cooper	W	Licking
	b. Licking						
8/21/1853	Amanda Bell Crain	F	A	John F. Crain	Latitia Dillon	W	Licking
	b. Licking (near)						
1/ /1853	Florinda Crain	F	A	John Crain	Florinda Markwell	W	near Licking
	b. near Licking						
4/30/1853	James McKee	M	A	Thomas C. McKee	Evalinda Casey	W	Licking
	b. Licking						
10/27/1853		M	A	Hiram McGlothin	Kesiah Cooper	W	Licking
	b. Licking						
3/19/1853		F	D	James Carey	Eliza J. Cassity	W	Licking
	b. Licking						
7/ /1853	David Delba	F	A	Thos. Green		B	Licking
	b. Licking, Re. slave.						
9/20/1853	Francis	M	A	Thos. Green		B	Licking
	b. Licking, Re. slave.						
9/22/1853	Elizabeth Harbor	F	A	John Harbor	Catharine Duett	W	Licking
	b. Licking						
9/ /1853		F	A	Fielding Green Sen.		M	
	Re. slave.						
1/22/1853	Mary F. B. Clack	F	A	Thompsin Clack	Cervia Myres	W	Licking
	b. Licking						
4/ 4/1853	Louisania Myres	F	A	Wilburn Myres	Mahala Myres	W	Licking
	b. Licking						
12/ /1853		F	A	John Myres	Eliza J. Markwell	W	Licking
	b. Licking						
5/ /1853	Sarah F. Hawkins	F	A	John Hawkins	Deliba White	W	Licking
	b. Licking						
5/ /1853		F	A	G. W. Razor		M	Licking
	b. Licking, Re. slave.						
	Martha H. Green	F	A	Sampson Green	Eliza Ann Bailey	W	Licking
	b. Licking						

COUNTY Fleming

S Sex
C Condition A-Alive D-Dead

DATE	NAME OF CHILD	S	C	NAME OF FATHER	NAME OF MOTHER	CO.	RESIDENCE
4/ 6/1853	James H. Norris b. Licking	M	A	William Norris	Lucy Ann Logan	W	Licking
/ /1853	Almira Kissick b. Licking	F	A	William Kissick	Amanda Reeves	W	Licking
7/ 7/1853	Mary Ann Fawns b. Licking	F	A	John Fawns	Sarah Kissick	W	Licking
4/ 7/1853	James S. Tinbley b. Licking	M	A	Samuel Tinbley	Mary Cannattin	W	Licking
1/ 7/1853	Asa S. Atchison b. Licking	M	A	Thos. J. Atchison	E. C. Maxey	W	Licking
8/ 5/1853	Sarah M. Estill b. Licking	F	A	Samuel Estill	Mary Rice	W	Licking
Spring	Sarah E. Demoss b. Licking	F	A	Lewis Demoss	Delilah D. Annow	W	Licking
10/ /1853	Selucius G. Johnson b. Licking	M	A	Adgedent Johnson	Caroline Atchisin	W	Licking
5/ 2/1853	Sarah E. Johnson b. Licking	F	A	William Johnson	Harriet Lytte	W	Licking
7/ 7/1853	Mary B. Denton b. Licking	F	A	William P. D.	Malinda Jones	W	Licking
8/ /1853	 b. Licking	M	A	John M. Gray	Elizabeth Davis	W	Licking
4/30/1853	 b. Licking, Re. Died when 2 weeks old.			George W. Gray		W	Licking
1/16/1853	Louisa Barksdale b. Hillsboro	F	A	Daniel Barksdale	Elizabeth Crain	W	Hillsborough
3/16/1853	Harvy D. Edwards b. near Poplar Plains	M	A	William Edwards	Nancy Whesley	W	near P. Plains
3/16/1853	Ebanor V. Hinton b. near Poplar Plains	F	A	James Hinton	Louisa Lewis	W	near P. Plains
4/ 7/1853	George N. Callahan b. Fox	M	A	Sonnett Calahan	Sarah S. Raves	W	Fox
4/17/1853	Kenten C. Porter b. Locust	M	A	William Porten	Sally Ann Straham	W	Locust
7/22/1853	Amelia Beaucamp b. Poplar Plains	F	A	William Beaucamp	Nancy Hinton	W	Poplar Plains
7/29/1853	Mary Jane Fulton b. Poplar Plains	F	A	George Fulton	Jemima Sampson	M	Poplar Plains

COUNTY Fleming

S Sex
C Condition A-Alive D-Dead

DATE	NAME OF CHILD	S	C	NAME OF FATHER	NAME OF MOTHER	CO.	RESIDENCE
8/12/1853	Florence A. Crain b. Hillsborough	F	A	Thomas Crain	Jemima Stanesfer	W	Hillsborough
8/ /1853	b. Poplar Plains, Re. slave.	M	A	Dr. William Armstrong		B	P. Plains
8/18/1853	b. near Hillsborough	F	A	John Lyons		W	near Hillsborough
9/ 6/1853	b. near P. Plains	F	A	Lewis Markwell	Nancy Crain	W	near Hillsborough
9/20/1853	b. near P. Plains	M	A	William Leforge	Eliza J. Straham	W	near Hillsborough
9/ 7/1853	Emiline b. near P. Plains, Re. slave.	F	A	Wilford Taylor	Celia	B	near Hillsborough
9/27/1853	Paulina Graham b. near P. Plains	F	A	Robt. Graham	Caroline Matthew	W	near Hillsborough
10/ 5/1853	Lucretia Northcott b. near Hillsborough	F	A	Joseph B. Northwitt	Louisa Emmons	W	near Hillsborough
11/16/1853	b. Pop;ar Plains, Re. slave.	M	A	O. A. Kendall		B	P. Plains
11/17/1853	Charles H. Davis b. near Hillsborough	M	A	Col. F. R. Davis	Markwell	W	near Hillsborough
11/23/1853	Sarah A. Leforge b. near Hillsborough	F	A	Lewis Leforge	Hester Ann Leaford	W	Hillsborough
10/12/1853	b. Poplar Plains, Re. Father a slave, mother free.	F	A	Joshua Triplett (slave)	Fanny Hackley	M	Poplar Plains
	b. Hillsborough	F	A			W	near Hillsborough
11/11/1853	b. Re. Born at 7 months & died at 15 days.	N	A	Simpson Dearing	Joanna Downie	W	
12/10/1853	b. Flemingsburg	M	A	E. T. Hall	Jones	W	Flemingsburg
10/15/1853	William W. Lucas b. near Tilton	M	A	George W. Lucas	Nancy Hysong	W	near Tilton
11/13/1853	b. near Tilton	F	A	William Duley	Matilda Wood	W	near Tilton
10/25/1853	James H. Wood b. near Tilton	M	A	Andrew T. Wood	Matilda Picksel	W	near Tilton
11/ 2/1853	b. near Tilton	F	A	William Groves		W	near Tilton

23

S Sex

COUNTY Fleming

C Condition A-Alive D-Dead

DATE	NAME OF CHILD	S	C	NAME OF FATHER	NAME OF MOTHER	CO.	RESIDENCE
10/15/1853	Mary E. Dillon b. near Tilton	F	A	Isaiah Dillon	Mary Ann Todd	W	near Tilton
1/28/1853	James Bowman b. Flemingsburg	M	A	James M. Bowman	Harriet Jones	W	Flemingsburg
2/12/1853	b. near Flemingsburg, Re. slave.	F	A	Abram Gooding	Julia Ann	B	near Flemings-burg
2/11/1853	Emily b. near Flemingsburg, Re. slave.	M	A	Wm. H. Smith	Debila	B	near Flemings-burg
11/16/1853	b. near Flemingsburg	M	A	Kiah Brown	Elizabeth Epile	W B	near Flemings-burg
11/ 6/1853	Albert T. Smith b. near Flemingsburg	M	A	James E. Smith	Angeline Thompson	W	near Flemings-burg
12/10/1853	Mary P. Bishop b. Flemingsburg	F	A	Henry Bishop	Lucy Porter	W	Flemingsburg
10/12/1853	Larkin b. Flemingsburg, Re. slave.	M	A	W. H. Smith	Annie	B	Flemingsburg
5/ 7/1853	b. near Flemingsburg	M	A	John Bishop		W	near Flemings-burg
5/ 2/1853	b. near Flemingsburg	F	A	Wilford McRoberts	Conrod	W	Flemingsburg
12/27/1853	b. Flemingsburg	M	A	Joseph M. Alexander	Metcalf	W	Flemingsburg
7/22/1853	Harry Kirth b. near Tilton	M	A	James A. Kirth	Mahala Overley	W	near Tilton
4/ 3/1853	b. Flemingsburg	F	A	John Dale	Sarah Jacobs	W	Flemingsburg
3/20/1853	b. near Flemingsburg, Re. slave.	M	A	Mrs. Sowarel of masen	Mary	M	near Flemingsburg
3/27/1853	b. Flemingsburg, Re. slave.	M	A	Henry Bishop	Adaline	M	Flemingsburg
8/28/1853	Louisa C. Elston b. near Flemingsburg	F	A	Edward Elston	Anny E. Strode	W	near Flemings-burg
8/ 9/1853	b. near Flemingsburg, Re. Premature ?.	F	D	Patrick Cantby	Margaret	W	near Flemings-burg
2/ 8/1853	Hester Ann Watts b. near Flemingsburg	F	A	John A. Watts	Nancy Ann Foxworthy	W	near Flemings-burg

24

S Sex
C Condition A-Alive D-Dead

COUNTY Fleming

DATE	NAME OF CHILD	S	C	NAME OF FATHER	NAME OF MOTHER	CO.	RESIDENCE
5/18/1853	Mary G. Tibbs b. near Flemingsburg	F	A	William T. Tibbs	Louisa Farrner	W	near Flemingsburg
12/28/1853	William H. DeBell b. near Mt. Carmel	M	A	William J. DeBell	Lewellyn Dougherty	W	Mt. Carmel
12/ 5/1853	b. Wilsons Run		A	John C. Jones	Susanah BAird	W	near Mt. Carmel
9/16/1853	Samuel H. Craig b. Wilsons Run	M	A	David Craig	Malva Doyle	W	Mt. Carmel (near)
	Virginia M. Farris b. near P. Plains	F	A	Harvey Farris	Paulina Dale	W	near P. Plains
1/ 2/1853	Eliza J. Markwell b. near Hillsborough	F	A	Alfred Markwell	Mary Alexander	W	near Hillsborough
10/10/1853	Sarah C. McJlrain? b. near P. Plains	F	A	James McJlacrim	Mary Morgan	W	near P. Plains
1/ 3/1853	William T. Ham b. near P. Plains	M	A	Samuel D. Ham	C. H. Faris	W	near P. Plains
12/17/1853	G. W. Conrod b. near P. Plains	M	A	Reuben Conrod	Lucinda Lewis	W	near P. Plains
10/25/1853	b. near P. Plains			Joseph Beamithon		W	near P. Plains
4/19/1853	Harriet A. McGregor b. near Hillsborough	F	A	Alex McGregor	Mary Steel	W	near Hillsborough
12/15/1853	Mary Keeny b. near Hillsborough	F	A	Michael C. Keerey	Sarah Ann Neal	W	near Hillsborough
5/24/1853	Lemuel T. Graham b. near Hillsborough	M	A	A. F. Graham	Martha Stovy	W	near Hillsborough
1/ 9/1853	Samuel M. Woodard b. Licking	M	A	J. W. Woodard	Sarah Ann Anderson	W	Licking
8/17/1853	Mary E. J. Hopkins b. Licking	F	A	Herod Hopkins	Emily J. Hopkins	W	Licking
2/17/1853	Almanza M. Grose b. Locust	F	A	Braceton Grose	Mary J. Faris	W	Locust
6/ 8/1853	Joseph Helphinstine b. near P. Plains	M	A	W. P. Helphinstine	Milky Doyl	W	near P. Plains
3/16/1853	Reubena Re. slave.	F	A	Laurence Triplett	Linda	M	P. Plains

S Sex
C Condition A-Alive D-Dead

COUNTY Fleming

DATE	NAME OF CHILD	S	C	NAME OF FATHER	NAME OF MOTHER	CO.	RESIDENCE
11/ /1853	William Planck b. near Licking	M	A	John Planck	Matilda Arnold	W	Licking
6/15/1853	Mary McClain b. Licking	F	A	J. W. McClain	Mary Ann Dillon	W	Fleming Co.
12/23/1853	James W. H. Oberley b. near Tilton	M	A	Jonathan Overby	France A. Gardner	W	Tilton
	James Webster b. Tilton	M	A	James Webster	Clarissa A. Gardner	W	Tilton
2/ 7/1853	Fanny S. Hendricks b. P. Plains (near)	F	A	William Hendricks	Elizabeth Howe	W	near P. Plains
9/ /1853	Susan b. P. Plains, Re. slave.	F	A	William Hendricks	Parthena	B	near P. Plains
9/24/1853	- - - - b. Flemingsburg	M	A			W	
9/ /1853	- - - - b. Flemingsburg, Re. twins.	F	D	Dennis Belt	Mary Eckles	W	near Flemingsburg
12/ 2/1853	Elizabeth Hukle b. near Mt. Carmel	F	A	Wm. Hukle	Mary A. Brooks	W	near Mt. Carmel
3/17/1853	Francis Plummer b. near Mt. Carmel	M	A	George Plummer	Julia A. Power	W	near Mt. Carmel
10/ /1853	Mary Alice Thomas b. near Mt. Carmel, Re. Illegitimate.	F	A		Susannah Thomas	W	near Mt. Carmel
7/ 4/1853	John T. France b. b. near Tilton	M	A	Jonas France	Rebecca Jackson	W	Tilton
	 b. P. Plains, Re. Premature.		D	J. C. Hardy		W	P. Plains
7/ 5/1853	Charles Pearce b. P. Plains	M	A	J. M. Pearce	Jastena Darnall	W	P. Plains
12/ 1/1853	Jim b. P. Plains, Re. slave.	M	A	O. A. Kendall	Mariah	B	P. Plains
	Harrison b. near Poplar Plains, Re. slave.	M	A	Jerry Hall		B	near P. Plains
1/ /1853	 b. near Flemingsburg, Re. slave.	F	A	John S. Botts		B	near Flemingsburg
4/20/1853	 b. near Flemingsburg, Re. slave.	M		Amy Botts		B	
5/ 9/1853	Queen America b. Fox	F	A	William Kissick	Rosana Jamison	W	Fox

COUNTY Fleming

DATE	NAME OF CHILD	S	C	NAME OF FATHER	NAME OF MOTHER	CO.	RESIDENCE
11/ /1853	William T. Fulkerson b. Fox	M	A	J. D. Fulkerson	Mallissa	W	Fox
	Mary Joice b. Flemingsburg	F	A	Michael Jorice		W	Flemingsburg
10/27/1853	Clarissa Miller b. Locust	F	A	Henry Miller	Hannah Dalryanple	W	Locust
4/26/1853	John Chrisman b. Locust	M	A	Andrew Chrisman	Malinda Chrisman	W	Locust
4/ /1853	John or Green b. Wilsons Run, Re. slave.	M	A	Mrs. Harriet Evans		M	Wilson Run
5/ /1853	Lucy b. near Mt. Carmel, Re. slave.	F	A	Joel Debell		B	near Mt. Carmel
3/ /1853	 b. near Mt. Carmel, Re. slave.	M	A	Abram McGowan		M	near Mt. Carmel
	 b. near Mt. Carmel, Re. slave.	M	A	Abram McGowan		M	near Mt. Carmel
	 b. near Mt. Carmel, Re. slave.	F	A	Abram McGowan		B	near Mt. Carmel
4/ 5/1853	Harriet J. Riley b. P. Plains	F	A	John S. Riley	Matilda Sutton	W	P. Plains
1/ 6/1853	Mahaba E. Crain b. near Hillsborough	F	A	Marshall Crain	Louisa E. Hopkins	W	near Hillsborough
3/ 7/1853	Charles Doods b. near P. Plains	M	A	James Dodds	Mary Evans	W	near P. Plains
3/ /1853	Phebe F. b. near Flemingsburg, Re. slave.	F	A	Joseph Farrow		B	Flemingsburg
	Elijah b. near Flemingsburg, Re. slave.	M	A	Joseph Farrow		B	near Flemingsburg
3/ 4/1853	James H. Farrow b. near Flemingsburg	M	A	Joseph Farrow	Rosanna Ann Hood	W	Flemingsburg
7/25/1853	Rosanna McJlvain b. near Flemingsburg	F	A	William McJlvain	Mary E. Farrow	W	Lewisburg, Mason
8/15/1853	Thomas R. Comwell b. near Flemingsburg	M	A	James Comwell	Amanda Plummer	W	near Flemingsburg
8/27/1853	Lewellyn Davis b. Fox	F	A	Elias Davis	Mary Lyons	W	near Hillsborough
8/ 5/1853	Mary Barber b. Licking	F	A	Daniel Barber	Catharine Folland	W	Licking

COUNTY Fleming

S Sex
C Condition A-Alive D-Dead

DATE	NAME OF CHILD	S	C	NAME OF FATHER	NAME OF MOTHER	CO.	RESIDENCE
8/ /1853		F	A	Dr. E. Logan		B	P. Plains
	b. P. Plains, Re. slave.						
8/28/1853	Margaret Hutson	F	A	J. W. Hutson	Mary Day	W	Fox
	b. Fox						
4/ 3/1853	Atha J. Johnson	F	A	John H. Johnson	Emily Naylor	W	Fox
	b. Fox						
11/22/1853	John T. Vansant	M	A	John K. Vansant	Nancy Markwell	W	near Flemingsburg
	b. near Flemingsburg						
9/ 7/1853	Isabella P. Mahew	F	A	William Mahew	Angeline Riggs	W	Mt. Carmel
	b. near Mt. Carmel						
3/22/1853	Daniel	M	A	James M. Triplett	Harriet	B	near P. Plains
	b. near P. Plains, Re. slave.						
7/ 3/1853	Russel M. Rawlings	M	A	Anthony Rawlings	Suaan Walton	W	near P. Plains
	b. near P. Plains						
6/28/1853	Elizabeth S. Christy	F	A	William E. Christy	Olivia Gray	W	near P. Plains
	b. near P. Plains						
5/ /1853		F	A	Gamaliel Freeman	Sarah Overton	W	near P. Plains
	b. near P. Plains						
11/18/1853	Charles H. Davis	M	A	Col. F. R. Daris	Evaline Markwell	W	near Hillsborough
	b. near Hillsborough						
12/12/1853	Martha A. Robertson	F	A	F. P. Robertson	Martha E. Fruley	W	Maysville
	b. near Blue Licks						
6/22/1853	Maranda R. Pearce	F	A	Rawleigh W. Pearce	Betsy Johnson	W	Cincinnati
	b. near Cincinnati						
9/12/1853	Martha Reeves	F	A	William Reeves	Cynthia Ann Smith	W	near Flemingsburg
	b. near Maysville						
10/24/1853	Mary E. Belt	F	A	James Belt	Amanda Cooper	W	near Flemingsburg
	b. near Flemingsburg						
7/17/1853	Eliza Bell Overton	F	A	Creed Overton	Eliza Vansant	W	Fox
	b. Fox						
9/19/1853	Edward Roberts	M	A	Edward Roberts	Margaret A. Thompson	W	Fox
	b. Fox						
9/24/1853	Malinda S. Reeves	F	A	Benj. J. Reeves	Mary R. Jimison	W	Fox
	b. Fox						
Summer			A	J. W. Foudry	-- Havens	W	Fox
	b. Fox						
9/22/1853	Amanda J. Rawlings	F	A	Sanford Rawlings	Mary Dawson	W	near Hillsborough
	b. near Hillsborough						

COUNTY Fleming

S Sex
C Condition A-Alive D-Dead

DATE	NAME OF CHILD	S	C	NAME OF FATHER	NAME OF MOTHER	CO.	RESIDENCE
10/ 9/1853	Atha C. Kearns b. near Hillsborough	F	A	Thomas Kearns	Vian Johnson	W	near Hillsborough
5/ 5/1853	G. W. Barber b. Licking	M	A	George Barber	Sarah Johnson	W	Licking
6/ 4/1853	Mary D. Nate b. near Mt. Carmel	F	A	Charles Nute	Malinda Glasscock	W	near Mt. Carmel
4/21/1853	Mary J. Downs b. near Mt. Carmel	F		Edward Downs	Nancy Clary	W	near Mt. Carmel
12/29/1853	b. Flemingsburg, Re. slave.			John J. Rodgers		B	Flemingsburg
11/19/1853	Sophia A. Pickert b. near Mt. Carmel	F	A	John Pickert	Sophia A. Carstin	W	Charles Marshalls
	Abram Alexander b. Flemingsburg	M	A	Joseph M. Alexander	Elizabeth McCalf	W	Flemingsburg
7/ 5/1853	Theodore Fischer	M	A	John G. Fischer	Mary Hoenig	W	Flemingsburg
7/ 5/1853	Victor Fischer b. Flemingsburg, Re. Twins.	M	A	John G. Fischer	Mary Hoenig	W	Flemingsburg
6/17/1853	Kitty b. near Flemingsburg, Re. slave.	F	A	James M. Kenman		B	near Flemingsburg
9/ 2/1853	Jack b. near Flemingsburg, Re. slave.	M	A	Henry Hart		B	near Flemingsburg
1/ 7/1853	b. Flemingsburg	F	A	Enoch Kirtland	Abbie Powell	W	Flemingsburg
3/21/1853	b. Flemingsburg	F	A	Jacob Bishop	Mary Hart	W	near Flemingsburg
5/ 7/1853	Eliza Morgan b. Flemingsburg, Re. slave.	F		L. D. Anderson		B	Flemingsburg
7/ 9/1853	b. near Mt. Carmel, Re. slave.	M	A	Charles Marshall		B	near Mt. Carmel
8/13/1853	b. near Mt. Carmel	M	A	Edward Down	Mary --	W	near Flemingsburg
2/15/1853	G. W. Elliott b. Fox	M	A	George Elliott	Poly Ann Bramel	W	Fox
9/ /1853	Rebecca E. Royse b. Fox	F	A	William T. Royse	Mary Ann Bailey	W	Fox
12/25/1853	Isabella Roys. b. Fox	F	A	Samuel H. Roys	Robata Bailey	W	Fox

COUNTY Fleming

DATE	NAME OF CHILD	S	C	NAME OF FATHER	NAME OF MOTHER	CO.	RESIDENCE
9/ /1853	Rebecca Roys. b. Fox	F	A	William Roys	Polly Ann M. Ross?	W	Fox
11/20/1853	Matilda S. Farons b. Fox	F	A	William Farons	Lucinda Boyd	W	Fox
10/23/1853	Sophia Hartley b. Fox	F	A	John Hartley	Sophia Fouche	W	Fox
10/ 9/1853	Logan O. Jones b. Fox	M	A	A. C. Jones	Eliza J. Kissick	W	Fox
12/25/1853	-- Royse b. Fox	M	A	Anthony Royse	Sarah Boys	W	Fox
2/13/1853	-- Carpenter b. Fox	M	A	John S. Carpenter		W	Fox
10/10/1853	Nancy J. Williams b. Fox	F	A	Harrison Williams	Malissa Fouche	W	Fox
4/18/1853	Bramble b. Fox	F	A	Z. W. Bramble	Hinton	W	Fox
3/ /1853	Sever. b. Fox	F	D	Casper H. Sever	Eliza Shoult	W	Fox
12/20/1853	John S. Newman b. Fox	M	A	John D. Newman	Minerva J. Littleton	W	Fox
9/19/1853	Gardner b. Triplett	M	A	Harrison Gardner	Mary Tribby	W	Triplett
12/ 9/1853	Lee b. Triplett	F	D	Hiram Lee	Kentey Ann Campbell	W	Triplett
6/ 9/1853	Eliza Kinder b. Triplett	F	A	William G. Kinder	Lucinda Raiburn	W	Triplett
12/10/1853	Johnson b. Triplett	M	D	Jefferson Johnson	Rachel Sorrel	W	Triplett
2/16/1853	Elizabeth E. Cogswell b. Licking	F	A	Thomas Cogswell	Elizabeth Day	W	Licking
3/10/1853	Sarah E. Sorrel b. Licking	F	A	John H. Sorrel	Polly Ann Johnson	W	Licking
4/26/1853	Sally Ann Myres b. Licking	F	A	K. R. Myres	Amelia Carey	W	Licking
5/ /1853	Eliza Ann Whitte b. Triplett	F	A	Robt. White	E. D. Goodan	W	Triplett

S Sex
C Condition A-Alive D-Dead

COUNTY Fleming

DATE	NAME OF CHILD	S	C	NAME OF FATHER	NAME OF MOTHER	CO.	RESIDENCE
11/20/1853	Elizabeth Hedrick b. Triplett	F	A	Michael Hedrick	Elizabeth Razor	W	Triplett
12/29/1853	James M. Thomas b. Triplett	M	A	T. J. Thomas	Mary Ann Flood	W	Triplett
9/24/1853	James A. Cassity b. Triplett	M	A	A. R. Cassity	J. Hedges	W	Triplett
10/28/1853	America C. Markwell b. Triplett	F	A	Landa. Markwell	Diana Logan	W	Triplett
10/ 1/1853	Samuel Hardiman b. Triplett	M	A	William Hardiman	Nancy Colbert	W	Triplett
12/ /1853	Nelly Ann Johnson b. Triplett	F	A	J. W. R. Johnson	Nancy Lee	W	Triplett
3/18/1853	Azrilla Humphries b. Triplett	F	A	Daniel Humphries	Susan Stanford	W	Triplett
11/ /1853	Mary J. Phelps b. Fox	F	A	J. B. Phelps	Nancy Sanders	W	Fox
8/12/1853	James A. Saunders b. Fox	M	A	Hiram Saunders	Abigail Saunders	W	Fox
8/28/1853	Tompkins Logan b. Triplett	M	A	William W. Logan	Elizabeth Giodan	W	Triplett
11/12/1853	Jonathan S. Walker	M	A			W	
11/12/1853	Johnson S. Walker b. Fox, Re. Twins.	M	A	Samuel Walker	Polly Ann Dale	W	Fox
12/ /1853	Thomas D. Sutton b. Fox	M	A	Richard Sutton	Tabitha J. Rigdon	W	Fox
8/ 1/1853	Andrew Gooding b. Fox	M	A	James Gooding	Phebe Hurst	W	Fox
3/ 5/1853	Charlotte Hurst b. Fox	F	A	Miles Hurst Jr.	Ann E. Carpenter	W	Fox
11/26/1853	Sarah M. Reeves b. Fox	F	A	John Reeves	Nancy Hughes	W	Fox
1/17/1853	Edna A. Carpenter b. Fox	F	A	Richard E. Carpenter	Harriett Estill	W	Fox
12/16/1853	Lucinda Hinton b. Fox	F	A	David Hinton	Jane Hickerson	W	Fox
8/ /1853	Mary E. Carpenter b. Fox	F	A	Marshall Carpenter	Pakerson	W	Fox

31

S Sex
C Condition A-Alive D-Dead

COUNTY Fleming

DATE	NAME OF CHILD	S	C	NAME OF FATHER	NAME OF MOTHER	CO.	RESIDENCE
7/20/1853	Martha Hinton b. Fox	F	A	Brice Hinton	Evaline Jourdan	W	Fox
12/ 3/1853	Miles Doyl b. Fox	M	A	John Doyl	Elizabeth A. McCann	W	Fox
1/18/1853	Winefield Hickerson b. Fox	M	A	Marshall Hickerson	Malinda Lewman	W	Fox
12/ 2/1853	Harriet A. Jourdan b. Fox	F	A	William S. Jourdan	Eliza Ross	W	Fox
11/ /1853	Plummer b. Fox	M	A	Joseph Plummer	Elizabeth Mase	W	Fox
8/ 2/1853	Susan Gourley b. Fox	F	A	E. D. Gourley	Minerva R. Brow.	W	Fox
12/ /1853	Ashael M. McRoberts b. Triplett	M	A	Trumbo McRoberts	Susanah Ham	W	Triplett
8/ /1853	b. Triplett	F	D	Edmund Portey	Cynthia Stovy	W	Triplett
7/18/1853	Portey b. Triplett	M	A	George Portey	Margaret Young	W	Triplett
9/ 2/1853	James M. Callahan b. Fox	M	A	Edward Callahan	Priscilla Joudan	W	Fox
2/24/1853	Edward T. Gregor b. Triplett	M	A	Nathanel Gregory	Mahala Templeman	W	Triplett
8/12/1853	b. Triplett, Re. slave.	F	A	Barnet Seamons		B	Triplett
7/ /1853	Martha M. N. Power b. Triplett	F	A	John D. Power	Martha Coyl	W	Triplett
4/ 1/1853	Rebecca S. Pugh b. Triplett	F	A	Mariah Pugh	Cydrova? C. Wood	W	Triplett
11/13/1853	Robt. G. Reeves b. Fox	M	A	George Reeves	Eliza Plummer	W	Fox
8/17/1853	Edward Webster b. Fox	M	A	John A. Webster	Angeline Havens	W	Fox
7/ /1853	Greenup Nickle b. Triplett	M	A	William Nickle	Lucinda Pearce	W	Triplett
8/ /1853	Elizabeth Nickle b. Triplett	F	A	Robt. Nickle	Rachael Coggwell	W	Triplett
8/ /1853	William Bartlett b. Triplett	M	A	Silas Bartlett	Barbary McDonald	W	Triplett

COUNTY Fleming

DATE	NAME OF CHILD	S	C	NAME OF FATHER	NAME OF MOTHER	CO.	RESIDENCE
6/ /1853	John C. Atchison b. Triplett	M	A	Wm. P. Atchison	Abigail Moore	W	Triplett
6/27/1853	James M. Patterson b. Triplett	M	A	James B. Patterson	Sally Powers	W	Triplett
7/ /1853	b. Triplett, Re. slave.	M	D	Mrs. Rebecca Wilson		B	Triplett
9/ /1853	b. Triplett, Re. slave.	F	D	Rebecca Wilson		B	Triplett
11/ /1853	b. Triplett, Re. slave.	F	A	Rebecca Wilson		B	Triplett
12/ 8/1853	Victoria Johnson b. Triplett	F	A	Z. Johnson	Amanda A. Sanders	W	Triplett
7/13/1853	Jeremiah F. Johnson b. Triplett	M	A	Samuel P. Johnson	Elizabeth Saunders	W	Triplett
6/24/1853	Nancy A. Purvis b. Triplett	F	A	James Purvis	Nancy J. White	W	Triplett
12/19/1853	Benjamin F. Johnson b. Triplett	M	A	Z. P. Johnson	Frances L. Logan	W	Triplett
5/ /1853	Purvis b. Triplett	M	D	William Purvis	Dehla White	W	Triplett
3/13/1853	Charles M. Staggs b. Fox	M	A	Thomas Staggs	Polly Ann Jourdan	W	Fox
11/ 4/1853	Rachael Jones b. Fox	F	A	William F. Jones	Rachael Hinton	W	Fox
1/ 1/1853	Samuel Emmons b. Fox	M	A	William Emmons	Anfield Gregory	W	Fox
5/12/1853	b. Fox, Re. slave.	M	A	William Emmons		M	Fox
8/ /1853	Lucinda Robinson b. Fox	F	A	William P. Robinson	Rachael Simons	W	Fox
8/15/1853	Mary A. Nudigate b. Fox	M	A	William Nudigate	Mary Nickle	W	Fox
12/ 2/1853	Martha J. Davis b. Fox	F	A	John M. Davis	Sarah A. Penland	W	Fox
10/12/1853	Rebecca Callahan b. Fox	F	A	Anderson Callahan	Aridlla F. Hughes	W	Fox
3/14/1853	George Ann McRee b. Fox	M	A	Joseph McKee	Rebecca Fenton	W	Fox

33

COUNTY Fleming

S Sex
C Condition A-Alive D-Dead

DATE	NAME OF CHILD	S	C	NAME OF FATHER	NAME OF MOTHER	CO.	RESIDENCE
2/17/1853	Hiram Yasel b. Fox	M	A	Joseph Yasel	Martha J. Anderson	W	Fox
4/19/1853	James D. Muse b. Fox	M	A	James B. Muse	Sarah Walker	W	Fox
5/ /1853	Elliott b. Fox	F	D	James Elliott		W	Fox
10/31/1853	Humphries b. Fox	F	D	Wm. Humphries	Nancy Walker	W	Fox
8/15/1853	Amanda Evans b. Fox	F	A	Wm. B. evans	Matilda Plummer	W	Fox
11/24/1853	Susan Evans b. Fox	F	A	James B. Evans		W	Fox
2/ 4/1853	Franklin P. Bowen b. Fox	M	A	Morton Bourn	Evaline Smith	W	Fox
6/30/1853	-- Phelps b. Fox	M	A	Samuel R. Phelps	Sarah Plummer	W	Fox
9/ 3/1853	Mary Catharine Graham b. near P. Plains	F	A	William S. T. Graham	Lydia Mae Dearing	W	near P. Plains
5/20/1853	Slave b. Mt. Carmel	F		Richard Soward	Slave	M	Fleming
11/29/1853	Slave b. Mt. Carmel	F		Richard Soward	Slave	M	Fleming
3/20/1853	Slave b. Mt. Carmel	M		Richard Soward	Slave	M	Fleming
12/25/1853	Charles H. Dobyns b. Elizavill	M		Henry Dolyns	-- Umstadt	W	Fleming
8/25/1853	Martha A. Terhune b. Elizavill	F		Barnett Terhune	Martha Hicks	W	Fleming
8/ 3/1853	Ger. H. McCarty b. Oakwoods	M		John McCarty	Lucy Ann Cammins	W	Fleming
9/16/1853	Malinda McCarty b. Oakwoods	F		John R. McCarty	Martha Collins	W	Fleming
12/ /1853	Slave b. Elizavill	M		Simeon B. Allen	Slave	B	Fleming
12/ /1853	Slave b. Elizavill	M		Simeon B. Allen	Slave	B	Fleming
5/ 4/1853	Lucinda Hmmonds b. Fleming	F		W. W. Hammonds	Mary Spencer	W	Fleming

S Sex
C Condition A-Alive D-Dead

COUNTY __Fleming__

DATE	NAME OF CHILD	S	C	NAME OF FATHER	NAME OF MOTHER	CO.	RESIDENCE
11/17/1853	Jane Field	F		John Fields	Jane McCord	W	All residents
9/ 7/1853	Slave	F		Lunia Alexander	Slave	B	Fleming Co.
6/ 6/1853	Burns	M		Dennis & Mary Burns	Mary Wilson	W	
6/13/1853	Sullivan	M		Pat & Jonna Sullivan	Joanna Dillon	W	
6/24/1853	Slave	M		Geo. S. Bruce	Slave	B	
6/27/1853	Gairey	M		Saml. Gairey	Rebecca Gray	W	
6/29/1853	Farrow	M		Nimrod Farrow	Susan Farrow	W	
5/13/1853	Spencer	F		William Spencer	Harriet Shockey	W	
5/ 3/1853	Brown	F		Cummins Brown	Mary Saunders	W	
5/ 4/1853	Slave	F		Jno. H. Botts	Slave	B	
5/ 7/1853	Cullin	F		Cullin	Cullin	W	Re. Irish
5/10/1853	John Nash	M		John Nash	Sally Williams	W	
5/10/1853	Henry Thomas	M		William Thomas	Minvervy Brown	W	
5/10/1853	Slave	M		James Patton	Slave	B	
5/19/1853	Thos. Cochran	M		James Cochran Jr.	Isabella Sousley	W	
5/26/1853	Cochran	M		Robert Cochran	Margaret Adams	W	
5/29/1853	Amelia Botts Taylor	F		Charles Taylor	Sabina Blair	W	
4/ 7/1853	Shockney	M		William Shockney	Winifred Hayden	W	Re. Irish
4/11/1853	G. Slicer	M		A. G. Slicer	Elanor Frank	W	
4/16/1853	Sullivan	M		Not known	Mary Sullivan	W	Re. Irish
4/15/1853	Daniel Bush	M		Daniel Bush free	Eliza (cold. woman)	B	Re. Free
4/27/1853	William Cole	M		William Cole	Mary Wells	W	
7/ 1/1853	Ross	M		James Ross	Hannah Ford	W	
7/ 4/1853	Scott	F		John P. Scott	Lydia Jackson	W	
7/ 7/1853	Slave	M		John H. Wells	Slave	B	
7/ 7/1853	Ann McCarty	F		Frank McCarty	Sarah Myres	W	
7/14/1853	Slicer	F		Alfd. G. Slicer	Caroline Yost	W	
7/17/1853	Jemmia Caywood	F		Randolph Caywood	Jemmia Scott	W	
7/17/1853	Mary McIntyre	F		Geo. McIntyre	Mary McIntyre	W	
7/20/1853	Thos. Wiggins	M		Lawson Wiggins	Eliza S. Bishop	W	
7/23/1853	Geo. H. B. Loury	M		Geo. G. Lourey	Nancy Bruce	W	
7/24/1853	Jno. F. Bett	M		Hickerson Belt	Martha Fant	W	
7/25/1853	Catharine C. Hitt	F		Wilson W. Hitt	Catharine Cole	W	
7/26/1853	Saunders	M		Squire Saunders	Rachael Williams	W	
7/29/1853	James Nash	M		James Nash	Mary Williams	W	
8/ 1/1853	Bush	M		Pat Bush	Isabella Rednik	W	

Re. 7 mos. child.

COUNTY Fleming

S Sex
C Condition A-Alive D-Dead
G-Good

DATE	NAME OF CHILD	S	C	NAME OF FATHER	NAME OF MOTHER	CO.	RESIDENCE
8/11/1853	Lawson	F		John Larwson	Julian Hughes	W	All residents
8/27/1853	Terhune	F		Barnett Terhune	Sarah Hicks	W	Fleming Co.
8/29/1853	Bently	M		Campbell Bently	M. Graves	W	
9/ 1/1853	Slave	M		John Early	Slave	B	
9/16/1853	Wells	M		Mat. Wells	Elzh. Cord	W	
9/26/1853	Berry	M		Henry Berry	Louisa Armstrong	W	
	Re. 6 mos. child						
9/26/1853	Slave	F	D	John Sherwood	Slave	M	
9/28/1853	Cook	F		Edward Cook	Mary -- Irish	W	Re. Irish
9/30/1853	James Lee	M		John H. Lee	Eliza Potts	W	
10/11/1853	Slave	F	G	W. T. Dudley	Slave	B	
	b. William Dudley						
4/17/1853	Black	M	G	W. J. Howe	Slave	B	
4/27/1853	Jeff Foudry	M	G	Jeff Foudry	Mary Bell	W	
3/21/1853	Howe	F		W. T. Howe	Emily Proctor	W	
	Condition - not good						
3/23/1853	Miranda Taylor	F	A	Geo. A. Taylor	Miranda Washburn	W	
3/28/1853	Morganthaw	F	A	Henry Morganthaw	Not known	W	
11/15/1853	Slave	M	A	Mrs. A. Howe	Slave	B	
7/17/1853	Paxton	M	A	Granville	Mary Clinsman	W	
7/10/1853	Slave	M	A	Geo. W. Taylor	Slave	B	
2/12/1853	Philips	M	A	Martin Philips	Nancy Lawson	W	
8/ 4/1853	Slave	M	A	Sally Howe Mrs.	Slave	B	
9/ 9/1853	John Alexander	M	A	Wm. P. Blair	Nancy McIlvaine	W	
10/14/1853	Beam	M	A	Eli Beam	Mary Wilson	W	
12/31/1853	McCann	F	A	Marshall McCann	Nancy Hull	W	
11/28/1853	Arnold	M	A	Leuis Arnold	Nancy Rankin	W	
12/23/1853	James Wilson	M	A	Jonathan Overly	Frances Garner	W	
12/26/1853	Jas. D. Palmer	M	A	Philip O. Palmer	Lucinda Overby	W	
10/20/1853	Slave	M	A	Roley S. Porter	Slave	B	
6/ 5/1853	Sarah Ormstadt	F	A	Geo. Ormstadt	Nancy Pepper	W	
5/ 3/1853	Slave	F	A	Geo. Ormstadt	Slave	B	
5/ 2/1853	Martha McCord	F	A	David McCord	Margt. Sullivan	W	
11/25/1853	Slave	M	A	Mary Faris	Slave	B	
6/ 7/1853	Martha Duvall	F	A	Mosen Duvall	Frances Payne	W	
11/ 4/1853	Slave	F	A	J. G. Bishop Senr.	Slave	B	
12/14/1853	Mary Bishop	F	A	A. D. Bishop	Airey Ficklen	W	
5/ 6/1853	White Girl name not known	F	A	Thos. Cullin	Not known	W	

COUNTY <u>Fleming</u>   C Condition A-Alive D-Dead

DATE	NAME OF CHILD	S	C	NAME OF FATHER	NAME OF MOTHER	CO.	RESIDENCE
4/10/1853	Sarah Willett	F	A	Walker Willett	Matilda Rawlings	W	All residents
12/17/1853	Myres	F	A	Jas. Myres	Nancy Wilson	W	Fleming Co.
4/23/1853	Girl not known on the rail road	F	A	Michael Heman	Not known	W	
7/14/1853	Slave	M	A	Henry Bruce	Slave	B	
9/ 6/1853	Luan King	F	A	Enoch. King	Nancy Ann Campbell	W	
3/ 4/1853	Eli Howe	M	A	David L. Howe	Harriet Planek	W	
6/ 7/1853	Jno. G. Kane	M	A	Silas W. Kane	Martha Marsh	W	
10/20/1853	Slave	F	A	Polly Hornbock	Slave	B	
5/26/1853	Rice	M	A	Jackson Rice	Mary Tribby	W	
7/ 5/1853	Eliza Ann McIntyre	F	A	Barnett McIntyre	Mary Turney	W	
4/ 1/1853	John S. Finley	M	A	James Finley	Margaret Ricketts	W	
4/15/1853	Mary E. Peek	F	A	John Peck	Sarah Robinson	W	
9/ 1/1853	Marshall Hull	M	A	Moses Hull	Tobitha Rash	W	
2/20/1853	Miranda Rash	F	A	William Rash	Margaret Brothers	W	
3/17/1853	Wm. T. Dougherty	M	A	Thos. Dougherty	Elizabeth Ricketts	W	
8/28/1853	Juliett Ricketts	F	A	N. Harris	Amanda Ricketts	W	
9/28/1853	Slave	M	A	Nelson Gant	Slave	M	
9/28/1853	Slave	M	A	B. T. McIntyre	Slave	M	
4/27/1853	Carlotte Lapeley b. Flemingsburg	F	A	Jas. T. Lapsley	Elizabeth Brushell	W	
7/ 4/1853	John Scott b. Fleming	M	A	Wm. Scott	Maria Dillon	W	
11/11/1853	Tho. Hurst b. Fleming	M	A	Wm. Hurst	Susan E. Evans	W	
7/25/1853	Cathn. Hitt	F	A	Wilson Hitt	Cathn. Cole	W	
3/ /1853	Slave b. Flemingsburg	F	A	L. D. Stockton	Slave	M	
9/25/1853	Wm. G. Nute b. Flemingsburg	M	A	Wm. G. Nute	Phebe Stockton	W	
3/10/1853	Slave b. Fleming	F	A	Mary Mills	Slave	M	
6/20/1853	Mary Ryan b. Fleming	F	A	Tos. Ryan	Mary Taylor	W	
9/ /1853	Mary Bramwell b. Fleming	F	A	Henry Bramwell	Jane Taylor	W	
9/ /1853	Slave b. Mt. Carmel	F	A	B. C. Foxworthy	Slave	M	

COUNTY _Fleming_

DATE	NAME OF CHILD	S	C	NAME OF FATHER	NAME OF MOTHER	CO.	RESIDENCE
10/ /1853	Slave b. Mt. Carmel	F	A	Nelson Morehead	Slave	M	Fleming Co.
1/ 9/1853	Slave b. Elizaville	F		America Howe	Slave	B	Flemingsburg
1/30/1853	Cowan b. near Elizaville	M		John Cowan	Elizabeth Harper	W	near Elizaville
2/ 2/1853	Kirk b. near Elizaville	F		Reasen S. Kirk	Levina Moore	W	near Elizaville
2/21/1853	Ann Prather b. near Elizaville	F		Walter Prather	Cynthia Callahan	W	near Elizaville
2/24/1853	Sousley b. near Elizaville	M		John E. Sousley	Susan Rash	W	near Elizaville
3/19/1853	Ewing b. near Elizaville	M		William Weing	Sarah Jane Allen	W	near Elizaville
10/29/1853	Mary Clark b. near Elizaville	F		John Clark	Lucinda Chrismen	W	near Elizaville
10/29/1853	Rock b. near Elizaville	F		Charles Rock	Melvina Hays	W	near Elizaville
10/15/1853	Hammonds b. near Elizaville	M		John Hammonds	Myra Barton	W	near Elizaville
10/16/1853	Slave b. near Elizaville	F		A. M. Patton	Slave	B	near Elizaville
10/17/1853	Wm. Franklin Williams b. near Elizaville	M		Jno. W. Williams	Elanor James	W	near Elizaville
11/ 3/1853	Maston b. near Elizaville	F		Thomas Maston	Caroline Kenner	W	near Elizaville
11/ 7/1853	Cline b. near Elizaville	F		Harrison Cline	Elizabeth Galligher	W	near Elizaville
11/ 8/1853	Spencer b. Elizaville	F		Zaddock Spencer	Mary Ann Taylor	W	Elizaville
11/25/1853	Mallory b. near Elizaville	F		Wilford Mallory	Rasana Hinton	W	Elizaville
12/ 4/1853	Wilson b. Nicholas Co.	M		Michael Wilson	Ebanor K. Lockridge?	W	Nicholas
12/ 7/1853	Chapell b. Elizaville	F		James Chapell	Lucy P. Bruce	W	Elizaville
12/14/1853	Margt. Botts b. Flemingsburg	F		Ben Botts	Juliett Dorsey	W	Flemingsburg

COUNTY Fleming

S Sex
C Condition A-Alive D-Dead

DATE	NAME OF CHILD	S	C	NAME OF FATHER	NAME OF MOTHER	CO.	RESIDENCE
12/15/1853	Payne b. Johnson Fork	F		Robert Payne	Rachael Burgess	W	Johnsons Fork of Licking
12/18/1853	Price b. Elizaville	F		Eliha Price	Elizabeth Courtney	W	Elizaville
12/18/1853	Dobyns b. Elizaville	M		Henry Dobyns	Ann Umstadt	W	Elizaville
12/29/1853	Morgan b. Elizaville	M		William F. Morgan	Ann Umstadt	W	Elizaville
12/20/1853	Susan Worrick b. Elizaville	M		Hurst Worrick	Mary Early	W	Elizaville
12/30/1853	Slave b. Elizaville	M		Free woman	Free woman	B	Elizaville
12/30/1853	Sousley b. Elizaville	F		Franklin Sousley	Susan Peck	W	near Blue Licks

Fleming County Sct.
    I certify that the foregoing is a correct copy of the List of Births for the year 1853 as returned by the Commissioner for said County. June 6, 1854.
                    W. T. Dudley CCK, Fleming County Court

DATE	NAME OF CHILD	S	C	NAME OF FATHER	NAME OF MOTHER	CO.	RESIDENCE
6/ /1855	Mahala Emmons	F	A	Joseph Belt Emmons	Polly Riggs	W	Fleming Co.
	Jane	F	A	Joseph Belt Emmons		B	All residents
5/ /1855	No name b. Nicholas County	F	D	E. E. Riggs		B	
3/23/1855	Joseph Franklin West	M	A	John H. West	Rebecca Hamilton	B	
9/26/1855	Alice	F	A	Eli Evans		M	
8/17/1855	Aridale Ingraham	F	A	Jean Ingraham	Sarah D. Armstrong	W	
3/12/1855	Lewellyn Northcut	F	A	Joseph B. Northcut	Louisa Emmons	W	
1/ /1855	Alfred Davis Foudery	M	A	Adison M. Foudery	Nancy D. Havens	W	
6/ /1855	Sarah E. J. Roberts	F	A	Edward Roberts	Margaret Ann Thompson	W	
5/25/1855	James C. M. Vinsant	M	A	George W. Vinsant	Isabel Cooper	W	
2/25/1855	Harrison Dudly Finsley	M	A	Samuel Finsley	Sarah Vannatten	W	
7/22/1855	Amanda Burke	F	A		Nancy Ann Burke	W	
10/ 4/1855	Mahilda G. Keerans	F	A	Thomas Keerans	Viana Johnson	W	
1/13/1855	Patsey Jane Emmons	F	A	William S. F. Emmons	Susan Reeves	W	
5/26/1855	Sarah Jane Goodpasture	F	A	Tennett Goodpasture	Margaret Nailor	W	
5/11/1855	John James Barbour	M	A	George Barbour	Sarah Johnson	W	
6/ 5/1855	John A. Powell	M	A	Absolyn Powell	Minerva Jones	W	

S Sex
C Condition A-Alive D-Dead

COUNTY___Fleming___

DATE	NAME OF CHILD	S	C	NAME OF FATHER	NAME OF MOTHER	CO.	RESIDENCE
2/ 5/1855	James R. McKee	M	A	Andrew McKee	Susan Roden	W	All residents
3/ 2/1855	Jonathan Denton	M	A	Frances Denton	Frances Rawlings	W	Fleming Co.
7/ 7/1855	Louisa Fons	F	A	John Fons	Sarah Kissick	W	
8/16/1855	Elvira Catharine Barbour	F	A		Sarah Jane Hunt	W	
	Re. George Bartour reputed father.						
9/ /1855	Luther Markwell	M	A	Marshall Markwell	Mystillia Walton	W	
7/25/1855	John Wally Hiley	M	A	William Hiley	Dorhia Ann Barnett	W	
11/17/1855	No name	M	A	Thomas J. Johnson	Malinda Jane Alexander	W	
6/22/1855	James Edin Humphreys	M	A	Richard Humphreys	Frances Arigen	W	
3/ 2/1855	Phebe Thomas Gooding	F	A	James R. Gooding	Phebe Hurst	W	
4/22/1855	George Maxwell Filson	M	A	Lewis D. Filson	Mary Jane Thompson	W	
12/30/1855	Marion Staggs	M	A	Thomas Staggs	Polly Ann Jordon	W	
11/ 4/1855	Rebecca Calvert	F	A	James Calvert	Jinnetta Razor (Kazor?)	W	
7/ 1/1855	Frances Marion Davis	M	A	James W. Davis	Martha Ann Davis	W	
7/27/1855	Henry Clay Crain	M	A	John F. Crain	Luticia Dillon	W	
9/28/1855	Israel W. Hargit	M	A	Whitfield Hargit	Lucinda Smoot	W	
5/23/1855	Juliett Zimmerman	F	A	J. Barnett Zimmermon	Juliett Marshall	W	
9/ 7/1855	Evaline McVesbit	F	A	John McVesbit	Sarah Atchison	W	
12/15/1855	James William Shields	M	A	James L. Shields	Harriet A. Gray	W	
6/10/1855	Sally Ann Markwell	F	A	Joel Markwell	Ester Rice	W	
5/21/1855	Trumbs Cooper	M	A	William Cooper	Hulda Swain	W	
11/20/1855	No name	M	A	Tobias Logan	Eliza Jane Christy	W	
10/15/1855	Serene Henry Johnson	F	A	Zachariah R. Johnson	Amanda Ann Sanders	W	
6/10/1855	Harvey Sanders Norris	M	A	William Norris	Lucy Ann Logan	W	
2/13/1855	William Trumbo	M	A	Oliver H. Trumbo	Nancy Manley	W	
3/ 8/1855	Ann Eliza Stone Lee	F	A	Hiram Lee	Margaret J. Hawkins	W	
10/ 5/1855	Lewis Elder Cogswell	M	A	Henry Cogswell	Louisa Johnson	W	
12/15/1855	Mary Elizabeth Shouch	F	A	G. B. Shouch	Lydia Myers	W	
1/10/1855	Melvina Sorrell	F	A	John Sorrell	Polly Amanda Johnson	W	
3/12/1855	Mary Catharine Ringo	F	A	William W. Ringo	Susan Heflin	W	
5/ 5/1855	Lewellyn Davis	F	A	Harry Davis	Nancy Smoot	W	
8/15/1855	Sarah Jane Royse	F	A	William Roys	Rebecca Royse	W	
3/12/1855	Samuel Kenton Royse	M	A	Abràm Royse	Margaret Jane Smith	W	
10/ 1/1855	Nancy Jane Royse	F	A	William Royse	Polly Ann Royse	W	
12/17/1855	Caroline	F	A	William Emmons		M	
12/ /1855	Frank	M	A	Jane Markwell		M	
/ /1855	Alice	F	A	Rebecca Wilson		B	
/ /1855	Jinny	F	A	Rebecca Wilson		B	

KENTUCKY COUNTIES VITAL STATISTICS   S Sex

COUNTY   Fleming   C Condition A-Alive D-Dead

DATE	NAME OF CHILD	S	C	NAME OF FATHER	NAME OF MOTHER	CO.	RESIDENCE
5/11/1855	Austin Davis	M	A	Elias G. Davis	Mary Ann Lyons	W	All residents
3/25/1855	George Fleming Royse	M	A	Hiram T. Royse	Artimena Moore	W	Fleming Co.
4/ /1855	James N. Calvert	M	A	Marion Calvert	Emily Fawns	W	
4/ 4/1855	William Logan	M	A	Henry Logan	Lucinda F. Gray	W	
12/24/1855	Farris M. Looman	M	A	James P. Looman	Charlotte Davis	W	
5/23/1855	Mary Ellen Shields	F	A	Samuel Shields	Elizabeth J. Nealis	W	
10/ /1855	No name	F	D	Thompson Chadwick	Sarah J. Faun	W	
5/26/1855	Franklin Cooper	M	A	George Cooper	Mary Likes	W	
8/27/1855	James Moses Bailey Swim	M	A	H. S. Swim	Mary Johnson	W	
8/27/1855	Leuilda Jane Humphreys	F	A	Not given	Eliza Humphreys	W	
	Re. Born out of wedlock.						
3/27/1855	Claud Powers	M	A	Ben F. Powers	Elizabeth McIlhany	W	
11/23/1855	Florence Jane Kendall	F	A	William A. Kendall	Mary C. Dailey	W	
4/26/1855	Davis C. Christian	M	A	John B. Christian	Eliza Branham	W	
10/ 9/1855	Louisa Lander Power	F	A	John D. Powers	Martha Coil	W	
9/26/1855	Lilla Bell White	F	A	John D. White	Elizabeth Harn (Ham?)	W	
2/25/1855	Sally Summers Ham	F	A	William M. Ham	Rebecca Humphreys	W	
10/30/1855	Amazel J. Ham	F	A	Thomas Ham	Emily Thacher	W	
12/ 9/1855	Not named	F	A	William Kinder	Lucinda Barbour	W	
6/22/1855	Joseph M. Wright	M	A	T. M. Wright	Matilda J. Swim	W	
6/26/1855	Eliza J. Swim	F	A	John W. Swim	Harriet Wright	W	
10/ 3/1855	Emily F. Jones	F	A	Samuel B. H. Jones	Martha Plummer	W	
3/11/1855	Mary F. Christy	F	A	Robert A. Christy	Amanda Newman	W	
5/10/1855	William Hendrick	M	A	William H. Kendrick	Elizabeth Howe	W	
11/ /1855	Not named	M	A	William H. Kendrick		B	
9/ 9/1855	Eli Sandford Rigden	M	A	Eli Rigden	Dicey Hurst	W	
8/ 4/1855	James D. Manchester	M	A	Abel B. Manchester	Othela Muse	W	
6/16/1855	Fanny Staggs	F	A	William Staggs	Teressa Estill	W	
7/ 4/1855	Elbert Gousby	M	A	E. D. Gourby	Minerva Brown	W	
8/ /1855	Eliza Jane Gulby	F	A	George Gulby	Martha Burns	W	
11/13/1855	Jededia Foster Hickerson	M	A	James Hickerson	Polly Loorman	W	
7/29/1855	Simon Peter Jonas Mark	M	A	Silas Mark	Malinda Thurman	W	
11/29/1855	Amelia B. Tibbs	F	A	W. T. Tibbs	Louisa Turner	W	
5/17/1855	Armild Arnold	F	A	Samuel J. Arnold	Serrilda McCan	W	
8/17/1855	Nancy Bell Elston	F	A	Edward Elston	Ann E. Strode	W	
12/ /1855	Nancy	F	A	Robert H. Couser		B	
12/29/1855	Amanda Elliott	F	A	James Elliott	Addaide Muse	W	

41

COUNTY   Fleming

S Sex
C Condition A-Alive D-Dead

DATE	NAME OF CHILD	S	C	NAME OF FATHER	NAME OF MOTHER	CO.	RESIDENCE
12/11/1855	Robert Evans	M	A	William B. Evans	Malinda Plummer	W	All residents
2/10/1855	George Early Conway	M	A	Peter Conway	Charlotte Jordan	W	Fleming Co.
5/ 3/1855	Robert A. McGregor	M	A	Brasferd McGregor	Sarah Denton	W	
6/20/1855	Tilas Keath Ham	M	A		Harriet Ham	W	
7/28/1855	Not named	F	A	Daniel Thacher	America Newgen	W	
12/ 4/1855	Sally Jane Ham	F	A	Smith P. Ham	Martha Heflin	W	
12/ 3/1855	Edward DeBell Brayfield	M	A	Obed. Brayfield	Elizabeth J. Hopper	W	
8/18/1855	Mary Susan Obanion	F	A	James T. Obanion	Catherine A. Myers	W	
10/25/1855	Eliza G. Norwood	F	A	Alfred Norwood	Sarah J. Dobyns	W	
8/ 3/1855	Henry F. Belt Doyle	M	A	William Doyle	Rebecca Helvenstine	W	
9/10/1855	Mary Isabel Hudson	F	A	George Hudson	Rachel Fenton	W	
6/ 7/1855	Mary Mahala Muse	F	A	Hiram Muse	Martha Eliott	W	
1/ 8/1855	Frances M. McKee	M	A	John A. McKee	Eliza Braunner	W	
12/ 4/1855	Mariah Humphreys	F	A	Alfred Humphreys	Rebecca Humphrys	W	
11/17/1855	Simon Dudley McKee	M	A	Joseph McKee	Rachel Fenton	W	
2/ 5/1855	William Edward McKee	M	A	William McKee	Emily Lorman	W	
3/25/1855	Sarah Alice Carpenter	F	A	John Carpenter	Milly Ann Berry	W	
9/22/1855	John William Lee	M	A	Granville Lee	Ann A. Shanklin	W	
4/ /1855	Elizabeth C. Mark	F	A	Titus Mark	Drucila Hinton	W	
1/ 9/1855	Jane Foxworthy	F	A	Alexander Foxworthy	Sarah Goddard	W	
12/23/1855	Calvin	M	A	James Wallingsford		B	
2/23/1855	George Ann Clary	F	A	Warner Clary	Mary Gulich	W	
6/ 2/1855	Osa Lewellyn Williamson	F	A	Thomas Williamson	Elvira Curtis	W	
6/ 3/1855	John William Farrow	M	A	Kenas M. Farrow	Margaret Wallingford.	W	
8/28/1855	Not named	M	A	John Terry	Nancy H. Farrow	W	
10/13/1855	George	M	A	Richard Soward		B	
	Isabel	F	A	William Wallingford		B	
2/ /1855	Jennette Looman	F	A	Jonathan R. Looman	Mary Elston	W	
8/27/1855	Mary Elizabeth Davis	F	A	Reese Davis	M. J. Foxworthy	W	
5/ /1855	Not named	F	A	John Foxworthy		B	
4/20/1855	Nancy M. Turner	F	A	Robert Turner	Lydia McGowan	W	
3/27/1855	Granny Ann Arnold	F	A	James Arnold		B	
7/ /1855	Livey Ann Walker	F	A	Levin Walker	Emily Owens	W	
10/21/1855	Anna Bell Calvert	F	A	G. W. Calvert	Clarissa Foxworthy	W	
12/ /1855	Not named	F	D	Fielding Goodman		B	
11/ /1855	James Henry	M	A	M. P. Wallingford		B	
12/ /1855	Oscar Barnett Alexander	M	A	James M. Alexander	Elizabeth M. Redden	W	

COUNTY Fleming   C Condition A-Alive D-Dead

DATE	NAME OF CHILD	S	C	NAME OF FATHER	NAME OF MOTHER	CO.	RESIDENCE
11/ 6/1855	James Williams	F	A	Joshua W. Williams	Almedia Wyatt	W	All residents
9/18/1855	Sarah Isabel	F	A	Salathiel Burnis		B	Fleming Co.
4/ 8/1855	William	M	A	Salathiel Burnis		B	
3/20/1855	Marcus Bramell	M	A	Mathew Bramel	Sally Lineher	W	
9/26/1855	Joann Glass	F	A	Andrew Glass	Eliza Ann Tutton	W	
10/ /1855	Robert	M	A	Joseph D. Farrow		B	
9/ 6/1855	Elizabeth Edna Deering	F	A	Burgess Diering	Amanda Emmons	W	
12/26/1855	Roby P. Bishop	M	A	Henry Bishop	Lucy Porter	W	
12/ /1855	Hannah	F	A	Fanz Ham		B	
4/ /1855	Samuel B. Lyons	M	A	Daniel T. Lyons	Margaret Dillon	W	
3/28/1855	Robert P. Humphreys	M	A	Daniel Humphreys	Susan Staniford	W	
5/23/1855	William Darnall Bradley	M	A	Hiram Bradley	Amanda C. C. Filson	W	
10/20/1855	Charles Robert Hall	M	A	E. F. Hall	America J. Jones	W	
12/27/1855	James Alfred Reeves	M	A	William G. Reeves	Mary Hall	W	
5/10/1855	Mary V. Chord	F	A	William H. Chord	Virginia Dupery	W	
/ /1855	Alice P. Bowman	F	A	John Bowman	Fanny M. Hall	W	
8/ 4/1855	Henrietta	F	A	L. D. Anderson		M	
2/ /1855	Richard	M	A	L. D. Anderson		B	
6/14/1855	Mary Catherine Kane	F	A	Silas W. Kane	Nanno Walsh	W	
6/ /1855	Fanny	F	A	Alexander Hart		B	
6/ /1855	Elizabeth	F	A	Elijah Hart		B	
6/ /1855	Sarah	F	A	Mary Catherine Hart		B	
8/25/1855	Jerusha Silvey	F	A	Harrison Silvey	Frances Jane French	W	
2/ /1855	Clarissa	F	A	Joel DeBell		B	
9/ /1855	Sam	M	A	Joel DeBell		B	
7/28/1855	John Crotty	M	A	Patrick Crotty	Margaret Rooney	W	
9/ /1855	Rosanna Alexander	F	A	Joseph M. Alexander	Elizabeth Metcalf	W	
	Not named	F	A	L. W. Andrews		B	
10/ /1855	Not named	F	A	L. W. Andrews		B	
12/24/1855	Granville	M	A	Jonathan Cooper		B	
11/ 7/1855	Nancy Morgan	F	A	John Morgan	Mary Lyons	W	
10/27/1855	William Henry Hamilton	M	A	William Hamilton	Mary Green	W	
9/12/1855	Hiram Fleming Saunders	M	A	Hiram Sanders	Abigall Sanders	W	
10/15/1855	John Trumbo Myers	M	A	John Myers	Eliza Jane Markwell	W	
8/15/1855	Edward L. Hinton	M	A	John Hinton	Sarah A. Fitch	W	
6/ /1855	Henry	M	A	E. Logan		B	
11/31/1855	Billy	M	A	D. A. Kendall		B	

43

COUNTY Fleming

S Sex
C Condition A-Alive D-Dead

DATE	NAME OF CHILD	S	C	NAME OF FATHER	NAME OF MOTHER	CO.	RESIDENCE
11/31/1855	Ann Armstrong	F	A	Samuel E. Armstrong	Adeline Kendall	W	All residents
6/25/1855	Emmy Lucy Pearce	F	A	James M. Pearce	Justine Darnall	W	Fleming Co.
8/ /1855	Henry	M	A	James M. Pearce		B	
3/27/1855	Anna Stamper Danley	F	A	Leroy C. Danley	Juliet Durke	W	
6/ 6/1855	William Henry	M	A	America Moss		B	
6/ 4/1855	Mariah	F	A	Thomas Oliver		B	
12/ 4/1855	Roby Porter Bishop	M	A	Henry Bishop	Lucy Porter	W	
6/21/1855	Silas C. W. Ham	M	A	Dunitt Ham	Rebecca McRoberts	W	
12/ 4/1855	Sally Jane Ham	F	A	Smith Ham	Martha Heflin	W	
9/ /1855	Harriet	F	A	Squire Million		B	
3/24/1855	Elisha D. Butler	M	A	John H. Butler	Elizabeth Ham	W	
11/27/1855	Eolin Swim Daley	F	A	James C. Daley	Saurin W. Neuland	W	
3/ 5/1855	Ervin J. Sousley b. on Johnson	M	A	Geo. D. Sousley	Malinda Cochran	W	on Johnson Creek
9/ /1855	(colored) b. on Johnson	M	A	Geo. D. Sousley		B	on Johnson Creek
6/16/1855	Mary F. Griffith b. on Fleming Creek	F	A	Willoughby Griffith	Julian Hall	W	on Fleming Creek
10/27/1855	Mahaly Bell b. on Southlick	F	A	Danl. Dalrymple	Jane Newman	W	near Tilton
8/31/1855	name none b. in Tilton	F	A	A. T. Wood	Matilda Pickrel	W	near Tilton
2/ /1855	Elisha France b. Tilton	M	A	Jonas France	Rebecca Jucson	W	near Tilton
1/28/1855	Eli H. Browning b. on Licking	M	A	John Browning	Jane Ewing	W	on Licking near Sherburn
1/ 2/1855	William T. Wood b. Tilton	M	A	John Wood	Eliza Ann Pickrel	W	Tilton
11/ 4/1855	William A. Rice b. on Licking	M	A	Henry Rice	Lucinda Jane Rice	W	on Licking
9/26/1855	Harrison Kendal b. Fleming Creek	M	A	Henry Kendall	Mary Ann Sutton	W	on Fleming Creek
5/16/1855	name none b. near Tilton	M	A	Eli Wilson	Nancy Ann Tarbet	W	near Tilton
6/ /1855	Andrew b. on Three Mile	M	A	Edward Morman	Roda Powell	W	on Three Mill Creek
10/26/1855	George T. Willson b. near Tilton	M	A	Jesiah Wilson	Eliza Porter	W	near Tilton

S Sex
C Condition A-Alive D-Dead

COUNTY ___Fleming___

DATE	NAME OF CHILD	S	C	NAME OF FATHER	NAME OF MOTHER	CO.	RESIDENCE
8/ 7/1855	Nettie b. near Tilton	F	A	James D. Webster	Clarissa A. Gardner	W	Tilton
1/11/1855	Sarah Alice b. on Licking	F	A	James W. Tribby	Minerva Mars	W	on Licking River
11/12/1855	Richard N. Daily b. Sherburn, Ky.	M	A	Samuel Thomas Daily	Sarah Dailey	W	Sherburn, Ky.
3/ /1855	(Colored) b. Sherburn, Ky.	F	A	Nelson Fant		M	
/ /1855	Ania (colored) b. Sherburn, Ky.	F	A	H. S. Wilson		B	
3/ 3/1855	Allen H. Enilry b. Sherburn, Ky.	M	A	R. M. Enilry	Mary E. Hill	W	Sherburn
10/27/1855	Rollen C. Garey b. on Fleming Creek	M	A	Wm. Garey	Isabella Alexander	W	on Felming creek
2/15/1855	A. T. Lee b. on Locut Creek	M	A	W. R. Lee	Margaret Todd	W	on Locust
7/31/1855	Martha E. Rice b. on Licking	F	A	Wm. Rice	Reda Johnson	W	on the waters of Licking
	Chambers E. Saunders b. near Sherburn	M	A	Sylvania Saunders	Nancy Buckley	W	near Sherburn
9/ 8/1855	name none b. on South Lick	F	D	James T. Farris	Sarah Williams	W	on South Lick
	 b. on Fleming Creek	F	A	James Kennan		B	
8/ 5/1855	John W. Wilson b. near Tilton	M	A	W. S. Wilson	Emily T. Loyd	W	near Tilton
1/10/1855	George McKee b. on Locust	M	A	A. T. McKee	Letitia Faqua	W	on Locust
The Fall	Cay (colored) b. near Tilton	M	A	Sephen Bowles (Stephen ?)		B	
9/ 3/1855	name none b. near Sherburn, Re. 7 months pregnant.	M	D	David McCabe	Jane Finley	W	near Sherburn
7/ /1855	name none b. near Tilton	M	A	H. O. Kendall	Elizabeth McCan	W	near Tilton
3/16/1855	Lucy Bell Williams b. on Locust	F	A	Peter Williams	Susanna White	W	on Locust Creek
3/25/1855	Mary Jane b. on Fleming	F	A	Jacson Rice	Lucinda Tribby	W	on the waters of Fleming Crk.

COUNTY Fleming

S Sex
C Condition A-Alive D-Dead

DATE	NAME OF CHILD	S	C	NAME OF FATHER	NAME OF MOTHER	CO.	RESIDENCE
8/23/1855	James E. McCall b. on the waters of Licking	M	A	Jacson McCall	Dolly Hysong	W	on the waters of Licking
7/ /1855	Betty T. Howe b. near Tilton	F	A	W. S. Howe	Emily Proctor	W	near Tilton
1/25/1855	Edwin C. Smith b. on Fleming	F	A	E. T. Smith	Margaret Cooper	W	on Fleming
/ /1855	Jo (colored) b. Tilton	M	A	James T. Dearing		B	
3/13/1855	James Todd b. Tilton	M	A	Thomas Todd	Sophrona Browning	W	near Tilton
8/ 8/1855	Albert W. Campbell b. Tilton	M	A	Stephen Campbell	Resa Hinton	W	Tilton
10/20/1855	b. on Locust Creek, Re. Full Time.	M	D	Moses Saunders	Nancy Smith	W	on Locust Creek
1/18/1855	John Porter b. on Three Mile	M	A	Andrew Porter	Martha Wilson	W	on Three Mile Creek
/ /1855	Marshall Hull b. on Three Mile	M	A	Moses Hull	Tabath Rash (Bash?)	W	on Three Mile Creek
12/ /1855	Peter F. Williams b. on Licking	M	A	Joseph J. Williams	Elizabeth Japp (Sapp?)	W	on Licking
4/ /1855	b. on Fleming Creek	M	A	R. T. Kirk	Lavena Moore	W	on Fleming Creek
12/ /1855	b. on Licking River	M	A	Wm. Smith	Louisa Ross ?	W	on Licking
12/11/1855	Jeremiah S. Hunt b. on Licking River	M	A	John Hunt	Jane Campbell	W	on Licking
3/17/1855	Berry F. Ross b. on Fox Creek	M	A	Silas Ross	Armilda Duncan	W	on Fox Creek
1/26/1855	b. on Fleming Creek	M	A	Isaac Plank	Nancy Howe	W	on Fleming Creek
5/15/1855	b. on Fleming Creek	M	A	John H. Plank	Mary E. Casida	W	on Fleming Creek
2/24/1855	James M. Newman b. near Tilton	M	A	Alexander Newman	Sarah J. Williams	W	near Tilton
12/ 1/1855	Mary J. Todd b. near Tilton	F		George W. Todd	Mary R. Whitney	W	near Tilton
9/25/1855	b. on the waters of Fleming Creek	M		John F. Clark	Lucinda Chrisman	W	on waters Fleming Creek

S Sex
C Condition A-Alive D-Dead

COUNTY __Fleming__

DATE	NAME OF CHILD	S	C	NAME OF FATHER	NAME OF MOTHER	CO.	RESIDENCE
9/ /1855			D	J. H. Lee	M. E. Potts	W	Fleming Creek
	b. on Fleming						
2/15/1855	Liza Ann	F	A	D. B. Shepherd	Minerva Todd	W	on Locust
	b. on waters of Locust						
9/ 8/1855	James J. Crain	M	A	Hiram Crain	Mary L. Hopkins	W	on Locust
	b. on Locust						
9/ /1855	Walter M.	M	A	Walter Prather	Cintha Calhan ?	W	on Fleming
	b. on Fleming, Re. Father died 2 months before birth.						
8/ 9/1855	Elizabeth	F	A	N. A. Kirk		W	on Fleming
8/ 9/1855	Wallace	M	A	N. A. Kirk		W	on Fleming Creek
	b. on Fleming Creek, Twins.						
5/ /1855	Liza	F	A	W. H. Smith		M	
	b. on Allison						
6/ /1855	Henry	M	A	W. H.? Smith		B	
	b. on Allison						
11/ 3/1855	Matthew W. Smith	M	A	James E. Smith	Angeline Thompson	W	on Allison Creek
	b. on Allison						
7/27/1855	Lucy H. Thomas	F	A	Joseph Thomas	Sarah C. Liter	W	on Johnson
	b. on Johnson						
4/ 7/1855	Emily J. Shockley	F	A	W. H. Shockley	Ann E. Dickey	W	near Elizaville
	b. near Elizaville						
7/16/1855	Jno. L. McClain	M	A	Joseph McClain	Eliza Jane Clark	W	near Elizaville
	b. near Elizaville						
1/ 5/1855	James H. Grannis	M	A	William Grannis	Narcississ Hurst	W	on waters Locust Creek
	b. on waters Locust						
10/10/1855	Monroe D. Saunders	M	A	James A. Saunders	Mariah A. Arnold	W	on Three Mile Creek
	b. on Three Mile Creek						
3/16/1855	Louisa E. Hopkins	F	A	Herod Hopkins	Emily Hopkins	W	on Locust Creek
	b. on Locust Creek						
7/25/1855	Mary A. Harman	F	A	John W. Harman	Sarah Kearns	W	on Locust Creek
	b. on Locust Creek						
11/28/1855	George W. Smith	M	A	Thomas E. Smith	Catharine Wilson	W	in Tilton
	b. in Tilton						
4/ 1/1855	Charles (colored)	M	A	L. T. Hix		B	
	b. Martha Mills						
2/ /1855	Rolly (colored)	M	A	James Triplett		M	
	b. Bald Hill						
4/ /1855	name none	M	A	James Triplett		M	
	b. Bald Hill						

47

COUNTY __Fleming__   C Condition A-Alive D-Dead

DATE	NAME OF CHILD	S	C	NAME OF FATHER	NAME OF MOTHER	CO.	RESIDENCE
5/ /1855		M	A	James Triplett		B	
	b. Bald Hill						
5/ /1855		F	A	James Triplett		B	
	b. Bald Hill						
4/23/1855	Isaac W. Smith	M	A	Henry Smith	Mary E. Sapp	W	on Licking River
	b. on Licking River						
7/ /1855	James A. Jaeson	M	A	James A. Jackson	Eliza A. Sapp	W	on Licking River
	b. on Licking River						
9/19/1855	Aaron Williams	M	A	James Williams	Harriet Saunders	W	on the waters of Licking
	b. on Licking River						
5/ 3/1855		M	A	Sylvanus Painter	Ruth Minerva Saunders	W	on the waters of Licking
	b. on Licking River						
8/15/1855	Squire	M	A	John W. Story	Angeline Harman	W	on Licking
	b. on Licking River						
8/18/1855	Charles E.	M	E	J. Ringo	Matilda Saunders	W	T.?Grove Mills
	b. J.?Grove Mills						
11/30/1855	Cordelia F. Harper	F	A	Wm. W. Harper	Nancy E. Story?	W	on Buchannan
	b. on Buchannan Creek						
11/25/1855	James C. Dougherty	M	A	Thomas Daugherty	Elizabeth Rickets	W	Sherburn
	b. Sherburn						
3/ 5/1855	John S. Brown	M	A	Cummins Brown	Mary A. Saunders	W	on Fleming Creek
	b. on Felming Creek						
3/ /1855	name none	M	D	J. W. Burk	Miranda A. Lee	W	on Licking
	b. on Licking						
6/21/1855	Benj. F. Tribby	M	A	George T. Tribby	Nancy Myers	W	on Licking
	b. Mires Mill, Licking						
8/ 9/1855		M	A	Matison Flora	Amanda Jolly	W	on Fleming
	b. on Fleming						
	Elias J. Blake	M	A	Thomas Blake	Abigal Robertson	W	on Fleming Creek
	b. on Fleming						
12/25/1855		M	A	James Parsons	Martha J. Hicks	W	on Fleming
	b. on Fleming						
/ /1855	William Cline	M	A	Harrison Cline	Elizabeth Gallaher	W	on Fleming Creek
	b. on Fleming						
9/ /1855	name none	M	A	A. Bishop	A. Fricklin	W	Bishops Mills
	b. Bishops Mills						

COUNTY Fleming   C Condition A-Alive D-Dead

DATE	NAME OF CHILD	S	C	NAME OF FATHER	NAME OF MOTHER	CO.	RESIDENCE
12/ /1855	(colored) b. Fleming	M	A	J. T. Walker		B	
5/27/1855	Elizabeth Dickson b. Maysville & Lex. Pike	F	A	James Dickson	Elizabeth P. Golden	W	on Elk Creek
5/ 5/1855	Franklin Bate b. Elk Creek	M	A	John H. Bate	Nancy Casida	W	on Elk Creek
9/15/1855	Jno. H. Abner b. Buchanan	M	A	Lincoln Abner	Margaret Evans	W	Buchanan Creek
11/21/1855	James Sullivan b. Elizaville Toll Gate	M	A	Patrick Sullivan	Joanne Dillon	W	Elizaville Pike
6/18/1855	Martha B. Shockley b. Buchannan Creek	F	A	H. B. Shockley	Lucinda Hammons	W	on Buchannan
	Sarah M. Bently b. Elk Creek	F	A	George Bently	E. M. McCord	W	Elk Creek
11/14/1855	name none b. Buchannan Creek	F	A	Michael Overley	Mary J. Ross	W	Buchannan Creek
1/15/1855	Sarah T. Overly b. Buchannan Creek, Condition unhealthy.	F		Michael Overley	Mary J. Ross	W	Buchannan Creek
8/ /1855	Mary C. Mc Cord b. Elk Creek	F	A	Alfred McCord	Julie Farrin	W	Elk Creek
12/16/1855	Elias Hickman b. Fair View	M	A	Leroy Hickman	Louisa Young	W	Fair View
4/ /1855	b. near Elizaville	M	D	W. H. Caywood	Lucy E. Plater?	W	near Elizaville
8/22/1855	b. at the Poor House	F	A	Sinet Collohan	Sarah J. Reeves	W	at Poor House
/ /1855	Mose (colored) b, near Elizaville	M	a	H. C. Sousley		M	
	Mary Jane Berry b. near Fair View, Re. Illegitimate.	F	A	Wesley Berry	Dianah Pitts	W	near Fairview
5/ /1855	Edgar Turner b, ib Licking	M	A	John Turner	Rachel Eden	W	on Licking
5/ /1855	(colored) b. near Elizaville	M	A	Wm. H. Darnall		M	near Elizaville
2/ 6/1855	Rosanna Spencer b. on Fleming Creek	F	A	W. H. Spencer	Harriet Shockley	W	on Fleming Creek
5/ /1855	Colored b. near Elizaville	M	A	John Botts		B	near Elizaville

S Sex
C Condition A-Alive D-Dead

COUNTY __Fleming__

DATE	NAME OF CHILD	S	C	NAME OF FATHER	NAME OF MOTHER	CO.	RESIDENCE
5/ /1855	(colored) b. Flemingsburg	F	A	Thomas R. Botts		B	Flemingsburg
12/ /1855	(colored) b. P. Plains	M	A	Isaac Pierce		B	P. Plains
4/ /1855	(colored) b. P. Plains	M	A	Wm. Armstrong		B	P. Plains
12/22/1855	b. near Hillsborough	M	A	Thomas Roberts	Mary J. Emmons	W	Hillsborough
8/20/1855	Colored b. Alison	M	A	Henry Hart		B	Allison
2/15/1855	b. on Locust Creek	F	A	James Summitt		W	on Locust
7/25/1855	Edwin Pearce b. Poplar Plains	M	A	E. L. Pearce	Eliza Cochran	W	P. Plains
9/ 7/1855	Mary E. Patton b. on Johnson	F	A	John Patton	Nancy Fitzgerald	W	on Johnson
/ /1855	Jula D. Ross b. on Johnson	F	A	James Ross	Hennetts Matthews	W	on Johnson
4/ 3/1855	b. on Fleming		A	James A. Tully	Elizabeth Rasney	W	on Fleming Creek
2/23/1855	b. on Johnson	F	D	Wm. Bell	Lucinda Bruce	W	on Johnson
1/18/1855	Wm. Shearwood b. on Johnson	M	A	John Shearwood	Hannah Blair	W	on Johnson
1/20/1855	Elis (colored) b. on Johnson	N	A	John Shearwood		B	on Johnson
	Lucy (colored) b. on Johnson	F	A	Charles Bell		B	on Johnson
11/22/1855	Margaret M. Lane b. on Johnson	F	A	Craven Lane	Mary Próter	W	on Johnson
11/ 2/1855	b. b. Fair View	M	D	W. S. Case	Mariah Payne	W	Fair View
11/11/1855	Walter W. Chandler b. on Johnson	M	A	Henry Chandler	Mary J. McCarty	W	Fair View
4/ /1855	Viers Buckler b. Fair View	M	A	W. P. BUCKLER	Matilda Gill	W	near Fair View
4/20/1855	Lucy Pipper b. on Johnson	F	A	Joseph J. Pipper	Elizabeth J. Allen	W	on Johnson

COUNTY Fleming

S Sex
C Condition A-Alive D-Dead

DATE	NAME OF CHILD	S	C	NAME OF FATHER	NAME OF MOTHER	CO.	RESIDENCE
11/ /1855	name none b. near Elizaville	M	D	Charles Taylor	Sabina Blair	W	near Elizaville
12/12/1855	 b. near Elizaville	F	A	A. B. Vansant	Jerusha Markwell	W	near Elizaville
12/23/1855	Sally Ann Fleming b. Elizaville	F	A	Jno. T. Fleming	Mary Stewart	W	Elizaville
1/29/1855	Charlotte J. Howe b. on Fleming	F	A	David D. Howe	Harriet Plank	W	on Fleming Creek
12/ /1855	Colored b. Flemingsburg	F	A	James Eckles		B	Flemingsburg
11/ /1855	Amelia Botts b. Flemingsburg	F	A	Ben Botts	Julia Dorsey	W	Flemingsburg
	Margaret McDonald b. Flemingsburg	F	A	Robert McDonald	Avina Martin	W	Flemingsburg
9/26/1855	Lilie Dudley b. Flemingsburg	F	A	W. T. Dudley	Kitty DeBell	W	Flemingsburg
10/ /1855	Colored b. Flemingsburg	F	A	W. T. Dudley		B	Flemingsburg
1/ 1/1855	Caroline Sarah b. on Southlick	F	A	W. M. Harman	Elizabeth Dillon	W	on Licking near Sherburn

Fleming County Sct.
    I, William T. Duley Clerk of the Court for the County Court of Fleming
certify that the foregoing is a true copy of the Registration of Births made
by the commissioner of Tax for Fleming County for the year 1855. June 13th
1856. Att. W. Dudley CFCC

2/ 8/1856	James T.	M	A	John W. Doyle	Elizabeth Arins	W	Fleming Co.
4/20/1856	Mary Ann	F	A	Nelson Hurst	Malinda Staggs	W	All residents
1/11/1856	Ann Eliza	F	A	Walter W. Hurst	Lucinda Hurst	W	
6/ /1856	Matilda	F	A	Miles Hurst Senr.	Mary Doyle	W	
7/30/1856	Pamelian	F	A	Joseph F. Doyle	Eliza Jane Haws (Hams?)	W	
4/11/1856	Charlotte	F	A	Samuel J. Carpenter	Emily Jorden	W	
12/13/1856	Rebecca Jane	F	A	Samuel Hamilton	Ricy Ann Choat	W	
6/ 8/1856	William Stuart	M	A	Alexander Montgomery	Elastima Prateman	W	
9/ 3/1856	Reuben Samuel	M	A	Alexander Ham	Sarah Hartly	W	
12/10/1856	Tobe	M	A	James E. Dodds	Mary E. Evans	W	

COUNTY Fleming

S Sex
C Condition A-Alive D-Dead

DATE	NAME OF CHILD	S	C	NAME OF FATHER	NAME OF MOTHER	CO.	RESIDENCE
10/ 4/1856		M	A	Joseph B. Northcutt	Louisa Emmons	W	All residents
7/ 1/1856	Burgess Dudley	M	A	Samuel Humphreys	Criller Jane Calvert	W	Fleming Co.
12/ 1/1856	Not named	M	A	Abram Yazle	Elizabeth Foudray	W	
10/16/1856	David R.	M	A	Richard Carpenter	Harriet Estill	W	
11/30/1856	George William	M	A	Charles L. Carpenter	Sophia Looman	W	
7/10/1856	William Franklin	M	A	Zacheus Bramwell	Nancy Jorden	W	
3/21/1856	Mary E.	F	A	George W. Markwell	Levina Clupper	W	
4/15/1856	Malinda	F	A	Greenup Jordan	Minerva Dougherty	W	
9/12/1856	Adalaska	M	A	L. P. Royse	Sarah Horget	W	
3/11/1856	Wm. Jasper	M	A		Eliza Fawns	W	
8/28/1856	John Z.	M	A	James P. Phields	Jennett Payne	W	
1/ 1/1856	Marion	M	A	Thomas Staggs	Polly Ann Jorden	W	
/ /1856	Lizzie C.	F	A	S. H. Fizer	Lewellyn Crain	W	
/ /1856	Virginia	F	A	Wm. Fizer	Rebecca T. Arnold	W	
7/ /1856	David C.	M	A	Benjamin Ross	Celia Holland	W	
12/25/1856	Mary Ann	F	A	James O. Ravik	Mary Amorn	W	
3/12/1856	Drucilla	F	A	Charles Arnold	Rachel M. Carpenter	W	(twins)
3/12/1856	Sarah	F	A	Charles Arnold	Rachel M. Carpenter	W	
12/12/1856	Not named	M	D	G. Triplett	Mary Mills	W	
/ /1856	Sarah Matilda	F	A	M. Purnell	Sarah A. Ross	W	
6/15/1856	Not named	F	D	W. F. Jorden	Matilda Hammond	W	
12/25/1856	Lydia Ann	F	A	Lawrance Triplett		B	
1/ /1856	Robert	M	A	Alexander McGregor	Mary Steete	W	
2/15/1856	James Franklin	M	A	Casper H. Seevers	Armeda Berekfield	W	
8/18/1856	Levi Buchanan	M	A	J. W. Lansdown	Sarah M. Overly	W	
8/17/1856	Hiram Vincent	M	A	Johnathan Stratten	Sarah Lansdown	W	
7/13/1856	Flavins B	M	A	J. B. Evans	Susan Knapp	W	
8/ 4/1856	Unice Ann	F	A	Faritty R. Muse	Susan H. Lee	W	
3/ /1856	Amanda	F	A	James B. Muse	Sarah Walker	W	
4/21/1856	Clay Northcutt	M	A	Alfred Hurst	Susan Swim	W	
2/13/1856	Elizabeth Margarett	F	A	Jackson Kirk	Sally J. Humphreys	W	
12/10/1856	Not named	F	D	Joseph Yazle	Martha J. Anderson	W	
9/29/1856	Not named	M	A	Harrison Gardner	Mary Trebby	W	
5/ 1/1856	Mary	F	A	Elijah L. Carpenter	Mahala Jorden	W	
8/15/1856	Anna	F	A	Samuel W. Stephens	Elenor A. Tanner	W	
	b. Mason County						
5/10/1856	Marshall	M	A	L. J. Arnold	Sarelda McCan	W	

COUNTY __Fleming__

DATE	NAME OF CHILD	S	C	NAME OF FATHER	NAME OF MOTHER	CO.	RESIDENCE
10/ /1856	Anna	F	A	James R. Bell	Elizabeth Farrow	W	All residents
8/21/1856	John	M	A	Edward Calahan	Priscilla Jorden	W	Fleming Co.
1/22/1856	Mary Amanda	F	A	G. W. Vansant	Isabelle Cooper	W	
4/22/1856	Mary Alice	F	A	Ruben Coonrod	Lucinda Lewis	W	
4/15/1856	Nancy Bell	F		A. P. Helphenstine	Martha J. Doyle	W	
3/17/1856	Rebecca Jane	F	A	Samuel Jones	Priscilla Jones	W	
10/30/1856	Elizabeth Susan	F	A	David Hamilton	Rachel Yazle	W	(next name ?)
12/20/1856	Isadore	F	A	R. M. Thomas	Mirian Day	W	
7/2/1856	Rebecca Jane	F	A	Allen Story	Malinda J. Markwell	W	
12/29/1856	Not named	F	A	William Pierce	Mary Ann Davis	W	
2/ /1856		M	A	N. L. Andrews		M	
9/ 6/1856	Wm. Fleming	M	A	John Story	Margaret Day	W	
9/ /1856	Not named	M	A	Henry Tabis	Nancy Smoot	W	
12/25/1856	Charlotte	F	A	Wm. Emmons	Anfield Gregor	W	
3/11/1856	Mary Alice	F	A	Samuel Royse	Roberty Bair	W	
3/18/1856	Parthena	F	A	Robert W. Hayden	Jane Reeves	W	
12/27/1856	James Buchannan	M	A	Samuel Cline	Elizabeth Ann Harget	W	
5/29/1856	Milton	M	A	Noah Reeves	Queen A. Hayden	W	
12/22/1856	Martha Jane	F	A	Jackson Kipack	Polly Claine	W	
2/13/1856	Mary E.	F	A	George F. Mooney	Mary E. Eckles	W	
1/ 5/1856	Susan Mariah	F	A	Marshall Stubblefield	Mary Pilgrim	W	
11/10/1856	Julian	M	A	Thomas T. Atchison	Elizabeth C. Marcy	W	
/ /1856	Robert	M	A	Alfred Jacobs	Rachel Asbury	W	
8/ /1856	James P.	M	A	Marshall Hickerson	Matilda Looman	W	
6/22/1856	John Thomas	M	A	John A. Watts	Nancy M. Foxworthy	W	
6/10/1856	Richard Carpenter	M	A	Wm. M. Carpenter	Eliza Ann Kurst	W	
2/25/1856	Emily M.	F	A	Fielding Jones	Catharine Moore	W	
5/ 1/1856	Mary J.	F	A	Joel Sanders	Surtilda Looman	W	
8/17/1856	Marion b. Lewis Co.	M	A	Aron Quicksall	Elizabeth Prater	W	
6/16/1856	John W. b. Fleming Co.	M	A	Daniel Carpenter	America Hurst	W	
11/ 1/1856	Lowreny	F		Sarah Sybold		B	
4/15/1856	Not named	M	D	Obed P. Nute		B	
10/13/1856	Rosa Jane	F	A	Nathaniel Thomas	America Holland	W	
3/ 1/1856	Ann	F	A	W. M. Foxworthy	Alice H. Everett	W	
7/23/1856	James Edward	M	A	Wm. C. R. Harrison	Caroline Reed	W	
2/22/1856	Ida Bell	F	A	William Mayhew	Angeline Riggs	W	

KENTUCKY COUNTIES VITAL STATISTICS   S Sex

COUNTY Fleming   C Condition A-Alive D-Dead

DATE	NAME OF CHILD	S	C	NAME OF FATHER	NAME OF MOTHER	CO.	RESIDENCE
10/ 2/1856	Jesie L.	M	A	Wm. B. O. Bannon	Mary F. Wallingford	W	All residents
12/18/1856	Ban P. Trav	M	A	Joseph R. Glasscock		M	Fleming Co.
12/ /1856	Martin	M		Joel DeBell		B	
3/17/1856	Not named	M	D	Clark B. Mark	Amelia Wallingford	W	
1/ 1/1856	Joel T.	M	A	Alfred DeBell	Susan P. Turner	W	
1/ /1856	Leander Cos	M	A	James Hickerson	Mary Looman	W	
10/20/1856	James Thomas	M	A	Thomas J. Jones	Amelia Freeman	W	
7/ 1/1856	Mary Ellen	F	A	George Hartly	Elizabeth Ham	W	
11/23/1856	William Addison	M	A	Thomas P. Sutton	Celia Gooding	W	
2/ /1856	Mary Virginia	F	A	W. H. Ingraham	Virginia Evans	W	
2/24/1856	Ann Eliza	F	A	William DeBelt	Lewellyn Dougherty	W	
1/ 1/1856	Bill	M	A	Alfred Morehead		B	
5/18/1856	Charles	M	A	Charles Nute	Malinda A. Glasscock	W	
1/16/1856	Elizabeth Florence	F	A	James M. Becket	Mary Browning	W	
2/24/1856	Bilvy	F	A	Richard Soward		B	
7/ 4/1856	Nancy Darnell	F	A	Thornton Davenport	Ruth Meredith	W	
7/12/1856	Cleon	M	A	A. Duley Ross	Penelope Strode	W	
7/12/1856	Lilly Florence	F	A	Landen D. Farrar	Sarah A. Wallingford	W	
12/14/1856	Sarah Jane	F	A	Andrew Mattingly	Malinda Ewbanks	W	
5/ 3/1856	Harriett Louisa	F	A	John Reeves	Nancy Hughes	W	
2/22/1856	Joseph Thornton	M	A	Mark Wallingford	Elizabeth Farrow	W	
3/13/1856	Emma	F	A	S. T. Fitch	Delia B. Fitch	W	
1/14/1856	Lucina	M	A	Fielding Goodman	Elizabeth Wallingford	W	
1/30/1856	Amanda Belt	F	A	William Bridges	Nancy Hamnestid	W	
2/ 8/1856	Charles	M	A	Joseph S. Wallingford	Helen Morrison	W	
2/26/1856	Walter	M	A	S. J. Hammonds	Levina J. Fitch	W	
8/ 5/1856	James Taylor b. Mason Co.	M	A	Trusidale Carmichael	Delila Henderson	W	
6/ 5/1856	Martin	M	A	Thomas Ward	Catharine Haynie	W	
8/10/1856	Not named	M	A	J. L. Foudray	Amanda Davis	W	
12/12/1856	William H.	M	A	Charles Lynum	Jane Vannatten	W	
12/ /1856	Sarah E.	F	A	Alfred L. Havens	Sarah Loyd	W	
11/30/1856	Leah E.	F	A	K. P. Jones	Lydia R. Havens	W	
10/ 3/1856	James F.	M	A	John Heithly	George Ann Nailor	W	
9/16/1856	Martha Ann	F	A	James F. Likes	Polly Ann Rice	W	
8/19/1856	Harriett K.	F	A	Wm. Vanlandingham	Penelope Moore	W	
8/ /1856	Mary M.	F	A	Presly Walton	Elizabeth Jinkins	W	

54

COUNTY Fleming

S Sex
C Condition A-Alive D-Dead

DATE	NAME OF CHILD	S	C	NAME OF FATHER	NAME OF MOTHER	CO.	RESIDENCE
8/ /1856	Not named	F	A	Henry Hart	Elizabeth Jinkins	B	All residents
/ 1/1856	Alfred H.	M	D	John A. Davis	Sarah A. Hinton	W	Fleming Co.
5/22/1856	Not named	M	A	Daniel Johnson	Charlotte Pearce	W	
12/17/1856	John A.	M	A	Fieling W. Gray	Maria L. Crafford	W	
7/ /1856	Susan	F	A	W. H. Hendrix	Maria L. Cafford	B	
4/ /1856	Phebe	F	A	Leroy Kenner	Mary Bell	W	
4/ 8/1856	Kate	F	A	Leroy Kenner		B	
6/12/1856	Harriett	F	A	James Kidwell	Amelia Hinton	W	
4/ 9/1856	Henry	M	A	Ethebert Logan		B	
9/ /1856	Louisa	F	A	Joel R. Turner	Margaret Ross	W	
4/ 4/1856	John R.	M	A	Van Dodge	Elmira Sampson	W	
8/17/1856	Henry	M	A	J. S. Lanagan	Catharien Shay	W	b. Mason Co.
/ /1856	John	M	A	Mrs. Lucy C. Lee		B	
10/25/1856	Thomas Bell	F	A	Thomas Maxey	Malinda Atchison	W	
4/ 1/1856	Alvin	M	A	Elias Roberson	Louisa Atchison	W	
7/ 4/1856	Sarah Amanda	F	A	Abner Boyd	Elizabeth Smoot	W	
3/12/1856	Charles P.	M	A	Simpson Vice	Elizabeth Day	W	
11/10/1856	Madison Marion	M	A	Dudley Davis	Phidilla Newman	W	
9/11/1856	Martha Bell	F	A	Lilas T. Keith	Maria J. Humphreys	W	
8/ 1/1856	Nancy	F	A	Garnet Hickerson		M	
3/ 3/1856	John S.	M	A	Robert A. Gooding	A. James	W	
10/ /1856	Not named	M	A	Robert A. Gooding		B	
12/ /1856	Name none b. on Fleming Creek	F	A	James M. Shockey	Augusta Ross	W	on Fleming Creek
12/ /1856	Benj. F. b. on Fleming Creek	M	A	R. G. Spencer	Rasa Shockley	W	on Fleming Creek
12/ /1856	name none b. on Licking	M	A	Saml. Gray	Gray	W	Licking
4/20/1856	Margaret b. on Johnson	F	A	W. H. Graves	Gary	W	on Johnson
12/27/1856	Charles W. b. on Johnson	M	A	Moses Givens	Ann Rodgers	W	on Johnson
/ /	b. on Johnson	M	A	Jno. B. Kendrick		B	on Johnson
11/27/1856	John H. b. on Johnson	M	A	Santford Stockdale	Fields	W	on Johnson
8/12/1856	Henry M. b. Fleming Creek	M	A	C. C. Hanemans	Lucinda Himes	W	Fleming Creek

55

COUNTY Fleming

DATE	NAME OF CHILD	S	C	NAME OF FATHER	NAME OF MOTHER	CO.	RESIDENCE
8/26/1856	John W. b. Fleming Creek	M	A	Wm. H. Shockley	Eliza Dickey	W	Fleming Creek
10/15/1856	Geo. W. b. on Licking	M	A	James B. McIntire	Dorinda McIntire	W	on Licking
2/25/1856	Jno. T. b. Licking	M	A	E. P. Bunies	Mary Finley	W	near U.B. Lick
2/14/1856	Lucy F. b. on Licking	F	A	F. P. Sousley	Susan Peck	W	on Licking
10/ /1856	name none b. Mudlick	F	A	H. C. Sousley		B	Licking
9/ /1856	name none b. Mudlick	F	A	T. B. McIntire		B	Licking
3/29/1856	Charles	M	A	W. H. H. Williams	Dudley	W	Fleming
10/15/1856	Mary J. b. Johnson	F	A	John Dale	Mary Duncan	W	Johnson
5/10/1856	Eliza J. b. Fleming	F	A	J. H. H. Myers	Sally Ann Cord	W	on Fleming
10/29/1856	Charles W. b. on Johnson	M	A	P. W. Odohorty	Margaret McCord	W	on Fleming
11/10/1856	Ann b. on Johnson	F	A	Henry Cassidy	Ann Craig	W	on Johnson
9/ /1856	Sarah F. b. on Fleming	F	A	J. H. Lee	Sarah Potts	W	on Fleming
12/16/1856	Ann E. b. on Johnson	F	A	Jonson Ross	Ross	W	Johnson
9/ /1856	Susan b. Johnson	F	A	Joseph Jackson	Mary Swain	W	on Johnson
4/ /1856	Albert b. near Elizaville	M	A	T. S. Farrow	Eliza Bentley	W	near Elizaville
10/ 8/1856	Irvan b. Fleming Creek	M	A	Levi C. Moore	Eliza Williams	W	on Fleming
7/ /1856	Marand J. b. Licking	F	A	John N. Burk	Mary Lee	W	on Licking
4/23/1856	Anida J. b. Jonson Creek	F	A	Joseph Sims	Nancy Wise	W	on Johnson
10/16/1856	William H. b. on Licking	M	A	John M. Cord	Susan Ross	W	Licking

COUNTY __Fleming__

S Sex
C Condition A-Alive D-Dead

DATE	NAME OF CHILD	S	C	NAME OF FATHER	NAME OF MOTHER	CO.	RESIDENCE
4/14/1856	Eli S.	M		R. F. Parker	Mary Stephens	W	near Elisaville
	b. near Elizaville						
5/19/1856	Benj.	M		Elias Early	Eliza Givens	W	near Centerville
	Centerville						
10/ /1856	Charles	M		Geo. D. Sousley	Malinda Cochran	W	near Elizaville
	b. near Elizaville						
10/ /1856				Geo. D. Sousley		B	near Elizaville
6/11/1856	Henry C.V.	M		Bell Wm.	Lucinda Bruce	W	on Johnson
	b. near Elizaville						
9/ /1856	Robt. S.	M		Joseph Pepper	Lorinda Alen	W	near Elizaville
	b. near Elizaville						
1/ /1856	James A.	M		Thos. Felhome?		W	on Licking
	b. Licking						
9/ /1856	Negro	M		Lavina Alexander		B	on Licking
	b. on Fleming						
9/ /1856	Negro	M		Lucy B. Pepper		B	on Licking
	b. on Jonson						
9/ /1856	Negro	M		Lucy B. Pepper		B	on Licking
9/ /1856	Negro	M		Danl. Clark		B	
	b. on Johnson						
1/ /1856	James	M		Danl. Clark		B	
	b. near Fairview						
/ /1856				Jno. Fitchgerld	Rosa A. Moore	W	Fairview
9/ /1856	Martha O.	F		David Weaver		W	on Johnson
	b. Fairview						
4/ /1856	John O.	M		Wm. Bowlan	L. Leek	W	Elk Creek
	b. on Elk Creek						
4/ /1856	Janes T.	M		Robt Staimford	Parkstone	W	Elk Creek
	b. Elk Creek						
2/13/1856	Andrew J.	M		J. McCarty	Lucy A. Cummons	W	Elk Creek
	b. Elk Creek						
7/15/1856	Andrew	M		J. McCarty		B	Elk Creek
	b. Elk Creek						
5/ /1856	Ann	F		W. H. Morgan	Ann Bruce	W	near Elizaville
	b. near Elizaville						
5/ /1856	Colored	M		Fanny Mulay		B	
	b. Johnson						

S Sex
C Condition A-Alive D-Dead

COUNTY __Fleming__

DATE	NAME OF CHILD	S	C	NAME OF FATHER	NAME OF MOTHER	CO.	RESIDENCE
1/ /1856	William b. on Licking	M		Nat Peck	Charlette Crain	W	U.B. Lick
9/ 5/1856	James F. b. on Licking	M		Babbett W. J.	Sophia Sousley	W	on Licking
6/11/1856	Mary E. b. near Centerville	F		J. N. Reeves	Julia Ann Cord	W	near Centerville
6/ /1856	Colored	F		G. W. Bishop		B	
12/ /1856	John b. Fleming Creek	M		Jno. Bishop	Morgan	W	Fleming Creek
9/ /1856	Edward D. b. near F. Burg	M		Thomas Andrews	Sabina Metcalf	W	Flemingsburg
9/ /1856	Colored	M		Thos. Andrews		B	
7/ /1856	Amanda J. b. on Licking	F		J. N. Burk	Ann Lee	W	on Licking
4/ 9/1856	Amanda J. b. Johnson	F		Jno. N. Johnson	Wise	W	Johnson
9/ 6/1856	John P. b. on Johnson	M	A	Elbridg Bell	E. Taylor	W	on Johnson
7/12/1856	Mary A. b. Johnson	F	A	Mason Caywood	Ross	W	near Fairview
3/ 2/1856	Morgan J. b. Fleming	M	A	Thomas Blake	Mers	W	Fleming Creek
2/25/1856	Robert B. b. Fleming Creek	M	A	John May	Malinda Cochran	W	on Fleming Creek
5/16/1856	Sarah C. b. on Fleming Creek	F	A	L. B. Williams	Amanda Rallins	W	Fleming Creek
10/ /1856	Araar b. Fleming Creek	F	A	A. D. Bishop	Ary Ficklin	W	on Fleming Creek
9/17/1856	Lucy H. b. on Fleming	F	A	James Tully	Casey Ramey	W	on Fleming
3/10/1856	Thomas b. Fleming Creek	M	A	Michael Hekoe	Bridget	W	on Fleming
6/ 7/1856	James A. b. Fleming Creek	M	A	Henry Dixon	Mary Jolly	W	on Fleming
5/20/1856	 b. Johnson	M	A	James Hurst	Adamson, Betsey	W	on Johnson
1/ /1856	 b. Johnson	M	A	John Murs	Susan Hunt	W	on Johnson

COUNTY__Fleming____

S Sex
C Condition A-Alive D-Dead

DATE	NAME OF CHILD	S	C	NAME OF FATHER	NAME OF MOTHER	CO.	RESIDENCE
9/ 1/1856	Mary E. b. on Fox Creek	F	A	B. F. Reeves	Mary A. Jimison	W	on Licking
9/ 8/1856	Elew Ann b. Tilton, Ky.	F	A	Joseph Overly	Judath Crain	W	Tilton, Ky.
3/ 4/1856	Julia b. Sherborne, Ky.	F	A	S. D. Baird	Nancy Cosby	W	Sherburne
11/ /1856	 b. near Tilton, Ky.	F	D	E. Thomas		B	Sherburne
10/25/1856	Allen b. on Locust Creek	M	A	John Wilson	Emily Pickerel	W	Tilton
/ /1856	John (colored) b. Tilton, Ky.	M	A	Archabald Hall		B	Tilton
3/15/1856	John S. b. Tilton	M	A	Thomas J. Dillon	Amanda T. Wilson	W	Tilton
8/ /1856	Lucy Bell b. on Locust	F	A	Geo. S. Story	Mary Wills	W	on Locust
12/26/1856	Wm. C. b. Hillsburough	M	A	James V. Payne	Amanda Freeman	W	Hillsburough
3/ /1856	Jo (colored) b. Sherburn	M	A	Sarah Marple		B	Hillsburough
11/ /1856	Jno. (colored) b. on Fleming Creek	M	A	Wm. Crain		B	Hillsburough
10/10/1856	 b. on Fleming Creek	M	A	John K. Vansant	Nancy Markwell	W	on Fleming
7/28/1856	John b. near Hillsborough	M	A	John Crawford	Martha Payne	W	on Locust
8/ 1/1856	John on Fleming	F	A	R. R. Bell		B	
6/20/1856	John b. near F. Burg	M	A	James Comwell	Amanda Plummer	W	on Fleming
3/ /1856	Charles b. Fleming Co.	M	A	W. T. Walker		B	
9/ 4/1856	Mary b. Flemingsburg	F	A	John T. Wall	Elizabeth Dudley	W	Flemingsburg
5/ /1856	Ann G. b. Paris, Ky.	F	A	C.K.B. Duncan	Zeller A. Carter	W	Flemingsburg
5/17/1856	Henry M. b. Flemingsburg	M	A	A. J. Stephens	Sarah F.McDonald	W	Flemingsburg

COUNTY __Fleming__

S Sex
C Condition A-Alive D-Dead

DATE	NAME OF CHILD	S	C	NAME OF FATHER	NAME OF MOTHER	CO.	RESIDENCE
5/18/1856	Emma Wilson	F	A	E. A. Lee	Mary J. Lee	W	Flemingsburg
	b. near Flemingsburg						
11/ /1856	Malissa Ann	F	A	Jef Preston	Elizabeth Talrymple	W	on Licking
	b. on Licking						
9/ 5/1856	John R. T.	M	A	Jonathan Overly	Frances A. Gardner	W	Tilton, Ky.
	b. Tilton						
11/ 8/1856	Wm. B.	M	A	John King	Sarath Walson (Wilson?)	W	Three Mile Creek
	b. on Three Mile Creek						
5/ /1856		F	D	Patrick Tearney	Ellan Rily	W	near Tilton
	b. near Tilton						
9/ /1856	Saml. W.	M	A	Joseph A. Miller	Hannah Dalrymple	W	on South Lick
	b. on South Lick						
10/ /1856	Virginia	F	A	John Wood	Ann E. Pickerel	W	near Tilton
	b. Tilton						
11/30/1856	Margaret E.	F	A	John Ishmall	Mary A. Hunt	W	on Licking
	b. on Licking						
1/19/1856	Saml. H.	M	A	Wm. S. Pearce	Amilda Janders	W	on Licking
	b. near Elizaville						
6/ /1856	Elizabeth	M	A	John Rice	Elizabeth Rigdon	W	on Three Mile
	b. on Three Mile						
5/ /1856	Maranda (colored)	F	A	E. A. Robertson		B	
	b. near Tilton						
3/24/1856	Wm. H.	M	A	W. N. Duley	Matilda Wood	W	near Martha Mills
	b. near Martha Mills						
11/ 5/1856	Charles W.	M	A	S. P. Carpenter	Amanda J. Crain	W	near Martha Mills
	b. near Martha Mills						
11/19/1856	Elizabeth Helen (Aelen?)	F	A	Columbus Tribby	Anjeline Perdoo	W	on South Lick
	b. on South Lick						
6/19/1856	Danl. Boon	M	A	Not known	unknown	W	unknown
	b. unknown, Re. Left at Jents Door.						
2/16/1856	Elijah Foster	M	A	Green Harmon	Jane Ross	W	on South Lick
	b. on South Lick						
2/11/1856	Charles Edward	M	A	Britain Dillon	Ruth A. Nealis	W	on Three Mile
	b. on Three Mile						
5/ /1856	James J.	M	A	Lewis Gully	Elizabeth Overly	W	near Titlton
	b. near Tilton						
11/25/1856	J. C. Buckenridge	M	A	G. T. Paxton	Mary Chrisman	W	on Fleming Creek
	b. on Fleming Creek						

COUNTY Fleming

S Sex
C Condition A-Alive D-Dead

DATE	NAME OF CHILD	S	C	NAME OF FATHER	NAME OF MOTHER	CO.	RESIDENCE
7/16/1856	Permelia A. b. Tilton	F	A	Franklin Bridges	Elizabeth J. Lee	W	Tilton, Ky.
6/24/1856	Granville T. b. on Fleming	M	A	G. W. Overley	Sarah E. Kincurt	W	on Fleming
7/23/1856	Sarah E. b. on Licking	F	A	Wesley H. Harmon	Ellan J. Scott	W	on Licking
6/ 1/1853	Wm. A. b. on South Lick	M	A	Standfield Jones	Evaline Harman	W	on South Lick
8/ 7/1856	Carline Magnire b. on Three Mile	F	A	James W. McCan	Mary Dillon	W	on Three Mile
9/ /1856	Mary R. b. Sherburn	F	A	Peter Sapp	Martha Rice	W	Sherburn
6/ /1856	J. C. Breckinridge b. on Three Mile	M	A	Salvanus Pointer	Manerva Saunders	W	on Three Mile
9/ /1856	Eliza Ann b. on South Lick	F	A	Wm. Jones	Nancy A. Kearns	W	on South Lick
5/11/1856	Elizabeth J. b. on South Lick	F	A	Joseph H. Faris	Mary A. Todd	W	on South Lick
2/29/1856	Sarah Jane b. Sherburn, Ky.	F	A	Jno. W. Williams	Elizabeth F. James	W	on Licking
1/ 1/1856	Mary Thomson b. on Three Mile	F	A	James Porter	Amanda Chrisman	W	on Three Mile
10/ /1856	Mary Frances b. on Locust Creek	F	A	Fletcher Davis	Mariah J. Mark	W	on South Lick
6/19/1856	Archabald T. b. Tilton, Ky.	M	A	S. D. Gardner	Mariam Hull	W	Tilton, Ky.
3/11/1856	Rebeca Bell b. on Locust	F	A	Saml. R. Lytte	Elizabeth Todd	W	on Locust
1/ 8/1856	Margaret Caroline b. on Locust	F	A	Isaiah Ditton	Mary A. Todd	W	on Locust
9/ /1856	Roobt. b. near Sherburn	M	A	Alfred Williams	Elizabeth Mauzey	W	on Licking
/ /1856	Harret (colored) b. Sherburn, Ky.	F	A	Geo. Aitkin		B	on Licking
10/15/1856	Levi b. on Three Mile	M	A	Geo. Reeves	Elizabeth Williams	W	on Three Mile

COUNTY   Fleming   C Condition A-Alive D-Dead

DATE	NAME OF CHILD	S	C	NAME OF FATHER	NAME OF MOTHER	CO.	RESIDENCE
9/21/1856	Wm. C. b. on Licking	M	A	L. S. Saunders	Sarah Morgan	W	on Licking
6/28/1856	Wm. b. on Licking	M	A	Joshua Lovel	Jane Burk	W	on Licking
9/20/1856	Daniel Daring b. on South Lick	M	A	James Rankin	Kejiah Harmon	W	on South Lick
5/25/1856	Sarah b. Hillsborough	M	A	David R. Nealis	Sarah A. Nealis	W	near Hillsborough
6/17/1856	Joy Lee b. Ringos Mill on Licking	F	A	Wm. Denton	Malinda Jones	W	on Licking
12/ /1856	 b. on Locust Creek	F	A	James Thompson	Sarah Denton	W	on Locust
10/28/1856	James b. on Fleming	M	A	John Plank	Mary E. Cassidy	W	Fleming
8/18/1856	Anna b. on Fleming	F	A	Marshal Hurst	Jane Ricketts	W	on Fleming
11/25/1856	name none b. near Flemingsburg	M	A	James M. Walker	Luisa Strode	W	near Flemings-burg
11/12/1856	Ardela b. on Fleming	F	A	Samuel Hunt	Hilda A. Williams	W	on Fleming
11/24/1856	Elmira M. b. near Flemingsburg	F	A	Wm. Smith	Jane Worick	W	near Flemings-burg
11/24/1856	Bill (colored)	M	A	E. E. Pearce		B	
11/24/1856	(colored)	M	A	Wineford Pearce		M	
11/24/1856	Charles (colored) b. Flemingsburg	M	A	John Gray		B	
4/22/1856	Albert b. near P. Plains	M	A	Rufus Emmons	Louisa Hendrix	W	near P. Plains
9/ /1856	Nancy (colored) b. near P. Plains	F		Jery Story		B	
1/ /1856	name none b. near Hillsborough	F	D	D. S. Backadale	E. J. Crain	W	near Hillsborough
12/ /1856	Lydia (colored) b. near Tilton	F	A	W. T. Howe		B	
3/20/1856	John W. b. near Tilton	M	A	Wm. B. McCracken	Frankey Dogget	W	near Tilton
11/24/1856	Martha M. b. near Tilton	F	A	Jackson McCall	Dolly Hysong	W	near Tilton

COUNTY   Fleming

Fleming County Sct.
    I certify that the foregoing 6 pages contains a true copy of the
Registration of Births for 1857 for Fleming as returned by the commissioner
of Tax.   Att. W. T. Dudley C.F.C.C.

DATE	NAME OF CHILD	S	C	NAME OF FATHER	NAME OF MOTHER	CO.	RESIDENCE
10/24/1857	James Harrison	M	A	Richard King	Margaret T. Smoot	W	All residents
4/28/1857	Not named	M	A	Alex McGregor	Mary Sheel	W	Fleming Co.
1/ 5/1857	Eliza Catharine	F	A	James Reeves	Elizabeth P. Matchel	W	
4/19/1857	Elizabeth Finley	F	A	Daniel Yazle	Alice Humphrey	W	
11/ 4/1857	Aaron Philps	M	A	Moses Saunders	May Day	W	
6/11/1857	David	M	A	Wm. P. Helponstine	Milky Doyle	W	
3/20/1857	Eliza	F	A	Jas. M. Pearce	Jautina Darrnall	W	
11/23/1857	Malinda Jane	F	A	Ruben Hartley	Mary Bramble	W	
11/15/1857	Eliza Jane	F	A	George Muse	Sarah Newman	W	
12/23/1857	John	M	A	John Story	Margaret Day	W	
10/12/1857	Charles	M	A	Alfred Jordan	Margaret Hutchison	W	
5/24/1857	Mirnerva	F	A	H. W. Hinton		M	
8/24/1857	Mary	F	A	Benj. Ham	Mary E. Hinton	W	
2/25/1857	Nelson	M	A	Thos. Staggs	Polly Ann Gorden	W	
8/18/1857	William Henry Sampson	M	A	Saml. P. Shields	Jeannett Payne	W	
11/15/1857	James William	M	A	Henry Markwell	Mardolete Razor	W	
3/ 2/1857	Andrew Jackson	M	A	Sylvester Estill	Elizabeth McKee	W	
5/ 7/1857	Eliza Jane	F	A	Saml. G. Davis	Lucinda Estill	W	
1/10/1857	John Wesley	M	A	Abel Markwell	Margaret Wright	W	
1/28/1857	Thomas B.	M	A	Absolem Powell	Minerva Jones	W	
10/10/1857	Not named	M	A	Robert Hayden	Jane Reeves	W	
5/25/1857	Hiram Bruce	M	A	Barnesford McGregor	Sarah Denton	W	
4/30/1857	John Mason	M	A	Hiram W. Royal	Sibby Horgeth	W	
6/17/1857	Jas. William	M	A	Hiram W. Royal	Sibby Harged	W	
7/13/1857	Thos. Bruce	M	A	John Myers	Eliza G. Markwell	W	
9/25/1857	Not named	M	A	John Kissick	Henrietta Reeves	W	
10/20/1857	Amanda Irabell	F	A		Joanna Crawford	W	
9/15/1857	Charles Simpson	M	A	James Boyce	Louisa Davis	W	
11/ 8/1857	Manduville	F	A	Fomtty R. Mual	Susan Lee	W	
7/21/1857	Nancy Jane	F	A	Hiram T. Royas	Artimeso Moore	W	
11/ /1857	Jemimia O.	F	A	F. R. Davis	Evaline Markwell	W	
3/11/1857	Celia	F	A	Aaron Gardner	Elizabeth Jordan	W	

COUNTY   Fleming

S Sex
C Condition A-Alive D-Dead

DATE	NAME OF CHILD	S	C	NAME OF FATHER	NAME OF MOTHER	CO.	RESIDENCE
7/10/1857	Mary Alice	F	A	Fielding Jones	Catharine Moore	W	All residents
2/28/1857	Not named	F	A	George Reeves	Mary C. Hall	W	Fleming Co.
10/ 1/1857	Not named	F	A	George Gully	Martha Burroughs	W	
10/20/1857	Samuel Perry	M	A	Asa Ham	Louisa Hartley	W	
9/16/1857	Not named	F	D	Saml. Cunningham	Amanda Colwell	W	
10/ 1/1857	Evaline Lewis	F	A	Elijah Carpenter	Mahala Jorden	W	
2/19/1857	Raleigh	M	A	Hiram Staggs	Elizabeth Jorden	W	
9/30/1857	Dudley Bell	M	A	Robert Saunders	Priscille E. Lewman	W	
7/ 5/1857	William	M	A	W. S. Beaucamp	Nancy J. Hinton	W	
10/20/1857	James Monroe	M	A	Wm. McKee	Emily Lewman	W	
10/ 7/1857	Martha Ellen	F	A	James P. Lewman	Charlotte Davis	W	
10/19/1857	Not named	M	A	Zacheus Evans	Sally McCleing	W	
4/20/1857	Charles Wm.	M	A	William Maddex	Elizabeth M. Kirk	W	
7/27/1857	Silas	M	A	Alfred Humphreys	Rebecca Humphreys	W	
10/16/1857	Dorcus D.	F	A	John Bowman	Fanny N. Hall	W	
6/19/1857	Charles	M	A	Jackson Everett	Mary E.	W	
8/28/1857	George A.	M	A	Andrew Glass	Jane Sutton	W	
12/ /1857	Louisa	F	A	J. B. Emmons		B	
12/ /1857	Not named	F	D	J. B. Emmons		B	
7/ 7/1857	Henry	M	A	J. S. Dunbar	Lucy P. Dudley	W	(twins)
7/ 7/1857	Elizabeth	F	A	J. S. Dunbar	Lucy P. Dudley	W	
9/ /1857	Lilly Frances	F	A	C. W. Browning	Nancy Mattingly	W	
10/12/1857	Richard Henry	M	A	Titus B. Chandler	Mary Winder	W	
9/10/1857	William	M	A	William M. Foxworthy	Alice Everett	W	
9/10/1857	Van	M	A	Nelson Morehead		M	
8/ /1857	Hester	F	A	Harrison Silvey	Jane French	W	
8/15/1857	John W.	M	A	Joseph Dixon	Eliza Hubanks	W	
10/ 5/1857	Nelson	M		Joseph Glasscock	Mary Foxworthy	W	
12/15/1857	Daniel	M		Joseph Glasscock		B	(twins)
12/18/1857	Traverse	M		Joseph Glasscock		B	
5/ /1857	Lewis	M		Joseph Glasscock		B	
2/21/1857	Mary Jane	F		Abram Denton	Evaline Jones	W	
2/26/1857	Joseph	M		Ephraim Phillips	Elizabeth Royse	W	
5/ 7/1857	T. J. Crain	M		John F. Crain	L. Dillon	W	
11/ 8/1857	Leander Coleman	M		Salem J. Smoot	Phidela Smoot	W	
11/13/1857	Mary Goldsmith	F		St. Clair Smoot	Barber A. Rawlings	W	
10/21/1857	Lewis Russell	M		Mathew G. Jones	Mary R. Stone	W	

S Sex
C Condition A-Alive D-Dead

COUNTY __Fleming__

DATE	NAME OF CHILD	S	C	NAME OF FATHER	NAME OF MOTHER	CO.	RESIDENCE
8/ 5/1857	Anna Bell	F	A	Jane Crain		M	All residents
4/15/1857	Betty Kate	F	A	Northcott Rawlings	Alice E. Lewis	W	Fleming Co.
12/25/1857	Not named	F	.	O. A. Kewtall		M	
7/15/1857	Cepbas A.	M		Anthony Rawlings	Susan Walton	W	
6/26/1857	Emily B.	F		James Jorden	Delily Lewman	W	
9/16/1857	Charles	M		James Boyd	Louisa Davis	W	
11/ 2/1857	George Washington	M		William Newdigate	Mary Nickie	W	
3/21/1857	Daniel Webster	M		Miles Hurst	Ann E. Carpenter	W	
3/21/1857	Joseph N.	M		Haroz Farris	Pellina Dale	W	
4/22/1857	Oscar L.	M		John James	Mary C. Jorden	W	
11/ 5/1857	Not named	M		Joel Saunders	Matild Lewman	W	
5/ 6/1857		F		Andrew Fountain	Louisia Robb	W	
5/ 6/1857		F		Andrew Fountain	Louisia Robb	W	
10/11/1857				James Dalrymiple	Margaret Gooding	W	
10/ /1857	Robe B.	M	A	John L. May	Malinda Cockran	W	
3/27/1857	James	M	A	David Howe	Harriet Plank	W	
11/ /1857	Louisa	F	A	Thos. Stockdale	Bridges	W	
3/ /1857	Mason	M	A	Thos. A. Crywood	Moore	W	
12/25/1857	John	M	D	Thos. Hilligoss	Darnall	W	
2/ /1857	John T.	M	A	Alfd. McCord	Farren	W	
7/12/1857	Abasha J.	F	A	Rearon Kirk	Moore	W	
1/16/1857	Samuel T.	M	A	Jn. H. McIntyre	McIntyre	W	
12/ /1857	Evaline J.	F	A	James M. Shockley	Ross	W	
1/23/1857	William H.	M	A	Ssmuel R. Mears	William	W	
9/ 8/1857	Elvin	M	A	Thos. E. Blake	Mears	W	
9/ 4/1857	James F.	M	A	W. W. Robert	Sousley	W	
10/ 6/1857	Margaret A.	F	A	John Johnson	Cochran	W	
2/25/1857	John A.	M	A	John A. Farrow	Park	W	
12/ /1857	Sarah Ann	F	A	David Brown	Farrow	W	
4/ /1857	Ann	F	A	Thos. Blake	Robertson	W	
6/30/1857	Ametia	F	A	John F. Belt	Wilson	W	
2/12/1857	Amanda E.	F	A	David Jolly	Stepheson	W	
10/ /1857	Alfred	M	A	Harrison Cline	Gollaher	W	
12/ 2/1857	Mary V.	F	A	B. L. Williams	Rolland	W	
4/ /1857	Mary	F	A	A. J. Goodplastone	Rolland	W	
5/27/1857	William W.	M	A	Ben H. Shockley	Holland	W	
4/ 4/1857	William W.	M	A	Hiram Moore	Bruce	W	
6/ 4/1857		F	A	G. G. Lowery	Williams	W	

S Sex
C Condition A-Alive D-Dead

COUNTY Fleming

DATE	NAME OF CHILD	S	C	NAME OF FATHER	NAME OF MOTHER	CO.	RESIDENCE
11/22/1957	Not named	F	A	Samuel Farris	Glenn	W	All residents
10/ /1857	Edwind	M	A	Wm. Ewing		B	Fleming Co.
10/ /1857	Edwind	M	A	Thos. B. McIntyre	Cachman	W	
12/ 4/1857	W. B. Sousley	M	A	H. C. Sousley	Fitzgeral	W	
9/ 6/1857	Josephine	F	A	Isaac K. Powers	McIntyre	W	
12/ /1857	Not named	F	A	David Howe	Rachel Wilson	W	
4/ 4/1857	Not named	F	D	Hiram Moore	Sillvena	W	
3/ 8/1857	Charles b. Mason Co.	M	A	David McCord	Farris	W	
9/13/1857	Albert James	M	A	G. W. Edwards	Sarah Flarity	W	
8/24/1857	Kate	F	A	James Gudding	Bridget	W	
12/28/1857	James	M	A	B. Glorky		B	
7/28/1857		M	A	G. W. Bishop	Nancy Long	W	Bath Co.
9/10/1857	Alfred C.	M	A	W. H. Berry	Payne	W	
3/10/1857	Mary E.	F	A	J. C. Hysong		W	
7/ /1857	Osber H.	M	A			W	
7/ /1857	Not named	F	A			B	
7/22/1857	Nancy E.	F	A		Sherrod	W	
6/ /1857	Martha	F	A	Wm. Huff	Mary Evans	W	
12/ 8/1857	Mary F.	F	A	Gincolen, Abner	Dotron	W	
4/13/1857	Mary V.	F	A	Buckhannon	Overly	W	
11/18/1857		F	D	Bently		W	
9/15/1857	Frans A.	F	A	T. S. Farrow	Bently	W	
1/21/1857	Amy B.	F	A	Willoughby Griffith	Julian Hall	W	
1/16/1857	Elizabeth R.	F	A	S. L. Crain	Louellan Taber	W	
12/ /1857	Colored	F	A	James Taber	Louellan	B	
1/ 1/1857	William	M	A	Alex Hart	Jane Anderson	W	
1/ /1857	Colored	M	A	Hart		B	
6/16/1857	Seth	M	A	Thos. R. Botts	Mary T. Fleming	W	
3/ /1857	Colored	M	A	Thos. R. Botts		B	
7/ /1857	Colored	M	A	T. R. Botts		B	
9/ 9/1857	Lucinda Hardin b. Frankford, Ky.	F	D	H. W. Bruce	Lizzie Barber Helm	W	
11/ /1857	Elizabeth	F	A	Ben Botts	Juliet E. Dorsey	W	
4/ 4/1857	Bruce	M	A	John W. Harmon	Sarah Keerns	W	
12/ /1857	Mary	F	A	Peter Joyce	Rosanah Casady	W	
7/ 1/1857	John	M	A	James Riley	Ann Moran	W	

66

COUNTY   Fleming

S Sex
C Condition A-Alive D-Dead

DATE	NAME OF CHILD	S	C	NAME OF FATHER	NAME OF MOTHER	CO.	RESIDENCE
6/ 1/1857	George Ann	F	A	G. W. Basken	Deborah Bedell	W	All residents
9/ /1857	Henry B. Keal	M	A	Saml. J. Real	Mary L. Fouch	W	Fleming Co.
5/27/1857	Martha F.	F	A	Thos. Dillon	Martha F. Williams	W	
9/ 2/1857	Elijah W.	M	A	Wesley H. Harmon	Ellen J. Scott	W	
1/ /1857	name none	M	D	Jas. D. Ringo	Emily Plank	W.	
1/ 5/1857	Alice	F	A	Benj. Pierce	Mary Dean	W	
5/ /1857	Mary A.	F	A	Eli Beam	Mary J. Wilson	W	
6/ 9/1857	Ema	F	A	G. B. Perkins	Margaret Clark	W	
11/ 3/1857	Julia A.	F	A	John Peck	Sarah A. Robertson	W	
8/ 6/1857	Andrew F.	M	A	John W. Williams	Elaner James	W	
	Martha Morter	F	A	Jackson McCall	Dally Hysong	W	
11/ /1857	Robert A.	M	A	Geo. E. Reeves	Elizabeth Williams	W	
4/ 4/1857	Lucina Jane	F	A	Jno. Moren	Matilda Rankins	W	
6/12/1857	Mary E.	F	A	Jno L. Bridges	Sarah T. Wilson	W	
12/11/1857	Sarah L.	F	A	Robt. Clinkinheard	Lucinda D. Bames	W	
8/ 5/1857	Tilton	M	A	Wm. Rice	Roda Jonson	W	
4/16/1857	Alford	M	A	John W. Woodard	Sarah Anderson	W	
5/ 5/1857	Mary A.	F	A	Wm. Bateman	Louisa Prater	W	
12/22/1857	Thos. M.	M	A	B. M. Embry	Mary E. Hull	W	
12/ /1857	John F.	M	A	Patrick Dougherty	Margaret McCord	W	
4/22/1857	Charley	M	A	Stephen D. Gardner	Maureen Hull	W	
12/29/1857	name none	M	D	Alfred Williams	Elizabeth Mauzy	W	
3/27/1857	Anne Lizzie	F	A	A. D. Miller	Martha M. Freelan	W	
9/17/1857	Sarah C.	F	A	John Hunt	Jane Campbell	W	
3/28/1857		F	A	James Lyman	Elizabeth Wills	W	
8/ 7/1857	Isaac E.	M	A	Joseph Buckanan	Nancy Ishmall	W	
5/ /1857	Jno M.	M	A	Jas. W. Tribby	Manerva Mers	W	
7/26/1857	Sarah Frances	F	A	James Porter	Amanice Chrisman	W	
9/14/1857	Louisa L.	F	A	Jesse Ingrham	Sarah Armstrong	W	
10/26/1857	Robert W.	F	A	Josiah W. Wilson	Eliza Porter	W	
11/24/1857	Martha M.	F	A	Jackson McCall	Dally Hysong	W	
3/25/1857	Ruth	F	A	John Porter	Angeline Moren	W	
3/13/1857	Lija (col.)	F	A	Jonathan Clinkinton		B	
4/ 8/1857	Henry	M	A	Jas. A. Keith	Mahala Overly	W	
4/28/1857	Charles	M	A	Theodore Hart	Amanda Kendall	W	
3/ 6/1857	Moris A.	M	A	John F. Armstrong	Elizabeth Rash	W	
9/ 2/1857	Ethelbert Logan	M	A	J. C. Sousley	Ann J. Finley	W	

COUNTY Fleming

S Sex
C Condition A-Alive D-Dead

DATE	NAME OF CHILD	S	C	NAME OF FATHER	NAME OF MOTHER	CO.	RESIDENCE
4/22/1857	Maranda	F	A	W. S. T. Graham	Lyia Dearing	W	All residents
9/12/1857	Mary E.	F	A	W. H. Webster	Susan M. Triplett	W	Fleming Co.
9/17/1857	Hannah	F	A	Danl. Danrymple	Jane Newman	W	
10/30/1857	Elizabeth Walker	F	A	Wm. Graves	Helan Sutton	W	
7/ /1857	Faully Ball	F	A	A. W. Day	Rebeca Saunders	W	
4/ 6/1857	Ervin W.	M	A	P. M. Grose	Mary J. Faris	W	
8/ 4/1857	Sarah Alice	F	A	Jno. Pirkins	Rebeca Storz	W	
11/ 8/1857	Lafaette	M	A	Silas Ross	Armilda Duncan	W	
6/ /1857	Sophronia	F	A	Thomas Todd	Sophrania Browning	W	
10/21/1857	Sanford A.	M	A	Wm. P. Denton	Malinda Jones	W	
9/ 5/1857	Henry Finley	M	A	F. P. Robertson	Martha A. Finley	W	
10/30/1857	(Colored)	M	A	St. Clair Emons		M	
11/ /1857	Margaret	F	A	S. B. Lyons	Martha A. Day	W	
8/11/1857	Martha Ann	F	A	Jas. Newman	Mary A. Havins	W	
10/ /1857	(Colored)	M	A	Theadore Hart		B	
3/ /1857	Lord Hester	F	A	Hiram McKee	Sarah Ledford	W	
6/ 5/1857	Nancy	F	A	D. S. Barksdale	Elizabeth Crain	W	
4/ 2/1857	Henry	M	A	Jas. D. Webster	Clarissa A. Gardner	W	
6/ /1857	(colored child)	M	A	Archibald Hull		B	
10/ /1857	(colored)	M	A	Nelson Fant		B	
5/15/1857	John	M	A	Jas. M. Roby	Nancy C. Armstrong	W	
1/ 3/1857	William	M	A	S. W. Irvin	Cornelia Logan	W	
10/ /1857	Catharine Thomas	M	A	Thos. E. Smith	Catharine Wilson	W	
5/ /1857	(colored child)	M	A	James M. Triplet		B	
	Milliard Allen	M	A	Wm. Eden	Nancy J. Gray	W	
10/ /1857	Catharine Francis	F	A	Adam C. Gray	Abigal Woods	W	
10/ /1857	name none	F	D	Bratain	Elizabeth McCabe?	W	
11/ /1857	Nannie	F	A	John W. Dulin	Elizabeth Barns	W	
1/ /1857	Jno (colored)	M	A	Polly Hornback		B	
1/ /1857	(colored)	F	A	Ralleigh Kendall		M	
4/18/1857	Charles L.	M	A	John McCartney	Mary D. Dent	W	
8/ 1/1857	Gross R.	M	A	R. A. Lightfoot	Sallie E. Stockwell	W	

State of Kentucky, Fleming County Sct.
    I, William T. Dudley, Clerk of the Court for the county aforesaid certify
that the foregoing four pages contain a true list of the Births returned by the
Comm. of Tax for 1858. June 22, 1858.
                    W. T. Dudley CCK

COUNTY __Fleming__

S Sex
C Condition A-Alive D-Dead

DATE	NAME OF CHILD	S	C	NAME OF FATHER	NAME OF MOTHER	CO.	RESIDENCE
2/ 7/1858	Abram	M	A	William R. Denton	Rebecca Lyons	W	All residents
5/31/1858	Francis M.	M	A	Jas. H. West	Rebecca Hamilton	W	Fleming Co.
2/21/1858	Elizabeth	F	A	Lawrence Triplett		B	
10/15/1858	Enora	F	A	Samuel L. Carpenter	Sophia Lewman	W	
9/29/1858	Francis	F	A	J. B. Phelps	Nancy N. Sauders	W	
12/ /1858	Alaam	F	A	William S. T. Emmons	Susan Reeves	W	
5/17/1858	Boon	M	A	William Kissich	Amanda Reeves	W	
5/13/1858	Thomas F.	M	A	Presley Rawlings	Sary Vanlaninghour	W	
11/20/1858	John W.	M		Charles Shurlock	Milly Gillispie	W	
1/10/1858	Joseph L.	M		Thomas Keesans	Vianna Johnson	W	
10/11/1858	Joseph D.	M	D	Henry Kissich	Sarah J. Pleak	W	
10/12/1858	John W.	M	A	Henry Kissich	Sarah J. Pleak	W	(twins)
6/10/1858	Mary D.L.	F	A	George R. Barber	Sarah A. Johnson	W	
3/25/1858	Jacob V.	M	A	Samuel P. Tinsley	Sary Wannitton	W	
6/15/1858		M	D	James McGregor	Eliza Pickeral	W	
3/31/1858	Mirinda	F	A	John M. Pearce	Mary A. Reeves	W	
4/18/1858	Barney	M	A	Noah Reeves	Queen America Horgot	W	
12/21/1858	Hiram	M	A	Samuel L. Cline	Elizabeth A. Horgot	W	
11/ 1/1858	John W.	M	A	Michael Jamison	Nancy Pickerall	W	
9/27/1858	William	M	A	John T. Crain	Luticia Dillon	W	
1/ 8/1858	Vac'ory T.	M	A	David Shrout	Melinda Atchison	W	
4/ 5/1858	Nicholas	M	A	Tim Haflin	Briget Cook	W	
1/17/1858	Rebecca	F	A	Abel Markwell	Marget Bight	W	
2/20/1858	Jesse	M	A	Abram Magowan		B	
4/24/1858	William	M	A	John Van Cline	Martha J. Heming	W	
10/ /1858	Mary S.	F	A	Joseph Yazell	Martha J. Anderson	W	
8/ 7/1858	David H.	M	D	Andrew T. McKee	Elizabeth Hartley	W	
6/29/1858	Nancy A.	F	A	Elimigh Lewman	Harriet Hickerson	W	
6/10/1858	James F.	M	A	Francis Plummer	Ellen Lewman	W	
12/16/1858	Rolan	M	A	ELlijah Thomas	July Ann Dyre	W	
9/22/1858	Malvina C.	F	A	Johnathan Stratton	Sarah J. Lansdown	W	
6/26/1858	Mary E.	F	A	James Reeves	Elizabeth Matchett	W	
3/ 9/1858	William N.	M	A	George Elliott	Mary Bramer	W	
3/29/1858	Mary A.	F	A	Silas T. Keith	Mariah J. Humphries	W	
10/10/1858	Nancy J.	F	A	John McLain	Sebby Ann Reeves	W	
5/23/1858	Mary C.	F	A	William Doyle	Rebecca Helphenstine	W	
4/28/1858	Martha B.	F	A	David Morrison	Eliza A. Hayter	W	
10/15/1858	Henry A.	M	A	A. P. Helphenstine	Martha J. Doyle	W	

69

KENTUCKY COUNTIES VITAL STATISTICS

S Sex
C Condition A-Alive D-Dead

COUNTY Fleming

DATE	NAME OF CHILD	S	C	NAME OF FATHER	NAME OF MOTHER	CO.	RESIDENCE
12/20/1858	Ann E.	F	A	Addison Hedges	Nancy Day	W	All residents
5/31/1858	Elizabeth	F	A	Jeremiah Murphy	Sarah Hayden	W	Fleming Co.
					(Next name)		
3/ 2/1858	Elizabeth E.	F	A	A. F. Shields	Elizabeth Gray	W	
7/ 2/1858	William B.	M	A	R. L.McGregor	Emily Rawlings	W	
8/ 2/1858	Crilla	F	A	Lander Smoot	Naraissa Thompson	W	
10/27/1858	Jaspar C.	M	A	Drison T.G. Crawford	Mary A. McCracken	W	
10/15/1858	Malinda J.	F	A	Dudley Davis	Fidella Newman	W	
12/17/1858	Nancy J.	F	A	John L. Davis	Delila Shoat	W	
10/20/1858	Nelson M.	M	A	G. W. Vansanett	Isabella A. Cooper	W	
6/22/1858	Enoch	M	A	Alexander Shields	Lucinda Crain	W	
12/ 1/1858	Lucinda A.	F	A	Henry Helphenstine	Emily Glover	W	
4/ 1/1858	Mary E.	F	A	Samuel Shields	Elizabeth J. Mills	W	
5/31/1858	R. Jane	F	A	C. W. Foudray	Lucinda Lee	W	
12/28/1858	James	M	A	A. G. Lewis	Roda A. Crain	W	
11/18/1858		M	A	B. F. Reeves	Mary D. Jamison	W	
11/25/1858	Vernitta	F	A	J. G. Overton	July Ann Harman	W	
9/ 9/1858	Eliza B.	F	A	D. N. Skinner	Sarah Thompson	W	
4/27/1858	Mary E.	F	A	J. B. Northcut	Louisa Emmons	W	
3/15/1858	Gareld	F	A	Alfred Markwell		B	
10/10/1858	Henry	M	A	John S. Botts		B	
1/23/1858	Mary D.	F	A	John H. Gulick	Clementine Downs	W	
1/26/1858	Mary Ann	F	A	Wm. M. Walker		B	
7/ /1858	Zekiel	M	A	Rosanna T. Bradford		B	
6/20/1858	Sarah E.	F	A	G. W. Ross	Nancy Powers	W	
5/ 1/1858	Richard W.	M	A	John F. Lander	Sary M. Scott	W	
12/26/1858	Margret E.	F	A	John Moran	Margret Howe	W	
10/15/1858	Catharine	F	A	William A. Morrison		B	
6/ /1858	Alfred	M	A	M. P. Wallingford		B	
7/18/1858	John W.	M	A	G. W. Calvert	Clarissa Foxworthy	W	
11/ 8/1858	William	M	A	James R. Bell	Elizabeth Turner	W	
8/12/1858	Jerry	M	D	James Walingford		B	
5/13/1858	George	M	A	James Watingford		B	
12/23/1858	James W.	M	A	Walter Wallingford	Clarinda Johnson	W	
3/22/1858		M	D	B. F. Wallingford	Parthean Robison	W	
9/22/1858	Howard H.	M	A	D. C. Forrow	Mary Terry	W	
11/ 7/1858	Catharine	F	A	William Clary	Eveline Foxworthy	W	
10/ 1/1858	Robert	M	A	Thomas S. Hughes	Amanda Hurst	W	

COUNTY ___Fleming___

S Sex
C Condition A-Alive D-Dead

DATE	NAME OF CHILD	S	C	NAME OF FATHER	NAME OF MOTHER	CO.	RESIDENCE
1/16/1858	James W.	M	A	James H. Fizer	Lucinda Crain	W	All residents
12/13/1858	Brant R.	M	A	Samuel Walker	Mary Ann Dale	W	Fleming Co.
9/25/1858	Gilford S.	M	A	James Jordon	Martha E. Carpenter	W	
4/22/1858	Alice	F	A	Hiram Staggs	Elizabeth Jordan	W	
4/16/1858	George R.	M	A	John F. Haws	Permelia A. Brammel	W	
12/26/1858	William	M	D	William Hickerson	Nancy Carpenter	W	
6/28/1858	America	F	A	Miles Hurst	Mary Doyle	W	
11/ 6/1858	Mat Andrews	M	A	Marshall Hickerson	Malinda Lewman	W	
1/17/1858	Daniel	M	A	Walter W. Hurst	Lucinda Doyle	W	
8/ /1858	John	M	A	Daniel Morgan		B	
10/ /1858	Milly	F	A	Daniel Morgan		B	
11/ /1858	Sary C.	F	A	Daniel Morgan		B	
3/ 9/1858		F	D	Patrick O'Gar	Elizabeth Reed	W	
1/ /1858	Pheba A.	F	A	Obed P. Nute		B	
3/13/1858	Ann M.	F	A	Reese Davis	Melvy J. Foxworthy	W	
4/15/1858	Lucy J.	F	D	William H. Hinton	Amanda Jones	W	
12/ /1858	William	M	A	Harvey M. Farris	Perline Dale	W	
1/15/1858	Allen	M	A	J. B. Muse	Sary Walker	W	
1/20/1858	Malinda	F	A	William B. Arnold	Sary A. Arnold	W	
10/ 4/1858		F	A	Louiza Stockwell		B	
1/ /1858	Margret	F	A	A. K. Marshall		B	
3/27/1858	Minnie	F	A	Leroy W. Kenner	Mary Bell	W	
12/20/1858	Ophelia	F	A	W. C. R. Harrison		B	
6/ 1/1858	John D.	M	A	William T. Mayhugh	Angeline Riggs	W	
8/ 1/1858	Lybby B.	F	A	William H. Wallingford	Clarissa Segbold	W	
4/27/1858	Wesley	M	A	N. D. Glasscock		B	
9/11/1858	Luella	F	A	Car. B. White	Sary Power	W	
	b. Mason Co.						
9/ /1858	Arminda	F	A	Aaron Quicksall	Elizabeth Prater	W	
10/30/1858	Amelia	F	A	Samuel Williams	Elizabeth Alexander	W	
2/20/1858	Ellen	F	A	William F. Jordan	Matilda Hammons	W	
2/16/1858	Rebecca A.	F	A	John W. Doyle	Elizabeth Haws	W	
12/18/1858	Ida	F	A	Dudley Jordan	Ellen Sweet	W	
8/ 8/1858	Louisa	F	D	Thomas Staggs	Polly A. Jordan	W	
8/27/1858	Prissilla	F	A	Joseph F. Doyle	Eliza J. Haws	W	
12/ 5/1858	William	M	A	James Kidwell	Emeline Hinton	W	
3/15/1858	Jack	M	D	R. P. Samuels		B	
12/11/1858	Nancy	F	A	Thomas Oliver		B	

S Sex
C Condition A-Alive D-Dead

COUNTY __Fleming__

DATE	NAME OF CHILD	S	C	NAME OF FATHER	NAME OF MOTHER	CO.	RESIDENCE
7/ 8/1858	Burgis D.	M	A	Benjamin H. Ross	Cely Holland	W	All residents
8/ 5/1858	Hattie	F	A	William F. Lewis	Margret Evans	W	Fleming Co.
7/15/1858	Will	M	A	Alexander H. Brand		B	
7/16/1858	Mary E.	F	A	Joshua Stableton	Charity Blanton	W	
6/16/1858	Wesley B.	M	A	William B. Evans	Matilda Plummer	W	
3/ 1/1858	Mariah	F	A	Samuel Humphreys	Crilla J. Colvert	W	
11/ /1858		M	A	Benjamin J. Plummer	Martha A. Muse	W	
9/ 5/1858	William A.	M	A	Joseph D. McKee	Rachel Fenton	W	
11/10/1858	James	M	A	J. T. Standiford	Luann Maises	W	
1/30/1858	Abram	M	A	John F. Carpenter	Elizabeth Hopper	W	
3/22/1858	Laura	F	A	Elijah Ham	Margret J. Lightfood	W	
3/11/1858	Nancy E.	F	A	Charles B. Anold	Rachel M. Carpenter	W	
9/16/1858	Ann Eliza	F	A	Silas Mark	Malinda Thurman	W	
9/12/1858	Milton B.	M	A	Samuel G. Mark	Roxa J. Purnell	W	
1/10/1858	Tarissa A.	F	A	Granville See	Ann A. Shanklin	W	
12/12/1858	Daniel C.	M	A	Jonathan Lewman	Mary Elston	W	
1/22/1858	John	M	A	William Huclé	Mary A. Brooks	W	
2/ 2/1858	George H.	M	A	James M. Clary	Malinda Jackson	W	
8/10/1858	Eliza	F	A	Joel BeBell		B	
8/10/1858		F	D	Patrick Crotty	Margret Roney	W	
2/12/1858	Adison	M	A	Robert Gooding	Amanda Jones	W	
9/20/1858	Thomas	M	A	Robert Gooding		B	
3/16/1858	William B.	M	A	W. M. Harmon	Elizabeth Dillon	W	
8/20/1858	Benjamin G.	M	A	Samuel B. H. Jones	Martha Plummer	W	
12/28/1858	Thomas	M	A	Samuel Cunningham	Amanda Colwell	W	
3/18/1858		F	A	Abram Gooding		B	
3/ 4/1858	James Ella	F	A	James Belt	Amanda Cooper	W	
8/ 6/1858	Lewis H.	M	D	Jacob Reeder	Polly White	W	
11/14/1858	Ellen	F	A	Silas W. Kane	Nanna Walsh	W	
12/26/1858	William	M	A	John G. Fischer	Mary C. Koenig	W	
6/16/1858	Hugo G.B.	M	A	B. G. Village	R.G.J.F. Hacker	W	
8/12/1858	Alburty	F	A	Harrison Bowman	Nancy A. Shockley	W	
11/ 8/1858	Allice	F	A	Fanny M. Armstrong		B	
3/25/1858	Wesley	M	A	William H. Henrick		B	
4/10/1858	Maggie B.	F	A	Alfred W. Nowood	Sarah J. Dobyno	W	
8/10/1858		F	D	William S. Jordan	Sary Ann	W	
1/15/1858	Wm. Morgan	M	A	Wm. Morgan	Ann Bruce	W	

COUNTY Fleming

DATE	NAME OF CHILD	S	C	NAME OF FATHER	NAME OF MOTHER	CO.	RESIDENCE
7/21/1858	Lizza D. Smith	F	A	Thomas B. Smith	Sarah Lindsey	W	All residents
7/ /1858	Edward	M	A	Thos. Dougherty		B	Fleming Co.
10/ /1858	Mary	F	A	John Porter		B	
7/15/1858	Jane Adams	F	A	Jacob Adams	Mary J. Brown	W	
11/ /1858	Elizabeth B. Biddle	F	A	Stephen Biddle	Evaline Ross	W	
7/ /1858	Sarah Jane	F	A	John Tanner		B	
5/ /1858	Eliza	F	A	Geo. D. Loury		B	
10/25/1858	(not named)	F	A	Tilford Barne	Nancy Lowry	W	
4/13/1858	Martin M. Jackson	M	A	James Jackson	Lucinda Faris	W	
10/22/1858	Harrison	M	A	Benj. Johnson		B	
8/ /1858	Mary	F	A	G. D. Loury		B	
9/14/1858	Bertha Allen	F	A	Henry G. Allen	Mary Bolts	W	
9/10/1858	Mary Payne	F	A	James Payne	Maranda Payne	W	
3/ 3/1858	Lear	F	A	Levina Alexander		B	
9/19/1858	(not named)	F	A	Wm. Hopkins	Eliza Jones	W	
/ /			D	Joseph Skillman	Lavena Wilson	W	
3/29/1858	Mary Allis	F	A	John D. Hopkins	Lucinda Davis	W	
2/10/1858	John Joice	M	A	Patrick Joice	Katharine Cusick	W	
10/21/1858		F	A	Ira Dillon	Mary Ann Todd	W	
12/15/1858	Betty Allen	F	A	Andrew T. Wood	Matilda Pickrell	W	
6/10/1858	Barbery Ellen	F	A	George W. Overly	Sarah E. Kincart	W	
11/25/1858	Louisa Florence	F	A	Jessey Ingram	Sarah Armstrong	W	
5/ 1/1858	Mary	F	A	Jas. A. Wilson	Susan Arnald	W	
10/ 6/1858	Lucy Ricketts	F	A	Coleman Preston	Margaret J. Miller	W	
9/11/1858	Luellen	F	A	Columbus Tribby	Angeline Pedue	W	
8/20/1858	Wm. Marion	M	A	Jackson Cassidy	Luellen Darnall	W	
8/ 6/1858	(not named)	M	D	Edward Moren	Rhoda Powel	W	(d. 3 days old)
11/ 3/1858	Josephine Jones	F	A	Wm. Jones	Nancy A. Kerns	W	
2/21/1858	George W. Kogers	M	A	John Rogers	Mary Ham	W	(b. Carter Co.)
3/30/1858	Oliver Hickson	M	A	Moses T. Clack	Lenna Myer	W	
3/30/1858	Eliza Clack	F	A	Moses T. Clack	Lenna Myer	W	
	Re. Twin children male & female. b. Rowan Co.						
3/25/1858	William Andrew Newman	M	A	Alexander Newman	Sarah Jane Williams	W	
2/26/1858	Amanda West	F	A	John T. Wall	Elizabeth Dudley	W	
6/23/1858	William Lewis	M	A	Johnathan Wilson	Enfield R. Wilson	W	
10/ 8/1858	Presley Landers	M	A	Asa Sauders	Eliza J. Harman	W	
11/ /1858	Mary Shockley	F	A	William H. Shockley	Eliza Dickey	W	

COUNTY Fleming

S Sex
C Condition A-Alive D-Dead

DATE	NAME OF CHILD	S	C	NAME OF FATHER	NAME OF MOTHER	CO.	RESIDENCE
11/ /1858	Isabell J. Williams	F	A	James Williams	Harriet Sauders	W	All residents
10/28/1858	John Brooks	M	A	Theodore Hart	Amanda Kendall	W	Fleming Co.
2/28/1858	H. Clay	M	A	Sennet Callahan	Sarah J. Reeves	W	
4/15/1858	Elizabeth Finley	F	A	Enoch Barns	Mary J. Finley	W	
11/ 3/1858	Virginia Allis	F	A	John H. Planck	Mary Cassidy	W	
4/ /1858	Lizzie Minie	F	A	Wm. Grannis	Narcissa Hurst	W	
12/ /1858	Henry P. Emmons	M	A	Rufus Emmons	Louisa Hendrix	W	
5/30/1858	Henry Cassidy	M	A	Henry Cassidy	Ellen Crowley	W	(Irish)
9/27/1858	Mary A. Maher	F	A	Wm. Maher	Mary Marshall	W	
4/17/1858	James W. Birk	M	A	John N. Birk	Mary A. Lee	W	
11/20/1858	Henry	M	A	Richard Spencer		B	
7/ /1858	Anna	F	A	Harvey T. Wilson		B	
7/ /1858	Amanda	F	A	Harvey T. Wilson		B	
2/ 3/1858	Henry C. Ringoe	M	A	Joseph P. Ringoe	Matilda C. Sauders	W	
4/ 2/1858	Clarra H. Miller	F	A	Alfred D. Miller	Martha A. Freelan	W	
3/ 6/1858	Wm. Beard	M	A	Samuel Beard	Nancy Cooby	W	
7/27/1858	John Learney	M	A	Pat Learney (Tearney?)	Ellen Riley	W	(Irish)
12/20/1858	Mary Graham	F	A	Robt. Graham	Rebecca Porter	W	
7/23/1858	Thomas Crawford	M	A	John Crawford	Martha Payne	W	
9/11/1858	(not named)	F	A	Samuel Lytle	Elizabeth Todd	W	
10/ 2/1858	Ellen B. Powel	F	A	John Powel	Jane McCann	W	
10/23/1858	Elizabeth S. McLane	F	A	Jos. McLane	Mary A. Dillon	W	
10/15/1858	Timothy Riley	M	A	Jas. Riley	Ann Moren	W	(Irish)
8/22/1858	Harrison Sousley	M	A	John E. Sousley	Susan Bush	W	
12/27/1858	Lucinda	F	A	John E. Sousley		B	
6/ 1/1858	Isaac	M	A	Harrison Sousley		B	
6/12/1858	Albert	M	A	Richard Parker		B	
12/ 1/1858	(not named)	F	A	Henry Hart		B	
8/ 1/1858	(not named)	F	D	John Allen		B	
11/ /1858	Sally	F	A	Wm. Fleming		B	
9/ /1858	Eliza	F	A	O'Banion Kendall		B	
12/23/1858	Margaret	F	A	H. J. Darnall		B	
/ /	Joe	M	A	John H. Wells (time not recollected)		B	
9/ /1858			D	John H. Wells		B	
12/25/1858	Sam	M	A	Alexander Hart		B	
12/ /1858	George	M	A	Wilson Buckler		B	
9/13/1858	Clarissa	F	A	Robert Harper		B	

COUNTY   Fleming

S Sex
C Condition A-Alive D-Dead

DATE	NAME OF CHILD	S	C	NAME OF FATHER	NAME OF MOTHER	CO.	RESIDENCE
6/ 1/1858	Wm. H. Parker	M	A	Ricard Parker	Mary Stephenson	W	All residents
8/15/1858	John Sousley	M	A	Franklin Sousley	Susan Peck	W	Fleming Co.
8/25/1858	Wm. R. Smith	M	A	James E. Smith	Anjeline Thomson	W	
11/25/1858	Charles H. Berry	M	A	Henry Berry	Louisa Armstrong	W	
8/ 2/1858	Mary V. Dint	F	A	Wm. R. Dent	Martha Robertson	W	
4/20/1858	James E. Sapp	M	A	Wm. Sapp	Susan Hule	W	
10/12/1858	Sarah A. Williams	F	A	Wm. Williams	Rebecca Wrenchy	W	
9/ /1858	Jos. P. McIntire	M	A	Francis M. McIntyre	Sarah E. Patton	W	
1/21/1858	Wm. C. Morgan	M	A	Rawleigh Morgan	Amanda Hendrix	W	
4/21/1858	Wm. McCrary	M	A	John McCrary	Elizabeth	W	
2/ 7/1858	John T. Evans	M	A	O. V. Evans	Susan Evans	W	
9/11/1858	Wm. F. Sims	M	A	Duncan Simms	Martha Robertson	W	
11/26/1858	Wm. A. Williams	M	A	Alfred Williams	Elizabeth Mawzy	W	
7/11/1858	Charles F. Taylor	M	A	George A. Taylor	Maranda Washburn	W	
	Re. Taylor is keeper of the Poor House						
2/26/1858	Elijah Hart	M	A	Alexander Hart	Jane Anderson	W	
4/20/1858	George W. Supplee	M	A	Wm. Supplee	Mary Sapplee	W	
6/28/1858	Lear. M. Watton	F	A	John Hatton	Oleah Havens	W	
8/21/1858	Effa Lilian Smith	F	A	J. B. Smith Dr.	M. Addie Ball	W	
5/10/1858	Delila Bartlett	F	A	James Bartlett	Margery Barrett	W	
5/ 1/1858	Allis Buckler	F	A	Wilson Buckler	Malinda Gill	W	
10/21/1858	Lucinda Staniford	F	A	Robt. Staniford	Rubena Paxton	W	
4/ 9/1858	Louisa Stanfield	F	A	Pleasant Stanfield	Sarah Hammons	W	
1/18/1858	John E. H. P. English	M	A	James M. English	Sarah J. McCowan	W	
6/ 7/1858	John F. Case	M	A	Walter Case	Maria Payne	W	
9/15/1858	Lucy E. Stogdale	F	A	Thomas Strogdale	Sarah S. Stout	W	
5/ 2/1858	Thomas Lane	M	A	Craven Lane	Mary Prather	W	
6/29/1858	James T. Eckman	M	A	Danl. Eckman	Elizabeth Thomas	W	
6/15/1858	Ally Grace Simms	F	A	Jos. Simms	Mary E. Wise	W	
4/ 9/1858	James W. Dickson	M	A	John Dickson	Elizabeth E. Ballard	W	
8/10/1858	(not named)	M	A	Thomas T. More	Delila Stout	W	
7/24/1858	Samuel B. Adamson	M	A	John Adamson	Crissia White	W	
11/17/1858	Harlents Lovel	F	A	Joshua Lovel	Jane Birk	W	
11/26/1858	Eliza Emma Bentley	F	A	Ricard Bentley	Ann Overly	W	
4/29/1858	Lewis Frank	M	A	Henry Frank	Caroline Black	W	
7/27/1858	Elizabeth Campbell	F	A	James Campbell	Matilda Campbell	W	
12/28/1858	Mari. F. Adamson	F	A	Jas. H. Adamson	Lucy J. Barnett	W	
10/15/1858	Samuel Hildreth	M	A	Aquilla Hildreth	Martha J. Spencer	W	

COUNTY Fleming

DATE	NAME OF CHILD	S	C	NAME OF FATHER	NAME OF MOTHER	CO.	RESIDENCE
8/11/1858	Edmance P. McCarty	M	A	John E. McCarty	Polly A. Groves	W	All residents
12/ 3/1858	Lizzie M. Scott	F	A	Danl. N. Scott	Isabel Sousley	W	Fleming Co.
3/17/1858	Mary Mers	F	A	Samuel Mers	Adaline Williams	W	
8/12/1858	Benjamin Ross	M	A	Jas. D. Ross	Sarah A. Shockley	W	
9/13/1858	Nancy E. Harmon	F	A	Edward Harmon	Lucinda Keenins	W	
1/30/1858	(not named)	M	A	David L. Howe	Harriet Plauck	W	
10/25/1858	James C. Blair	M	A	Wallis Blair	Belinda Sousley	W	
7/23/1858	John C. Gairy	M	A	Wm. Gairy	Isabell Alexander	W	
7/ 4/1858	Sarah E. Galliher	F	A	John Galliher	Ellen McKee	W	
10/15/1858	Katharine Biddle	F	A	Elias Biddle	Mary Price	W	
12/27/1858	Wm. Morris	M	A	George V. Morris	Mary A. Bishop	W	
3/17/1858	Sary G. Kechley	F	A	Cephas Kechley	Virginia Williams	W	
10/15/1858	Charles Ross	M	A	James Ross	Henrietta Matthews	W	
4/17/1858	Thomas G. Falkner	M	A	George Falkner	Ann Baggot	W	
2/23/1858	James M. Watton	M	A	Rawleigh Watton	Nancy Newman	W	
7/28/1858	Wm. McClintock	M	A	Alexander McClintock	Cornelia Darnall	W	

Fleming County Sct.
    I certify that the foregoing is a true copy of the registration
of Births returned by the Comm. of Tax in the year 1859 for this
county. June 20th, 1859.
        Att. W. T. Dudley CCK County Court

12/28/1859	Fannie	F	A	George S. Fleming		B	
10/ 8/1859	Robert S.	M	A	James H. Fizer	Lucinda Crain	W	
12/ 8/1859	Robert	M	A	Phillip Helphenstine	Priscilla Doyle	W	
9/12/1859	Eliza	F	A	Mary Kidwell		B	
8/25/1859	Amanda E.	F	A	Dudley Brothers	Julia Queen	W	
3/ 3/1859	Amanda F.	F	D	Alexander Ham	Sary Hartley		
3/ 3/1859	Armelda B.	F	A	Alexander Ham	Sary Hartley	W	(twins)
6/27/1859	Jerry	M	A	Oliver Atchison		B	
5/ 5/1859	Hugh J.	M	A	Patrick O'Gar	Mary Reed	W	
4/14/1859	Frank S.	M	A	William H. Morrison	Mary E. Lyons	W	
10/14/1859	Not named	F	A	John Moore	Eliza J. Markwell	W	
3/16/1859	John G.	M	A	Alfred Jones	Eliza A. Humphries	W	
4/ 2/1859	Margaret Ann	F	A	Abner Boyd	Elizabeth Snoot	W	
10/ 1/1859	William S.	M	A	Samuel K. Philps	Sary Plummer	W	

COUNTY __Fleming__

S Sex
C Condition A-Alive D-Dead

DATE	NAME OF CHILD	S	C	NAME OF FATHER	NAME OF MOTHER	CO.	RESIDENCE
1/18/1859	George W.	M	A	James M. Ham	Mary J. Margett	W	All residents
8/25/1859	Mary Jane	F	A	Robert L. McGregor	Emily M. Rawlings	W	Fleming Co.
8/25/1859	David M. Shields	M	A	James L. Shields	Harriett E. Gray	W	
8/15/1859	Sara M.	F	A	Gamaliel Freeman	Sary Overton	W	
11/ 6/1859	Not named	M	A	James Shields	Jenetta Payne	W	
5/ 5/1859	Richard M.	M	A	Eli E. Busby	Emily Downey	W	
10/14/1859	Francis A.	M	A	James Downey	Eliza J. Rawlings	W	
7/ 1/1859	James W.	M	A	Basford McGregor	Sara Denton	W	
3/ 3/1859	Lula	F	A	George W. Hudson	Mary Day	W	
7/28/1859	Sylvester	M	A	James H. Davis	Nancy Estill	W	
6/15/1859	Mary E.	F	A	Samuel Davis	Lucinda Estill	W	
4/ 9/1859	Not named Re. Illegitimate	M	D		Elvine Hargett	W	
12/ 1/1859	George D.	M	A	William Royce	Polly Royce	W	
9/28/1859	Thos. W.	M	A	William McRoberts	Cyntha Walton	W	
2/12/1859	John C.B.	M	A		Angeline Vannatten	W	
9/ 1/1859	John B.	M	A	Whitfield Hargus	Lucinda Smoot	W	
10/12/1859	Fauttey T.	M	A	Fautty R. Stuse	Susan Lee	W	
12/29/1859	Not named	F	A	Elijah Ham	Margaret J. Lightfoot	W	
10/20/1859	Not named	F	A	George Hartley	Elizabeth Ham	W	
8/ /1859	Louisa Ann	F	A	William Jordan	Eliza Ann Ross	W	
2/25/1859	Jessett J.	M	A	James E. Carpenter	Cyntha J. Jordan	W	
1/13/1859	James Anna	F	D	Edward Elston	Ann Eliza Strode	W	
2/18/1859	Ellen	F	A	Samuel J. Carpenter	Emily Jordan	W	
4/25/1859	Keen R. (Dudley?)	M	A	John B. Dualey	Penuelia A. Palmer	W	
5/ 7/1859	Lucy	F	A	Ben W. Durrett	Bettie W. Hodges	W	b. Franklin
4/19/1859	William F. b. Mason Co.	M	A	Jacob Myers	Cristina Phissenhammer	W	
12/ /1859	Elijah	M	A	William Groves	Ellen Sutton	W	
12/24/1859	Thomas Sadler	M	A	William C. Sadler	Martha J. Dudley	W	
10/25/1859	Not named Re. Premature	M	D	Patrick Crotty	Margaret Roney	W	
5/15/1859	Maria	F	A	W. J. Mullay	Phebe S. Barnes	W	
12/16/1859	George R.	M	A	Elijah Reeves	Mathilda Bochett	W	
5/30/1859	Pickett	F	A	James Jones		B	
7/12/1859	David	M	A	James Jones		B	
9/ /1859	Not named	M	D	Abram Gooding		B	

COUNTY   Fleming   C Condition A-Alive D-Dead

DATE	NAME OF CHILD	S	C	NAME OF FATHER	NAME OF MOTHER	CO.	RESIDENCE
5/26/1859	Louisa	F	A	Fannie T. Mullay		B	All residents
3/14/1859	Not named b. Lewis	M	D	Henry Harrison	Margret Williams	W	Fleming Co.
12/17/1859	Not named	F	A	H.J. Perry		M	
7/27/1859	William	M	A	William H. Hendrick	Elizabeth Howe	W	
8/18/1859	Mary Ann	F	A	George W. Horton	Teletha Foxworthy	W	
12/28/1859	Elizabeth	F	A	Jacob C. Lee		B	
11/15/1859	Matilda	F	A	James R. Alexander		B	
1/27/1859	Bettie	F	A	Jerry Hall		B	
6/15/1859	Permelice Williams	F	A	Thos. J. Williams	Elvira Curtis	W	
8/ 8/1859	Not named	F	A	Angeline Tully		B	
7/ 5/1859	Emily	F	A	William H. Hinton	Amanda Jones	W	
12/27/1859	John	M	A	Richard Carpenter		B	
10/ 5/1859	Helen Wallingford	F	A	Joseph S. Wallingford	Helen Morrison	W	
4/10/1859	Henry	M	A	Joseph S. Wallingford		B	
8/17/1859	Mary Shofe	F	A	George W. Shope	Mary Conley	W	
12/13/1859	Maria	F	A	Thos. Wells		B	
10/ 6/1859	Jerry O.	M	A	Andrew Glass (Glap ?)	Eliza Ann Sutton	W	
7/23/1859	Maria	F	A	Dennis Belt		B	
12/ 7/1859	Eliza	F	A	Dennis Belt		B	
8/24/1859	Catharine	F	A	William A. Morrison	Julia Ann Wallingford	W	
11/25/1859	Mary E.	F	A	William H. Duncan	Martha Murry	W	
12/12/1859	Not named	F	A	Thos. B. McIntire		B	
11/15/1859	Not named	M	D	John J. Potts		B	
5/ 4/1859	Debby Jane	F	A	Johnson Ross (Rop?)	Debby Jane Ross	W	
7/ 7/1859	Not named	M	D	William N. Gillaspie	Sara R. Powers	W	
11/16/1859	James W.	M	A	Jarvis Standiford	Lucinda Myers	W	
3/20/1859	William T.	M	A	William B. Arnold	Sary Ann Arnold	W	
6/24/1859	Minnie Kate	F	A	Charles E. Goddard	Mary Carr	W	
4/ 6/1859	Emma	F	A	Green B. Triplett	Mary Mills	W	
8/10/1859	Not named	F	D	E. D. Gourley	Manerva Brown	W	
2/16/1859	Marietta	F	A	James P. Ham	Eliza Jones	W	
3/ 1/1859	Edwin	M	A	Nelson H. Hurst	Martha Harsk	W	
7/15/1859	Sue Bell	F	A	Thos. P. Sutton	Celia Gooding	W	
7/22/1859	James Thomas	M	A	Hiram Staggs	Elizabeth Jordan	W	
10/12/1859	Susan Bell	F	A	George Muse	Sarah Newman	W	
3/31/1859	Elizabeth Ellis	F	A	Daniel Pickett	Lucy Barris	W	

COUNTY Fleming

S Sex
C Condition A-Alive D-Dead

DATE	NAME OF CHILD	S	C	NAME OF FATHER	NAME OF MOTHER	CO.	RESIDENCE
11/17/1859	Rosa Bell	F	A	Matthew Bramel	Sarah Tincher	W	All residents
3/ 7/1859	Alexander	M	A	Armstead Campbell	Ann E. Wyatt	W	Fleming Co.
5/ 8/1859	George	M	A	Richard Ross	Mary Rigdon	W	
9/16/1859	Not named	F	D	James M. McGregor	Eliza Pickrell	W	
10/25/1859	James	M	A	John H. Gulick	Clemintine Downs	W	
8/26/1859	Joseph D.	M	A	James M. Alexander	Elizabeth M. Redden	W	
8/26/1859	Delila A.	F	A	John Jones	Mary C. Jordan	W	
2/ 2/1859	Charles W.	M	A	Reuben Hartly	Mary Bramel	W	
9/ 7/1859	Margaret	F	A	John F. Fitch	Sarah Dickey	W	
2/ 9/1859	Pheba	F	A	Obed P. Nute		B	
12/24/1859	Not named	M	D	Thomas Druman		B	
12/ 5/1859	Not named	M	A	Thos. Menick	Mary A. Witty	W	
9/10/1859	Anna B.	F	A	Harrison Magowan	Bettie A. Hutton	W	
8/ 1/1859	William F.	M	A	Amos Browning		B	
11/12/1859	Not named	F	A	Andrew Matingly	Malinda Hughbanks	W	
5/ 7/1859	Waller C.	M	A	Fill. Goodman	Elizabeth Goodman	W	
6/ 4/1859	Sara E.	F	A	Kenis M. Forrow	Mary M. Wallingford	W	
5/ 6/1859	Oscar	M	A	John Worrick	Amanda Lukins	W	
3/10/1859	Joseph W. b. Lewis	M	A	Samuel T. Lonley	Martha J. Johnson	W	
7/25/1859	John J.	M	A	L. D. Forrow	Sarah A. Wallingford	W	
10/ 8/1859	Emma	F	A	W. B. O'Bannon	Mary F. Wallingford	W	
2/22/1859	Charles B.	M	A	William DeBell	Louellen Dougherty	W	
12/ 6/1859	Dick Lee	M	D	Rosanna Bradford		B	
8/19/1859	Malinda J.	F	A	Thos. J. Jones	Amelia Freeman	W	
10/16/1859	Thos. C.	M	A	Titus Mark	Russella Hinton	W	
1/20/1859	Not named	M	D	William W. Fizer	Rebecca J. Arnold	W	
3/29/1859	Leander	M	A	John W. Lightfoot	Jaretta C. Lewman	W	
4/ 9/1859	Emily A.	F	A	Clark B. Mark	Amelia Wallingford	W	
6/17/1859	Phebe	F	A	Alfred Morehead		B	
9/ 8/1859	Wesley	M	A	Alfred Morehead		B	
2/16/1859	Jim	M	A	Alfred Morehead		B	
2/16/1859	Catharine V.	F	A	Charles Nute	Malinda Glasscock	W	
7/28/1859	Joshua B.	M	A	Newman Glasscock	Louisa Nute	W	
8/ 6/1859	Not named	M	D	Joel T. Lewman	Harriett Clary	W	
7/25/1859	Robert M. b. Mason	M	A	Thornton Davenport	Rutha Merideth	W	

COUNTY   Fleming

S Sex
C Condition A-Alive D-Dead

DATE	NAME OF CHILD	S	C	NAME OF FATHER	NAME OF MOTHER	CO.	RESIDENCE
9/24/1859	Louellen	F	A	Daniel Carpenter ?	America J. Hurst	W	All residents
3/21/1859	Daniel	M		Joseph W. Webster	Julia Ann Enix	W	Fleming Co.
10/ 7/1859	Not named Re. Premature	M	D	Fredrick Lamarr	Hester Hinton	W	
8/ 2/1859	Joshua	M	A	Joel Saunders	Matilda Lewman	W	
8/29/1859	Greenup	M	A	Hardin Gooding	Martha A. Gardner	W	
5/16/1859	Franklin W.	M	A	Obed Brayfield	Elizabeth J. Hopper	W	
8/18/1859	Samuel L.	M	A	E. G. Davis	Mary A. Lyons	W	
10/ 4/1859	Robert A.	M	A	William T. Hiett	Louisa Hedgel	W	
10/15/1859	Judith F.	F	A	William M. Carpenter	Eliza A. Hurst	W	
6/24/1859	Thomas D.	M	A	William Staggs	Teressa Estill	W	
10/26/1859	James A.	M	A	John B. Kirk	Ann Elizabeth Gardner	W	
10/ 1/1859	George H.	M	A	Jeremiah Owens	Mary J. McKee	W	
2/11/1859	James M.	M	A	Anderson Callahan	Arilla J. Hughes	W	
9/ 5/1859	William A.	M	A	Joseph D. McKee	Rachel Fenton	W	
6/20/1859	Elizabeth E.	F	A	John A. McKee	Eliza J. Braman	W	
11/11/1859	William P.	M	A	Alfred Humphries	Rebecca Humphries	W	
11/16/1859	Mary Alice	F	A	Samuel H. Geazle	Elizabeth E. Humphries	W	
8/ 9/1859	Not named	M	A	Martin Blanton	Eliza Vale	W	
11/27/1859	Not named	M	D	William W. Callahan	Ann E. Davis	W	
4/ 9/1859	Amanda E.	F	A	Ashal Ham	Louisa Hartly	W	
10/ 8/1859	Andrew B.C.	M	A	Willis Morgan	Elizabeth Hill	W	
9/ 7/1859	Sarah Bell	F	A	Sylvester Estill	Elizabeth McKinney	W	
10/12/1859	Benjamin M.	M	A	Hiram W. Royse	Sibby Hargett	W	
1/22/1859	Laben T.B.	M	A	William Vanlundingham	Penelope Hulloon	W	
3/26/1859	Alice E.	F	A	John M. Gray	Elizabeth J. Davis	W	
10/11/1859	Not named	M	A	Jackson Kissick	Mary Cline	W	
10/ 3/1859	Louisa	F	A	William F. Dickson	Mary J. Reeves	W	
2/16/1859	Martha A.	F	D	William Grimsley	Louisa Barbee	W	
10/24/1859	Elijah	M	A	Robert W. Hayden	Jane Reeves	W	
6/ 5/1859	Not named	M	A	John O. Jackson	Mary Kerringbrick ?	W	
11/20/1859	Jonathan T.	M	A	Hiram P. Jones	Lydda R. Havens	W	
11/29/1859	James A.	M	A	John McAdams	Mary J. Addams	W	
10/19/1859	Louellen	F	A	Thos. J. Johnson	Malinda J. Allender	W	
7/ 5/1859	William R.	M	A	Mathias Lee	Margaret J. Hawkins	W	
11/ 3/1859	Permelia	F	A	Henry C. Marshall	Mersolete Razor	W	
4/13/1859	John	M	A	Alfred Markwell		B	

COUNTY Fleming

S Sex
C Condition A-Alive D-Dead

DATE	NAME OF CHILD	S	C	NAME OF FATHER	NAME OF MOTHER	CO.	RESIDENCE
11/ 4/1859	Charley	M	D	William T. Walker		B	All residents
8/ 5/1859	Maria P.	F	A	William T. Dudley	Kittie DeBell	W	Fleming Co.
12/20/1859	Mary Elizabeth	F	A	David W. Howe		B	
10/25/1859	William Farrow b. Mason	M	A	Thornton S. Farrow	Eliza J. Bentley	W	
8/12/1859	Ellen	F	A	Eli Liking		B	
6/15/1859	Elizabeth H. Miller	F	A	Joseph Miller	Harriett Daldymple	W	
5/20/1859	Thomas Markwell	M	A	F. M. Markwell	Harriett Harmon	W	
2/11/1859		M	A	Mary Hombeck		B	
6/20/1859		M	A	Alexander Hart		B	
1/ 1/1859		M	A	Alexander Hart		B	
1/12/1859	Evan Griffith	M	A	Willoughby Griffith	Julia Ann Hall (Nall?)	W	
6/ 6/1859	Virginia Vansant	F	A	John K. Vansant	Nancy Markwell	W	
12/15/1859	Mary J. Clinkenbeard	F	A	Robert Clinkenbeard	Lucinda Barnes	W	
1/27/1859		M	A	Jonathan Clinkenbeard		B	
7/20/1859	J. H. Morgan	M	A	Raleigh Morgan	Amanda J. Hendrick	W	
9/18/1859	Not named	M	D	John W. Darnall	Isabella Crain	W	
10/18/1859	Albert Eaton	F	D	William Eaton	Nancy J. Gray	W	
12/30/1859	Not named	M	A	Moses T. Clark	Sary O. Myers	W	
12/ 7/1859	John A. Ingram	M	A	Jeses Ingram	Sary D. Armstrong	W	
5/18/1859	Esskine Porter	M	A	William Porter	Sally Ann Strahan	W	
6/26/1859	James Purkins	M	A	Isaac Ruskins	Mary Ann Eaton	W	
7/13/1859	John A. Ingram	M	A	F. A. Ingram	Martha Wells	W	
6/13/1859	Not named	F	D	Nelson Storz	Rosanna Storz	W	
12/ 9/1859	Oliver Storz	M	A	Alfred Story	Acrist Vanlandingham	W	
3/ 3/1859	Ira Goodwin	M	A	William Goodwin	Mathilda Faris	W	
11/20/1859	Jesse Logan	M	A	E. Logan	Eliza J. Pearce	W	
3/ /1859		F	A	Raleigh Kendall Jr.		B	
12/ 7/1859	Jolson Kendall	M	A	Raleigh Kendall, Jr.	Peachie Bendem	W	
12/ /1859		M	A	Raldigh Kendall Jr.		B	
6/15/1859	Amanda F. Payne	F	A	F. J. Payne	Lou Ellen Emmans	W	
5/11/1859	Samuel P. Porter	M	A	Andrew Porter	Francis Rankin	W	
3/18/1859	Joseph F. Bett	M	A	John F. Bett	Mary H. Willson	W	
11/15/1859	John W. Callahan	M	A	Sennett Callahan	Sary J. Reeves	W	
7/10/1859	Sanford B. Myers	M	A	Samuel Myers	Adeline Williams	W	
1/ 9/1859	Francis A. English	F	A	John M. English	Sary J. McGowan	W	
1/ 7/1859	G. F. Pyles	M	D	Milton Pyles	Jane R. Caywood	W	
11/ 3/1859	W. V. E. McCarty	M	D	Gabriel McCarty	Rebecca Graves	W	

KENTUCKY COUNTIES VITAL STATISTICS   S Sex

COUNTY   Fleming   C Condition A-Alive D-Dead

DATE	NAME OF CHILD	S	C	NAME OF FATHER	NAME OF MOTHER	CO.	RESIDENCE
5/26/1859	Jerry Power	F	A	James M. Power	Lucy Hull	W	All residents
2/26/1859	Manda E. Discon	F	A	James A. Discon	Elizabeth Golden	W	Fleming Co.
3/22/1859	William H. Abner	M	A	Lincoln Abner	Margaret Evans	W	
4/16/1859	James Carpenter	M	A	Peter Carpenter	Amanda J. Crain	W	
1/27/1859	Henry Rice	M	A	Samuel Rice	Mary J. Holland	W	
8/29/1859	John W. McIlvain	M	A	James McIlvain	Mary Morgan	W	
9/ 6/1859	John W. Todd	M	A	George Todd	Mary R. Whitney	W	
3/24/1859	Henry W. Lee	M	A	W. R. Lee	Margaret Todd	W	
5/ 9/1859	Jonathan F. Overly	M	A	Jonathan Overly	Francis Gardner	W	
12/ 5/1859	Charles M. Jones	M	A	Wm. B. Jones	Sarah K. Straban	W	
4/31/1859	Inez B. Peck	F	A	Nathaniel Peck	Charlotte Flerain	W	
4/31/1859		M	A	Nathaniel Peck		B	
11/15/1859	George D. Peck	M	A	John Peck	Sary A. Robertson	W	
10/17/1859	Not named	F	A	James McCann	Sarah Hull	W	
1/21/1859	Thomas Gardner	M	A	Stephen Gardner	Miram Hull	W	
1/ 3/1859	James A. Dunn	M	A	John Dunn	Amanda Hendrik	W	
1/ 6/1859	Laben M. Wood	M	A	John Wood	Martha Pickrell	W	
8/16/1859	Moses Hurst	M	A	Lewis Hurst	Martha Perkins	W	
8/30/1859	John H. Porter	M	A	John Porter	Angeline Moren	W	
1/28/1859	Francis M. Call	M	A	Daniel Call	Margaret Walson	W	
3/20/1859	Daniel W. Preston	M	A	Jefferson Preston	Elizabeth Dalrgniple	W	
6/10/1859	Jeff P. Gregory	M	A	Natheen Gregory	Sarah Wibby	W	
12/12/1859	Not named	F	A	James V. Payne	Amanda Freeman	W	
7/ /1859	Not named	M	A	Samuel B. Lyons		B	
12/25/1859	Not named	F	A	Samuel B. Lyons	Martha A. Day	W	
10/25/1859	Not named	F	D	Samuel Clark	Martha E. Chrisman	W	
9/ 3/1859	Miriam Storz	F	A	John Storz	Margaret Day	W	
6/17/1859	John E. Moren	F?	A	James Moren	Lucinda Harmon	W	
7/ 1/1859	Elizabeth H. Miller	F	A	Joseph Miller	Hannah Dalrgniple	W	
1/18/1859		F	A	Britton Dunn	Elizabeth McCabe	W	(Miscarriage)
4/13/1859	Henry D. Dayley	M	A	Covington Daily	Elizabeth Pearce	W	
10/ 9/1859	Mary Lightfoot	F	A	Dr. R. A. Lightfoot	Sarah E. Stockwell	W	
2/24/1859	Louisa Griffith	F	A	William Griffith	Mary E. David	W	
4/30/1859	Mark McGath	F	A	John McGath	Ellen Dillen	W	
2/18/1859	Bettie Armstrone	F	A	John Armstrong	Elizabeth Rash	W	
9/28/1859	Mary K. Skillman	W	A	Joseph Skillman	Lavinia Willson	W	
8/ 3/1859	Lilly A. Todd	F	A	James L. Todd	Mary J. Leforgee	W	
5/31/1859	Rhoda A. Wibby	F	A	Samuel Wibby	Lucinda Hambrick	W	

82

COUNTY __Fleming__

S Sex
C Condition A-Alive D-Dead

DATE	NAME OF CHILD	S	C	NAME OF FATHER	NAME OF MOTHER	CO.	RESIDENCE
8/25/1859	Lydia A. Graham	F	A	Ambrose Graham	Lucinda Shepherd	W	All residents
8/ 1/1859	Mary V.	F	A	Daniel Dalrgniple	Amanda Newman	W	Fleming Co.
8/ 7/1859	Sarah C. Buchanan	F	A	Joseph Buchanan	Nancy Ishmeal	W	
5/10/1859	Daniel E. Harmon	M	A	Joseph Harmon	Martha Harmon	W	
7/20/1859	Bittie C. Deering	F	A	James T. Deering	Elizabeth Thompson	W	
7/ 4/1859	Henry	M	D	James Keith	Mahala Overly	W	
10/15/1859	Nancy J. Hull	F	A	Moses Hull	Tabitha Rash	W	
6/15/1859	Not named	M	D	James Jones	Elizabeth Chrisman	W	
6/15/1859	Mary A. Spencer	F	A	R. G. Spencer	Roseta Spencer	W	
/ /1859		N	A	R. G. Spencer		B	
/ /1859	Not named	F	D	M. J. N. Myers	Sarah Ann Cord	W	
9/15/1859		M	A	James Armstead		B	
6/15/1859	Micheal Keyheo	M	A	Michael Keyhoe	Bridgett Bropha	W	
9/24/1859	Not named	F	A	James Jackson	Elizabeth Crawford	W	
5/21/1859	William L. Bentley	F	A	Geo. B. Bentley	Sarah F. Overly	W	
5/21/1859	Gusta Stephens	F	D	Andrew J. Stephens	Sarah F. McDonald	W	
9/20/1859		F	A	John Pardum		B	
6/15/1859	Alice Lenaghen	F	A	James Lenaghen	Catharine Lenaghen	W	
1/ /1859		M	A	E. T. Smith		B	
4/16/1859	Robert C. Smith	M	A	E. T. Smith	M. Alexander	W	
4/10/1859	Virginia B. Day	F	A	Squire A. Day	Maranda Jones	W	
6/15/1859	Martha Campbell b. Nicholas	F	A	George N. Campbell	Mary Alexander	W	
8/ 1/1859	Eliza E. Faris	F	A	Samuel Faris	Lucy H. Williams	W	
2/ 2/1859	Mary A. Mascey	F	A	Henry L. Mascey	Prudence Mascey	W	
8/ 1/1859	Margaret E. Cline	F	A	Wm. H. Cline	Elizabeth Galliher	W	
4/20/1859		M	A	Wm. G. Price		B	
3/20/1859	John M. Cord	M	A	John M. Cord	Susan F. Ross	W	
11/ 1/1859	Richard L. McDonald	M	A	James M. McDonald	Nancy Crump	W	b. Nicholas
5/15/1859	Not named	M	D	James H. Groves	Mary E. Williams	W	
10/20/1859	Mary Eliza Piles	F	A	Milton Piles	Jane R. Caywood	W	
7/ 1/1859	John J. Allen	M	A	John J. Allen		B	
5/10/1859		M	A	Thos. D. Andrews		B	
12/15/1859		M	D	Wm. T. Howe	Emily Proctor	W	(still born)
3/23/1859	Not named	M	A	D. C. Sousley	Ann J. Finley	W	
5/10/1859		M	D	James Cudihi	Sarah Flaherty	W	(still born)
3/10/1859	Daniel Sherwood	M	A	John Sherwood	Hannah M. Blair	W	

COUNTY   Fleming

DATE	NAME OF CHILD	S	C	NAME OF FATHER	NAME OF MOTHER	CO.	RESIDENCE
9/28/1859	Not named	M	A	William H. Stockdale	Lucinda M. Groves	W	Fleming Co.
2/21/1859	Addy B. Groves	F	A	William H. Groves	Caroline Swart	W	Fleming Co.
10/13/1859	James Alexander	M	A	William Alexander	Mary Swain	W	
4/29/1859	Nancy W. Walker	F	A	R. H. Walker	Fannie Ringo	W	
4/24/1859	Reuben S. Weaver	M	A	David Weaver	Nancy Ball	W	
12/15/1859		F	A	W. T. Buckler		B	
2/12/1859	Not named	M	A	Joseph Stuckrod	Elizabeth M. Williams	W	
2/12/1859	Not named	F	A	Harrison Sousley		B	
6/ /1859	Not named	F	A	James Smith		B	
9/12/1859	Emma Wiles	F	A	Peter B. Wiles	Jane Jones	W	
6/ 2/1859	Not named	F	A	George Summers	Mary Ficklin	W	
4/20/1859	James Cassiday	M	A	Henry Cassiday	Ann Joyce	W	
5/ 7/1859	William H. Williams	M	A	William K. Williams	F. A. Dudley	W	
8/ 1/1859	Not named	F	A	John Kedrick		B	
10/30/1859	Mary S. Dougherty	F	A	Barney Dougherty	Bridget Amonow	W	
11/ 3/1859	Catharine A. Lander	F	A	Joseph Lander	Catharine Robnet	W	
5/23/1859	Mary M. Mers	F	A	John Mers	-- Wibby	W	
12/15/1859		M	A	Benjamin Johnson		B	
12/15/1859		M	A	Benjamin Johnson		B	
12/ /1859		M	A	Thomas R. Potts		W	
6/24/1859	Evy Coliver	F	A?	James Coliver	Mary J. Overly	W	
5/17/1859	Catherine E. McCartney	F	A	John McCartney	Mary D. Dent	W	
5/17/1859		M	A	William Fant		B	
1/10/1859	James P. A. Dillen	M	A	Britton Dillin	Rushan Nealis	W	
7/15/1859		M	A	James P. Hendrick		B	
2/14/1859		M	A	James Kennon		B	
10/ 1/1859		M	A	John H. Wells		B	
12/ 1/1859		M	A	John H. Wells		B	
2/14/1859	Lizzie D. Hendrick	F	A	James P. Hendrick	Sophia Darnall	W	

Fleming County Sct.
   I, William T. Dudley, Clerk of the Court for the county aforesaid certify that the foregoing 6 pages contain a true copy of the Registration of Births returned by the Commissioner of Tax for the year 1860. Given under my hand this 20th day of June 1860.
     W. T. Dudley CCK

COUNTY __Fleming__

DATE	NAME OF CHILD	S	C	NAME OF FATHER	NAME OF MOTHER	CO.	RESIDENCE
8/26/1874	Not given b. Fleming Co.	M	A	Geo. C. Runyon b. Fleming Co.	Sarah J. Robertson b. Mason Co., Ky.	W	All residents Fleming Co.
11/30/1874	Ezekiel F. Runyon b. Fleming Co.	M	A	Jno H. Runyon b. Bourbon Co., Ky.	Susan R. Moore b. Mason Co., Ky.	W	
9/10/1874	James G. Williams b. Fleming Co.	M	A	J. W. Williams b. Bourbon Co., Ky.	Wiley? E. Williams b. Mason Co., Ky.	W	
7/ 6/1874	Andrew J. Hinton b. Fleming Co.	M	A	John D. Hinton b. Fleming Co.	Ellen C. Emmons b. Fleming Co.	W	
4/30/1874	Not Given b. Fleming Co.	M	A	Saml. Taibby b. Fleming Co.	Louisa Kemrick b. Fleming. Co.	W	
11/15/1874	Maggie H. McKee b. Fleming Co.	M	A	G. W. McKee b. Fleming Co.	Leannor Watts b. Fleming Co.	W	
10/ 3/1874	Alkia H. Allen b. Nicholas Co.	F	A	Garrett Allen b. Fleming Co.	Cynthia Potts b. Nicholas Co.	W	
1/23/1859	Jeri Gray b. Fleming Co.	F	A	Leuis Gray b. Brown Co., Ohio	Susan Lawvile b. Brown Co., Ohio	W	
9/15/1874	Lucy E. Liton b. Fleming Co.	F	A	Joseph D. Liten b. Bourbon Co., Ky.	Mary R. Johnson b. Fleming Co.	W	
1/25/1874	Thos. Fife b. Fleming Co.	M	A	Harry Fife b. Fleming Co.	Mahala Bush b. Fleming Co.	M	
7/21/1874	Phebe Williams b. Fleming Co.	F	A	Lawrence Williams b. Fleming Co.	Mary E. Williams b. Bourbon Co., Ky.	W	
12/25/1874	M. A. Howe b. Fleming Co.	F	A	John M. Howe b. Fleming Co.	Elizth. Stewart b. Fleming Co.	W	
6/15/1874	Not given b. Fleming Co.	F	A	Sandey Brom ? b. Fleming Co.	Lucy Hill b. Fleming Co.	B	
4/10/1874	Lucy E. Romey b. Fleming Co.	F	A	John A. Rooney b. Bourbon Co., Ky.	Mary Cochran b. Fleming Co.	W	
10/13/1874	Nannie W. Puter b. Fleming Co.	F	A	R. S. Porter b. Fleming Co.	M. M. Morris b. Ray Co., Mo.	W	
12/24/1874	James C. Alexander b. Fleming Co.	M	A	Jno. T. Alexander b. Fleming Co.	Lanna Sanley b. Fleming Co.	W	
6/12/1874	John S. Ricketts b. Fleming Co.	M	A	John R. Ricketts b. Fleming Co.	Elizth. Peck b. Fleming Co.	W	
5/14/1874	William F. Robertson b. Fleming Co.	M	A	James W. Robertson b. Fleming Co.	Anna Arnold b. not known	W	
12/15/1874	Not named b. Fleming Co.	M	A	James S. Burgess b. Indiana	Minerva Lauson b. Fleming Co.	W	

DATE	NAME OF CHILD	S	C	NAME OF FATHER	NAME OF MOTHER	CO.	RESIDENCE
2/ 2/1874	Robt. M. Lewis b. Fleming Co.	M	A	John T. Lewis b. Mason Co., Ky.	Mattie White b. Roman Co., Ky.	W	All residents Fleming Co.
1/27/1874	Charles F. Thornton b. Fleming Co.	M	A	Frank Thornton b. Fleming Co.	Emily Thomas b. Fleming Co.	M	
8/11/1874	John Stewart b. Fleming Co.	M	A	Daniel T. Stewart b. Fleming Co.	Mary F. Kirk b. Fleming Co.	W	
4/21/1874	Emma S. Stockdale b. Fleming Co.	M	A	S. C. Stockdale b. Fleming Co.	Sarah A. McCord b. Fleming Co.	W	
5/ 5/1874	Wm. F. Courtney b. Fleming Co.	M	A	Wm. E. Courtney b. Fleming Co.	Laura D. Dye b. Mason Co., Ky.	W	
9/ 3/1874	Herman F. Courtney b. Fleming Co.	M	A	Geo. L. Courtney b. Fleming Co.	Emarine McCarty b. Fleming Co.	W	
11/15/1874	Mary F. Buchanan b. Fleming Co.	F	A	Coleman Buchanan b. Nicholas Co., Ky.	Malinda Cash b. Not known	W	
2/ 9/1874	Ellis F. Biddle b. Fleming Co.	F	A	Thos. W. Biddle b. Fleming Co.	Margaret V. Pattern b. Maryland	W	
1/24/1874	Guy A. Biddle b. Fleming Co.	F	A	John Biddle b. Fleming Co.	Maria E. Burriss b. Fleming Co.	W	
11/15/1874	Ada M. Biddle b. Fleming Co.	F	A	Robt. P. Biddle b. Fleming Co.	Ann C. Bentley b. Fleming Co.	W	
11/ 7/1874	Not named b. Fleming Co.	F	A	Martin McDonald b. Ireland	Margt. A. Frazier b. Missouri	W	
6/15/1874	Anna M. Garey b. Fleming Co.	F	A	Wm. Garey b. Maryland	J. H. Alexander b. Fleming Co.	W	
5/ 7/1874	Sueda Brown? b. Fleming Co.	F	A	Leuis H. Bowen b. Lewis Co., Ky.	Aluretta H. Gross b. Bourdon Co., Ky.	W	
8/22/1874	Sarah E. Alexander b. Fleming Co.	F	A	Columbus Alexander b. Virginia	Mary J. McIntyre b. Fleming Co.	W	
9/10/1874	Not named b. Fleming Co.	F	A	E. B. Myres b. Nicholas Co., Ky.	Elizth. Buchannan b. Nicholas Co., Ky.	W	
8/ 3/1874	Ruth M. Gray b. Fleming Co.	F	A	Moses Gray b. Fleming Co.	Francis Froggs b. Fleming Co.	W	
6/21/1874	Mary E. Herrin b. Fleming Co.	F	A	Thos. Herrin b. Nicholas Co., Ky.	Ellen A. Kearans b. Nicholas Co., Ky.	W	
9/ 1/1874	Jerry? P. Kirk b. Fleming Co.	M	A	Wm. M. Kirk b. Fleming Co.	Julia A. Jones b. Fleming Co.	W	
9/17/1874	Lettie Duffey b. Fleming Co.	F	A	Wm. Duffey b. Fleming Co.	Julia A. Jones b. Fleming Co.	W	

COUNTY Fleming

S Sex
C Condition A-Alive D-Dead

DATE	NAME OF CHILD	S	C	NAME OF FATHER	NAME OF MOTHER	CO.	RESIDENCE
12/10/1874	Mary A. Cartmell b. Fleming Co.	F	A	W. W. Cartmell b. Bath Co., Ky.	Mary E. Vaughn b. Fleming Co.	W	All residents Fleming Co.
3/ 4/1874	Maggie Watkins b. Nicholas Co.	F	A	John Watkins b. Fleming Co.	Elizth. Mitchell b. Nicholas Co., Ky.	W	
2/14/1874	Ruth A. Pearce b. Bath Co., Ky.	F	A	Isaac E. Pearce b. Fleming Co.,	Marie Dailey b. Fleming Co.	W	
2/12/1874	Eliza Jones b. Fleming Co.	F	A	Joseph M. Jones b. Pennsylvania	Allie Overley b. Fleming Co.	W	
8/16/1874	Lucinda Hendrick b. Fleming Co.	F	A	Oliver Hendrix b. Bath Co., Ky.	Catharine Janus b. Bath Co., Ky.	M	
4/ 4/1874	Sallie Peck b. Fleming Co.	F	A	George Peck b. Fleming Co.	Rebecca Burgoss b. Fleming Co.	W	
5/31/1874	Henry P. Rogers b. Indiana	M	A	James F. Rogers b. Ohio	Clara C. Bishop b. Fleming Co.	W	
2/ 7/1874	Not named b. Fleming Co.	F	A	James Lauson b. Fleming Co.	Elizth. Pickrell b. Fleming Co.	W	
7/28/1874	James S. Rice b. Fleming Co.	M	A	John H. Rice b. Fleming Co.	Margaret Porter b. Fleming Co.	W	
7/25/1874	Wm. T. Moren b. Fleming Co.	M	A	John Moren b. Fleming Co.	Cynthia Vice b. Fleming Co.	W	
12/26/1874	Edgar Thomson b. Fleming Co.	M	A	John Thompson b. Virginia	Millie Overley b. Fleming Co.	W	
11/27/1874	Everest L. Hefflin b. Fleming Co.	M	A	James M. Hefflin b. Virginia	Mary L. Hitt b. Virginia	W	
3/25/1874	Loda Faris b. Fleming Co.	F	A	Joseph H. Faris b. Fleming Co.	Malinda D. Moren b. Fleming Co.	W	
9/20/1874	Mary D. Vice b. Nicholas Co., Ky.	F	A	Wm. Vice b. Bath Co., Ky.	Mary H. Beam b. Fleming Co.	W	
2/ 3/1874	Jno. Evans b. Fleming Co.	F	A	James T. Evans b. Fleming Co.	Louise Perkins b. Fleming Co.	W	
9/ 4/1874	Walter P. Hendrix b. Fleming Co.	M	A	W. F. Hendrix b. Fleming Co.	Eliza J. Barnes b. Fleming Co.	W	
5/ 4/1874	Rebecca B. Todd b. Fleming Co.	F	A	Joseph Todd b. Fleming Co.	Sarah J. Harmon b. Fleming Co.	W	

A Copy Attest. M. M. Teagar CCK, Fleming Co. Ct.

S Sex

C Condition A-Alive D-Dead

COUNTY __Fleming__

DATE	NAME OF CHILD	S	C	NAME OF FATHER	NAME OF MOTHER	CO.	RESIDENCE
8/28/1874	Orlando Payne b. Fleming Co.	M	A	Edwin Payne b. Fleming Co.	Elizabeth Graham b. Fleming Co.	W	All residents Fleming Co.
12/28/1974	Not named b. Fleming Co.	F	A	O. S. Moore b. Bath Co., Ky.	Edna A. Stoddard b. Fleming Co.	W	
10/25/1874	Lida B. Turner b. Fleming Co.	F	A	Harry Turner b. Bourbon Co., Ky.	Addie E. Franklin b. Fayette Co., Ky.	W	
10/16/1874	F. T. Huston b. Fleming Co.	M	A	R. G. Hinton b. Indiana	Mary E. Samuel b. Franklin Co., Ky.	W	
6/ 4/1874	Norah & Flora Kimberley b. Fleming Co.	F	A	G. S. Kimberly b. Ohio	Nancy M. Coy b. Ohio	W	
3/ 7/1874	Celia A. Gray b. Fleming Co.	F	A	John E. Gray b. Fleming Co.	Lucinda J. Gardner b. Fleming Co.	W	
9/10/1874	Alson T. Bowing b. Fleming Co.	M	A	S. T. Bowing b. Ohio	G. A. Shears b. Virginia	W	
4/ 2/1874	Edgar L. Lytle b. Fleming Co.	M	A	Wm. P. Lytle b. Fleming Co.	Delia B. Morgan b. Fleming Co.	W	
3/ 9/1874	Louisa F. Hedrick b. Fleming Co.	F	A	Holman Hedrick b. Fleming Co.	Louisa H. Lytle b. Fleming Co.	W	
8/31/1874	Jennie C. Walton b. Fleming Co.	F	A	Thos. H. Walton b. Fleming Co.	Mary V. Oliver b. Bourbon Co., Ky.	W	
11/ 3/1874	E. P. Davis b. Fleming Co.	M	A	A. T. Davis b. Fleming Co.	Gertrude A. Auxier b. Johnson Co., Ky.	W	
5/ 9/1874	Ella & Eva Zimmerman b. Fleming Co.	F	A	Richd. Zimmerman b. Jessamini Co., Ky.	Mary E. Hedrick b. Fleming Co.	W	
9/ 7/1874	Chas. Davis b. Fleming Co.	F	A	Basil Davis b. Fleming Co.	Lizzie L. Sunnitt b. Fleming Co.	W	
9/10/1874	Etta Davis b. Fleming Co.	F	A	Fletcher Davis b. Fleming Co.	Maria J. Mark b. Fleming Co.	W	
1/ 1/1874	Louisa L. Dougherty b. Fleming Co.	F	A	J. M. Dougherty b. Bath Co., Ky.	Mahala E. Crain b. Fleming Co.	W	
12/ 4/1874	Juda Goodwin b. Fleming Co.	F	A	Wm. H. Goodwin b. Fleming Co.	P. A. Ham b. Fleming Co.	W	
5/ 8/1874	Rebecca R. Crain b. Fleming Co.	F	A	Jno. H. Crain b. Fleming Co.	Mary F. Bains b. Fleming Co.	W	
1/ 5/1874	Ida Proctor b. Fleming Co.	F	A	J. N. Proctor b. Fleming Co.	Maria L. Richardson b. Fleming Co.	W	
9/25/1874	Louisa W. Andrews b. Fleming Co.	F	A	Watson Andrews b. Fleming Co.	Mary E. Willson b. Bath Co., Ky.	W	

COUNTY Fleming

DATE	NAME OF CHILD	S	C	NAME OF FATHER	NAME OF MOTHER	CO.	RESIDENCE
8/ 8/1874	Mary F. Lander b. Fleming Co.	F	A	E. H. Lander b. Fleming Co.	Ellen Anderson Montgomery Co., Ky.	W	All residents Fleming Co.
9/23/1874	Mary L. Willeroy b. Fleming Co.	F	A	J. W. Willeroy b. Virginia	S. M. Estill b. Fleming Co.	W	
10/23/1874	Julia D. Walton b. Fleming Co.	F	A	R. R. Walton b. Fleming Co.	Nancy J. Newman b. Fleming Co.	W	
6/27/1874	Minnie Crawford b. Fleming Co.	F	A	Leandor Crawford b. Fleming Co.	Adaline Hall b. Fleming Co.	W	
10/15/1874	Sarah E. Adams b. Fleming Co.	F	A	John M. Adams b. Fleming Co.	Mary J. Adams b. Fleming Co.	W	
6/19/1874	Mary H. Markwell b. Fleming Co.	F	A	E. W. Markwell b. Fleming Co.	Sarah A. Whitney b. Bath Co., Ky.	W	
8/20/1874	Daniel Findry b. Fleming Co.	M	A	John H. Findry b. Fleming Co.	Nancy L. Helphentine b. Fleming Co.	W	
1/24/1874	Robert Wite b. Fleming Co.	M	A	Robert Wite b. Pennsylvania	Mirtil Rogers b. Bath Co., Ky.	W	
5/ 6/1874	Geo. S. Muse b. Fleming Co.	M	A	George Muse b. Fleming Co.	Martha Stiry b. Fleming Co.	W	
6/10/1874	Minnie Hammonds b. Fleming Co.	F	A	Saml. Hammonds b. Fleming Co.	Martha Hinton b. Fleming Co.	W	
11/17/1874	Alice T. Dillon b. Fleming Co.	F	A	T. J. Dillon b. Fleming Co.	Vinicia M. Cabe b. Fleming Co.	W	
8/12/1874	Flora Belle b. Fleming Co.	F	A	Robt. Cochran b. Fleming Co.	Anna Morrison b. Mason Co., Ky.	W	
9/ 7/1874	Not given b. Fleming Co.	F	A	Joseph Buchanan b. Fleming Co.	Not known b. Fleming Co.	W	
10/ 7/1874	Not given b. Fleming Co.	F	A	Fielder Brauch b. Nicholas Co., Ky.	Belle Paxten b. Fleming Co.	W	
9/ 1/1874	Not given b. Fleming Co.	F	A	Milton Kirk b. Fleming Co.	Julia Jones b. Fleming Co.	W	
10/ 6/1874	Not given b. Fleming Co.	F	A	Robt. T. Finley b. Fleming Co.	Eliza Denton b. Fleming Co.	W	
10/24/1874	Not given b. Fleming Co.	M	A	Tandy Lyons b. Fleming Co.	Parthenia Lytle b. Fleming Co.	W	
5/28/1874	Not given b. Fleming Co.	F	A	Joseph T. Faris b. Fleming Co.	-- Day b. Fleming Co.	W	
5/30/1874	Not given b. Fleming Co.	F	A	Robt. McKee b. Fleming Co.	Sarah L. Stiry (Story?) b. Fleming Co.	W	

COUNTY__Fleming__   C Condition A-Alive D-Dead

DATE	NAME OF CHILD	S	C	NAME OF FATHER	NAME OF MOTHER	CO.	RESIDENCE
6/23/1874	Not given b. Fleming Co.	F	A	Frank Thornton b. Fleming Co.	Sarah ? b. Fleming Co.	M	All residents Fleming Co.
6/17/1874	Not given b. Fleming Co.	F	A	Saml. Watson b. Fleming Co.	Sarah Jones b. Fleming Co.	W	
7/28/1874	Not given b. Fleming Co.	M	A	John Henry Rice b. Fleming Co.	Margt. Portor b. Fleming Co.	W	
8/ 5/1874	Not given b. Fleming Co.	M	A	Levi O.Williams b. Fleming Co.	b. Fleming Co.	W	
2/ 2/1874	Not given b. Fleming Co.	M	A	John T. Lewis b. Fleming Co.	b. Fleming Co.	W	
2/16/1874	Not given b. Fleming Co.	M	A	Andrew Grose b. Fleming Co.	Anna Belt b. Fleming Co.	W	
3/25/1874	Flora D. b. Fleming Co.	F	A	Jos. H. Faris b. Fleming Co.	Malinda Muir b. Fleming Co.	W	
2/10/1874	Not given b. Fleming Co.	F	A	Chas. Watson b. Fleming Co.	Henrietta Call b. Fleming Co.	W	
6/ 6/1874	Henry C. Malery b. Fleming Co.	M	A	Chas. Malery b. Fleming Co.	Louisa Caywood b. Fleming Co.	W	
6/12/1874	Jno. B. Ricketts b. Fleming Co.	M	A	John R. Ricketts b. Fleming Co.	Elizth. Peck b. Fleming Co.	W	
6/16/1874	Not given b. Fleming Co.	F	A	Wm. Hughes b. Fleming Co.	Not given b. Fleming Co.	M	
8/30/1874	Silvester Barm b. Fleming Co.	F	A	Sandy Bram b. Fleming Co.	Lucy Dudley b. Fleming Co.	B	
12/25/1874	Martha A. Howe b. Fleming Co.	F	A	Jno. M. Howe b. Fleming Co.	Elizth. E. Ferguson b. Fleming Co.	W	
12/24/1874	Jas. C. Alexander b. Fleming Co.	M	A	Jas. T. Alexander b. Fleming Co.	Louisa Sousley b. Fleming Co.	W	
11/21/1874	James Bush b. Fleming Co.	M	A	Tobin Bush b. Fleming Co.	Elizth. E. Ferguson b. Fleming Co.	W	
9/ 7/1874	Wm. Mullarkey b. Fleming Co.	M	A	Jas. Mullarkey b. Ireland	Mary Casey b. Mason Co.	W	
11/15/1874	Not given b. Fleming Co.	M	A	Thos. A. Caywood b. Fleming Co.	Sarah E. Hawther b. Indiana	W	
1/12/1874	Ranny T. Williams b. Fleming Co.	M	A	Abner C. Williams b. Fleming to.	Derindor Adams b. Fleming Co.	W	

A Copy Attest. M. M. Teagar CCK, Fleming Co. Ct.

S Sex
C Condition A-Alive D-Dead

COUNTY Fleming

DATE	NAME OF CHILD	S	C	NAME OF FATHER	NAME OF MOTHER	CO.	RESIDENCE
7/ 7/1874	Nannie Plummor b. Fleming Co.	F	A	James Plummor b. Fleming Co.	Olivia Lauder b. Ky.	W	Poplar Plains
7/25/1874	Jennie Mae Plummor b. Fleming Co.	F	A	Henry Plummor b. Fleming Co.	Lizzie Mills b. Mason Co., Ky.	W	Poplar Plains
2/24/1874	Lizzie Samuel b. Fleming Co.	F	A	B. F. Samuel b. Alabama	Edna Armstrong b. Fleming Co.	W	Poplar Plains
10/15/1874	Not named b. Fleming Co.	M	A	Chas. Hopper b. Ky.	S. F. Edwards b. Ky.	W	Fleming Co.
9/ 3/1874	Lenora Ross b. Fleming Co.	F	A	J. W. Ross b. Ky.	Emily Pollard b. Texas	W	Ky.
9/ 5/1874	Not named b. Fleming to.	M	A	E. F. Bradley b. Ky.	b. Ky.	W	Ky.
6/ 4/1874	Nannie Earles b. Fleming Co.	F	A	A. J. Earles b. Virginia	Rosannah McCord b. Fleming Co.	W	Fleming Co.
1/ 1/1874	Not named b. Fleming Co.	F	A	Neuton Greene b. not known	b. not known	B	Ky.
9/ 5/1874	Lida Ellen Biddle b. Fleming Co.	F	A	James H. Biddle b. Fleming Co.	Maggie E. McLave b. Mason Co., Ky.	W	Fleming Co. All residents
5/15/1874	Not named b. Fleming Co.	M	A	Samuel Gallahan b. Fleming Co.	Nancy Myres b. Mason Co., Ky.	W	
4/18/1874	Not named b. Fleming Co.	M	A	Joseph Shepard b. Fleming Co.	Susan Davis b. Mason Co., Ky.	W	
4/10/1874	Not named b. Fleming Co.	M	A	Wm. Walker b. Robertson Co., Ky.	Elijth. Bradford b. Robertson Co., Ky.	W	
3/11/1874	Not named b. Fleming Co.	F	A	John Bailey b. Ky.	Artemisa Fields b. Fleming Co., Ky.	W	
3/29/1874	Ethral Stoat b. Fleming Co.	F	A	Thos Stoat b. Robertson Co.	Laura B. Stiles b. Mason Co., Ky.	W	
2/ 3/1874	Not named b. Fleming Co.	M	A	Andrew Cameron b. Ky.	Milly Eubanks b. Nicholas Co., Ky.	W	
2/25/1874	Gertrude Hynes b. Fleming Co.	F	A	Granville H. Swantz b. Fleming Co.	Katie Cogan b. Ireland	W	
1/12/1874	Nancy Elizth. b. Fleming Co.	F	A	Marion Payne b. Fleming Co.	Elzth. Thomas b. Fleming Co.	W	
1/ 8/1874	No name b. Fleming Co.	M	A	William Cinneys? b. Nicholas Co., Ky.	Hageline Caywood b. Fleming Co.	W	
6/ 3/1874	Not named b. Fleming Co.	F	A	Henry Hawkins b. Mason Co., Ky.	b. Nicholas Co.	B	Mason Co.

COUNTY Fleming

S Sex
C Condition A-Alive D-Dead

DATE	NAME OF CHILD	S	C	NAME OF FATHER	NAME OF MOTHER	CO.	RESIDENCE
5/27/1874	Not named b. Fleming Co.	F	A	James Mulliken b. Robertson Co.	Elizabeth Raukins b. Robertson Co., Ky.	W	All residents Fleming Co.
1/18/1874	Not named b. Fleming Co.	M	A	Wm. McCamack b. Ireland	Mary Cogan b. Ireland	W	
7/22/1874	Not named b. Fleming Co.	F	A	Thos. Hawkins b. Fleming Co.	Rebecca Flora b. Fleming Co.	W	
7/20/1874	Not named (Bastard) b. Fleming Co.	M	A	Not known	Sarah Hawkins b. Fleming Co.	W	
7/24/1874	Not named b. Fleming Co.	M	A	George Hedge b. Nicholas Co., Ky.	Matilda Bushler b. Robertson Co., Ky.	W	
8/26/1874	Not named b. Fleming Co.	M	A	George C. Runyon b. Fleming Co.	Sarah Robertson b. Fleming Co.	W	
10/ 5/1874	Terissa b. Fleming Co.	F	A	John H. Payne b. Fleming Co.	Anna Pumphery b. Mason Co., Ky.	W	
10/12/1874	Not named b. Fleming Co.	M	A	John E. McCord b. Fleming Co.	Jane Hughes b. Nicholas Co., Ky.	W	
11/ 2/1874	Not named b. Fleming Co.	M	A	Owen Myres b. Vermont	Ann Bartlett b. Robertson Co., Ky.	W	
11/15/1874	Not named b. Fleming Co.	F	A	Lamar Spriggs b. Fleming Co.	Eliza White b. Robertson Co., Ky.	W	
11/22/1874	Not named b. Fleming Co.	M	A	Saml. McCunack b. Nicholas Co., Ky.	Bettie Morgan b. Nicholas Co., Ky.	W	
11/20/1874	Not named b. Fleming Co.	F	A	Wm. H. Shepard b. Fleming Co.	Mary C. Ross b. Fleming Co.	W	
11/22/1874	Chris b. Fleming Co.	M	A	Chris Hahn b. Germany	Christine Kackler b. Germany	W	
12/19/1874	Not named b. Fleming Co.	M	A	Richd. F. Lane b. Fleming Co.	Martha A. McCord b. Fleming Co.	W	
4/12/1874	Not named b. Fleming Co.	M	A	Wm. S. McCord b. Fleming Co.	Elizth. Stockdale b. Fleming Co.	W	
4/16/1874	Etta May McCord b. Fleming Co.	F	A	Edward McCord b. Fleming Co.	Paulina J. Richards b. Mason Co., Ky.	W	
3/30/1874	Amos S. Stamper b. Fleming Co.	M	A	John W. Stamper b. Bath Co., Ky.	Rachl. Mann b. Nicholas Co.	W	
1/ 2/1874	Zettie Albany b. Fleming Co.	F	A	John A. McCord b. Fleming Co.	Margaret M. Stockdale b. Fleming Co.	W	
1/13/1874	George C. Sherwood b. Fleming Co.	M	A	John Sherwood b. Fleming Co.	Hannah M. Blair b. Fleming Co.	W	

COUNTY __Fleming__

DATE	NAME OF CHILD	S	C	NAME OF FATHER	NAME OF MOTHER	CO.	RESIDENCE
7/30/1874	Not named b. Fleming Co.	F	A	Ben Shepard b. not known	Martha Shepard b. not known	B	All residents Fleming Co.
8/ 3/1874	William E. Lindsay b. Fleming Co.	M	A	Henry P. Lindsay b. Mason Co., Ky.	Harriet Bett b. Fleming Co.	W	
8/ 7/1874	Mary Francis Lander b. Fleming Co.	F	A	E. Henry Lander b. Fleming Co.	Ellen Anderson b. Fleming Co.	W	
8/23/1874	Not given b. Fleming Co.	F	A	Chas. Hammond b. Fleming Co.	-- Jones b. Fleming Co.	W	
9/12/1874	David Wall Fitch b. Fleming Co.	M	A	David Fitch b. Fleming Co.	Kate Cooper b. Fleming Co.	W	
7/12/1874	Robert b. Fleming Co.	M	A	Alexander Gains b. Fleming Co.	Maria Botts b. Fleming Co.	B	
6/ 6/1874	Lucien Mc. D. Howe b. Fleming Co.	M	A	Dunlap Howe b. Fleming Co.	Adaline C. McDarell b. Mason Co., Ky.	W	
4/15/1874	No name b. Fleming Co.	M	A	Not known b. Not known	Ann Frizzell b. Carter Co., Ky.	B	
10/15/1874	Juliet Fletcher b. Fleming Co.	F	A	Dusey Fletcher b. Fleminsburg, Ky.	Jane Husston b. Cinti, Ohio	M	
12/21/1874	Geo. D. P. Ashton b. Fleming Co.	M	A	Charlton H. Ashton b. Lexington, Ky.	Harriet Dudley b. Flemingsburg, Ky.	W	
9/17/1874	Lucien Reeves b. Fleming Co.	M	A	Jesse Reeves b. Fleming Co.	Hannah Jackson b. Fleming Co.	W	
5/ 7/1874	No name b. Fleming Co.	M	A	Wm. E. Jones b. Fleming Co.	Mary Stephens b. Fleming Co.	W	
11/12/1874	No name b. Fleming Co.	M	A	John Berry? b. Fleming Co.	Cami Wright b. Fleming Co.	M	
11/25/1874	No name b. Fleming Co.	F	A	W. W. Blair b. Fleming Co.	Malinda Sousley b. Fleming Co.	W	
12/13/1874	Franklin B. Faucett b. Fleming Co.	M	A	Saml. Faucett b. Bath Co.	Mary F. Sousley b. Fleming Co.	W	
7/ 1/1874	Mary Jockey b. Fleming Co.	F	A	Jacob Jockey b. Germany	Mary Goodwin b. Indiana	W	

A Copy Attest. M. M. Teagar CCK, Fleming Co. Ct.

DATE	NAME OF CHILD	S	C	NAME OF FATHER	NAME OF MOTHER	CO.	RESIDENCE
1/ 3/1874	Lutie L. Collins b. Fleming Co.	F	A	Wm. Collins b. Fleming Co.	Rica Stilla b. Ohio	W	

S Sex

C Condition A-Alive D-Dead

COUNTY Fleming

DATE	NAME OF CHILD	S	C	NAME OF FATHER	NAME OF MOTHER	CO.	RESIDENCE
3/24/1874	No name b. Fleming Co.	F	A	Robt. L. Dryden b. Mason Co., Ky.	Eliza J. Logan b. Carter Co., Ky.	W	All residents Fleming Co.
1/ /1874	Mary E. Davenport b. Fleming Co.	F	A	Joseph Davenport b. Mason Co., Ky.	Louisa Johnson b. Carter Co., Ky.	W	
1/18/1874	Not named b. Fleming Co.	M	A	Jas. F. Doyle b. Fleming Co.	Paulina Walker b. Fleming Co.	W	
2/ 2/1874	Nannie D. Overley b. Fleming Co.	F	D	Jas. H. Overley b. Fleming Co.	Alice J. Beckett b. Fleming Co.	W	
4/ 2/1874	Ella Gorden b. Fleming Co.	F	A	Perry Gorden b. Fleming Co.	Mary Clary b. Lewis Co., Ky.	W	
12/26/1874	Jas. M. Wallingford b. Fleming Co.	M	A	Edward O. Wallingford b. Lewis Co., Ky.	Sarah Rugless Lewis Co., Ky.	W	
11/ 3/1874	Nathaniel Kirk b. Fleming Co.	M	A	Wm. T. Kirk b. Lewis Co., Ky.	Nancy C. Rayborns b. Lewis Co., Ky.	W	
9/12/1874	Watt A. Ham b. Fleming Co.	M	A	Jeremiah Ham b. Fleming Co.	Lavina Underwood b. Lewis Co., Ky.	W	
9/ 7/1874	Lucy Ellen Ham b. Fleming Co.	F	A	Jno. A. Ham b. Carter Co., Ky.	Sarah Weeks b. Virginia	W	
7/19/1874	Margt. Baker b. Ohio	F	A	Alexr. Baker b. Luncince Co., Ky.	Lucy Haney b. Carter Co., Ky.	W	
11/23/1874	Mary F. Martin b. Fleming Co.	F	A	Wm. G. Martin b. Virginia	Mary E. Davis b. Greenup Co., Ky.	W	
7/27/1874	Wm. A. Ham b. Fleming Co.	M	A	Fautley R. Ham b. Fleming Co.	Mary A. Thomas b. Fleming Co.	W	
9/24/1874	Owen B. Carpenter b. Fleming Co.	M	A	Jas. Carpenter b. Fleming Co.	Eliza A. Dlary b. Fleming Co.	W	
7/ 4/1874	Florence J. Peid b. Fleming Co.	F	A	Francis D. Peid b. Fleming Co.	Emily Kidesco? b. Fleming Co.	W	
9/20/1874	Chas. Fizer b. Fleming Co.	M	A	Wm. W. Fizer b. Fleming Co.	Rebecca J. Arnold b. Fleming Co.	W	
4/ 3/1874	Claudie C. Watts b. Fleming Co.	F	A	Jno. A. Watts b. Fleming Co.	Nancy N. Foxworthy b. Fleming Co.	W	
8/ 4/1874	Chas. P. Mattinley b. Mason Co., Ky.	M	A	Jno T. Mattingly b. Mason Co., Ky.	Francis B. Mattingley b. Mason Co., Ky.	W	
1/ 6/1874	Malinda M. Strode b. Fleming Co.	F	A	Jno. Strode b. Fleming Co.	Mellisia Weir b. Fleming Co.	W	
2/12/1874	Chas. G. Debill b. Fleming Co.	M	A	Johua H. Debell b. Fleming Co.	Eliza M. Fleming b. Fleming Co.	W	

COUNTY Fleming

S Sex
C Condition A-Alive D-Dead

DATE	NAME OF CHILD	S	C	NAME OF FATHER	NAME OF MOTHER	CO.	RESIDENCE
7/21/1874	Jas. B. Nash b. Fleming Co.	M	A	Jas. S. Nash b. Fleming Co.	Ada L. Walker b. Fleming Co.	W	All residents Fleming Co.
12/15/1874	Taylor L. Spurgson b. Fleming Co.	M	A	Moses Spurgson b. Lewis Co., Ky.	Amanda J. Cox b. Fleming Co.	W	
4/ 9/1874	Dorcas K. Weir b. Fleming Co.	F	A	Wm. Weir b. Fleming Co.	Lucinda Luman b. Fleming Co.	W	
6/ /1874	Cora Monroe b. Fleming Co.	F	A	Chas. Monroe b. Fleming Co.	Harriet Butte b. Bath Co., Ky.	C	
6/24/1874	Chas. A. Gardner b. Fleming Co.	M	A	St. Clair Gardner b. Fleming Co.	Mary Jones b. Fleming Co.	W	
11/30/1874	Wm. Carpenter b. Fleming Co.	M	A	Jno. C. Carpenter b. Fleming Co.	Amelia A. Perry b. Lewis Co., Ky.	W	
11/14/1874	Anna T. Jones b. Fleming Co.	F	A	Rufus H. Jones b. Fleming Co.	Matilda Carpenter b. Fleming Co.	W	
2/12/1874	Edward E. Hawes b. Fleming Co.	M	A	Jno. F. Hawes b. Fleming Co.	Cornlia M. Brammel b. Fleming Co.	W	
4/24/1874	Monroe Hawes b. Fleming Co.	M	A	Wm. T. Hawes b. Fleming Co.	Lida M. Williams b. Fleming Co.	W	
9/ 3/1874	Mary J. Staggs b. Fleming Co.	F	A	Thos. D. Staggs b. Fleming Co.	Lucinda Reeves b. Fleming Co.	W	
3/17/1874	Dora A. Harmon b. Fleming Co.	F	A	Wm. T. Harmon b. Fleming Co.	Margt. Melforst b. Ohio	W	
3/17/1874	b. Fleming Co.	F	A	David Gorman b. Carter Co., Ky.	Mary McCoy b. Ohio	W	
4/26/1874	Oscar Gooding b. Fleming Co.	M	A	Wesley Gooding b. Fleming Co.	Elizth. M. Carpenter b. Fleming Co.	W	
9/18/1874	Alex P. Ross b. Fleming Co.	M	A	Geo. S. Ross b. Fleming Co.	Elizth. R. Gooding b. Fleming Co.	W	
5/19/1874	Jos. A. Hartley b. Fleming Co.	M	A	Reuben Hartley b. Fleming Co.	Mary Brammel b. Fleming Co.	W	
4/ 4/1874	Rosetta Kirk b. Fleming Co.	F	A	Shelby T. Kirk b. Wolfe Co., Ky.	Sophia D. Hartley b. Fleming Co.	W	
1/24/1874	Martin P. Plunner b. Fleming Co.	F	A	Jno. S. Plunner b. Fleming Co.	Louisa Humpheys b. Fleming Co.	W	
10/24/1874	Sarah Barnes b. Fleming Co.	F	A	Jas. W. Barnes b. Carter Co.	Louisa Evans b. Fleming Co.	W	
11/30/1874	John W. Kissick b. Fleming Co.	M	A	Isaac Kissick b. Fleming Co.	Mary Hefflin b. Fleming Co.	W	

S Sex
C Condition A-Alive D-Dead

COUNTY Fleming

DATE	NAME OF CHILD	S	C	NAME OF FATHER	NAME OF MOTHER	CO.	RESIDENCE
12/ 1/1874	Jackson G. Henderson b. Fleming	M	A	Jas. M. Henderson b. Carter Co., Ky.	Elizth. Qualls b. Virginia	W	All residents Fleming Co.
9/15/1874	Miam Hartley b. Fleming Co.	M	D	Simpson Hartley b. Fleming Co.	Nancy Brinegan b. Carter Co., Ky.	W	
3/12/1874	Martha L. Evans b. Fleming Co.	F	A	St. Clair Evans b. Fleming Co.	Lida M. Emmons b. Fleming Co.	W	
7/ /1874	 b. Fleming Co.	M	A	Levi F. McKee b. Fleming Co.	Mary A. Humpheys b. Fleming Co.	W	
1/ 1/1874	Chas. S. Jones b. Illinois	M	A	James H. Jones b. Fleming Co.	Sarah F. Thompson b. Virginia	W	
5/21/1874	No name b. Fleming Co.	M	D	Geo. S. McKee b. Fleming Co.	Susan A. Haw b. Carter Co., Ky.	W	
12/20/1874	Marshall K. Humpheys b. Fleming Co.	M	A	Francis M. Humpheys b. Fleming Co.	Barbara Haw ? b. Rowan Co., Ky.	W	
2/22/1874	Corilla J. Humpheys b. Fleming Co.	F	A	Wm. H. Humpheys b. Fleming Co.	Barbara Million b. Fleming Co.	W	
5/24/1874	Daisey A. Petty b. Fleming Co.	F	A	Elijah Petty b. Virginia	Martha J. Griffith b. Virginia	W	
4/14/1874	Sarah A. Muse b. Fleming Co.	F	A	Wm. M. Muse b. Fleming Co.	Charlotte Hurst b. Fleming Co.	W	
6/ 9/1874	Louisa Hord b. Fleming Co.	F	A	Adison P. Hord b.Mason Co., Ky.	Harriet Wallingford b. Mason Co., Ky.	W	
2/ 9/1874	James Broadwell b. Fleming Co.	M	A	Geo. W. Broadwell b. New Jersey	Nancy J. Purnell b. Ohio	W	
9/12/1874	Alexr. M. Cook b. Fleming Co.	M	A	Thos. A. Cook b. Mason Co., Ky.	Nellie Adams b. Fleming Co.	W	
12/16/1874	No name b. Fleming Co.	M	A	Leandor G. Cord b. Fleming Co.	Susan A. Stockdale b. Fleming Co.	W	
12/17/1874	Sterling P. McCord b. Fleming Co.	M	A	Jas. A. McCord b. Fleming Co.	Clainda A. McCarty b. Fleming Co.	W	
11/10/1874	Not named b. Fleming Co.	M	A	Jas. Thomas b. not known	Charlotte Hurst b. Fleming Co., Ky.	W	

A Copy Attest. M. M. Teagan CCK, Fleming Co. Ct.

| 11/14/1875 |
b. Fleming Co. | F | A | E. Mouey
b. Fleming Co. |
b. Fleming Co. | W | |

COUNTY__ Fleming___

DATE	NAME OF CHILD	S	C	NAME OF FATHER	NAME OF MOTHER	CO.	RESIDENCE
11/23/1875		M	A	Allen Boyse	Eliza Clarke	W	All residents
	b. Fleming Co.			b. Fleming Co.	b. Brown Co.		Fleming Co.
11/10/1875	Henry Ingram	M	A	Jesse Ingram	Sarah Armstrong	W	
	b. Fleming Co.			b. Fleming Co.	b. Fleming Co.		
5/14/1875	Slewellyn Boyse	F	A	William Boyse		W	
	b. Fleming Co.			b. Fleming Co.	b. Fleming Co.		
3/25/1875	Mattie S. Evans	F		Franklin Evans	Ella Hurton (Hinton?)	W	
	b. Fleming Co.			b. Fleming Co.	b. Fleming Co.		
10/14/1875		F	A	A. F. Vize	-- Emmons	W	
	b. Fleming Co.			b. Fleming Co.	b. Fleming Co.		
5/ 7/1874		F	A	Frank Fleuring		W	
	b. Fleming Co.			b. Fleming Co.	b. Fleming Co.		
3/22/1875	Allen S. Plummer	M	A	Benj. A. Plummer	Amanda N. Armstrong	W	
	b. Fleming Co.			b. Fleming Co.	b. Fleming Co.		
1/11/1875	Frank Howard	M	A		Mary D. Dent	W	
	b. Fleming Co.			b. Fleming Co.	b. Fleming Co.		
8/29/1874	Martin S. Harrison	M	A	William H. Harrison	Maggie McNelly	W	
	b. Fleming Co.			b. Fleming Co.	b. Fleming Co.		
4/21/1874	Henry P. Leforgee	M	A	James C. Leforgee	Sue Hendrix	W	
	b. Fleming Co.			b. Fleming Co.	b. Fleming Co.		
7/24/1875	Mary S. Bridges	F	A	John Bridges	Eliza Harrison	Negro	
	b. Fleming Co.			b. Fleming Co.	b. Fleming Co.		
12/18/1875		M	A	Abner Triplett	Margaret A. Burus	W	
	b. Fleming Co.			b. Fleming Co.	b. Fleming Co.		
10/25/1875		M	A	H. Clay Stone	Sarah Wallingford	W	Mason Co., Ky.
	b. Fleming Co.			b. Fleming Co.	b. Fleming Co.		
12/19/1875		M	A	Henry Mattingly	Annie Sweet	W	Mason Co., Ky.
	b. Mason Co., Ky.			b. Mason Co., Ky.	b. Mason Co., Ky.		
4/20/1875		M	A	Edward Breene		W	
	b. Fleming Co.			b. Fleming Co.	b. Fleming Co.		
9/20/1875	Lulu Francis	F	A	Francis Hopper	Elizabeth Wallingford	W	Mason Co., Ky.
	b. Mason Co., Ky.			b. Mason Co., Ky.	b. Mason Co., Ky.		
4/24/1875	Amos K. Mattingly	M	A	William Mattingly	Elizabeth Mattingly	W	Mason Co., Ky.
	b. Mason Co., Ky.			b. Mason Co., Ky.	b. Mason Co., Ky.		
1/13/1875		M	A	John Breeze	Lucy A. Browning	W	
	b. Fleming Co.			b. Fleming Co.	b. Fleming Co.		
8/29/1875		F	A	Abraham Stratton		W	
	b. Fleming Co.			b. Fleming Co.	b. Fleming Co.		

COUNTY Fleming

S Sex
C Condition A-Alive D-Dead

DATE	NAME OF CHILD	S	C	NAME OF FATHER	NAME OF MOTHER	CO.	RESIDENCE
1/ 1/1875		F	A	Franklin Blanton	E -- --.	W	All residents
	b. Fleming co.			b. Fleming Co.	b. Fleming Co.		Fleming Co.
2/ 2/1875	James W. Reeves	M	A	John Reeves	Ella Evans	W	
	b. Fleming Co.			b. Fleming Co.	b. Fleming Co.		
7/25/1875	Mary B. Thomas	F	A	Marsh Thomas	Mattie Tasson	Negro	Mason Co.
	b. Fleming Co.			b. Mason Co.	b. Mason Co.		
7/ 8/1875		M	A	Dudley Jordan	Sweet	W	
	b. Fleming Co.			b. Fleming Co.	b. Fleming Co.		
8/13/1875		M	A	James V. Jones		W	
	b. Fleming Co.			b. Fleming Co.	b. Fleming Co.		
3/15/1875	Cyrus Plummer	M	A	James M. Plummer	Mary Evans	W	
	b. Fleming Co.			b. Fleming Co.	b. Fleming Co.		
4/ 8/1875	Charles Wallingford	M	A	Benj. F. Wallingford	Bettie Glascock	W	
	b. Fleming Co.			b. Fleming Co.	b. Fleming Co.		
3/10/1875		F	A	Kenas M. Farrow	Margaret Wallingford	W	Mason Co.
	b. Mason Co.			b. Fleming Co.	b. Fleming Co.		
3/ 3/1875	Lucy Collins	F	A	William Collins	Rosa Mills	W	
	b. Fleming Co.			b. Mason Co.	b. Mason Co.		
7/26/1875	Catharine Dougherty	F	A	Charles Daugherty	Bridget O. Mann(O'Mann?)	W	Mason Co.
	b. Mason Co.			b. Ireland	b. Ireland		
10/ 1/1875	Millie Pugh	F	A	William A. Pugh	Caroline Farrow	W	Mason Co.
	b. Mason Co.			b. N.C.	b. Mason Co., Ky.		
7/27/1875	Fleming Carr	M	A		Lager Carr	negro	
	b. Fleming Co. Re. Bastard				Fleming Co.		
8/18/1875	Robert C. Grimes	M	A	Jerry Grimes	Lucy Cassidy	W	
	b. Fleming Co.			b. Fleming Co.	b. Fleming Co.		
11/28/1875		M	A	Edward Jacobs	Jennie McDonald	W	
11/28/1875		F	A	Edward Jacobs	Jennie McDonald	W	
	b. Fleming Co.			b. Fleming Co.	b. Fleming Co.		
12/ 1/1875	Robert S. Busby	M	A	Edward Busby	Emily Sourney	W	
	b. Fleming Co.			b. Fleming Co.	b. Fleming Co.		
3/28/1875	Mary Lyons	F	A	Daniel W. Lyons	Celia Warder	W	
	b. Fleming Co.			b. Ireland	b. Fleming Co.		
4/ 6/1875	Irvin J. King	M	A	Noah S. King	Elizabeth F. Lee (See?)	W	
	b. Fleming Co.			b. Fleming Co.	b. Fleming Co.		
3/25/1875	Henry E. Dobyns	M	A	Henry B. Dobyns	Nancy Goodman	W	
	b. Fleming Co.			b. Fleming Co.	b. Fleming Co.		

COUNTY Fleming

DATE	NAME OF CHILD	S	C	NAME OF FATHER	NAME OF MOTHER	CO.	RESIDENCE
1/20/1875	Charles F. Burns	M	A	Enoch P. Burns	Mary J. Finley	W	All residents
	b. Fleming Co.			b. Fleming Co.	b. Fleming Co.		Fleming Co.
3/ 1/1875	Thomas P. Garrison	M	A	Frank Garrison	Emily Jones	Negro	
	b. Fleming Co.			b. Fleming Co.	b. Fleming Co.		
4/21/1875		F	A	John OSullivan	Margaret Weir	W	
	b. Fleming Co.			b. Mason Co.	b. Fleming Co.		
3/ 6/1875		F	A	Daniel Bryant	Lizzie Darnall	Negro	
	b. Fleming Co.			b. Va.	b. Fleming Co.		
3/ 5/1875	Maggie	F	A	William H. Fogg	Adaline Summers	W	Nicholas Co.
	b. Nicholas Co., Ky.			b. Montgomery Co., Ky.	b. Bourban Co., Ky.		
7/25/1875		F	A	Patrick Dorain	Bridget Moore	W	
	b. Fleming Co.			b. Ireland	b. Ireland		
7/26/1875		F	D	Willoughby Griffith	Julia Hall	W	
	b. Fleming Co.			b. Fleming Co.	b. Fleming Co.		
9/25/1875	Maggie M. Momson	F	A	Charles B. Momson	Mary F. Jones	W	
	b. Fleming Co.			b. Fleming Co.	b. Fleming Co.		
8/10/1875	John R. Stewart	M	A	William H. Stewart	Amelia C. Stewart	W	
	b. Fleming Co.			b. Fleming Co.	b. Fleming Co.		
8/19/1875	Elizabeth Singleton	F	A	James W. Singleton	Eugene Sadler	W	
	b. Fleming Co.			b. Fleming Co.	b. Fleming Co.		
1/30/1875	Emily Tucker	F	A	John Hughes	Caroline tucker	Negro	
	b. Fleming Co.			b. Fleming Co.	b. Fleming Co.		
4/10/1875	John D. Sousley	M	A	John D. Sousley	Nannie Pearson	W	
	b. Fleming Co.			b. Fleming Co.	b. Clarke Co., Ky.		
3/ 7/1875	Annie E. Jones	F	A	Anderson Jones	Eliza Jackson	Negro	
	b. Fleming Co.			b. Fleming Co.	b. Mason Co., Ky.		
1/ 1/1875	Millie Branders	F	A	John Branders	Jennie Mack	M	
	b. Fleming Co.			b. not known	b. Fleming Co.		
6/18/1875	Benjamin Hawkins	M	A	John H. Hawkins	Jennie Hawkins	W	
	b. Fleming Co.			b. Fleming Co.	b. Fleming Co.		
2/ 3/1875	Johnston B. Kelly	M	A	John W. Kelly	Serilda E. Ross	W	
	b. Fleming Co.			b. Fleming Co.	b. Mo.		
2/19/1875	Lucy H. Green	F	A	Henry Bush	Mary C. Green	B	
	b. Fleming Co.			b. Fleming Co.	b. Fleming Co., Ky.		
9/ 9/1875		M	A	William Thomas	Elizabeth Art	W	
	b. Fleming Co.			b. Fleming Co.	b. Fleming Co.		
7/ 8/1875	Johannah	F	A	B. T. OHarn	Johnnah Sullivan	W	
	b. Fleming Co.			b. Ireland	b. Ireland		

S Sex
C Condition A-Alive D-Dead

COUNTY __Fleming__

DATE	NAME OF CHILD	S	C	NAME OF FATHER	NAME OF MOTHER	CO.	RESIDENCE
3/28/1875		M	A	William Johnson	Jemima Booth	W	All residents
	b. Fleming Co.			b. Ash Co. N.C.	b. Lee Co., Va.		Fleming Co.
5/22/1875		F	A	William O. Coryell	Nancy B. Elston	W	
	b. Fleming Co.			b. Mason Co., Ky.	b. Fleming Co.		
7/ 8/1875		F	A	Isaac Bird	Jetty Willis	B	
	b. Fleming Co.			b. Fleming Co.	b. Fleming Co.		
5/29/1875		F	A	Luther M. Strode	Margaret Foster	W	
	b. Fleming Co.			b. Fleming Co.	b. Campbell Co., Ky.		
10/17/1875		M	A	John H. Bush		Negro	
	b. Fleming Co.			b. Fleming Co.	b. Fleming Co.		
8/ 8/1875	Sarah McCord	F	A	John W. McCord	Sarah F. Dye	W	
	b. Fleming Co.			b. Fleming Co.	b. Fleming Co.		
11/24/1875	Letitia B. Raimey	F	A	John A. Raimey	Mary A. Cochran	W	
	b. Fleming Co.			b. Bourban Co., Ky.	b. Fleming Co.		
11/ 4/1875	Robert E. Ralston	M	A	John Ralston	Louisa Hamilton	W	
	b. Fleming Co.			b. Fleming Co.	b. Bath Co., Ky.		
3/ 2/1875	Winstow Flauglen	M	A	Francis M. Flauglen	Elizabeth McDaniel	W	Brown Co., O.
	b. Fleming Co.			b. Brown Co., Ohio	b. Brown Co., Ohio		
7/16/1875		M	A	John Mailey		W	
	b. Fleming Co.			b. Fleming Co., Ky.	b. Ireland		
12/27/1875	William D. Howe		A	John W. Howe	Lizzie A. Stewart	W	
	b. Fleming Co.			b. Fleming Co.	b. Fleming Co.		
11/ 8/1875		M	A	Leonard Clarke	Sarah WcMillen	W	
	b. Fleming Co.			b. Fleming Co.	b. Fleming Co.		
12/ 6/1875	M. Omar Sousley	M	A	James W. Sousley	Sallie E. McIntyre	W	
	b. Fleming Co.			b. Fleming Co.	b. Fleming Co.		
6/15/1875	Charles J. McIntyre	M	A	William J. McIntyre	Elizabeth S. Sousley	W	
	b. Fleming Co.			b. Fleming Co.	b. Fleming Co.		
8/16/1875	Maria Bryant	F	A	Gus Bryant	Martha Workman	W	Bracken Co., Ky.
	b. Nicholas Co., Ky.			b. Nich. Co., Ky.	b. Bath Co., Ky.		
4/ 3/1875	Alice G. Hurst	F	A	B. H. Hurst	Mary E. Davis	W	
	b. Fleming Co.			b. Fleming Co.	b. Fleming Co.		
3/16/1875	Patrick H. Doyle	M	A	John Doyle	Quille? Welch	W	
	b. Fleming Co.			b. Ireland	b. Ireland		
10/31/1875	Samuel C. Power	M	A	John S. Power	Alice B. Dudley	W	
	b. Fleming Co.			b. Fleming Co.	b. Fleming Co.		
11/ 7/1875	Alice S. Benltey	F	A	R. M. Bentley	Jane Overley	W	
	b. Fleming Co.			b. Fleming Co.	b. Fleming Co.		

COUNTY Fleming

DATE	NAME OF CHILD	S	C	NAME OF FATHER	NAME OF MOTHER	CO.	RESIDENCE
9/11/1875	William E. Conley b. Fleming Co.	M	A	Patrick Conley b. Ireland	Hannah Heffern b. Ireland	W	All residents Fleming Co.
12/14/1875	John Thomas Holland b. Fleming Co.	M	A	Newton Holland b. Fleming Co.	Susan Jackson b. Fleming Co.	W	
9/ 4/1875	W. C. Briggs b. Fleming Co.	M	A	George D. Briggs b. Bennington Co., Ky.	Annie F. Ross b. Bath Co., Ky.	W	Nicholas Co.
9/ 6/1875	Parly A. Alexander b. Fleming Co.	F	A	William D. Alexander b. Fleming Co.	Mary E. McIntyre b. Fleming Co.	W	
10/20/1875	William H. McDanall b. Fleming Co.	M	A	Isiah McDaniel b. Brown Co., O.	Mary J. Brootkover b. Brown Co., O.	W	
10/26/1875	Lillian H. Vansant b. Fleming Co.	F	A	John H. Vansant b. Fleming Co.	Mary E. Inlow b. Fleming Co.	W	
11/22/1875	b. Fleming Co.	F	A	George M. Caywood b. Fleming Co.	Sarah V. Power b. Fleming Co.	W	
12/25/1875	Mariah Mansfield b. Fleming Co.	F	A	Mortimer Marshall	Alice Hines b. Fleming Co.	Col.	
12/ 1/1875	b. Fleming Co.	M	A	Reuben S. Goodwin b. Fleming Co.	Ella F. Jones b. Fleming Co.	W	
10/31/1875	Arison W. Slicer b. Fleming Co.	M	A	James W. Slicer b. Fleming Co.	Laura Lee b. Fleming Co.	W	
11/18/1875	b. Fleming Co.	F	A	Lawson T. Lee (See?) b. Fleming Co.	Margt. J. Hurst b. Fleming Co.	W	
5/20/1875	b. Fleming Co.	F	A	James J. Overtow b. Fleming to.	Julia Harrison b. Fleming Co.	W	
8/ 9/1875	b. Fleming Co.	M	A	Austin Saunders b. Fleming Co.	Sarah M. Boyd b. Fleming Co.	W	
2/14/1875	Becca B. McCord b. Fleming Co.	F	A	David McCord b. Fleming Co.	Elizabeth Stockdale b. Fleming Co.	W	
6/28/1875	Claudy McCord b. Fleming Co.	M	A	W. S. McCord b. Fleming Co.	Elizabeth Stockdale b. Fleming Co.	W	
6/28/1875	b. Fleming Co.	F	D	W. S. McCord b. Fleming Co.	Elizabeth Stockdale b. Fleming Co.	W	
10/24/1875	b. Mason Co.	M	A	W. F. Peed b. Mason Co.	Burns b. Mason Co.	W	Mason Co.
5/13/1875	John C. Edwards b. Fleming Co.	M	A	John C. Edwards b. Montgomery Co., Ky	Sarah Toner b. Mason Co., Ky.	W	
8/26/1875	b. Fleming Co.	M	A	Richard D. Mouey b. Fleming Co.	Martha Kendall b. Fleming Co.	W	

S Sex
C Condition A-Alive D-Dead

COUNTY Fleming

DATE	NAME OF CHILD	S	C	NAME OF FATHER	NAME OF MOTHER	CO.	RESIDENCE
9/11/1875		M	A		Julia Harrison	M	All residents
	b. Fleming Co.			b. Fleming Co.	b. Fleming Co.		Fleming Co.
3/18/1875		M	A	John Parker	Emma Moore	W	
	b. Fleming Co.			b. Fleming Co.	b. Fleming Co.		
3/ 1/1875		F	A	Wm. B. Stevens	Caroline Wills	W	
	b. Fleming Co.			b. Fleming Co.	b. Fleming Co.		
3/ 1/1875		F	A	G. McMullin	Louisa Eden	W	
	b. Fleming Co.			b. Greene Co., Ohio	b. Fleming Co.		
5/16/1875		M	A	Aaron J. Phelps	Lucinda Barus	W	
	b. Fleming Co.			b. Fleming Co.	b. Fleming Co.		
4/15/1875		F	A	Joholen B. Hawkins	Drura Hedrick	W	
	b. Fleming Co.			b. Fleming Co.	b. Rowan Co., Ky.		
1/25/1875		M	A	Patrick Keerans	Ellen Shannon	W	
	b. Fleming Co.			b. Fleming Co.	b. Fleming Co.		
5/12/1875	Sarah E. Smith	F	A	Robert H. Smith	Mary S. Bowen	W	
	b. Fleming Co.			b. Foyatt, Ky.	b. Fleming Co.		
2/11/1875		M	A	Wyatt Berry	Ellen Summers	Col.	
	b. Fleming Co.			b. Fleming Co.	b. Fleming Co.		
1/ 7/1875	Walter Bradley	M	A	John Bradley	Delila Armstrong	Col.	
	b. Fleming Co.			b. Fleming Co.	b. Fleming Co.		
2/21/1875		F	A	Jas. P. Allen	Annie E. Wilson	W	
	b. Fleming Co.			b. Fleming Co.	b. Fleming Co.		
2/21/1875		F	D	John H. French	Lettie A. Rhodan	W	
	b. Fleming Co.			b. Scott Co.	b. Fleming Co.		
2/ 4/1875		M	A	J. B. Summons	Caroline Teetiers	W	
	b. Mason Co.			b. Brown Co. Ohio	b. Adams Co., Ohio		
2/21/1875	Annie Allen	F	A	Jas.P. Allen	Annie E. Wilson	W	
	b. Fleming Co.			b. Fleming Co.	b. Fleming Co.		
11/20/1875	David B. Mitchell	M	A	Alvin R. Mitchell	Lucy A. Brown	W	
	b. Fleming Co.			b. Fleming Co.	b. Adams Co., O.		
12/ 9/1875	Twins	M	A	Asa McRoberts	Lucy Pepper	W	
	b. Fleming Co.			b. Fleming Co.	b. Adams Co., O.		
2/27/1875		M	A	Charles M. Hughes	Mary M. Wallington	W	
	b. Fleming Co.			b. Mason Co., Ky.	b. Owing Co., Ind.		
6/ 3/1875		M	A	George McCormick	Eliza Hall	W	
	b. Fleming Co.			b. Mason Co.	b. Woodford Co., Ky.		
1/24/1875	Sarah Hickerson	F	A	Leroy M. Hickerson	Melvina Stitt	W	
	b. Fleming Co.			b. Mason Co., Ky.	b. Nicholas Co., Ky.		

COUNTY __Fleming__

DATE	NAME OF CHILD	S	C	NAME OF FATHER	NAME OF MOTHER	CO.	RESIDENCE
2/12/1875		F	A	William Leet (Seet?)	Sarah Hughbanks	W	All residents
	b. Fleming Co.			b. Fleming Co.	b. Fleming Co.		Fleming Co.
2/23/1875		M	A	John Umstaddt	Mary McCarty	W	
	b. Fleming Co.			b. Fleming Co.	b. Fleming Co.		
4/ 2/1875		F	A	Elza Caywood	Nancy Veach	W	
	b. Fleming Co.			b. Fleming Co.	b. Brown Co., Ohio		
3/28/1875			A	William Johnson	Jemima Bothe	W	(twins)
	b. Fleming Co.			b. Nash Co. N.C.	b. Lee Co., Va.		
10/13/1875	John Herbert Wigletman	M	A	Jno. E. Wightman	Martha J. Wells	W	
	b. Fleming Co.			b. Brown Co., Ohio	b. Brown Co., Ohio		
5/ 8/1875	James Burnis	M	A	Jno. Burns	Ellen Barnett	W	
	b. Fleming Co.			b. Fleming Co.	b. Nicholas Co., Ky.		
8/ 4/1875	Theodoria McCracken	F	A	William C. McCracken	Annie M. Jackson	W	
	b. Fleming Co.			b. Harrison Co., Ky.	b. Robertson Co., Ky.		
1/ 1/1875	Jennie B. Helphinstine	F	A	Samuel C. Helphinstine	Minerva Nealis	W	
	b. Fleming Co.			b. Fleming Co.	b. Fleming Co.		
11/28/1875		M	A	Jesse Markwell	Lizie Anderson	W	
	b. Fleming Co.			b. Fleming Co.	b. Montgomery Co., Ky.		
3/29/1875	Simeon P. Carpenter	M	A	Francis M. Caywood	Sarah E. McCarty	W	
	b. Fleming Co.			b. Fleming Co.	b. Fleming Co.		
7/19/1875		M	A	Lester A. bryant	Joseph A. Richard	W	Nicholas Co.
	b. Nicholas Co., Ky.			b. Nicholas Co., Ky.	b. Bath Co., Ky.		
3/ 2/1875		M	A	William Johnson	Sarah Fields	W	
	b. Fleming Co.			b. Fleming Co.	b. Nicholas Co., Ky.		
5/22/1875		M	A	Absolem Ryan	Emily Douglas	W	
	b. Fleming Co.			b. Fleming Co.	b. Fleming Co.		
4/14/1875	Virginia L. Stout	F	A	Shipman P. Stout	Sarah A. Caywood	W	
	b. Fleming Co.			b. Fleming Co.	b. Fleming Co.		
4/30/1875		F	A	Jacob Allison	Elizabeth Collins	W	
	b. Fleming Co.			b. Fleming Co.	b. Fleming Co.		
7/12/1875		M	A	William McCord	Rebecca Collins	W	
	b. Fleming Co.			b. Fleming Co.	b. Fleming Co.		
7/24/1875		M	A	Grant Stockdale	Mary A. Davis	W	
	b. Fleming Co.			b. Fleming Co.	b. Fleming Co.		
7/19/1875		F	A	Harrison Moore	Lucinda J. Konutz	W	
	b. Fleming Co.			b. Fleming Co.	b. Fleming Co.		
7/30/1875		M	A	Harrison McCormick	Jane Blake	W	
	b. Fleming Co.			b. Mason Co.	b. Nicholas Co., Ky.		

		S Sex
		C Condition A-Alive D-Dead

COUNTY   Fleming

DATE	NAME OF CHILD	S	C	NAME OF FATHER	NAME OF MOTHER	CO.	RESIDENCE
4/30/1875		M	A	Jno. R. Thompson		W	All residents
	b. Fleming Co.			b. Fleming Co.	b. Rowan Co., Ky.		Fleming
	(Copied list mothers name not given)						
7/11/1875		M	A	GeorgeC. Runyon	Sarah Robertson	W	
	b. Fleming Co.			b. Fleming Co.	b. Fleming Co.		
8/22/1875		F	A	John P. Moore	Louisa C. Swart	W	
	b. Fleming Co.			b. Fleming Co.	b. Fleming Co.		
9/ 1/1875		F	A	George McCord	Margaret Sane	W	
	b. Fleming Co.			b. Fleming Co.	b. Fleming Co.		
9/ 9/1875	Cliff Robertson	M	A	Lee Robertson	Liddie Cleft	W	
	b. Fleming Co.			b. Fleming Co.	b. Mason Co.		
11/ 9/1875		F	A	JeromeKirk	Elizabeth Emmons	W	
	b. Fleming Co.			b. Lewis Co., Ky.	Fleming Co.		
9/18/1875		M	A	Richard Williams	Lucy Stockdale	W	
	b. Fleming Co.			b. Fleming Co.	b. Fleming Co.		
9/30/1875		M	A	Samuel J. Groves	Sallie Stockdale	W	
	b. Fleming Co.			b. Fleming Co.	b. Fleming Co.		
10/12/1875		M	A	Milton Pyles	Jane Caywood	W	
	b. Fleming Co.			b. Mason Co., Ky.	b. Fleming Co.		
5/11/1875	Maggie Day	F	A	Truman S. Day	Lucinda Gray	W	
	b. Fleming Co.			b. Fleming Co.	b. Fleming Co.		
11/ 8/1875		M	A	James S. Swart	Sarey E. Bentley	W	
	b. Fleming Co.			b. Fleming Co.	b. Fleming Co.		
11/25/1875		M	A	Felix McCarty	Nancy Wise	W	
	b. Fleming Co.			b. Fleming Co.	b. Fleming Co.		
7/10/1875		M	A	Jno. E. Collins	Miss Mulliken	W	
	b. Fleming Co.			b. Fleming Co.	b. Nicholas Co., Ky.		
12/14/1875		F	A	Thomas Mtout	Laura B. Stiles	W	
	b. Fleming Co.			b. Robertson Co., Ky.	b. Mason Co., Ky.		
3/13/1875	Leislie B. Newman	M	A	James W. Newman	Florence Graham	W	
	b. Fleming Co.			b. Fleming Co.	b. Fleming Co.		
1/28/1875	John G. Todd	M	A	W. W. Todd	Amanda E. Walton	W	
	b. Fleming Co.			b. Fleming Co.	b. Fleming Co.		
11/17/1875	Milton Taylor	M	A	Frank Taylor	Liddie Jamison	W	
	b. Fleming Co.			b. Fleming Co.	b. Fleming Co.		
1/11/1875	Frank H. McCarty	M	A	John McCarty	Mary D. Dent	W	
	b. Fleming Co.			b. Fleming Co.	b. Fleming Co.		

COUNTY Fleming

DATE	NAME OF CHILD	S	C	NAME OF FATHER	NAME OF MOTHER	CO.	RESIDENCE
3/17/1875	Charles M. Downey b. Fleming Co.	M	A	Henry C. Downey b. Fleming Co.	Mary A. Phelps b. Fleming Co.	W	All residents Fleming Co.
2/6/1875	California Harrison b. Fleming Co.	F	A	Daniel Harrison b. Fleming Co.	Sybvina Selby b. Fleming Co.	W	
1/1/1875	Lottie A. Hutchison b. Fleming Co.	F	A	Robert T. Hutchison b. Fleming Co.	Lucinda C. Crain b. Fleming Co.	W	
5/8/1875	b. Fleming Co.	F	A	James McCord b. Fleming Co.	Mary McCarty b. Fleming Co.	W	
4/16/1875	Charles Powell b. Fleming Co.	M	A	Andrew M. Powell b. Fleming Co.	Phoebe Williams b. Mason Co., Ky.	W	
11/20/1875	Mary W. Shepard b. Fleming Co.	F	A	William H. Shepard b. Mason Co., Ky.	Mary C. Ross b. Robertson Co., Ky.	W	
11/21/1875	b. Fleming Co.	F	A	George W. Cord b. Fleming Co.	Isabella Donaldson b. Fleming Co.	W	
10/5/1875	Amelia Scott b. Fleming Co.	F	A	Daniel N. Scott b. Fleming Co.	J. H. Sousley b. Fleming Co.	W	
4/10/1875	John D. Sousley b. Fleming Co.	M	A	John D. Sousley b. Fleming Co.	Nancy Percell b. Clarke Co., Ky.	W	
11/28/1875	b. Fleming Co.	M	A	Alvin Mitchell b. Bath Co., Ky.	Lucy M. Brown b. Fleming Co.	W	
8/3/1876	Charles Tribby b. Fleming Co.	M	A	Samuel Tribby b. Fleming Co.	Eliza Jones b. Fleming Co.	W	
11/24/1876	J. G. Rankins b. Fleming Co.	M	A	W. M. Rankins b. Fleming Co.	Martha Rankins b. Fleming Co.	W	
10/26/1876	A. S. Todd b. Fleming Co.	W	A	W. B. Todd b. Fleming Co.	L. E. Story b. Fleming Co.	W	
5/21/1876	Alvin Rankins b. Fleming Co.	M	A	Jackson Rankins b. Bath Co.	Nan Rankins b. Fleming Co.	W	
12/18/1876	W. W. Emmons b. Fleming Co.	M	A	J. E. Emmons b. Bath Co., Ky.	T. A. Emmons b. Fleming Co.	W	
11/7/1876	Eliza H. Hopkins b. Fleming Co.	M	A	J. W. Hopkins b. Fleming Co.	Eliza A. Watkins b. Fleming Co.	W	
11/7/1876	Eddie E. Hopkins b. Fleming Co.	F	A	J. W. Hopkins b. Fleming Co.	Eliza A. Watkins b. Fleming Co.	W	
10/20/1876	Charles H. Moren b. Fleming Co.	M	A	John Moran b. Fleming Co.	Catharine Moren b. Fleming Co.	W	
10/22/1876	Lucy E. McLain b. Fleming Co.	F	A		Nancy McLain b. Bath Co., Ky.	W	

DATE	NAME OF CHILD	S	C	NAME OF FATHER	NAME OF MOTHER	CO.	RESIDENCE
9/11/1876	Ruth M. Porter b. Fleming Co.	F	A	Andrew M. Porter b. Fleming Co.	Sarah M. Sadwick b. Fleming Co.	W	All residents Fleming Co.
1/12/1876	b. Fleming Co.	M	A	Oliver B. Saunders b. Fleming Co.	Alberta Saunders b. Fleming Co.	W	
10/ 3/1876	b. Fleming Co.	M	A	Nimrod Call b. Bourbon Co., Ky.	Nancy J. Watson b. Fleming Co., Ky.	W	
9/18/1876	Annie Waugh b. Fleming Co.	F	A	George S. Waugh b. Nicholas Co., Ky.	Hannah S. Daugherty b. Fleming Co.	W	
5/ 7/1876	John S. Oakerson b. Fleming Co.	M	A	John H. Oakerson b. Fleming Co.	Tabitha J. Oakerson b. Fleming Co.	W	
5/ 7/1876	Seila H. b. Fleming Co.	F	A	John H. Oakerson b. Fleming Co.	Tabitha J. Oakerson b. Fleming Co.	W	
12/26/1876	Rhetta Brown b. Fleming Co.	F	A	Howard Brown b. Virg.	Maria Brown b. Bath Co., Ky.	Col.	
2/ 9/1876	D. A. Jones b. Fleming Co.	M	A	Rice James b. Fleming Co.	Sarah C. Jones b. Bath Co., Ky.	W	
8/10/1876	Ida B. Hull b. Fleming Co.	F	A	James A. Hull b. Ind.	Cynthia Rice b. Fleming Co.	W	
7/ 9/1876	Earnest Hillis b. Fleming Co.	M	A	Ceplias Hillis b. Ind.	Julia Peck b. Fleming Co.	W	
4/18/1876	A. B. McCormick b. Fleming Co.	F	A	W. F. McCormick b. Ind.	Mary E. Boyd b. Ind.	W	
10/ 8/1876	N. E. Lapp (Sapp ?) b. Fleming Co.	F	A	George A. Lapp b. Fleming Co.	Mary C. Jackson b. Nicholas Co., Ky.	W	
2/ 3/1876	R. T. Lapp b. Fleming Co.	M	A	John Lapp b. Fleming Co.	Mary Humphreys b. Nicholas Co., Ky.	W	
11/20/1876	Annie Carpenter b. Fleming Co.	F	A	Wm. Carpenter b. Ind.	M. A. Ulers b. Nicholdas Co., Ky.	W	
7/17/1876	N. C. Sapp (Lapp?) b. Fleming Co.	F	A	Wm. Sampp b. Fleming Co.	Susan Humphreys b. Nicholas Co., Ky.	W	
5/30/1876	Hattie Peck b. Fleming Co.	F	A	George Peck b. Fleming Co.	Rebecca Burgess b. Nicholas Co., Ky.	W	
8/ 1/1876	M. C. Dodge b. Fleming Co.	F	A	John J. Dodge b. Fleming Co.	Catharine Sousley b. Nicholas Co., Ky.	W	
9/ 2/1876	J. H. Steward b. Fleming Co.	M	A	J. T. Steward b. Mason Co., Ky.	E. J. Steward b. Va.	W	
12/10/1876	b. Fleming Co.	M	A	Francis M. Botterill b. Ohio	E. S. Spencer b. Fleming Co..	W	

COUNTY Fleming

DATE	NAME OF CHILD	S	C	NAME OF FATHER	NAME OF MOTHER	CO.	RESIDENCE
4/21/1876	E. L. Herrin b. Fleming Co.	M	A	Thomas Herrin b. Nicholas Co., Ky.	E. A. Kerrans b. Nicholas Co., Ky.	W	All residents Fleming Co.
8/29/1876	Charles Gray b. Fleming Co.	M	A	James Gray b. Nicholas Co., Ky.	M. J. Gray b. Fleming Co.	W	
10/18/1876	Lucien B. Adams b. Fleming Co.	M	A	David Adams b. Fleming Co.	S. A. Cochran b. Fleming Co.	W	
12/15/1876	H. E. Mitchell b. Fleming Co.	M	A	Wm. Mitchell b. Bath Co., Ky.	Susan A. Brown b. Fleming Co.	W	
9/ 1/1876	Amanda Y. Biddle b. Fleming Co.	F	A	Richard T. Biddle b. Fleming Co.	Ary C. Bentley b. Fleming Co.	W	
5/17/1876	James P. Barton b. Fleming Co.	M	A	William R. Barton b. Fleming Co.	Mollie Parsons b. Fleming Co.	W	
8/12/1876	M. A. Bishop b. Fleming Co.	F	A	J. C. Bishop b. Fleming Co.	M. O. Biddle b. Fleming Co.	W	
6/27/1876	Charles O. Biddle b. Fleming Co.	M	A	Thomas W. Biddle b. Fleming Co.	P. V. Parsons b. Md.	W	
5/25/1876	John Gay b. Fleming Co.	M	A	Samuel Gay b. Fleming Co.	Maggie Dillon b. Fleming Co.	W	
5/22/1876		F	A	J. N. Price	E. J. Runyon	W	
5/22/1876	b'. Fleming Co.	F	A	J. N. Price b. Fleming Co.	E. J. Runyon b. Mason Co., Ky.	W	
10/27/1876	b. Fleming Co.	M	A	Samuel P. Clarke b. Fleming Co.	Sarah J. McRoberts b. Rowan Co., Ky.	W	
9/ 2/1876	J. C. Clarke b. Fleming Co.	M	A	Thomas Clarke b. Fleming Co.	Susan Tibbs b. Fleming Co.	W	
5/15/1876	E. M. Allen b. Fleming Co.	F	A	John E. Allen b. Fleming Co.	Virginia A. Clarke b. Fleming Co.	W	
3/20/1876	L. M. Sherwood b. Fleming Co.	M	A	John Sherwood b. Fleming Co.	H. M. Blair b. Fleming Co.	W	
6/13/1876	Charles L. Moore b. Fleming Co.	M	A	George W. Moore b. Fleming Co.	Amelia B. Taylor b. Fleming Co.	W	
9/ 1/1876	W. Bush b. Fleming Co.	M	A	Tobias Bush b. Fleming Co.	L. E. Ferguson b. Fleming Co.	B	
8/17/1876	David T. Biddle b. Fleming Co.	M	A	John H. Biddle b. Fleming Co.	M. E. McLane b. Mason Co., Ky.	W	
2/ 7/1876	C. D. Eubanks b. Fleming Co.	M	A	Charles Eubanks b. Nicholas Co., Ky.	Malinda Barton b. Fleming Co.	W	

S Sex
C Condition A-Alive D-Dead

COUNTY __Fleming__

DATE	NAME OF CHILD	S	C	NAME OF FATHER	NAME OF MOTHER	CO.	RESIDENCE
10/19/1876	A. E. Hammonds b. Fleming Co.	F	A	C. W. Hammonds b. Fleming Co.	Martha Adams b. Fleming Co.	W	All residents Fleming Co.
1/18/1876	 b. Fleming Co.	M	A	W. R. Howard b. Nicholas Co., Ky.	Victoria Hammond b. Fleming Co., Ky.	W	
11/13/1876	George M. Ewing b. Fleming Co.	M	A	G. W. Ewing b. Nicholas Co., Ky.	S. Smart b. Nicholas Co., Ky.	W	
10/ 8/1876	E. M. McCarty b. Fleming Co.	F	A	James McCarty b. Fleming Co.	Mary Wise b. Fleming Co.	W	
8/27/1876	 b. Fleming Co.	M	A	John Biddle b. Fleming Co.	M. E. Burriss b. Fleming Co.	W	
4/20/1876	 b. Fleming Co.	M	A	G. B. Bentley b. Fleming Co.	Sarah Overley b. Fleming Co.	W	
9/27/1876	W. T. Hawkins b. Fleming Co.	M	A	T. W. T. Hawkins b. Nicholas Co., Ky.	Rebecca Flora b. Estill Co., Ky.	W	
9/ 1/1876	 b. Fleming Co.	M	A	Jasper Hughes b. Nicholas Co., Ky.	Mary Hunter b. Fleming Co.	W	
11/12/1876	J. T. Fields b. Fleming Co.	M	A	Wm. Fields b. Fleming Co.	S. M. Cory b. Bath Co., Ky.	W	
10/15/1876	E. J. Clarke b. Fleming Co.	M	A	B. D. Clarke b. Fleming Co.	S. A. Cluter b. Mason Co., Ky.	W	
2/ 7/1876	J. S. Setters b. Fleming Co.	M	A	J.P. Setters b. Carter Co., Ky.	N. J. Setters b. Carter Co., Ky.	W	
12/ 9/1876	 b. Fleming Co.	F	A	Elias Clarke b. Mason Co., Ky.	Annie B. Ratcliffe b. Bourbon Co., Ky.	W	
6/29/1876	Mattie Johnson b. Fleming Co.	F	A		Lucy Johnson b. Fleming Co.	B	
9/21/1876	Maggie M. Heflin b. Fleming Co.	F	A	James Heflin b. Va.	Mary L. Hitt b. Va.	W	
2/12/1878	Wm. Hinton b. Fleming Co.	M	A	William Hinton b. Fleming Co.	Henrietta Barnes b. Fleming Co.	W	
10/ 9/1876	 b. Fleming Co.	M	A	James Evans b. Fleming Co.	Louisa Perkins b. Fleming Co.	W	
7/31/1876	B. H. Bristow b. Fleming Co.	M	A	Andrew W. Bristow b. Bath Co., Ky.	America Hinton b. Fleming Co.	W	
3/ 4/1876	Wm. E. Faris b. Fleming Co.	M	A	Ira Faris b. Fleming Co.	Louisa Sweet b. Fleming Co.	W	
11/15/1876	John Parks b. Fleming Co.	M	A	Octavia Parks b. Ohio	Mary A. Grimes b. Ohio	W	

COUNTY Fleming

DATE	NAME OF CHILD	S	C	NAME OF FATHER	NAME OF MOTHER	CO.	RESIDENCE
5/26/1876	Andrew M. Triplett b. Fleming Co.	M	A	Wm. Daugherty b. Bath Co., Ky.	Lydia Triplett b. Fleming Co.	W	All residents Fleming Co.
9/ 5/1876	S. T. McKee b. Fleming Co.	M	A	Wm. McKee b. Fleming Co.	M. C. Dillon b. Fleming Co.	W	
5/11/1876	Wm. S. Porter b. Fleming Co.	M	A	Thomas Porter b. Fleming Co.	Martha Williams b. Bath Co., Ky.	W	
2/18/1876	Saml. T. Owens b. Fleming Co.	M	A	John Owens b. Mason Co., Ky.	Ann Power b. Fleming Co.	W	
6/17/1876	Florence Lawson b. Fleming Co.	F	A	James Lawson b. Fleming Co.	Matilda Pickrell b. Fleming Co.	W	
7/ 5/1876	b. Fleming Co.	M	A	Ed Denton b. Bath Co., Ky.	Sarah J. Crain b. Bath Co., Ky.	W	
5/12/1876	Bruce Payne b. Fleming Co.	M	A	Edward B. Payne b. Fleming Co.	Elizabeth Graham b. Fleming Co.	W	
1/ 3/1876	N. B. Rawlings b. Fleming Co.	F	A	Richard Rawlings b. Fleming Co.	Virginia Emmons b. Fleming Co.	W	
10/31/1876	N. R. McRoberts b. Fleming Co.	F	A	James McRoberts b. Fleming Co.	Alice Dearing b. Fleming Co.	W	
7/30/1876	M. S. Hurst b. Fleming Co.	F	A	Jesse Hurst b. Fleming Co.	Elizabeth McIlvain b. Fleming Co.	W	
12/19/1876	b. Fleming Co.	F	A	C. H. Spencer b. Fleming Co.	Evaline Planck b. Fleming Co.	W	
12/ 8/1876	Ory Drennan b. Fleming Co.	F	A	Jas. Drennan b. Ohio	Hattie Spencer b. Fleming Co.	W	
7/ 8/1876	b. Fleming Co.	F	A	H. M. Wallingford b. Lewis Co., Ky.	Mary Willett b. Fleming Co.	W	
7/31/1876	Wm. F. Williams b. Fleming Co.	M	A	J.P. Williams b. Fleming Co.	Mary L. Overley b. Fleming Co.	W	
9/17/1876	Carol A. Frank b. Fleming Co.	M	A	Joseph C. Frank b. Mason Co., Ky.	Sarah Darnall b. Fleming Co.	W	
12/22/1876	b. Fleming Co.	M	A	J. H. Rice b. Fleming Co.	Margaret Porter b. Fleming Co.	W	
10/ 9/1876	E. J. Dickey b. Fleming Co.	F	A	James I. Dickey b. Fleming Co.	Ann E. Kirk b. Fleming Co.	W	
9/ 6/1876	C. T. Campbell b. Fleming Co.	M	A	C. B. Campbell b. Fleming Co.	E. M. Howe b. Fleming Co.	W	
12/26/1876	M. B. Hedrick b. Fleming Co.	F	A	W. B. Hedrick b. Nicholas Co., Ky.	Jennie Sharpe b. Fleming Co.	W	

S Sex

C Condition A-Alive D-Dead

COUNTY __Fleming__

DATE	NAME OF CHILD	S	C	NAME OF FATHER	NAME OF MOTHER	CO.	RESIDENCE
4/15/1876	N. Proctor b. Fleming Co.	F	A	J. N. Proctor b. Fleming Co.	Maria Richardson b. Mason Co., Ky.	W	All residents Fleming Co.
3/16/1876	M. D. Williams b. Fleming Co.	F	A	John W. Williams b. Bourbon Co., Ky.	D. Glascock b. Mason Co., Ky.	W	
12/17/1876	b. Fleming Co.	M	A	Geo. B. Jackson b. Fleming Co.	Lucy C. Teagar b. Lewis Co., Ky.	W	
10/21/1876	J. M. Thompson b. Fleming Co.	M	A	B. M. Thompson b. Mason Co., Ky.	M. E. Sousley b. Fleming Co.	W	
4/25/1876	Annie Jockey b. Fleming Co.	F	A	Jacob Jockey b. Germany	Mary Goodwin b. Ind.	W	
6/ 4/1876	T. S. Jones b. Fleming Co.	M	A	F. Jones b. Mason Co., Ky.	E. A. Jones b. Fleming Co.	Col.	
1/28/1876	b. Fleming Co.	M	A	E. R. Burns b. Bath Co., Ky.	Eliza Whaley b. Bath Co., Ky.	W	
12/19/1876	J. H. Fredrick b. Fleming Co.	M	A	John Fredrick b. Penn.	N. F. Fredrick b. Fleming Co.	W	
9/15/1876	C. A. Norton b. Fleming Co.	M	A	Wm. Norton b. Geo.	N. A. Purvis b. Fleming Co., Ky.	W	
11/10/1876	J. A. Mills b. Fleming Co.	F	A	John Mills b. Fleming Co.	Mattie E. Burke b. Nicholas Co., Ky.	W	
6/ 9/1876	J. Scruggs b. Fleming Co.	M	A	J. W. Scruggs b. Bourbon Co., Ky.	Annie Johnson b. Fleming Co.	W	
1/ 5/1876	M. Pitts b. Fleming Co.	F	A	Wm. B. Pitts b. Lewis Co., Ky.	S. H. Evans b. Fleming Co.	W	
6/27/1876	M. B. Johnson b. Fleming Co.	F	A	J. S. Johnson b. Fleming Co.	Lucy Wells b. Fleming Co.	W	
4/15/1876	E. F. Bush b. Fleming co.	F	A	M. Bush b. Fleming Co.	Francis Burres b. Fleming Co.	Col.	
4/14/1876	S. Bell b. Fleming Co.	F	A	John Bell b. Fleming Co.	Martha Hendrix b. Fleming Co.	W	
1/ 6/1876	Robert Dudley b. Fleming Co.	M	A	James B. Dudley b. Fleming Co.	Jennie Taylor b. Fleming Co.	W	
9/28/1876	Seth Andrews b. Fleming Co.	M	A	Robert D. Andrews b. Fleming Co.	Anna Thompson b. Mason Co., Ky.	W	
9/28/1876	Anna Andrews b. Fleming Co.	F	A	Robert D. Andrews b. Fleming Co.	Anna Thompson b. Mason Co., Ky.	W	
5/ 4/1876	Albin Dorsey b. Fleming Co.	M	A	E. J. Dorsey b. Fleming Co.	Fannie Lukins (Sukins) b. Mason Co., Ky.	W	

COUNTY __Fleming__

DATE	NAME OF CHILD	S	C	NAME OF FATHER	NAME OF MOTHER	CO.	RESIDENCE
4/22/1876	Mollie Markwell b. Fleming Co.	F	A	J. S. Markwell b. Fleming Co.	Paulina Graham b. Mason Co., Ky.	W	All residents Fleming Co.
4/19/1876	Charles T. Crain b. Fleming Co.	M	A	Lewis P. Crain b. Bath Co., Ky.	Amanda Foster b. Mason Co., Ky.	W	
5/19/1876	Thomas Nealis b. Fleming Co.	M	A	S. M. Nealis b. Fleming Co.	Rebecca Todd b. Mason Co., Ky.	W	
3/ 5/1876	Chas. D. Barnaby b. Fleming Co.	M	A	Elias W. Barnaby b. Fleming Co.	Emma Dillon b. Mason Co., Ky.	W	
5/ 8/1876	Narah Thomson b. Fleming Co.	M	A	Allen G. Johnson b. Fleming Co.	M. A. Havens b. Mason Co., Ky.	W	
11/18/1876	Tilden Todd b. Fleming Co.	M	A	Joseph Todd b. Fleming Co.	S. J. Harmon b. Mason Co., Ky.	W	
1/ 1/1876	J. W. Hurst b. Fleming Co.	M	A	F. H. Hurst b. Bath Co., Ky.	R. H. Pearce b. Mason Co., Ky.	W	
5/20/1876	A. D. Rankins b. Fleming Co.	M	A	J. Rankins b. Fleming Co.	Nancy Barbee b. Bath Co., Ky.	W	
7/ 5/1876	M. M. Kimberly b. Fleming Co.	F	A	Wm. C. Kimberly b. Rowan Co., Ky.	M. J. McClanahan b. Bath Co., Ky.	W	
12/13/1876	R. B. Graham b. Fleming Co.	M	A	O. K. Graham b. Fleming Co.	Mahala Emmons b. Fleming Co.	W	
5/22/1876	Mary Kelly b. Fleming Co.	F	A	J. W. Kelly b. Mason Co., Ky.	Serilda Ross b. Mo.	W	
3/ 9/1876	b. Fleming Co.	F	A	Charles Paul b. Mason Co., Ky.	M. A. Campbell b. Bath Co., Ky.	W	
10/ 2/1876	W. D. Fitch b. Fleming Co.	M	A	S. E. Fitch b. Fleming Co.	F. M. Wallingford b. Fleming Co.	W	
3/ 3/1876	E. F. Browning b. Fleming Co.	M	A	J. E. Browning b. Fleming Co.	M. E. Moss b. Fleming Co.	W	
9/10/1876	James M. Harbeson b. Fleming Co.	M	A	W. P. Harbeson b. Fleming Co.	F. B. Harris b. Mason Co., Ky.	W	
7/14/1876	A. J. McCarty b. Fleming Co.	M	A	John McCarty b. Bath Co., Ky.	Jane Pervis b. Bath Co., Ky.	W	
11/20/1876	John Breene b. Fleming Co.	M	A	Martin Breene b. Ireland	Ann Tobe b. Ireland	W	
10/ 1/1876	S. B. Griffith b. Fleming Co.	F	A	W. Griffith b. Fleming Co.	J. A. Hull b. Fleming Co.	W	
7/10/1876	Bell O'Gar b. Fleming Co.	F	A	Patrick O'Gar b. Ireland	Elizabeth Reed b. Fleming Co.	W	

COUNTY   Fleming

DATE	NAME OF CHILD	S	C	NAME OF FATHER	NAME OF MOTHER	CO.	RESIDENCE
7/10/1876		F	A	Geo. S. Kimberly	Mary McClary	W	All residents
	b. Fleming Co.			b. Ohio	b. Ohio		Fleming Co.
6/22/1876	H. Price	M	A	Wm. A. Price	Sallie Lee	W	
	b. Fleming Co.			b. Carter Co., Ky.	b. Fleming Co.		
11/ 5/1876	S. A. Rawls	F	A	Taylor Rawls	M. Patterson	Col.	
	b. Fleming Co.			b. Bath Co., Ky.	b. Fleming Co.		
8/10/1876	M. E. Harmon	F	A	J. W. Harmon	S. Currans	W	
	b. Fleming Co.			b. Carter Co., Ky.	b. Bath Co., Ky.		
12/ 1/1876	C. B. Phelps	M	A	Z. J. Phelps	M. Barksdale	W	
	b. Fleming Co.			b. Carter Co., Ky.	b. Fleming Co.		
12/25/1876	T. J. Davis	M	A	F. Davis	M. J. Mark	W	
	b. Fleming Co.			b. Fleming Co.	b. Fleming Co.		
3/ 5/1876	Lewis Markwell	M	A	Lewis Markwell	Arnethia Swim	W	
	b. Fleming Co.			b. Fleming Co.	b. Fleming Co.		
11/24/1876	A. A. Hawkins	F	A	Richard Hawkins	America Gray	W	
	b. Fleming Co.			b. Jesamine Co., Ky.	b. Fleming Co.		
5/11/1876		M	A	W. D. McKinney	E. Adams	W	
	b. Fleming Co.			b. Fleming Co.	b. Fleming Co.		
11/23/1876	J. A. Lewis	M	A	J. J. Lewis	Delila Adams	W	
	b. Fleming Co.			b. Morgan Co., Ky.	b. Fleming Co.		
4/20/1876	J. C. Coliver	M	A	Wm. Coliver	Amanda Williams	W	
	b. Fleming Co.			b. Bath Co., Ky.	b. Fleming Co.		
1/ 1/1876	W. A. Razor	M	A	John H. Razor	M. E. Johnson	W	
	b. Fleming Co.			b. Rowan Co., Ky.	b. Fleming Co.		
3/10/1876	R. D. Palmer	M	A	P. O. Palmer	S. Overley	W	
	b. Fleming Co.			b. Mason Co., Ky.	b. Fleming Co.		
2/22/1876	B. M. Vanarsdale	F	A	Isaac Vanarsdale	S. Sislebrook	W	
	b. Fleming Co.			b. Bath Co., Ky.	b. Mason Co., Ky.		
8/ 1/1876	C. R. Heddleston	F	A	R. Heddleston	J. Durant	W	
	b. Fleming Co.			b. Fleming Co., Ky.	b. Ohio		
10/10/1876	M. M. Howe	F	A	Dunlap Howe	A. C. McDowell	W	
	b. Fleming Co.			b. Fleming Co.	b. Mason Co., Ky.		
4/ 1/1876	W. S. Overley	M	A	J. H. Overley	A. J. Beckett	W	
	b. Fleming Co.			b. Fleming Co.	b. Fleming Co.		
6/14/1876	E. S. T. Rose	F	A	R. R. Rose	J. F. Bramble	W	
	b. Fleming Co.			b. Mason Co., Ky.	b. Mason Co., Ky.		
7/20/1876		M	A	S. Hopper	S. Crain	W	
	b. Fleming Co.			b. Mason Co., Ky.	b. Mason Co., Ky.		

COUNTY __Fleming__

S Sex
C Condition A-Alive D-Dead

DATE	NAME OF CHILD	S	C	NAME OF FATHER	NAME OF MOTHER	CO.	RESIDENCE
6/20/1876	T. S. Spurgeon b. Fleming Co.	M	A	M. Spurgeon b. Lewis Co., Ky.	A. J. Cox b. Fleming Co., Ky.	W	All residents Fleming Co.
10/ 5/1876	 b. Fleming Co.	F	A	Thos. Glascock b. Fleming Co.	S. Howe b. Mason Co., Ky.	W	
10/20/1876	W. C. Beckett b. Fleming Co.	M	A	W. F. Beckett b. Fleming Co.	A. Towler b. Lewis Co., Ky.	W	
9/ 7/1876	Ida B. Wilkerson b. Fleming Co.	F	A	A. Wilkerson b. Ohio	Mary J. Reeves b. Fleming Co.	W	
10/17/1876	 b. Fleming Co.	F	A	Wm. Debell b. Fleming Co.	E. S. McIntyre b. Fleming Co.	W	
7/ 4/1876	L. S. Towler b. Fleming Co.	M	A	C. A. Towler b. Bath Co., Ky.	M. Hutchison b. Pendleton Co., Ky.	W	
4/ 5/1876	Adrian Payne b. Fleming Co.	F	A	J. V. Payne b. Fleming Co.	Elizabeth Rigdon b. Fleming Co.	W	
4/20/1876	W. H. Wallingford b. Fleming Co.	M	A	T. Wallingford b. Fleming Co.	Amanda Parker b. Lewis Co., Ky.	W	
12/ 1/1876	S. Jones b. Fleming Co.	F	A	S. S. Jones b. Fleming Co.	N. Lee b. Fleming Co.	W	
9/ 5/1876	B. B. Towler b. Fleming Co.	F	A	N. Towler b. Lewis Co.	Amanda Bridges b. Fleming Co.	W	
9/20/1876	 b. Fleming Co.	F	A	A. Pollett b. Mason Co., Ky.	Annie Baird b. Mason Co., Ky.	W	
9/16/1876	John Sterrett b. Mason Co., Ky.	M	A	J. Sterrett b. Ohio	Sharlott Taylor b. Ohio	W	
6/11/1876	J. J. Jones b. Fleming Co.	M	A	W. B. Jones b. Fleming Co.	Mattie A. Cox b. Fleming Co.	W	
5/15/1876	 b. Fleming Co.	M	A	Samuel Hiver b. Fleming Co.	Priscilla D. Jones b. Fleming Co.	W	
7/13/1875	R. H. Yantis b. Fleming Co.	M	A	R. H. Yantis b. Garrett Co., Ky.	M. Howe b. Fleming Co.	W	
11/ 6/1876	 b. Fleming Co.	F	A	W. Baize b. Ohio	Hannah Shoupe b. Ohio	W	
3/ 6/1876	E. D. Humphreys b. Fleming Co.	M	A	Taylor Humphreys b. Rowan Co., Ky.	Nancy Suman b. Fleming Co.	W	
5/ 5/1876	O. S. William b. Fleming Co.	F	A	J. S. William b. Fleming Co.	E. Gilkerson b. Fleming Co.	W	
9/ 1/1876	A. M. Earles b. Fleming Co.	M	A	Rees Earles b. Rowan Co., Ky.	J. M. Ham b. Va.	W	

S Sex
C Condition A-Alive D-Dead

COUNTY Fleming

DATE	NAME OF CHILD	S	C	NAME OF FATHER	NAME OF MOTHER	CO.	RESIDENCE
10/ 2/1876	H. E. Hurst b. Fleming Co.	F	A	John Hurst b. Fleming Co.	E. Humphreys b. Fleming Co.	W	All residents Fleming Co.
8/ 7/1876	Elizabeth Doyle b. Fleming Co.	F	A	Miles Doyle b. Fleming Co.	Edith Ross b. Fleming Co.	W	
6/ 6/1876	J. D. Gooding b. Fleming Co.	M	A	Nelson Gooding b. Fleming Co.	Maggie Hickerson b. Fleming Co.	W	
2/19/1876	John Raftery b. Fleming Co.	M	A	Dan Raftery b. Ireland	H. McDuavid b. Ireland	W	
8/27/1876	Edwin Giuty b. Ohio	M	A	Charles Guity b. Canada	A. Daugherty b. Ireland	W	
10/27/1876	D. W. McDonald b. Fleming Co.	M	A	J. E. McDonald b. Ohio	Alice Dixon b. Fleming Co.	W	
10/23/1876	M. D. Calrke b. Fleming Co.	F	A	Elias Clarke b. Mason Co., Ky.	Annie B. Ratcliffe b. Bourbon Co., Ky.	W	
1/29/1876	Mattie Johnson b. Fleming Co.	F	A		Lucy Johnson b. Fleming Co.	B	
6/26/1876	A. S. Caywood b. Fleming Co.	F	A	T. A. Caywood b. Fleming Co.	S. E. Hamilton b. Ind.	W	
1/ 7/1876	J. W. Powell b. Fleming Co.	M	A	A. M. Powell b. Fleming Co.	Phoebe Williams b. Mason Co., Ky.	W	
10/ 5/1876	Druzilla Lyons b. Fleming Co.	F	A	J. W. Lyons b. Fleming Co.	Elizabeth Clyne b. Fleming Co.	W	
2/15/1876	M. S. Atchison b. Fleming Co.	F	A	J. H. Atchison b. Rowan Co., Ky.	N. M. Porter b. Nicholas Co., Ky.	W	
1/14/1875	W. S. Towler b. Fleming Co.	M	A	A. S. Towler b. Va.	S. C. Cullipp b. Wt. Va.	W	
6/22/1876	J. M. Siuthercom b. Fleming Co.	M	A	W. T. Suithercom b. Ill.	Emma Clarke b. Nicholas Co., Ky.	W	
4/27/1876	C. E. Dotson b. Fleming Co.	F	A	J. W. Dotson b. Mason Co., Ky.	Mary Seever b. Fleming Co.	W	
8/21/1876	b. Fleming Co.	M	A	Wm. M. Cord b. Fleming Co.	E. J. Thomas b. Fleming Co.	W	
10/15/1876	Foster McCarty b. Fleming Co.	M	A	Alexander McCarty b. Fleming Co.	Miriam Warren b. Rowan Co., Ky.	W	
3/23/1876	F. V. Walker b. Fleming Co.	M	A	W. H. Walker b. Fleming Co.	E. A. Bradley b. Nicholas Co., Ky.	W	
4/19/1876	J. H. Thompson b. Fleming Co.	M	A	James Thompson b. N.Y.	E. H. Young b. Fleming Co.	W	

DATE	NAME OF CHILD	S	C	NAME OF FATHER	NAME OF MOTHER	CO.	RESIDENCE
1/31/1876	John T. Kackler b. Fleming Co.	M	A	John Kackler b. Germany	Mary McMann b. Ireland	W	All residents Fleming Co.
2/26/1876	B. P. Runyon b. Fleming Co.	F	A	John Runyon b. Mason Co., Ky.	C. Z. Davis b. Mason Co., Ky.	W	
4/15/1876	O. S. Arasmith b. Fleming Co.	F	A		Rachael Arasmith b. Bath Co., Ky.	W	
3/14/1876	M. S. Downey b. Fleming Co.	F	A	Richard Downey b. Fleming Co.	Eliza Foang b. Fleming Co.	W	
1/10/1876	Maud R. Cox b. Fleming Co.	F	A	William Cox b. Va.	R. C. Armstrong b. Va.	W	
12/10/1876	E. S. Moody b. Fleming Co.	M	A	J. W. Moody b. Bath Co., Ky.	S. R. Phelps b. Fleming Co.	W	
9/28/1876	O. A. Seever b. Fleming Co.	F	A	J. F. Seever b. Fleming Co.	D. J. Rankins b. Fleming Co.	W	
8/22/1876		M	A	Alfred Fawns	E. A. Humphreys	W	
8/22/1876	b. Fleming Co.	M	A	Alfred Fawns b. Fleming Co.	E. A. Humphreys b. Fleming Co.	W	
9/ 7/1876	E. E. Evans b. Fleming Co.	F	A	J. M. Evans b. Fleming Co.	Cordelia Pointer b. Fleming Co.	W	
4/11/1876	W. O. White b. Fleming Co.	F	A	R. White b. Penn.	Myrtle Rogers b. Bath Co., Ky.	W	
11/21/1876	Alma Littleton b. Fleming Co.	F	A	D. S. Littleton b. Lewis Co., Ky.	Eliza Muse b. Fleming Co.	W	
11/ 6/1876	Morris Evans	M	A	Franklin Evans	M. E. Hinton	W	
11/ 6/1876	Marion Evans b. Fleming Co.	M	A	Franklin Evans b. Fleming Co.	M. E. Hinton b. Kansas	W	
3/24/1876	Edgar Sykes b. Fleming Co.	M	A	D. F. Sykes b. Fleming Co.	J. F. Littleton b. Lewis Co., Ky.	W	
10/ 8/1876	O. L. Plummer b. Fleming Co.	F	A	J. S. Plummer b. Fleming Co.	S. S. Humphreys b. Fleming Co.	W	
9/22/1876	David Morrison b. Fleming Co.	M	A	W. H. Morrison b. Fleming Co.	Louisa Johnson b. Carter Co., Ky.	W	
11/21/1876	C. H. Marshall b. Fleming Co.	M	A	J. W. Marshall b. Grant Co., Ky.	Mary Porter b. Campbell Co., Ky.	W	
5/12/1876	Ann King b. Fleming Co.	F	A	J. W. King b. Harrison Co., Ky.	E. J. Wagenor b. Pendleton Co., Ky.	W	
6/17/1876	J. F. Spradling b. Fleming Co.	F	A	Henry Spradling b. Floyd Co., Ky.	Matilda Humphreys b. Fleming Co.	W	

COUNTY Fleming

Sex
C Condition A-Alive D-Dead

DATE	NAME OF CHILD	S	C	NAME OF FATHER	NAME OF MOTHER	CO.	RESIDENCE
10/22/1876	M. C. Petty	M	A	Mathew M. Petty	A. C. Saye	W	All residents
	b. Fleming Co.			b. W. Va.	b. W. Va.		Fleming Co.
7/25/1876	J. H. Ham	M	A	Wesley Ham	Amanda McKee	W	
	b. Fleming Co.			b. Rowan Co., Ky.	b. Fleming Co.		
5/16/1876	Hiram Stamper	M	A	William Stamper	Sarah Bar	W	
	b. Fleming Co.			b. Nich. Co., Ky.	b. Carter Co., Ky.		
11/30/1876	E. B. Jones	F	A	T. J. Jones	Hester White	W	
	b. Fleming Co.			b. Fleming Co.	b. Rowan Co., Ky.		
9/ 3/1876	C. H. Nudigate	M	A	Robert Nudigate	Nancy Reeve	W	
	b. Fleming Co.			b. Fleming Co.	b. McGoffin Co., Ky.		
2/29/1876	J. N. Williams	M	A	Miles Williams	S. P. Simon	W	
	b. Fleming Co.			b. Mason Co., Ky.	b. Floyd Co., Ky.		
12/31/1876	W. E. Saunders	M	A	C. T. Saunders	M. J. Plummer	W	
	b. Fleming Co.			b. Fleming Co.	b. Fleming Co.		
1/27/1876	W. J. Gulley	M	A	John Gulley	M. J. Duley	W	
	b. Fleming Co.			b. Fleming Co.	b. Ohio		
9/10/1876	A. J. Gooding	M	A	Wesley Gooding	M. E. Carpenter	W	
	b. Fleming Co.			b. Fleming Co.	b. Fleming Co.		
12/ 6/1876	M. T. Ingram	F	A	J. Ingram	S. E. Nealis	W	
	b. Flmeing Co.			b. Bath Co., Ky.	b. Flemihg Co., Ky.		
1/25/1876	C. B. Hammond	M	A	J. S. Hammond	V. M. Stewart	W	
	b. Fleming Co.			b. Fleming Co.	b. Fleming Co.		
3/ 1/1876	M. J. Selby	F	A	James Selby	Louella Day	W	
	b. Fleming Co.			b. Fleming Co.	b. Ind.		
6/ 9/1876	M. A. Perkins	F	A	Isaac Perkins	M. A. Eden	W	
	b. Fleming Co.			b. Fleming Co.	b. Fleming Co.		
4/13/1876	M. F. Saunders	F	A	A. D. Saunders	E. A. Yazel	W	
	b. Fleming Co.			b. Fleming Co.	b. Nich. Co., Ky.		
4/13/1876	F. S. Evans	M	A	J. S. Evans	E. Story	W	
	b. Fleming Co.			b. Rowan Co., Ky.	b. Fleming Co., Ky.		
6/11/1876	J. F. Bradley	M	A	W. A. Bradley	Emily Havens	W	
	b. Fleming Co.			b. Bourbon Co., Ky.	b. Fleming Co.		
5/16/1876	M. M. Ham	F	A	James Ham	Sarah Kissick	W	
	b. Fleming Co.			b. Lewis Co., Ky.	b. Fleming Co.		
3/29/1876	M. A. Denton	M	A	O. B. Denton	Seran Newman	W	
	b. Fleming Co.			b. Fleming Co.	b. Fleming Co.		
5/ 8/1876	M. Newman	F	A	Simpson R. Newman	Victoria Taber	W	
	b. Fleming Co.			b. Fleming Co.	b. Fleming Co.		

COUNTY <u>Fleming</u>

S Sex
C Condition A-Alive D-Dead

DATE	NAME OF CHILD	S	C	NAME OF FATHER	NAME OF MOTHER	CO.	RESIDENCE
5/10/1876	b. Fleming Co.	M	A	Joseph Crawford b. Fleming Co.	R. A. Pearce b. Fleming Co.	W	All residents Fleming Co.
1/ 1/1876	John Crawford b. Fleming Co.	M	A	Joab Crawford b. Fleming Co.	Elizabeth Claypoole b. Fleming Co.	W	
6/ 4/1876	Robert Moore b. Fleming Co.	M	A	Elisha Moore b. Va.	Nancy Hayden b. Fleming Co.	W	
1/ 1/1876	T. R. Richards b. Fleming Co.	M	A	E. W. Richards b. Bath Co., Ky.	M. R. Kinbro b. Nicholas Co., Ky.	W	
12/ 1/1878	George W. Peck b. Fleming Co.	M	A	George Peck b. Fleming Co.	Rbecca Burgess b. Fleming Co.	W	
11/ 7/1878	Wallace Sapp b. Fleming Co.	M	A	William Sapp b. Fleming Co.	Susan Hull b. Montgomery Co., Ky.	W	
12/ 4/1878	Charles M. Planck b. Fleming Co.	M	A	William Planck b. Fleming Co.	Sarah Hull b. Fleming Co.	W	
5/27/1878	Elizabeth M. Willis b. Fleming Co.	F	A	Columbus Willis b. Indiana	Julia Peck b. Fleming Co.	W	
10/ 6/1878	Mary C. Dunn b. Fleming Co.	F	A	John Dunn b. Fleming Co.	Caroline McClane b. Fleming Co.	W	
1/21/1878	Mary E. Dillon b. Fleming Co.	F	A	William Dillon b. Fleming Co.	Margaret Saunders b. Fleming Co.	W	
12/ 2/1878	John W. Ishmael b. Fleming Co.	M	A	John T. Ishmael b. Fleming Co.	Louisa E. Geose b. Fleming Co.	W	
5/30/1878	John S. Watson b. Fleming Co.	M	A	David Watson b. Fleming Co.	Caroline Duley b. Bath Co., Ky.	W	
2/ /1878	Lizzie Brown b. Fleming Co.	F	A	Lewis Brown b. Bath Co., Ky.	Matilda Bailey b. Mason Co., Ky.	B	
10/18/1878	Joseph P. Moran b. Fleming Co.	M	A	John Moran b. Fleming Co.	Cynthia Vice b. Bath Co., Ky.	W	
11/ /1878	Thomas H. Hopkins b. Fleming Co.	M	A	Thomas Hopkins b. Fleming Co.	Catherine Moran b. Fleming Co.	W	
3/26/1878	Andrew W. Lawson b. Fleming Co.	M	A	James Lawson b. Fleming Co.	Elizabeth Pickerell b. Fleming Co.	W	
9/14/1878	Annie Pearce b. Fleming Co.	F	A	Edward E. Pearce b. Fleming Co.	Annie Clark b.Mason Co., Ky.	W	
11/ 1/1878	James W. McDonald b. Fleming Co.	M	A	George W. McDonald b. Fleming Co.	Mary Powell b. Mason Co., Ky.	W	
8/15/1878	Louisa E. Payne b. Fleming Co.	M	A	Henry Payne b. Fleming Co.	Amelia McCall b. Mason Co., Ky.	W	

COUNTY Fleming

DATE	NAME OF CHILD	S	C	NAME OF FATHER	NAME OF MOTHER	CO.	RESIDENCE
1/ 1/1878	Robert Yantis b. Fleming Co.	M	A	Robert Yantis b. Ganard Co., Ky.	Mary Howe b. Mason Co., Ky.	W	All residents Fleming Co.
3/ /1878	Francis Calvert b. Fleming Co.	F	A	Burgess Calvert b. Rowan Co., Ky.	Miss Jackson b. Rowan Co., Ky.	W	
1/ 3/1878	Mary Y. Parker b. Fleming Co.	F	A	William Parker b. Fleming Co.	Malissa Emmons b. Fleming Co.	M	
2/26/1878	Octava Barnes b. Christian Co., Ky.	F	A	Cambridge C. Barnes b. Greenup Co., Ky.	Francis E. Hawkins b. Bath Co., Ky.	W	
1/14/1878	Lizzie McRoberts b. Fleming Co.	F	A	Weeks McRoberts b. Rowan Co., Ky.	Maranda Doyle b. Fleming Co., Ky.	W	
4/28/1878	Annie M. Hurst b. Fleming Co.	F	A	Daniel W. Hurst b. Fleming Co.	Fannie M. Staggs b. Fleming Co.	W	
4/ 9/1878	Robert M. Carpenter b. Fleming Co.	M	A	Richard Carpenter b. Fleming Co.	Amelia C. Hinton b. Fleming Co.	W	
4/ 6/1878	William G. Carpenter b. Fleming Co.	M	A	Charles Carpenter b. Fleming Co.	Rachael Jones b. Fleming Co.	W	
4/ 8/1878	Joseph Jones b. Fleming Co.	M	A	Joseph Jones b. Fleming Co.	Bell Plummer b. Lewis Co.	W	
4/10/1878	Benjamin Lucas b. Fleming Co.	M	A	G. B. Lucas b. Grant Co., Ky.	Margaret Jones b. Fleming Co.	W	
8/17/1878	Not named b. Fleming Co.	M	A	Thomas Jones b. Fleming Co.	Hester White b. Fleming Co.	W	
5/30/1878	Sarah M. Plummer b. Fleming Co.	F	A	Jeremiah Plummer b. Lewis Co., Ky.	Mary Martin b. Lewis Co., Ky.	W	
4/20/1878	James K. Cottingham b. Fleming Co.	M	A	James Cottingham b. Nicholas Co., Ky.	Mary Glascock b. Nicholas Co., Ky.	W	
5/17/1878	Berta A. Stidman b. Fleming Co.	F	A	James Stidman b. Wolf Co., Ky.	Bethsaba Bear b. Caster Co., Ky.	W	
3/ 6/1878	Minnie C. Hinton b. Fleming Co.	F	A	Squire Hinton b. Fleming Co.	Emma Carpenter b. Fleming Co.	W	
12/22/1878	Jessie Gooding b. Fleming Co.	M	A	Andrew Gooding b. Fleming Co.	Elizabeth Hickerson b. Fleming Co.	W	
7/11/1878	Not named b. Fleming Co.	M	D	Jacob Davis b. Ohio	Catherine Jones b. Harrison Co., Ky.	W	
7/12/1878	Not named b. Fleming Co.	F	D	Jacob Davis b. Ohio	Catherine Jones b. Harrison Co., Ky.	W	
11/ 5/1878	Jaley Thacker b. Fleming Co.	F	A	Abraham Thacker b. Laurel Co., Ky.	Barba S. Ham b. Fleming Co.	W	

S Sex
C Condition A-Alive D-Dead

COUNTY __Fleming__

DATE	NAME OF CHILD	S	C	NAME OF FATHER	NAME OF MOTHER	CO.	RESIDENCE
11/ 8/1878	Cynthia Y. Hurst b. Fleming Co.	F	A	Joseph Hurst b. Fleming Co.	Maggie G. Jones b. Fleming Co.	W	All residents Fleming Co.
8/22/1878	Fannie A. Ross b. Fleming Co.	F	A	George S. Ross b. Fleming Co.	Elizabeth Gooding b. Fleming Co.	W	
5/ 8/1878	Bailey Staggs b. Fleming Co.	M	A	Charles Staggs b. Fleming Co.	Nannie Williams b. Fleming Co.	W	
7/ 8/1878	Lauria B. Parker b. Fleming Co.	F	A	Shelton Parker b. Laurel Co., Ky.	Elizabeth Hartley b. Fleming Co.	W	
7/10/1878	William B. Jones b. Fleming Co.	M	A	James Jones b. Fleming Co.	Sarah F. Thompson b. Virginia	W	
9/18/1878	Charles S. McIntyre b. Fleming Co.	M	A	David McIntyre Fleming Co.	Eliza Reeves b. Fleming Co.	W	
12/21/1878	Bertha E. McIntyre b. Fleming Co.	F	A	Samuel McIntyre b. Fleming Co.	Mary C. Reeves b. Fleming Co.	W	
12/22/1878	Evaline Hammonds b. Fleming Co.	F	A	Samuel Hammonds b. Fleming Co.	Martha Hinton b. Fleming Co.	W	
10/ 6/1878	Nelson Hurst b. Fleming Co.	M	A	James Hurst b. Fleming Co.	Sarah Humphreys b. Fleming Co.	W	
2/27/1878	James M. May b. Fleming Co.	M	A	John H. May b. Pike Co., Ky.	Minerva Justis b. Floyd Co., Ky.	W	
10/13/1878	Miranda Cooney b. Fleming Co., Illegitimate	F	A	Joseph Cooney b. unknown	Jennie Story b. Fleming Co.	M	
10/ 2/1878	Elizabeth B. Todd b. Fleming Co.	F	A	William Todd b. Fleming Co.	Edna Crawford b. Fleming Co.	W	
12/15/1878	Lydia B. Denton b. Fleming Co.	F	A	Ed Denton b. Bath Co., Ky.	Sarah Crain b. Bath Co., Ky.	W	
3/ 9/1878	Michael Emmett b. Fleming Co., Illegitimate	M	A	Michael Hines b. Ireland	Minerva McClerg b. Rowan Co., Ky.	W	
11/21/1878	Adda L. Dailey b. Fleming Co.	F	A	Milton Dailey b. Bracken Co., Ky.	Ludie V. Moreland b. Bracken Co., Ky.	W	
3/26/1878	Emmett Payne b. Fleming Co.	M	A	Edwin Payne b. Fleming Co.	Elizabeth Graham b. Fleming Co.	W	
2/14/1878	John Deering b. Fleming Co.	M	A	William Deering b. Fleming Co.	Malvina Kirk b. Fleming Co.	W	
9/14/1878	Robert B. Moore b. Fleming Co.	M	A	John Moore b. Fleming Co.	Rebecca Helvestine b. Fleming Co.	W	
12/25/1878	Clarance Kimberly b. Fleming Co.	M	A	George Kimberly b. Ohio	Nancy McCoy b. Ohio	W	

COUNTY Fleming

S Sex
C Condition A-Alive D-Dead

DATE	NAME OF CHILD	S	C	NAME OF FATHER	NAME OF MOTHER	CO.	RESIDENCE
4/ /1878	Josie Briges b. Fleming Co.	F	A	John Budges (Bridges?) b. Fleming Co.	Elizabeth Harrison b. Fleming Co.	M	All residents Fleming Co.
12/20/1878	Eddie Madden b. Fleming Co.	M	A	Squire Madden b. Fleming Co.	Mary J. Elliott b. Fleming Co.	M	
11/ 1/1878	William B. Hopkins b. Fleming Co.	M	A	Marion Hopkins b. Fleming Co.	Maggie Edon b. Fleming Co.	W	
11/20/1878	Howard G. Pumphrey b. Fleming Co.	M	A	Thomas L. Pumphrey b. Maryland	Ella B. Dudley b. Fleming Co.	W	
9/24/1878	Atta B. White b. Fleming Co.,(Illegitimate)	F	A	unknown b. unknown	Eliza White b. Fleming Co.	M	
3/16/1878	Not named	M	A	James White	Ada Fletcher	M	
3/16/1878	Not named b. Fleming Co.	M	A	James White b. Fleming Co.	Ada Fletcher b. Fleming Co.	M	(twins)
3/ 9/1878	James O. Williams b. Fleming Co.	M	A	John Williams b. Fleming Co.	Mary Overley b. Fleming Co.	W	
4/ 2/1878	Emma Belt b. Fleming Co.	F	A	William S. Belt b. Fleming Co.	Helen Hall b. Fleming Co.	W	
5/24/1878	Aaron E. Fletcher b. Fleming Co.	M	A	Thomas Fletcher b. Fleming Co.	Lizzie Parker b. Fleming Co.	M	
8/20/1878	William Hussey b. Fleming Co.	M	A	Thomas Hussay b. Ireland	Ellen Scary b. Ireland	W	
10/ /1878	Not named b. Fleming Co.	M	D	Hiram Jones b. Ill.	Mary E. Hopper b. Mason Co., Ky.	W	
4/18/1878	Maggie B. Doyle b. Fleming Co.	F	A	Thomas Doyle b. Fleming Co.	Amelia Walker b. Fleming Co.	W	
1/21/1878	Estella Strode b. Fleming Co.	F	A	Luther Strode b. Fleming Co.	Nancy M. Boyd b. Campbell Co., Ky.	W	
12/16/1878	Albertie Coryell b. Fleming Co.	F	A	William O. Coryell b. Mason Co., Ky.	Nannie B. Elston b. Fleming Co.	W	
11/15/1878	Harrison W. Ross b. Fleming Co.	M	A	James Ross b. Mason Co., Ky.	Mattie Williams b. Fleming Co.	W	
12/10/1878	William M. Wallingford b. Fleming Co.	M	A	Valentine B. Wallingford b. Fleming Co.	Miranda Tune b. Nicholas Co., Ky.	W	
10/18/1878	Mariel W. Siter b. Fleming Co.	F	A	William Siter b. Bourbon Co., Ky.	Mary Wells b. Fleming Co.	W	
6/27/1878	Lulie Fitch b. Texas	F	A	Salathiel Fitch b. Fleming Co.	Fannie M. Wallingford b. Fleming Co.	W	

COUNTY Fleming

S Sex
C Condition A-Alive D-Dead

DATE	NAME OF CHILD	S	C	NAME OF FATHER	NAME OF MOTHER	CO.	RESIDENCE
6/30/1878	Mary A. Taylor	F	A	John Taylor	Elizabeth Smith	B	All residents
	b. Fleming Co.			b. Fleming Co.	b. Mason Co., Ky.		Fleming Co.
6/27/1878	Ollie Wren	M	A	Samuel Wren	Matilda Jones		
	b. Fleming Co.			b. Bath Co., Ky.	b. Bath Co., Ky.		
12/ /1878	Not named	F	A	Alber Ralls	Lizzie Sousley	B	
	b. Fleming Co.			b. Fleming Co.	b. Fleming Co.		
4/17/1878	Peter Green	M	A	Peter Green	Amanda Lawfton	B	
	b. Fleming Co.			b. Fleming Co.	b. Fleming Co.		
6/30/1878	Alberta Elliott	M	A	unknown	Caroline Elliott	M	
	b. Fleming Co. (Illegitimate)			b. unknown	b. Fleming Co.		
9/15/1878	Benjamin Taylor	M	A	Robert Taylor	Martha A. Harn (Ham?)	W	
9/15/1878	James Taylor	M	A	Robert Taylor	Martha A. Harn (Ham?)	W	(twins)
	b. Fleming Co.			b. Fleming Co.	b. Lewis Co., Ky.		
2/17/1878	Mary Vanarsdale	F	A	Isaac Vanarsdall	Laurea Sashbrook	W	
	b. Fleming Co.			b. Bath Co., Ky.	b. Mason Co., Ky.		
4/21/1878	Fannie A. Andrews	F	A	Thomas S. Andrews	Bettie Botts	W	
	b. Fleming Co.			b. Fleming Co.	b. Fleming Co.		
11/12/1878	Not named	F	A	David M. Vansant	S. F. Amos	W	
	b. Fleming Co.			b. Fleming Co.	b. Bath Co., Ky.		
11/ 1/1878	John S. Lightfoot	M	A	Robert A. Lightfoot	Sarah E. Stockwell	W	
	b. Fleming Co.			b. Fleming Co.	b. Fleming Co.		
11/20/1878	Emily Moore	F	A	Wesley Moore	Martha Doyle	W	
	b. Fleming Co.			b. Fleming Co.	b. Fleming Co.		
12/22/1878	Minerva Owens	F	A	A. R. Owens	Bell Jordan	W	
	b. Fleming Co.			b. Fleming Co.	b. Fleming Co.		
8/10/1878	Joseph H. Harbeson	M	A	William Harbeson	Julia Harris	W	
	b. Fleming Co.			b. Fleming Co.	b. Ohio		
11/24/1878	John Fee	M	A	John Fee	Fannie Combs	B	
	b. Fleming Co.			b. unknown	b. Mason Co.		
2/ /1878	Frank Taylor	M	A	Frank Taylor	Lydia Flinn	B	
	b. Fleming Co.			b. Fleming Co.	b. Fleming Co.		
12/ 1/1878	Nina Tibbs	F	A	Francis Tibbs	Ellen Taylor	B	
	b. Fleming Co.			b. Fleming Co.	b. Fleming Co.		
8/21/1878	Emaline Harrison	F	A	William Harrison	Maggie McNelly	W	
	b. Fleming Co.			b. Delaware	b. Delaware		
7/27/1878	Amanda Coleman	F	A	Eliha Coleman	Millie Shepherd	B	
	b. Fleming Co.			b. unknown	b. Fleming Co.		
	Re. Illegitimate						

121

DATE	NAME OF CHILD	S	C	NAME OF FATHER	NAME OF MOTHER	CO.	RESIDENCE
8/ 6/1878	Margaret Lyons b. Fleming Co.	F	A	Michael Lyons b. Ireland	Kate Brauch b. Minn.	W	All residents Fleming Co.
9/26/1878	Earnest Hall b. Fleming Co.	M	A	Thomas R. Hall b. Fleming Co.	Lucinda Moran b. Fleming Co.	W	
3/12/1878	Elizabeth Dudley b. Fleming Co.	F	A	William Dudley b. Nicholas Co., Ky.	Elizabeth Jacobs b. Mason Co., Ky.	W	
4/10/1878	Margaret Conden b. Fleming Co.	F	A	Bartholomew Conden b. Ireland	Annie Mackey b. Ireland	W	
12/14/1878	Julia B. Warren b. Fleming Co.	F	A	William H. Warren b. Rowan Co., Ky.	Amy Griffith b. Fleming Co.	W	
3/ 2/1878	Paul Heflin b. Fleming Co.	M	A	John Heflin b. Virginia	Mildred Robinson b. Montgomery Co., Ky.	W	
4/ 7/1878	Not named b. Fleming Co.	M	D	John Razor b. Bath Co., Ky.	Clara Lancaster b. Boone Co., Ky.	W	
4/ 8/1878	Mary V. Thompson b. Fleming Co.	F	A	Thomas Thompson b. Virginia	Martha Click b. Bath Co., Ky.	W	
3/23/1878	Eliza B. Gorman b. Fleming Co.	F	A	Archibald Gorman b. Penn.	Eliza Gorman b. Nicholas Co., Ky.	W	
1/ 30/1878	Joseph M. Bristow b. Fleming Co.	M	A	Andrew Bristow b. Bath Co., Ky.	America Hinton b. Fleming Co.	W	
11/ /1878	Motie Boyd b. Fleming Co.	F	A	Rees Boyd b. Fleming Co.	Bertha Crain b. Fleming Co.	B	
3/ 5/1878	Emma Story b. Fleming Co.	F	A	William Story b. Fleming Co.	Mary Stewart b. Fleming Co.	W	
6/12/1878	Birdie F. Ham b. Fleming Co.	F	A	Joseph Ham b. Lewis Co., Ky.	Mary Pearce b. Fleming Co.	W	
1/ 5/1878	William R. Fondray b. Fleming Co.	M	A	George W. Fondray b. Fleming Co.	California Dillon b. Fleming Co.	W	
8/17/1878	Georgie M. Arnold b. Fleming Co.	F	A	George Arnold b. Fleming Co.	Mary Emmons b. Bath Co., Ky.	W	
10/29/1878	Murtle Tubby b. Fleming Co.	F	A	Samuel Tubby b. Fleming Co.	Louisa Hamrick b. Fleming Co.	W	
12/20/1878	Minnie Daugherty b. Fleming Co.	F	A	James Daugherty b. Bath Co., Ky.	Fenton Emmons b. Bath Co., Ky.	W	
2/16/1878	Lucy E. Plauck b. Fleming Co.	F	A	Jacob Plauck b. Fleming Co.	Minnie Emmons b. Bath Co., Ky.	W	
12/24/1878	James M. Moren b. Fleming Co.	M	A	Daniel B. Moren b. Fleming Co.	Geneva Emmons b. Bath Co., Ky.	W	

COUNTY Fleming

S Sex
C Condition A-Alive D-Dead

DATE	NAME OF CHILD	S	C	NAME OF FATHER	NAME OF MOTHER	CO.	RESIDENCE
11/21/1878	James M. Watson b. Fleming Co.	M	A	Charles M. Watson b. Fleming Co.	Henrietta Call b. Bath Co., Ky.	W	All residents Fleming Co.
2/26/1878	Emery Caywood b. Fleming Co.	M	A	William Caywood b. Fleming Co.	Lucy Prater b. Fleming Co.	W	
12/16/1878	Lucy F. Collins b. Fleming Co.	F	A	John E. Collins b. Fleming Co.	Ruth Mullikin b. Nicholas Co., Ky.	W	
11/ 7/1878	Ida B. Ishmael b. Fleming Co.	F	A	Samuel Ishmael b. Nicholas Co., Ky.	Lydia A. Johnson b. Fleming Co.	W	
9/25/1878	Clauda A. Johnson b. Fleming Co.	F	A	John Johnson b. North Carolina	Martha Cochran b. Fleming Co.	W	
7/12/1878	Charles M. Eubanks b. Fleming Co.	M	A	William Eubanks b. Fleming Co.	Louisa Seet (Leet?) b. Fleming Co.	W	
9/22/1878	James C. Grimes b. Fleming Co.	M	A	Jerry Grimes b. Nicholas Co., Ky.	Jennie Cassidy b. Fleming Co.	W	
1/30/1878	Nannie Payne b. Fleming Co.	F	A	James Payne b. Fleming Co.	Rachael Cartwell b. Bath Co., Ky.	W	
8/ /1878	Eddie D. Payne b. Fleming Co.	M	A	William Payne b. Fleming Co.	Mary E. Thomas b. Fleming Co.	W	
5/ 4/1878	Miles B. McCormick b. Fleming Co.	M	A	William F. McCormick b. unknown	Mary E. Boyd b. Indiana	W	
2/ /1878	Not named b. Fleming Co.	F	A	Perry Jones b. Fleming Co.	Lucy Dent b. Fleming Co.	B	
3/16/1878	Leslie Bush b. Fleming Co., Illegitimate	M	A		Susana Bush b. Fleming Co.	B	
12/25/1878	Not named b. Fleming Co.	M	A	William H. Leet b. Fleming Co.	Hannan Hughbanks b. Nicholas Co., Ky.	W	
12/14/1878	Not named b. Fleming Co.	M	A	Bazel Britey b. Lewis Co., Ky.	Lydia Fredrick b. Lewis Co., Ky.	W	
4/13/1878	William H. Bryant b. Fleming Co.	M	A	John J. Bryant b. Fleming Co.	Amanda Hunter b. Fleming Co.	W	
5/ 2/1878	Frank Parker b. Fleming Co.	M	A	Frank Parker b. Bourbon Co., Ky.	Nancy Madison b. Bourbon Co., Ky.	M	
5/11/1878	John Scruggs b. Fleming Co.	M	A	Samuel P. Scruggs b. Bourbon Co., Ky.	Emma Johnson b. Fleming Co.	W	
3/ 7/1878	Rebecca E. Johnson b. Fleming Co.	F	A	James Johnson b. Fleming Co.	Josephine Flora b. Mason Co., Ky.	W	
7/ /1878	Emma Scruggs b. Fleming Co.	F	A	John Scruggs b. Bourbon Co., Ky.	Annie Johnson b. Fleming Co.	W	

COUNTY   Fleming

DATE	NAME OF CHILD	S	C	NAME OF FATHER	NAME OF MOTHER	CO.	RESIDENCE
6/10/1878	Henrietta W. Hildreth b. Fleming Co.	F	A	Robert Hildreth b. Nicholas Co., Ky.	Cassandre Campbell b. Mason Co., Ky.	W	All residents Fleming Co.
5/ 1/1878	Stella M. Smart b. Fleming Co.	F	A	Granville Swart b. Fleming Co.	Katie Cogan b. Mason Co., Ky.	W	
10/ 8/1878	Fredrick H. Kackler b. Fleming Co.	M	A	John Kackler b. Germany	Mollie McMahon b. Ireland	W	
6/ 2/1878	Robert M. Sherwood b. Fleming Co.	M	A	William Sherwood b. Fleming Co.	Laura Hughes b. Nicholas Co., Ky.	W	
4/24/1878	Oscar W. Johnson b. Fleming Co.	M	A	John Johnson b. Fleming Co.	Lucy Wells b. Fleming Co.	W	
4/23/1878	Yancy E. McCord b. Fleming Co.	M	A	James McCord b. Fleming Co.	Mary McCarty b. Fleming Co.	W	
4/12/1878	Pearly J. Stephens b. Fleming Co.	F	A	Richard Stephens b. Bath Co., Ky.	Sarah Flora b. Nicholas Co., Ky.	W	
3/ 4/1878	Ida Flora b. Fleming Co.	F	A	John Flora b. Lewis Co., Ky.	Malica Riggs b. Ohio	W	
10/20/1878	Not named b. Fleming Co.	F	A	John W. Dotson b. Mason Co., Ky	Mary Seever b. Fleming Co.	W	
1/23/1878	Clary B. Fisher b. Fleming Co.		A	Lewis Fisher b. Mason Co., Ky.	Sarah E. Fredrick b. Mason Co., Ky.	W	
6/25/1878	Effie Nolin b. Fleming Co.	F	A	William W. Nolin b. Mason Co., Ky.	Jane Sousley b. Fleming Co.	W	
8/15/1878	W. C. Graves b. Fleming Co.	M	A	Joseph A. Graves b. Fleming Co.	Sallie Aubrey b. Fayette Co., Ky.	W	
8/ 1/1878	Perry J. Thomas b. Fleming Co.	M	A	George W. Thomas b. Fleming Co.	Cynthia McClaus b. Mason Co., Ky.	W	
11/ 9/1878	Reuben Hawin b. Fleming Co.	M	A	John Hawin b. Virginia	Mary J. Dixon b. Fleming Co.	W	
9/29/1878	Carrie W. Graves b. Fleming Co.	F	A	William H. Graves b. Mason Co., Ky.	Caroline Swart b. Nicholas Co., Ky.	W	
7/ /1878	Mattie C. Courtney b. Fleming Co.	F	A	George L. Courtney b. Fleming Co.	Emerine McCarty b. Fleming Co.	W	
12/ 7/1878	Edward Cummins b. Mason Co., Ky.	M	A	Edward Cummins b. unknown	Mary E. Shields b. Nicholas Co., Ky.	W	
8/13/1878	Susie L. Courtney b. Fleming Co.	F	A	William Courtney b. Fleming Co.	Laura B. Dye b. Mason Co., Ky.	W	
12/13/1878	Susan S. Cord b. Fleming Co.	F	A	Leander G. Cord b. Fleming Co.	Susan Stockdale b. Fleming Co.	W	

COUNTY Fleming

S Sex
C Condition A-Alive D-Dead

DATE	NAME OF CHILD	S	C	NAME OF FATHER	NAME OF MOTHER	CO.	RESIDENCE
2/17/1878	James McRoberts b. Fleming Co.	M	A	Asa McRoberts b. Rowan Co., Ky.	Lucy E. Pepper b. Fleming Co.	W	All residents Fleming Co.
2/17/1878	Lida Frank b. Fleming Co.	F	A	Joseph Frank b. Mason Co., Ky.	Sallie Darnall b. Fleming Co.	W	
2/10/1878	Nellie B. Johnson b. Fleming Co.	F	A	Joseph Johnson b. Fleming Co.	Mollie Estill b. Bourbon Co., Ky.	W	
4/18/1878	Leslie B. Keel b. Fleming Co.	M	A	Leander C. Keel b. Fleming Co.	Mary Wheeler b. Mason Co., Ky.	W	
3/ /1878	Lula Daugherty b. Fleming Co. (Illegitimate)	F	A	Thomas Daugherty b. unknown	Elizabeth Brown b. Fleming Co., Ky.	B	
8/17/1878	Not named b. Fleming Co.	M	A	James Robertson b. Fleming Co.	Annie Arnold b. Logan Co., Ky.	W	
10/ 2/1878	Robert R. Belt b. Fleming Co.	M	A	Robert Belt b. Fleming Co.	Mary A. Inlow b. Fleming Co.	W	
6/ 6/1878	John P. Lewis b. Fleming Co.	M	A	John Lewis b. Morgan Co., Ky.	Martha White b. Fleming Co.	W	
10/ /1878	Willie Smith b. Fleming Co.	M	A	Warner Smith b. Fleming Co.	Nannie Gaskins b. Fleming Co.	M	
9/ /1878	Warner Smith	M	A	Charles Smith	Pickett Carr	M	
9/ /1878	Charles Smith b. Fleming Co.	M	A	Charles Smith b. Fleming Co.	Pickett Carr b. Fleming Co.		(twins)
1/31/1878	Susan L. Fleming b. Fleming Co.	F	A	Lewis Fleming b. Fleming Co.	Martha Jackson b. Maryland	B	
12/16/1878	Bettie C. Robertson b. Fleming Co.	F	A	Calvin Robertson b. Fleming Co.	Emma Cassidy b. Fleming Co.	W	
8/ 6/1878	Fitchie Beasley b. Fleming Co.	M	A	Mason Beasley b. Ohio	Lizzie Shelton b. Ohio	W	
3/ 1/1878	Lou b. Fleming Co. (Illegitimate)	F	A	unknown b. unknown	Ima Robertson b. Fleming Co.	B	
3/18/1878	James E. Meadows b. Fleming Co.	M	A	Rawleigh Meadows b. Virginia	Mary Griffith b. Fleming Co.	W	
6/ 2/1878	W. Harvey Belt b. Fleming Co.	M	A	Harvey Belt b. Fleming Co.	Eliza Smith b. Fleming Co.	W	
9/25/1878	Sadie B. Gardner b. Fleming Co.	F	A	B. H. Gardner b. Rowan Co., Ky.	Alice B. Hopper b. Fleming Co.	W	
1/ 9/1878	Thomas Sweeney b. Fleming Co.	M	A	Martin Sweeney b. Ireland	Mary Cummins b. Fleming Co.	W	

COUNTY Fleming

DATE	NAME OF CHILD	S	C	NAME OF FATHER	NAME OF MOTHER	CO.	RESIDENCE
11/ 1/1878	Lucy M. McIntyre b. Fleming Co.	F	A	William J. McIntyre b. Fleming Co.	Elizabeth Sousley b. Fleming Co.	W	All residents Fleming Co.
6/22/1878	Phenton C. Sousley b. Fleming Co.	F	A	George D. Sousley b. Fleming Co.	Maggie Hilligors b. Fleming Co.	W	
10/ /1878	Not named b. Fleming Co.	M	A	Alvin Mitchell b. Bath Co., Ky.	Lucy A. Brown b. Fleming Co.	W	
3/18/1878	Oliver T. McIntyre b. Fleming Co.	M	A	Joseph McIntyre b. Fleming Co.	Sallie Brown b. Fleming Co.	W	
10/20/1878	James T. Herron b. Fleming Co.	M	A	Thomas Herron b. Nicholas Co., Ky.	Ellen Kerns b. Nicholas Co., Ky.	W	
8/ 2/1878	James R. Sousley b. Fleming Co.	M	A	John B. Sousley b. Fleming Co.	Sallie Clark b. Fleming Co.	W	
9/17/1878	Samuel Woodford b. Fleming Co.	M	A	Buckner Woodford b. Bourbon Co., Ky.	Nannie Brooks b. Bourbon Co., Ky.	W	
2/11/1878	Rufus Kendall	M	A	Jessie Kendall	Jemima Parker	W	
2/11/1878	Opal Kendall b. Fleming Co.	F	A	Jessie Kendall b. Fleming Co.	Jemima Parker b. Fleming Co.	W	(twins)
2/14/1878	Mintie M. Argo b. Fleming Co.	F	A	John Argo	Bell Gilkison b. Fleming Co.	W	
3/19/1878	Charles C. Alexander b. Fleming Co.	M	A	George Alexander b. Ohio	Dorca Williams b. Fleming Co.	W	
8/18/1878	Ollie Faris	M	A	Kirk Faris	Caroline M. Grose	W	
8/18/1878	Watson Faris b. Fleming Co.	M	A	Kirk Faris b. Fleming Co.	Caroline M. Grose b. Nicholas Co., Ky.	W	(twins)
2/20/1878	William R. Grannis b. Fleming Co.	M	D	Harvey Grannis b. Fleming Co.	Sallie Blair b. Fleming Co.	W	
10/ 9/1878	Richard E. Mallory b. Fleming Co.	M	A	Stewart Mallory b. Fleming Co.	Hannah Williams b. Fleming Co.	W	
6/ 8/1878	John A. L. Kerns b. Fleming Co.	M	A	John W. Kerns	Amanda Burke b. Fleming Co.	W	
11/22/1878	Samuel M. Arnold b. Fleming Co.	M	A	Samuel Arnold b. Fleming Co.	Elizabeth Stanfield b. Fleming Co.	W	
3/17/1878	Amelia B. Taylor b. Fleming Co.	F	A	John Taylor b. Canada	Harriet Hill b. Fleming Co.	B	
8/ 8/1878	William Alexander b. Fleming Co.	M	A	John Alexander b. Fleming Co.	Elizabeth Cochran b. Fleming Co.	W	
8/12/1878	Ellie Gray b. Fleming Co.	F	A	Santford Gray b. Nicholas Co., Ky.	Elizabeth Williams b. Fleming Co.	W	

S Sex
C Condition A-Alive D-Dead

COUNTY __Fleming__

DATE	NAME OF CHILD	S	C	NAME OF FATHER	NAME OF MOTHER	CO.	RESIDENCE
4/30/1878	Tina J. Clarke b. Fleming Co.	F	A	Harry Clarke b. Fleming Co.	Elizabeth Bradford b. Fleming Co.	M	All residents Fleming Co.
7/ 7/1878	Lucy J. Dodge b. Fleming Co.	F	A	John Dodge b. Fleming Co.	Kate Sousley b. Fleming Co.	W	
7/ 6/1878	Louvina Eubanks b. Fleming Co.	F	A	Charles Eubanks b. Nicholas Co., Ky.	Matilda Barton b. Fleming Co., Ky.	W	
4/ 4/1878	Armstead Jolley b. Fleming Co.	M	A	Thomas Jolley b. Nicholas Co., Ky.	Rebecca Hopkins b. Nicholas Co., Ky.	W	
4/ 4/1878	Oscar Jolley b. Fleming Co.	M	A	Thomas Jolley b. Nicholas Co., Ky.	Rebecca Hopings b. Nicholas Co., Ky.	W	(twins)
7/ 9/1878	Maggie M. Howe b. Fleming Co.	F	A	John M. Howe b. Fleming Co.	Lizzie Stuart b. Fleming Co.	W	
8/17/1878	Maggie E. Wallingford b. Fleming Co.	F	A	Columbus Wallingford b. Lewis Co., Ky.	Mary Willett b. Fleming Co.	W	
3/17/1878	Lucy B. Moore b. Fleming Co.	F	A	James W. Moore b. Bourbon Co., Ky.	Pauline J. McGinnis b. Nicholas Co., Ky.	W	
8/29/1878	Lyda M. Howe b. Fleming Co.	F	A	James M. Howe b. Fleming Co.	Ettie Richards b. Ohio	W	
12/11/1878	Susan B. Thompson b. Fleming Co.	F	A	Bethuel M. Thompson b. Mason Co., Ky.	Mary E. Sousley b. Fleming Co.	W	
11/18/1878	Not named b. Fleming Co.	M	A	Thomas Biddle b. Fleming Co.	Margaret V. Patterson b. Maryland	W	
3/12/1878	Leland B. Barton b. Fleming Co.	M	A	William Barton b. Fleming Co.	Mary J. Parsons b. Fleming Co.	W	
5/ 4/1878	Thomas C. Caywood b. Fleming Co.	M	A	Thomas H. Caywood b. Mason Co., Ky.	Lucy M. OBannon b. Fleming Co.	W	
12/ 1/1878	Lydia H. Faris b. Fleming Co. (Illegitimate	F	A	James Faris b. Tenn.	Maria Clayborn b. Nicholas Co., Ky.	B	
1/ 7/1878	Thomas C. Darnall b. Fleming Co.	M	A	Gilbert Darnall b. Mason Co., Ky.	Sarah Cochran b. Fleming Co.	W	
4/30/1878	William C. White b. Fleming Co. (Illegitimate)	M	A	William White b. --	Sarah -- b. Fleming Co.	M	
11/10/1878	John A. Fox b. Fleming Co.	M	A	Daniel Fox b. Fleming Co.	Mary Bush b. Fleming Co.	M	
12/ 5/1878	Not named b. Fleming Co.	M	A	Daniel Fox b. Fleming Co.	Mary Bush b. Fleming Co.	M	
8/12/1878	Earnest V. McCord b. Fleming Co.	M	A	William McCord b. Fleming Co.	Elizabeth E. Stockdale b. Fleming Co.	W	

COUNTY   Fleming

DATE	NAME OF CHILD	S	C	NAME OF FATHER	NAME OF MOTHER	CO.	RESIDENCE
2/ 4/1878	Mary A. Moore b. Fleming Co.	F	A	George Moore b. Fleming Co.	Amelia B. Taylor b. Fleming Co.	W	All residents Fleming Co.
6/ /1878	Dalia Lowery b. Fleming Co.	M	A	Charles Lowery b. Fleming Co.	Elizabeth Robertson b. Fleming Co.	B	
4/ /1878	Ida M. Bush b. Fleming Co.	F	A	Tobias Bush b. Fleming Co.	Elizabeth E. Ferguson b. Fleming Co.	B	
9/ 8/1878	Edgus E. Cassidy b. Fleming Co.	M	A	Emmitt Cassidy b. Fleming Co.	Georgie Dreman b. Lewis Co., Ky.	W	
11/11/1878	Lucy K, Barnes b. Fleming Co.	F	A	Gabriel Barnes b. Fleming Co.	Caroline Carr b. Fleming Co.	B	
3/17/1878	William H. Lamar b. Fleming Co.	M	A	Elijah Lamar b. Mason Co., Ky.	Elizabeth Graves b. Fleming Co.	W	
10/22/1878	Rebecca J. Dillon b. Fleming Co.	F	A	Robert A. Dillon b. Mason Co., Ky.	Nancy Graves b. Fleming Co.	W	
2/22/1878	Lloyd A. McCarty b. Fleming Co.	M	A	Santford McCarty b. Fleming Co.	Mary Wise b. Fleming Co.	W	
8/27/1878	Lectia Richards b. Fleming Co.	F	A	Joseph Richards b. Mason Co., Ky.	Hester A. Bryant b. Bath Co., Ky.	W	
4/ 9/1878	Susan L. Fields b. Fleming Co.	F	A	Thomas Fields b. Fleming Co.	Mary J. Tolle b. --	W	
12/ 2/1878	John D. Clarke b. Fleming Co.	M	A	Benjamin Clarke b. Fleming Co.	Susan Cliff b. Mason Co., Ky.	W	
2/24/1878	Henry S. Songbottom b. Fleming Co.	M	A	Thomas Longbottom b. Virginia	Rebecca Reed b. Bath Co., Ky.	W	
3/ 4/1878	Silas McCord b. Fleming Co.	M	A	David McCord b. Fleming Co.	Elizabeth Stockdale b. Fleming Co.	W	
6/ /1878	Saran E. Fields b. Fleming Co.	F	A	Joseph Fields b. Fleming Co.	Matilda Howard b. Mason Co., Ky.	W	
6/14/1878	Minnie C. Flora b. Fleming Co.	F	A	James Flora	Armilda York b. Pendleton Co., Ky.	W	
12/ 8/1878	Clarance A. Latham b. Fleming Co.	M	A	Samuel C. Latham b. Mason Co., Ky.	Francis McCarty b. Fleming Co.	W	
3/ 3/1878	Charles D. Pugh b. Fleming Co.	M	A	George Pugh b. Harrison Co., Ky.	Eliza Jolly b. Adams Co. Ohio	W	
9/13/1878	Thomas Hutton b. Fleming Co.	M	A	George Hutton b. Harrison Co., Ky.	Lidia Arnold b. Fleming Co.	W	
10/ 6/1878	Eliza Rankin b. Fleming Co.	F	A	Robert Rankin b. Harrison Co., Ky.	Louisa Arnold b. Fleming Co.	W	

COUNTY __Fleming__   C Condition A-Alive D-Dead

DATE	NAME OF CHILD	S	C	NAME OF FATHER	NAME OF MOTHER	CO.	RESIDENCE
2/12/1878	James A. Hedger b. Fleming Co.	M	A	William Hedger 	Ruth Saunders b. Fleming Co	W	All residents Fleming Co.
1/ 6/1878	James F. Park b. Fleming Co.	M	A	John Park b. Carter Co., Ky.	Mary E. Saunders b. Fleming Co.	W	
11/22/1878	William Davis b. Fleming Co.	M	A	Taylor Davis b. Fleming Co.	Nancy Evans b. Fleming Co.	W	
7/ 4/1878	Samuel Manchester b. Fleming Co.	M	A	George Manchester b. Brown Co., Ohio	Mary Potman b. Fleming Co.	W	
11/ /1878	Mary E. Muse b. Fleming Co.	F	A	Marion Muse b. Fleming Co.	Margaret Rosor b. Fleming Co.	W	
6/14/1878	Mollie H. Conley b. Fleming Co.	F	A	John Conley b. Johnson Co., Ky.	Elizabeth Brammer b. Carter Co., Ky.	W	
7/27/1878	Frederick Ward b. Mason Co., Ky.	M	A	William Ward b. Fleming Co.	Martha E. Newman b. Fleming Co.	W	
3/ /1878	Sarah Davis b. Fleming Co.	F	A	Dudley Davis b. Bath Co., Ky.	Amanda Williams b. Bath Co., Ky.	W	
11/30/1878	Davis b. Fleming Co.	M	A	Taylor Davis b. Fleming Co.	Gertrude Alter b. Johnson Co., Ky.	W	
1/ 7/1879	William Maxey b. Fleming Co.	M	A	Oliver P. Maxey b. Bath Co., Ky.	Lucy A. Broughton b. Carke Co., Ky.	W	
8/ 5/1878	Simpson Ratcliffe b. Fleming Co.	M	A	William Ratcliffe b. Morgan Co., Ky.	Alice A. Keerans b. Fleming Co.	W	
4/ 2/1878	Linnie T. Rogers b. Fleming Co.	F	A	James Rogers b. Fleming Co.	Elenor Riddle b. Fleming Co.	W	
6/ 9/1878	Francis Crain b. Lewis Co., Ky.	F	A	Amant Crain b. Fleming Co.	- - - - b. Bath Co., Ky.	W	
10/ /1878	Mary E. Vice b. Fleming Co.	F	A	Marion Vice b. Fleming Co.	Sarah Vice b. Fleming Co.	W	
3/10/1878	Jones b. Fleming Co.	M	A	Thomas Jones b. Fleming Co.	Catherine Smith b. not known	W	
8/ 1/1878	John B. Keerans b. Cincinnati, O.	M	A	Blair Keerans b. Fleming Co.	Motie Vanden b. Mason Co., Ky.	W	
9/20/1878	Letta O. Barksdale b. Fleming Co.	F	A	Wm. H. Backsdale b. Fleming Co.	Mary F. Graham b. Fleming Co.	W	
4/ 6/1878	Zella G. Meeks b. Fleming Co.	F	A	William Meeks b. Nicholas Co., Ky.	Mary E. Martin b. Nicholas Co., Ky.	W	
5/ /1878	John W. Denton b. Fleming Co.	M	A	Thomas Denton b. Fleming Co.	Mary Oliver b. Fleming Co.	W	

S Sex

COUNTY   Fleming

C Condition A-Alive D-Dead

DATE	NAME OF CHILD	S	C	NAME OF FATHER	NAME OF MOTHER	CO.	RESIDENCE
12/ 8/1878	Milford Cox b. Fleming Co.	M	A	William Cox b. Adams Co. O.	Sarah E. Thomas b. Fleming Co.	W	All residents Fleming Co.
11/28/1878	Samuel Goodwin b. Fleming Co.	M	A	John B. Goodwin b. Fleming Co.	Mary E. Shields b. Fleming Co.	W	
3/ 6/1878	Miranda Patton b. Fleming Co.	F	A	John Patton b. Brown Co., O.	Mary A. Patton b. Bath Co., Ky.	W	
6/25/1878	Edith Crawford b. Fleming Co.	F	A	James Crawford b. Fleming Co.	Lucinda Davis b. Fleming Co.	W	
7/27/1878	William C. Willeroy b. Fleming Co.	M	A	John W. Willeroy b. King William Co., Va.	Sarah M. Estill b. Fleming Co.	W	
8/ 3/1878	Ninetta Powell b. Fleming Co.	F	A	Thos. J. Powell b. Fleming Co.	Emily Warner b. Fleming Co.	W	
3/28/1878	Mary P. Abney b. Fleming Co.	F	A	Lucien B. Abney b. S.C.	Jane Stuart b. Fleming Co.	W	
9/ /1878	Catherine Smith b. Fleming Co.	F	A	James Smith b. Fleming Co.	Francis Smith b. Fleming Co.	B	
8/26/1878	Not named b. Fleming Co.	F	A	Henry Mattingly b. Mason Co., Ky.	Anny Sweet b. Mason Co., Ky.	W	
3/23/1878	Benjamin H. Willett b. Fleming Co.	M	A	John M. Willett b. Fleming Co.	Mary E. Ham b. Lewis Co., Ky.	W	
1/11/1878	Amos A. Reeder b. Fleming Co.	M	A	Benjamin Reeder b. Lewis Co., Ky.	Alice Wallingford b. Lewis Co., Ky.	W	
4/27/1878	Mary J. Arnold b. Fleming Co.	F	A	Charles Arnold b. Lewis Co., Ky.	Rebecca Deatley b. Lewis Co., Ky.	W	
11/16/1878	James A. Edwards b. Fleming Co.	M	A	Martin Edwards b. Ohio	Fannie J. Patton b. Mason Co., Ky.	W	
7/19/1878	Sarepta Walker b. Mason Co., Ky.	F	A	Addison Walker b. Fleming Co.	Sarah Garrard (Ganard ?) b. Tenn.	W	
1/ 4/1878	Lulu Wallingford b. Fleming Co.	F	A	Joseph Wallingford b. Iowa	Nannie Strode b. Mason Co., Ky.	W	
2/ 7/1878	Claud Rash b. Fleming Co.	M	A	William Rash b. Fleming Co.	Suan Embry b. Fleming Co.	W	
9/ 5/1878	Stella E. Wallingford b. Fleming Co.	F	A	Benjamin F. Wallingford b. Fleming Co.	Elizabeth Glascock b. Fleming Co.	W	
4/28/1878	Boyd C. Foxworthy b. Fleming Co.	M	A	Squire Foxworthy b. Fleming Co.	Sarah C. Kelley b. Fleming Co.	W	
1/ 9/1878	Jessie Glascock b. Fleming Co.	M	A	Thomas Glascock b. Fleming Co.	Sallie Howe b. Mason Co., Ky.	W	

COUNTY Fleming

S Sex
C Condition A-Alive D-Dead

DATE	NAME OF CHILD	S	C	NAME OF FATHER	NAME OF MOTHER	CO.	RESIDENCE
7/10/1878	Minnie Truitt b. Fleming Co.	F	A	Andrew J. Truitt b. Mason Co., Ky.	Margaret A. Power b. Fleming Co.	W	All residents Fleming Co.
4/27/1878	Not named b. Fleming Co.	M	A	George Kelley b. Fleming Co.	Nannie Clary b. Lewis Co., Ky.	W	
11/ 2/1878	George W. Foxworthy b. Fleming Co.	M	A	John W. Foxworthy b. Fleming Co.	Sarah E. Wallingford b. Mason Co., Ky.	W	
4/18/1878	Not named b. Fleming Co.	F	D	Brice Hannah b. Lewis Co., Ky.	Francis A. Ruggles b. Lewis Co., Ky.	W	
6/24/1878	Bettie Carpenter b. Fleming Co.	F	A	William Carpenter b. Fleming Co.	Mary Smethers b. Virginia	W	
9/ 1/1878	Henry C. Arthur b. Fleming Co.	M	A	James A. Arthur b. Boyd Co., Ky.	Elizabeth Toller b. Boyd Co., Ky.	W	
7/ 8/1878	Robert B. Toller b. Fleming Co.	M	A	Joseph Toller b. Lewis Co., Ky.	Mary Carpenter b. Lewis Co., Ky.	W	
9/22/1878	Anola C. Ham b. Fleming Co.	F	A	F. R. Ham b. Fleming Co.	Mary A. Thomas b. Fleming Co.	W	
2/24/1878	George C. Million b. Fleming Co.	M	A	Isaac Million b. Rowan Co., Ky.	Alice Mortimee b. Virginia	W	
9/ 5/1878	John W. Gordon b. Fleming Co.	M	A	John Gordon b. Pendleton Co., Ky.	Victoria Erskin b. Virginia	W	
4/13/1878	Ollie D. Fizer b. Fleming Co.	M	A	William Fizer b. Virginia	Rebecca J. Arnold b. Fleming Co.	W	
6/12/1878	Florence B. Hurst b. Fleming Co.	F	A	Jessie Hurst b. Fleming Co.	Lizzie McIlvain b. Fleming Co.	W	
9/21/1878	Annie L. Lukins b. Fleming Co.	F	A	Joseph P. Lukins b. Fleming Co.	Mary L. Glascock b. Fleming Co.	W	
9/20/1878	Amanda Lewis b. Fleming Co. (Illegitimate)	F	A	Not known b. unknown	Martha Lewis b. Fleming Co.	M	
5/23/1878	Lillie Debell b. Fleming Co.	F	A	Jessie Debell b. Fleming Co.	Melvina McIntyre b. Fleming Co.	W	
1/19/1878	Elsie M. Ringo b. Fleming Co.	F	A	Charles E. Ringo b. Fleming Co.	Sarah E. McClure b. bath Co., Ky.	W	
3/23/1878	Clifton Pyles b. Fleming Co.	M	A	Milton Pyles b. Mason Co.	Jane R. Caywood b. Fleming Co.	W	
12/16/1878	John B. Thompson b. Fleming Co.	M	A	John W. Thompson b. Fleming Co.	Sarah Beckett b. Morgan Co., Ky.	W	
2/ 5/1878	Casper K. Seivers b. Fleming Co.	M	A	James Seivers b. Fleming Co.	Barinda Raukin b. Nicholas Co., Ky.	W	

COUNTY Fleming   C Condition A-Alive D-Dead

DATE	NAME OF CHILD	S	C	NAME OF FATHER	NAME OF MOTHER	CO.	RESIDENCE
9/ 5/1878	John R. Abrams	M	A	John Abrams	Ester Blackburn	W	All residents
	b. Fleming Co.			b. Madison Co., Ky.	b. Harrison Co., Ky.		Fleming Co.
11/12/1878	Annie Evans	F	A	Allen M. Evans	Amanda V. Muse	W	
	b. Fleming Co.			b. Fleming Co.	b. Fleming Co.		
4/28/1878	Elizabeth Barnes	F	A	Wellington Barnes	Louisa Havens	W	
	b. Covington,			b. Magoffin Co., Ky.	b. Fleming Co.		
12/25/1878	Saunders Walton	M	A	John Walton	Lidia Markwell	W	
	b. Fleming Co.			b. Robertson Co., Ky.	b. Fleming Co., Ky.		
7/25/1878	William B. Freeman	M	A	William Freeman	Mary Ann McClure	W	
	b. Fleming Co.			b. Bath Co., Ky.	b. Bath Co., Ky.		
3/25/1878	George P. Kimberly	M	A	William Kimberley	Martha J. Gray	W	
	b. Fleming Co.			b. Ohio	b. Bracken Co., Ky.		
	Re. Illegitimate (This could belong to next name, might be on wrong line)						
9/ /1878	Hall	F	A	Not known	Nancy Hall	W	
	b. Fleming Co.			b. unknown	b. Morgan Co., Ky.		
6/ 1/1878	Edna F. Humphreys	F	A	Marshall Humphreys	Maggie McKee	W	
	b. Fleming Co.			b. Fleming Co.	b. Fleming Co.		
12/25/1878	Walton	M	D	John Walton	Lidia Markwell	W	
	b. Fleming Co.			b. Robertson Co., Ky.	b. Mason Co., Ky.		
1/21/1878	Walter Gray	M	A	Fielding Gray	Mariah Gray	W	
	b. Fleming Co.			b. Fleming Co.	b. Fleming Co.		
1/ 3/1878	No name	M	A	Thomas Barber	Helen Atchison	W	
	b. Fleming Co.			b. Fleming Co.	b. Bath Co., Ky.		
7/ 1/1878	George F. Kirk	M	A	Lewis Kirk	Angeline Vailes	W	
	b. Fleming Co.			b. West Virginia	b. W. Virginia		
3/25/1878	Sarah M. Bradley	F	A	Walter A. Bradley	Emily Bradley	W	
	b. Fleming Co.			b. Bourbon Co., Ky.	b. Fleming Co.		
1/21/1878	Fred Gray	M	A	Fielding Gray	Mariah Gray	W	
	b. Fleming Co.			b. Fleming Co.	b. Fleming Co.		
1/10/1878	Francis M. Royce	M	A	Aaron Royce	Sarah Stevens	W	
	b. Fleming Co.			b. Fleming Co.	b. Fleming Co.		
11/18/1878	Effa Pitts	F	A	John T. Pitts	Elizabeth Pitts	W	
	b. Fleming Co.			b. Lewis Co., Ky.	b. Lewis Co., Ky.		
3/ 6/1878	Annie F. Burns	F	A	James Burns	Virginia Humphreys	W	
	b. Fleming Co.			b. Ohio	b. Fleming Co.		
10/ 8/1878	Marion F. Hurst	M	A	Allen P. Hurst	Nancy Ham	W	
	b. Fleming Co.			b. Fleming Co.	b. Carter Co., Ky.		

COUNTY Fleming

S Sex
C Condition A-Alive D-Dead

DATE	NAME OF CHILD	S	C	NAME OF FATHER	NAME OF MOTHER	CO.	RESIDENCE
9/ /1878	Not named b. Fleming Co.	M	D	Jas. C. Downey b. Ohio	Louisa Plummer b. Fleming Co.	W	All residents Fleming Co.
5/ 5/1878	John T. White b. Fleming Co.	M	A	Robert White b. Philadelphia, Penn.	Mertill Rodgers b. Bath Co., Ky.	W	
12/ 9/1878	Minnie H. Humphreys b. Fleming Co.	F	A	Chas. Humphreys b. Louisville, Ky.	Judy Higbee b. Bath Co., Ky.	W	
10/ 4/1878	Brown b. Fleming Co. Re. Not named yet.	M	A	Lafayette Brown b. Carter Co., Ky.	Ellen Bolen b. Wise Co., Va.	W	
10/ 3/1878	Minnie J. Nudigate b. Fleming Co.	F	A	Robert Nudigate b. Fleming Co.	Nancy Reed b. Magoffin Co., Ky.	W	
11/19/1878	Maud Williams b. Fleming Co.	F	A	Miles Williams b. Morgan Co., Ky.	Priscilla Simms b. Floyd	W	

ABNER, Jno. H. 49
ABNER, Lincoln 49
ABNER, Lincoln 82
ABNER, William H. 82
ABNEY, Lucian B. 130
ABNEY, Mary P. 130
ABRAMS, John 132
ABRAMS, John R. 132
ADAMS, David 107
ADAMS, Delila 112
ADAMS, Derindor 90
ADAMS, E. 112
ADAMS, Jacob 73
ADAMS, Jane 73
ADAMS, John M. 89
ADAMS, Lucien S. 107
ADAMS, Margaret 35
ADAMS, Martha 108
ADAMS, Mary J. 89
ADAMS, Nellie 96
ADAMS, Sarah E. 89
ADAMSON, Betsey 58
ADAMSON, Jas. H. 75
ADAMSON, John 75
ADAMSON, Mari. F. 75
ADAMSON, Samuel B. 75
ADDAMS, Mary J. 80
AITKIN, Geo. 61
ALEN, Lorinda 57
ALEXANDER, Abram 29
ALEXANDER, Charles C. 126
ALEXANDER, Columbus 86
ALEXANDER, Elizabeth 71
ALEXANDER, George 126
ALEXANDER, Isabell 76
ALEXANDER, Isabella 45
ALEXANDER, J. H. 86
ALEXANDER, James 84
ALEXANDER, James C. 85
ALEXANDER, James H. 42
ALEXANDER, James M. 79
ALEXANDER, James R. 78
ALEXANDER, Jas. C. 90
ALEXANDER, Jas. T. 90
ALEXANDER, Jno. T. 85
ALEXANDER, John 36
ALEXANDER, John 126
ALEXANDER, Joseph M. 24
ALEXANDER, Joseph M. 29
ALEXANDER, Joseph M. 43

ALEXANDER, Lavina 57
ALEXANDER, Levina 73
ALEXANDER, Lunia 35
ALEXANDER, M. 83
ALEXANDER, Malinda Jane 40
ALEXANDER, Mary 25
ALEXANDER, Mary 83
ALEXANDER, Oscar Barnett 42
ALEXANDER, Parly A. 101
ALEXANDER, Rosanna 43
ALEXANDER, Sarah E. 86
ALEXANDER, William 84
ALEXANDER, William 126
ALEXANDER, William D. 101
ALLEN, Alkia H. 85
ALLEN, Annie 102
ALLEN, Bertha 73
ALLEN, E. M. 107
ALLEN, Elizabeth J. 50
ALLEN, Garrett 85
ALLEN, Henry G. 73
ALLEN, Jas. P. 102
ALLEN, Jas. P. 102
ALLEN, John 74
ALLEN, John E. 107
ALLEN, John J. 83
ALLEN, S. B. 3
ALLEN, Sarah Jane 38
ALLEN, Simeon B. 34
ALLENDER, Malinda J. 16
ALLENDER, Malinda J. 80
ALLENDER, Polly 16
ALLISON, Jacob 103
ALTER, Gertrude 129
AMONOW, Bridget 84
AMORN, Mary 52
AMOS, S. F. 121
ANDERSON, Ellen 89
ANDERSON, Ellen 93
ANDERSON, Jane 66
ANDERSON, Jane 75
ANDERSON, L. D. 29
ANDERSON, L. D. 43
ANDERSON, Lizie 103
ANDERSON, Martha J. 34
ANDERSON, Martha J. 52
ANDERSON, Martha J. 69
ANDERSON, Sarah Ann 25
ANDRESON, Sarah 67
ANDREWS, Anna 110
ANDREWS, Fannie A. 121

ANDREWS, L. W. 43
ANDREWS, Louisa W. 88
ANDREWS, N. L. 53
ANDREWS, Robert D. 110
ANDREWS, Robert D. 110
ANDREWS, Seth 110
ANDREWS, Thomas 58
ANDREWS, Thomas S. 121
ANDREWS, Thos. D. 83
ANDREWS, Watson 88
ANNOW, Delilah D. 22
ANOLD, Charles B. 72
AOLEY, Celia Ann 15
ARASMITH, O. S. 115
ARASMITH, Rachael 115
ARGO, John 126
ARGO, Mintie M. 126
ARIGEN, Frances 40
ARINS, Elizabeth 51
ARMSTEAD, James 83
ARMSTRONE, Bettie 82
ARMSTRONG, Amanda N. 97
ARMSTRONG, Ann 44
ARMSTRONG, Delila 102
ARMSTRONG, Dr. William 23
ARMSTRONG, Edna 91
ARMSTRONG, Fanny M. 72
ARMSTRONG, Isaac P. 5
ARMSTRONG, John 82
ARMSTRONG, John F. 67
ARMSTRONG, Louisa 36
ARMSTRONG, Louisa 75
ARMSTRONG, Nancy C. 68
ARMSTRONG, R. C. 115
ARMSTRONG, Robt. 5
ARMSTRONG, Samuel E. 44
ARMSTRONG, Sarah 67
ARMSTRONG, Sarah 73
ARMSTRONG, Sarah 97
ARMSTRONG, Sarah D. 39
ARMSTRONG, Sary D. 81
ARMSTRONG, Wm. 50
ARNALD, Susan 73
ARNOLD, ----- 36
ARNOLD, Anna 85
ARNOLD, Annie 125
ARNOLD, Armild 41
ARNOLD, Charles 52
ARNOLD, Charles 130
ARNOLD, Chas. B. 15
ARNOLD, David 19

ARNOLD, George 122
ARNOLD, Georgie M. 122
ARNOLD, Granny Ann 42
ARNOLD, Henry 13
ARNOLD, James 42
ARNOLD, John 10
ARNOLD, L. J. 52
ARNOLD, Leander 10
ARNOLD, Leuis 36
ARNOLD, Lidia 128
ARNOLD, Louisa 128
ARNOLD, Lucinda 15
ARNOLD, Mariah A. 47
ARNOLD, Mary 2
ARNOLD, Mary J. 130
ARNOLD, Matilda 26
ARNOLD, Rebecca J. 79
ARNOLD, Rebecca J. 94
ARNOLD, Rebecca J. 131
ARNOLD, Rebecca T. 52
ARNOLD, Rolby Trully 13
ARNOLD, Samuel 126
ARNOLD, Samuel M. 126
ARNOLD, Sanuel J. 41
ARNOLD, Sary A. 71
ARNOLD, Sary Ann 78
ARNOLD, William B. 71
ARNOLD, William B. 78
ART, Elizabeth 99
ARTHUR, Henry C. 131
ARTHUR, James A. 131
ASBANY, Maranda 13
ASBURY, Rachel 53
ASH BER? L. Gallaher 5
ASHTON, Charleton H. 93
ASHTON, Geo. D.P. 93
ATCHISIN, Caroline 22
ATCHISON, Asa S. 22
ATCHISON, Helen 132
ATCHISON, J. H. 114
ATCHISON, John C. 33
ATCHISON, Louisa 55
ATCHISON, Lucinda 17
ATCHISON, M. S. 114
ATCHISON, Malinda 55
ATCHISON, Malinda 69
ATCHISON, Oliver 76
ATCHISON, Sarah 18
ATCHISON, Sarah 40
ATCHISON, Thomas T. 53
ATCHISON, Thos. J. 22

ATCHISON, Wm. P. 33
ATCKISON, Caroline 9
ATHOMAS, Elijah 69
ATHOMPSON, Susan B. 127
AUBREY, Sallie 124
AUXIER, Gertude A. 88
BABBETT, W. J. 58
BABBS, James 9
BABBS, Lewyllon 9
BACKDALE, D. S. 62
BACKSDALE, Wm. H. 129
BAGGOT, Ann 76
BAILEY, Eliza Ann 21
BAILEY, John 91
BAILEY, Mary Ann 29
BAILEY, Matilda 117
BAILEY, Robata 29
BAINS, Mary F. 88
BAIR, Roberty 53
BAIRD, Annie 113
BAIRD, S. D. 59
BAIRD, Susanah 25
BAIZE, W. 113
BAKER, Alexr. 94
BAKER, Betsey 16
BAKER, Margt. 94
BALL, M. Addie 75
BALL, Nancy 84
BALLARD, Elizabeth E. 75
BAMES, Lucinda D. 67
BANNON, Tabatha O. 14
BANNON, Wm. B.O. 54
BAR, Sarah 116
BARBEE, Louisa 80
BARBEE, Nancy 111
BARBER, Daniel 27
BARBER, G. W. 29
BARBER, George 29
BARBER, George R. 69
BARBER, Mary 27
BARBER, thomas 132
BARBOUR, Elvira Catharine 40
BARBOUR, George 39
BARBOUR, John James 39
BARBOUR, Lucinda 41
BARKSDALE, D. S. 68
BARKSDALE, Daniel 22
BARKSDALE, Danil 20
BARKSDALE, Letta O. 129
BARKSDALE, Louisa 22
BARKSDALE, M. 112

BARM, Silvester 90
BARNABY, Chas. D. 111
BARNABY, Elias W. 111
BARNE, Tilford 73
BARNES, Allice 2
BARNES, Cambridge C. 118
BARNES, Eliza J. 87
BARNES, Elizabeth 132
BARNES, Gabriel 128
BARNES, George F. 2
BARNES, Henrietta 108
BARNES, Inetta 2
BARNES, Jas. W. 95
BARNES, Lucinda 81
BARNES, Lucy K. 128
BARNES, Octava 118
BARNES, Phebe S. 77
BARNES, Sarah 95
BARNES, Wellington 132
BARNETT, Dorhia Ann 40
BARNETT, Ellen 103
BARNETT, Lucy J. 75
BARNS, Elizabeth 68
BARNS, Enoch 74
BARRETT, Margery 75
BARRIS, Lucy 78
BARTLETT, Ann 92
BARTLETT, Delila 75
BARTLETT, James 75
BARTLETT, Silas 32
BARTLETT, William 32
BARTON, James P. 107
BARTON, Leland B. 127
BARTON, Malinda 107
BARTON, Matilda 127
BARTON, Myra 38
BARTON, William 127
BARTON, William R. 107
BARTOUR, George 40
BARUS, Lucinda 102
BASH(?), Tabath 46
BASKEN, G. W. 67
BATE, Franklin 49
BATE, John H. 49
BATEMAN, Elastine 18
BATEMAN, Mary 18
BATEMAN, Wm. 67
BEAM, ----- 36
BEAM, Eli 36
BEAM, Eli 67
BEAM, Mary H. 87

BEAM, Ruth 2
BEAMITHON, Joseph 25
BEAR, Bethsaba 118
BEARD, Samuel 74
BEARD, Wm. 74
BEASLEY, Fitchie 125
BEASLEY, Mason 125
BEAUCAMP, Amelia 22
BEAUCAMP, Thomas M. 7
BEAUCAMP, W. S. 64
BEAUCAMP, William 22
BEAUCAMP, Wm. 7
BEBELL, Joel 72
BECKET, James M. 54
BECKETT, A. J. 112
BECKETT, Alice J. 94
BECKETT, Sarah 131
BECKETT, W. C. 113
BECKETT, W. F. 113
BEDELL, Deborah 67
BELL, Aletha 19
BELL, Charles 1
BELL, Charles 50
BELL, Edward 19
BELL, James P. 70
BELL, James R. 53
BELL, John 14
BELL, John 110
BELL, Martin P. Marshall 19
BELL, Mary 2
BELL, Mary 36
BELL, Mary 55
BELL, Mary 71
BELL, R. R. 59
BELL, S. 110
BELL, Wm. 50
BELLE, Flora 89
BELT, Anna 90
BELT, Dennis 26
BELT, Dennis 78
BELT, Emma 120
BELT, Harvey 125
BELT, Hickerson 35
BELT, James 28
BELT, James 72
BELT, John F. 65
BELT, Mary E. 28
BELT, Osburn 6
BELT, Osburn 6
BELT, Robert 125
BELT, Robert R. 125

BELT, W. Harvey 125
BELT, William S. 120
BENDEM, Peachie 81
BENLEY, Mary Jane 1
BENTLEY, ----- 66
BENTLEY, Alice S. 100
BENTLEY, Ann C. 86
BENTLEY, Ary C. 107
BENTLEY, Eliza 56
BENTLEY, Eliza Emma 75
BENTLEY, Eliza J. 81
BENTLEY, G. B. 108
BENTLEY, Geo. B. 83
BENTLEY, R. M. 100
BENTLEY, Richard 75
BENTLEY, Sarey E. 104
BENTLEY, William L. 83
BENTLY, ----- 36
BENTLY, Campbell 36
BENTLY, George 49
BENTLY, Sarah M. 49
BEREKFIELD, Armeda 52
BERRY(?)< John 93
BERRY, ----- 36
BERRY, Arthur 5
BERRY, Austin 5
BERRY, Charles H. 75
BERRY, Henry 36
BERRY, Henry 75
BERRY, Mary Jane 49
BERRY, Milly Ann 42
BERRY, Simpson Taylor 5
BERRY, W. H. 66
BERRY, Wesley 49
BERRY, Wm. H. 5
BERRY, Wyatt 102
BETT, Emily 2
BETT, Harriet 93
BETT, Hickison 2
BETT, Jno. F. 35
BETT, John F. 81
BETT, Joseph F. 81
BIDDLE, Ada M. 86
BIDDLE, Amanda Y. 107
BIDDLE, Charles O. 107
BIDDLE, David T. 107
BIDDLE, Elias 76
BIDDLE, Elizabeth B. 73
BIDDLE, Ellis F. 86
BIDDLE, Guy A. 86
BIDDLE, James H. 91

BIDDLE, John 86
BIDDLE, John 108
BIDDLE, John H. 107
BIDDLE, Katharine 76
BIDDLE, Lida Ellen 91
BIDDLE, M. O. 107
BIDDLE, Mary E. 5
BIDDLE, Richard T. 107
BIDDLE, Robt. P. 86
BIDDLE, Stephen 5
BIDDLE, Stephen 73
BIDDLE, Thomas 127
BIDDLE, Thomas W. 107
BIDDLE, Thos. W. 86
BIGHT, Marget 69
BIRD, Isaac 100
BIRK, James W. 74
BIRK, Jane 75
BIRK, John N. 74
BISHOP, A. 48
BISHOP, A. D. 36
BISHOP, A. D. 58
BISHOP, Clara C. 87
BISHOP, Eliza S. 35
BISHOP, G. W. 58
BISHOP, G. W. 66
BISHOP, Henry 24
BISHOP, Henry 24
BISHOP, Henry 43
BISHOP, Henry 44
BISHOP, J. C. 107
BISHOP, J. G. 36
BISHOP, Jacob 29
BISHOP, Jno. 58
BISHOP, John 24
BISHOP, M. A. 107
BISHOP, Mary A. 76
BISHOP, Mary P. 24
BISHOP, Roby P. 43
BISHOP, Roby Porter 44
BLACK, ----- 36
BLACK, Caroline 75
BLACKBURN, Ester 132
BLAIR, H. M. 107
BLAIR, Hannah 50
BLAIR, Hannah M. 83
BLAIR, Hannah M. 92
BLAIR, James C. 76
BLAIR, Sabina 35
BLAIR, Sabina 51
BLAIR, Sallie 126

BLAIR, W. W. 93
BLAIR, Wallis 76
BLAIR, Wm. P. 36
BLAKE, Elias J. 48
BLAKE, James 3
BLAKE, Jane 103
BLAKE, Lucinda J. 3
BLAKE, Thomas 48
BLAKE, Thomas 58
BLAKE, Thos. 65
BLANTON, Charity 72
BLANTON, Franklin 98
BLANTON, Martin 80
BOCHETT, Mathilda 77
BOLLEN, Ellen T. 1
BOLTS, Mary 73
BOON, Danl. 60
BOOTH, Jemima 100
BOTHE, Jemima 103
BOTTERILL, Francis M. 106
BOTTS, Amelia 51
BOTTS, Amy 26
BOTTS, Ben 38
BOTTS, Ben 51
BOTTS, Ben 66
BOTTS, Bettie 121
BOTTS, Jno. H. 35
BOTTS, John 49
BOTTS, John S. 26
BOTTS, John S. 70
BOTTS, Magt. 38
BOTTS, Maria 93
BOTTS, T. R. 66
BOTTS, Thomas R. 50
BOTTS, Thos. R. 66
BOURN, Morton 34
BOWEN, Franklin P. 34
BOWEN, Leuis H. 86
BOWEN, Mary S. 102
BOWING, Alson T. 88
BOWING, S. T. 88
BOWLAN, Wm. 57
BOWLES, Sephen 45
BOWMAN, Alice P. 43
BOWMAN, Harrison 72
BOWMAN, James 24
BOWMAN, James M. 24
BOWMAN, John 43
BOWMAN, John 64
BOYCE, James 63

BOYD, Abner 55
BOYD, Abner 76
BOYD, Emily 13
BOYD, Francis D. 18
BOYD, James 65
BOYD, Jas. 18
BOYD, Lucinda 30
BOYD, Mary E. 106
BOYD, Mary E. 123
BOYD, Motie 122
BOYD, Nancy M. 120
BOYD, Rees 122
BOYD, Sarah M. 101
BOYS, Sarah 30
BOYSE, Allen 97
BOYSE, Kitty 16
BOYSE, Slewellyn 97
BOYSE, William 97
BRADFORD, Elijth 91
BRADFORD, Elizabeth 127
BRADFORD, Rosanna 79
BRADFORD, rosanna T. 70
BRADLEY, E. A. 114
BRADLEY, E. F. 91
BRADLEY, Emily 132
BRADLEY, Herman 10
BRADLEY, Hiram 43
BRADLEY, J. F. 116
BRADLEY, John 102
BRADLEY, Sarah M. 132
BRADLEY, Shelton H. 10
BRADLEY, W. A. 116
BRADLEY, Walter 102
BRADLEY, Walter A. 132
BRADLEY, William Darnall 43
BRADLY, Mrs. Rosanna 18
BRAM, Sandy 90
BRAMAN, Eliza J. 80
BRAMBLE, ----- 30
BRAMBLE, J. F. 112
BRAMBLE, Mary 63
BRAMBLE, Z. W. 30
BRAMEL, Mary 79
BRAMEL, Mathew 43
BRAMEL, Matthew 79
BRAMEL, Poly Ann 29
BRAMEL, Zacharias 9
BRAMELL, Marcus 43
BRAMER, Mary 69
BRAMMEL, Cornlia M. 95
BRAMMEL, Mary 95

BRAMMEL, Permelia A. 71
BRAMMER, Elizabeth 129
BRAMWELL, Henry 37
BRAMWELL, Mary 37
BRAMWELL, Zacheus 52
BRANAS, Eliza Jane 10
BRAND, Alexander H. 72
BRANDERS, John 99
BRANDERS, Millie 99
BRANHAM, Eliza 41
BRAUCH, Fielder 89
BRAUCH, Kate 122
BRAUNNER, Eliza 42
BRAYFIELD, Edward Debell 42
BRAYFIELD, Obed 80
BRAYFIELD, Obed. 42
BRECKINRIDGE, J. C. 61
BREENE, Edward 97
BREENE, John 111
BREENE, Martin 111
BREEZE, John 97
BRIDGES(?), John 120
BRIDGES, ----- 65
BRIDGES, Amanda 19
BRIDGES, Amanda 113
BRIDGES, Franklin 61
BRIDGES, Jno. L. 67
BRIDGES, John 97
BRIDGES, Mary S. 97
BRIDGES, William 54
BRIGES, Josie 120
BRIGGS, George D. 101
BRIGGS, W. C. 101
BRINEGAN, Nancy 96
BRISTOW, Andrew 122
BRISTOW, Andrew W. 108
BRISTOW, B. H. 108
BRISTOW, Joseph M. 122
BRITEY, Bazel 123
BROADWELL, Geo. W. 96
BROADWELL, James 96
BROM(?), Sandey 85
BROOKS, Mary A. 26
BROOKS, Mary A. 72
BROOKS, Nannie 126
BROOTKOVER, Mary J. 101
BROPHA, Bridgett 83
BROTHERS, Dudley 76
BROTHERS, Margaret 37
BROUGHTON, Lucy A. 129
BROW, Minerva R. 32

BROWING, C. W. 64
BROWN(?), Sueda 86
BROWN, ----- 35
BROWN, Cummins 35
BROWN, Cummins 48
BROWN, David 65
BROWN, Elizabeth 125
BROWN, Howard 106
BROWN, John S. 48
BROWN, Kiah 24
BROWN, Lewis 117
BROWN, Lizzie 117
BROWN, Lucy A. 102
BROWN, Lucy A. 126
BROWN, Lucy M. 105
BROWN, Manerva 78
BROWN, Maria 106
BROWN, Mary J. 73
BROWN, Minerva 41
BROWN, Minvervy 35
BROWN, Rhetta 106
BROWN, Sallie 126
BROWN, Susan A. 107
BROWNING, Amos 79
BROWNING, Dr. W. G. 15
BROWNING, E. F. 111
BROWNING, Eli 2
BROWNING, Eli H. 44
BROWNING, Fidelia Ann 15
BROWNING, J. E. 111
BROWNING, John 44
BROWNING, Josiah 9
BROWNING, Lucy A. 97
BROWNING, Mary 54
BROWNING, Sophrania 68
BROWNING, Sophrona 46
BROWNING, Sophronia 20
BRUCE, ----- 65
BRUCE, Ann 57
BRUCE, Ann 72
BRUCE, Elvira 4
BRUCE, Geo. S. 35
BRUCE, H. W. 66
BRUCE, Henry 37
BRUCE, Henry (Sr.) 4
BRUCE, James 4
BRUCE, Lucinda 50
BRUCE, Lucinda 57
BRUCE, Lucy P. 38
BRUCE, Nancy 35
BRUSHELL, Elizabeth 37

BRYANT, Daniel 99
BRYANT, Gus 100
BRYANT, Hester A. 128
BRYANT, John J. 123
BRYANT, Lester A. 103
BRYANT, Maria 100
BRYANT, William H. 123
BUCHANAN, Coleman 86
BUCHANAN, Joseph 83
BUCHANAN, Joseph 89
BUCHANAN, Mary F. 86
BUCHANAN, Sarah C. 83
BUCHANNAN, Elizth. 86
BUCHANNON, ----- 66
BUCKANAN, Joseph 67
BUCKENRIDGE, J. C. 60
BUCKLER, Allis 75
BUCKLER, Viers 50
BUCKLER, W. P. 50
BUCKLER, W. T. 84
BUCKLER, Wilson 74
BUCKLER, Wilson 75
BUCKLEY, Nancy 2
BUCKLEY, Nancy 45
BUDGES, John 120
BUNIES, E. P. 56
BURGESS, James S. 85
BURGESS, Rachael 39
BURGESS, Rbecca 117
BURGESS, Rebecca 106
BURGOSS, Rebecca 87
BURK, Abram 16
BURK, J. N. 58
BURK, J. W. 48
BURK, Jane 62
BURK, John N. 56
BURKE, Amanda 39
BURKE, Amanda 126
BURKE, Mattie E. 110
BURKE, Nancy Ann 39
BURNES, James 132
BURNIS, James 103
BURNIS, Salathiel 43
BURNS, ----- 35
BURNS, ----- 101
BURNS, Annie F. 132
BURNS, Charles F. 99
BURNS, Dennis 5
BURNS, Dennis 35
BURNS, E. R. 110
BURNS, Enoch P. 99

BURNS, Jno. 103
BURNS, Martha 41
BURRES, Francis 110
BURRISS, Julia 8
BURRISS, M. E. 108
BURRISS, Maria E. 86
BURROUGHS, Martha 64
BURUS, Margaret A. 97
BUSBY, Edward 98
BUSBY, Eli E. 77
BUSBY, Robert S. 98
BUSH, ----- 35
BUSH, Daniel 35
BUSH, E. F. 110
BUSH, Henry 99
BUSH, Ida M. 128
BUSH, James 90
BUSH, John H. 100
BUSH, Leslie 123
BUSH, M. 110
BUSH, Mahala 85
BUSH, Mary 127
BUSH, Pat 35
BUSH, Susan 74
BUSH, Susana 123
BUSH, Tobias 107
BUSH, Tobias 128
BUSH, Tobin 90
BUSH, W. 107
BUSHLER, Matilda 92
BUTLER, Elisha D. 44
BUTLER, John H. 44
BUTTAR, Thos. 18
BUTTE, Harriet 95

CABE, Vinicia M. 89
CACHMAN, ----- 66
CALAHAN, Edward 53
CALAHAN, Sonnett 22
CALHAN(?), Cintha 47
CALL, Daniel 82
CALL, Francis M. 82
CALL, Henrietta 90
CALL, Henrietta 123
CALL, Nimroe 106
CALLAHAN, Anderson 33
CALLAHAN, Anderson 80
CALLAHAN, Cynthia 38
CALLAHAN, Edward 32
CALLAHAN, George N. 22
CALLAHAN, James M. 32
CALLAHAN, John W. 81

CALLAHAN, Martha A. 14
CALLAHAN, Rebecca 33
CALLAHAN, Sennet 74
CALLAHAN, Sennett 81
CALLAHAN, William W. 80
CALVERT, Anna Bell 42
CALVERT, Burgess 118
CALVERT, Crilla Jane 10
CALVERT, Criller Jane 52
CALVERT, Francis 118
CALVERT, G. W. 42
CALVERT, G. W. 70
CALVERT, James 40
CALVERT, James N. 41
CALVERT, Marion 41
CALVERT, Rebecca 40
CAMBPELL, Jane 67
CAMERON, Andrew 91
CAMMINS, Lucy Ann 34
CAMPBELL, Albert W. 46
CAMPBELL, Armstead 79
CAMPBELL, C. B. 109
CAMPBELL, C. T. 109
CAMPBELL, Cassandre 124
CAMPBELL, Elizabeth 75
CAMPBELL, George N. 83
CAMPBELL, James 75
CAMPBELL, Jane 46
CAMPBELL, Kentey Ann 30
CAMPBELL, M. A. 111
CAMPBELL, Martha 83
CAMPBELL, Matilda 75
CAMPBELL, Nancy Ann 37
CAMPBELL, Stephen 46
CANER, Louisa M. 17
CANNATTIN, Mary 22
CANTBY, Patrick 24
CAREY, Amelia 30
CAREY, James 21
CARMICHAEL, Trusidale 54
CARPENTER(?), Daniel 80
CARPENTER, ----- 30
CARPENTER, Ann E. 31
CARPENTER, Ann E. 65
CARPENTER, Annie 106
CARPENTER, Bettie 131
CARPENTER, Charles 118
CARPENTER, Charles L. 52
CARPENTER, Daniel 53
CARPENTER, Edna A. 31
CARPENTER, Elijah 64

CARPENTER, Elijah L. 13
CARPENTER, Elijah L. 52
CARPENTER, Elizth. M. 95
CARPENTER, Emma 118
CARPENTER, George 17
CARPENTER, Harvey 17
CARPENTER, James 82
CARPENTER, James E. 15
CARPENTER, James E. 77
CARPENTER, Jas. 94
CARPENTER, Jno. C. 95
CARPENTER, John 42
CARPENTER, John F. 72
CARPENTER, John S. 30
CARPENTER, M. E. 116
CARPENTER, Marilda 13
CARPENTER, Marshall 31
CARPENTER, Martha E. 71
CARPENTER, Mary 131
CARPENTER, Mary E. 15
CARPENTER, Mary E. 31
CARPENTER, Mary R. 15
CARPENTER, Matilda 95
CARPENTER, Nancy 71
CARPENTER, Owen B. 94
CARPENTER, Peter 82
CARPENTER, Rachel M. 52
CARPENTER, Rachel M. 72
CARPENTER, Ricahrd E. 31
CARPENTER, Richard 52
CARPENTER, Richard 53
CARPENTER, Richard 78
CARPENTER, Richard 118
CARPENTER, Robert M. 118
CARPENTER, S. P. 60
CARPENTER, Samuel J. 51
CARPENTER, Samuel J. 77
CARPENTER, Samuel L. 69
CARPENTER, Sarah Alice 42
CARPENTER, Simeon P. 103
CARPENTER, William 131
CARPENTER, William G. 118
CARPENTER, William M. 80
CARPENTER, Wm. 95
CARPENTER, Wm. 106
CARPENTER, Wm. M. 53
CARR, Caroline 128
CARR, Fleming 98
CARR, Lager 98
CARR, Mary 78
CARR, Pickett 125

CARSTIN, Sophia A. 29
CARTER, Caroline L. 6
CARTER, Zeller A. 59
CARTMELL, Mary A. 87
CARTMELL, W. W. 87
CARTWELL, Rachael 123
CASADY, Rosanah 66
CASE, John F. 75
CASE, W. S. 50
CASE, Walter 75
CASEY, Evalinda 21
CASEY, Mary 90
CASH, Malinda 86
CASIDA, Mary E. 46
CASIDA, Nancy 49
CASSIDAY, James 84
CASSIDY, Edgus E. 128
CASSIDY, Emma 125
CASSIDY, Emmitt 128
CASSIDY, Henry 56
CASSIDY, Henry 74
CASSIDY, Henry 84
CASSIDY, Jackson 73
CASSIDY, Jennie 123
CASSIDY, Lucy 98
CASSIDY, Mary 74
CASSIDY, Mary E. 62
CASSITY, A. R. 31
CASSITY, Eliza J. 21
CASSITY, Franklin 6
CASSITY, James A. 31
CASSITY, Jonathan M. 6
CAVAN, John A. 10
CAYWOOD, A. S. 114
CAYWOOD, Elza 103
CAYWOOD, Emery 123
CAYWOOD, Francis M. 103
CAYWOOD, George M. 101
CAYWOOD, Hageline 91
CAYWOOD, Jane 104
CAYWOOD, Jane R. 81
CAYWOOD, Jane R. 83
CAYWOOD, Jane R. 131
CAYWOOD, Jemmia 35
CAYWOOD, Louisa 90
CAYWOOD, Mason 58
CAYWOOD, Randolph 35
CAYWOOD, Sarah A. 103
CAYWOOD, T. A. 114
CAYWOOD, Thomas C. 127
CAYWOOD, Thomas H. 127

CAYWOOD, Thos. A.. 90
CAYWOOD, W. H. 49
CAYWOOD, William 123
CHADWICK, Thompson 41
CHANDER, Franklin P. 18
CHANDLER, Henry 50
CHANDLER, T. B. 18
CHANDLER, Titus B. 64
CHANDLER, Walter W. 50
CHAPELL, ----- 38
CHAPELL, James 38
CHOAT, Ricy Ann 51
CHORD, Mary V. 43
CHORD, William H. 43
CHRISINSON, Ellizabeth 3
CHRISMAN, Amanda 61
CHRISMAN, Amanice 67
CHRISMAN, Andrew 27
CHRISMAN, Elizabeth 83
CHRISMAN, John 27
CHRISMAN, Lucinda 46
CHRISMAN, Malinda 27
CHRISMAN, Martha E. 82
CHRISMAN, Mary 60
CHRISMEN, Lucinda 38
CHRISTIAN, Davis C. 41
CHRISTIAN, John B. 41
CHRISTY, Eliza Jane 40
CHRISTY, Elizabeth S. 28
CHRISTY, George W. 10
CHRISTY, Mary F. 41
CHRISTY, Robert A. 41
CHRISTY, William E. 10
CHRISTY, William E. 28
CINNEYS(?), William 91
CLACK, Mary F.B. 21
CLACK, Moses T. 73
CLACK, Thompsin 21
CLAINE, Polly 53
CLARK, Annie 117
CLARK, Danl. 57
CLARK, Eliza Jane 47
CLARK, John 38
CLARK, John F. 46
CLARK, Maranda 16
CLARK, Margaret 67
CLARK, Mary 38
CLARK, Moses T. 81
CLARK, Nancy 6
CLARK, Sallie 126
CLARK, Samuel 82

CLARKE, B. D. 108
CLARKE, Benjamin 128
CLARKE, E. J. 108
CLARKE, Elias 108
CLARKE, Elias 114
CLARKE, Eliza 97
CLARKE, Emma 114
CLARKE, Harry 127
CLARKE, J. C. 107
CLARKE, John D. 128
CLARKE, Leonard 100
CLARKE, M. D. 114
CLARKE, Samuel P. 107
CLARKE, Thomas 107
CLARKE, Tina J. 127
CLARKE, Virginia A. 107
CLARY, Ann E. 16
CLARY, George Ann 42
CLARY, Harriett 79
CLARY, James M. 72
CLARY, Mary 94
CLARY, Nancy 29
CLARY, Nannie 131
CLARY, Warner 16
CLARY, Warner 42
CLARY, William 70
CLAYBORN, Maria 127
CLAYPOOLE, Elizabeth 117
CLEFT, Liddie 104
CLICK, Martha 122
CLICK, Mary O. 12
CLIFF, Susan 128
CLINE, ----- 38
CLINE, Harrison 38
CLINE, Harrison 48
CLINE, Harrison 65
CLINE, Lucinda J. 18
CLINE, Margaret E. 83
CLINE, Mary 80
CLINE, Saml. F. 18
CLINE, Samuel 53
CLINE, Samuel L. 69
CLINE, William 48
CLINE, Wm. H. 83
CLINKENBEARD, Jonathan 81
CLINKENBEARD, Mary J. 81
CLINKENBEARD, Robert 81
CLINKIMBEARD, Jonthn. 18
CLINKINHEARD, Robert 67
CLINKINTON, Jonathan 67
CLINSMAN, Mary 36

COOPER, Margaret 46
COOPER, Margaret A. 15
COOPER, Sarah 15
COOPER, Sarah E. 9
COOPER, Susannah 12
COOPER, Trumbs 40
COOPER, William 40
CORA, --- 1
CORD, Elzh. 36
CORD, George W. 105
CORD, John M. 56
CORD, John M. 83
CORD, Julia Ann 58
CORD, Leander C. 124
CORD, Leandor G. 96
CORD, Sally Ann 56
CORD, Sarah Ann 83
CORD, Susan S. 124
CORD, Wm. M. 114
CORY, S. M. 108
CORYELL, Albertie 120
CORYELL, William O. 100
CORYELL, William O. 120
COSBY, Nancy 59
COTTINGHAM, James 118
COTTINGHAM, James K. 118
COURTNEY, Elizabeth 39
COURTNEY, Geo. L. 86
COURTNEY, George L. 124
COURTNEY, Herman F. 86
COURTNEY, Mattie C. 124
COURTNEY, Nancy 3
COURTNEY, Susie L. 124
COURTNEY, William 124
COURTNEY, Wm. E. 86
COURTNEY, Wm. F. 3
COURTNEY, Wm. F. 86
COUSER, Robert H. 41
COWAN, ----- 38
COWAN, John 38
COWSER, Robert 12
COX, A. J. 113
COX, Amanda J. 95
COX, John S. 1
COX, L. B. 1
COX, Mattie A. 113
COX, Maud R. 115
COX, Milford 130
COX, William 115
COX, William 130
COY, Nancy M. 88

COYL, Martha 32
CRAFFORD, Maria L. 55
CRAIG, Ann 56
CRAIG, David 25
CRAIG, Samuel H. 25
CRAIN, Amanda Bell 21
CRAIN, Amanda J. 60
CRAIN, Amanda J. 82
CRAIN, Amant 129
CRAIN, Bertha 122
CRAIN, Charles T. 111
CRAIN, Charlette 58
CRAIN, E. J. 62
CRAIN, Eleanor 14
CRAIN, Elizabeth 22
CRAIN, Elizabeth 68
CRAIN, Florence A. 23
CRAIN, Florinda 21
CRAIN, Francis 129
CRAIN, Henry Clay 40
CRAIN, Hiram 47
CRAIN, Isabella 81
CRAIN, James J. 47
CRAIN, Jane 19
CRAIN, Jane 65
CRAIN, Jno. H. 88
CRAIN, John 21
CRAIN, John F. 21
CRAIN, John F. 40
CRAIN, John F. 64
CRAIN, John T. 69
CRAIN, Judath 59
CRAIN, Lewellyn 52
CRAIN, Lewis P. 111
CRAIN, Lucinda 19
CRAIN, Lucinda 70
CRAIN, Lucinda 71
CRAIN, Lucinda 76
CRAIN, Lucinda C. 105
CRAIN, Mahaba E. 27
CRAIN, Mahala E. 5
CRAIN, Mahala E. 88
CRAIN, Marshall 5
CRAIN, Marshall 27
CRAIN, Nancy 23
CRAIN, Rebecca R. 88
CRAIN, Roda A. 70
CRAIN, S. 112
CRAIN, S. L. 66
CRAIN, Sarah 119
CRAIN, Sarah J. 109

CLOWELL, Amanda 72
CLOYD, Ezekiel 20
CLUPPER, Levina 52
CLUTER, S. A. 108
CLYNE, Elizabeth 114
COCHRAN, ----- 35
COCHRAN, ----- 65
COCHRAN, Eliza 15
COCHRAN, Eliza 50
COCHRAN, Elizabeth 126
COCHRAN, Elizth. T. 16
COCHRAN, James 35
COCHRAN, Malinda 44
COCHRAN, Malinda 57
COCHRAN, Malinda 58
COCHRAN, Martha 123
COCHRAN, Mary 20
COCHRAN, Mary 85
COCHRAN, Mary A. 100
COCHRAN, Robert 35
COCHRAN, Robt. 89
COCHRAN, S. A. 107
COCHRAN, Sarah 127
COCHRAN, Thos. 35
COCHRELL, Mary P. 15
COCKRAN, Malinda 65
COGAN, Katie 91
COGAN, Katie 124
COGAN, Mary 92
COGGWELL, Rachael 32
COGSWELL, Henry 40
COGSWELL, Lewis Elder 40
COGSWELL, Thomas 30
COIL, Martha 41
COLBERT, Jas. M. 17
COLBERT, Mary P. 17
COLBERT, Nancy 31
COLE, Catharine 35
COLE, Cathn. 37
COLE, William 35
COLEMAN, Amanda 121
COLEMAN, Elilha 121
COLIVER, Evy 84
COLIVER, J. C. 112
COLIVER, James 84
COLIVER, Wm. 112
COLLINS, Elizabeth 103
COLLINS, Jno. E. 104
COLLINS, John E. 123
COLLINS, Lucy 98
COLLINS, Lucy F. 123

COLLINS, Lutie L. 93
COLLINS, Mahala 11
COLLINS, Martha 34
COLLINS, Rebecca 103
COLLINS, William 98
COLLINS, Wm. 93
COLLOHAN, Sinet 49
COLVERT, Crilla J. 72
COLWELL, Amanda 64
COMADY, John F. 18
COMADY, Peter 18
COMBS, Fannie 121
COMWELL, James 27
COMWELL, James 59
COMWELL, Thomas R. 27
CONDEN, Bartholomew 122
CONDEN, Margaret 122
CONDIFF, ----- 13
CONDIFF, Walter M. 13
CONLEY, John 129
CONLEY, Mary 78
CONLEY, Mollie H. 129
CONLEY, Patrick 101
CONLEY, William E. 101
CONROD, ----- 24
CONROD, G. W. 25
CONROD, Rueben 25
CONWAY, George Early 42
CONWAY, Peter 42
COOBY, Nancy 74
COOK, ----- 36
COOK, Alexr. M. 96
COOK, Briget 69
COOK, Edward 36
COOK, Thos. A. 96
COONEY, Joseph 119
COONEY, Miranda 119
COONROD, Ruben 53
COOPER, Amanda 28
COOPER, Amanda 72
COOPER, Franklin 41
COOPER, George 9
COOPER, George 41
COOPER, Isabel 39
COOPER, Isabella A. 70
COOPER, Isabella Ann 9
COOPER, Isabelle 53
COOPER, Jonathan 43
COOPER, Kate 93
COOPER, Kesiah 21
COOPER, Kesiah 21

DARNELL, Thomas C. 127
DARNELL, Wm. H. 1
DARRNALL, Jautina 63
DAUGHERTY, A. 114
DAUGHERTY, Charles 98
DAUGHERTY, Hannah S. 106
DAUGHERTY, James 122
DAUGHERTY, Lula 125
DAUGHERTY, Thomas 48
DAUGHERTY, Thomas 125
DAUGHERTY, Wm. 109
DAVENPORT, Joseph 94
DAVENPORT, Mary E. 94
DAVENPORT, Thornton 54
DAVENPORT, Thornton 79
DAVID, Mary E. 82
DAVIS, A. T. 88
DAVIS, Amanda 54
DAVIS, Ann E. 80
DAVIS, Austin 41
DAVIS, Basil 88
DAVIS, C. Z. 115
DAVIS, Charles H. 23
DAVIS, Charles H. 28
DAVIS, Charlotte 41
DAVIS, Charlotte 64
DAVIS, Chas. 88
DAVIS, Col.F. R. 23
DAVIS, Debora 6
DAVIS, Dudley 55
DAVIS, Dudley 70
DAVIS, Dudley 129
DAVIS, E. G. 80
DAVIS, E. P. 88
DAVIS, Elias 27
DAVIS, Elias G. 41
DAVIS, Elizabeth 22
DAVIS, Elizabeth J. 80
DAVIS, Etta 88
DAVIS, F. 112
DAVIS, F. R. 63
DAVIS, Fletcher 61
DAVIS, Fletcher 88
DAVIS, Frances Marion 40
DAVIS, Harry 40
DAVIS, Jacob 118
DAVIS, James H. 77
DAVIS, James W. 40
DAVIS, John A. 55
DAVIS, John L. 70
DAVIS, John M. 33

DAVIS, Lewellyn 27
DAVIS, Lewellyn 40
DAVIS, Louisa 63
DAVIS, Louisa 65
DAVIS, Lucinda 73
DAVIS, Lucinda 130
DAVIS, Martha Ann 40
DAVIS, Martha J. 33
DAVIS, Mary A. 103
DAVIS, Mary Ann 53
DAVIS, Mary E. 94
DAVIS, Mary E. 100
DAVIS, Mary Elizabeth 42
DAVIS, Reese 42
DAVIS, Reese 71
DAVIS, Saml. G. 63
DAVIS, Samuel 77
DAVIS, Sarah 129
DAVIS, Susan 91
DAVIS, T. J. 112
DAVIS, Taylor 129
DAVIS, Taylor 129
DAVIS, William 129
DAWSON, Mary 28
DAY, ------ 89
DAY, A. W. 68
DAY, Diana R. 12
DAY, Eliza J. 8
DAY, Elizabeth 30
DAY, Elizabeth 55
DAY, Louella 116
DAY, Maggie 104
DAY, Margaret 53
DAY, Margaret 63
DAY, Margaret 82
DAY, Martha 18
DAY, Martha A. 68
DAY, Martha A. 82
DAY, Mary 28
DAY, Mary 77
DAY, May 63
DAY, Mirian 53
DAY, Nancy 70
DAY, Rebecca 17
DAY, S. A. 12
DAY, Squire A. 83
DAY, Truman S. 104
DAY, Virginia B. 83
DAYLEY, Henry D. 82
DEAN, Mary 67
DEANING, Allan 11

CRAIN, T. J. 64
CRAIN, Thomas 23
CRAIN, William 1
CRAIN, Wm. 59
CRAWFORD, Drison T.G. 70
CRAWFORD, Edith 130
CRAWFORD, Edna 119
CRAWFORD, Elizabeth 83
CRAWFORD, James 130
CRAWFORD, Joab 117
CRAWFORD, Joanna 63
CRAWFORD, John 8
CRAWFORD, John 59
CRAWFORD, John 74
CRAWFORD, John 117
CRAWFORD, Joseph 117
CRAWFORD, Leandor 89
CRAWFORD, Luther Burgess 14
CRAWFORD, M. L. 14
CRAWFORD, Minnie 89
CRAWFORD, Sarah 8
CRAWFORD, Thomas 74
CROTTY, Catharine 8
CROTTY, John 43
CROTTY, Patrick 8
CROTTY, Patrick 43
CROTTY, Patrick 72
CROTTY, Patrick 77
CROWLEY, Ellen 74
CRUMP, Nancy 83
CRYWOOD, Thos. A. 65
CUDIHI, James 83
CULLIN, ----- 35
CULLIN, Thos. 36
CULLIPP, S. C. 114
CUMMINS, Edward 124
CUMMINS, Mary 125
CUMMONS, Lucy A. 57
CUNNINGHAM, Saml. 64
CUNNINGHAM, Samuel 72
CURRANS, S. 112
CURTIS, Elvira 42
CURTIS, Elvira 78
CUSICK, Katharine 73

DABYINPLE, Danl. 16
DABYINPLE, Matilda C. 16
DAILEY, Adda L. 119
DAILEY, Marie 87
DAILEY, Mary C. 41
DAILEY, Milton 119
DAILEY, Sarah 45

DAILY, Covington 82
DAILY, Richard N. 45
DAILY, Samuel Thomas 45
DAIRS, Louisa 18
DALDYMPLE, Harriett 81
DALE, Asa P. 13
DALE, John 24
DALE, John 56
DALE, Mary Ann 71
DALE, Paulina 25
DALE, Pellina 65
DALE, Perline 71
DALE, Polly Ann 6
DALE, Polly Ann 31
DALEY, Eolin Swim 44
DALEY, James C. 44
DALRGNIPLE, Daniel 83
DALRGNIPLE, Elizabeth 82
DALRGNIPLE, Hannah 82
DALRYANPLE, Hannah 27
DALRYMIPLE, James 65
DALRYMPLE, Danl. 44
DALRYMPLE, Hannah 60
DANIS, Maranda 13
DANLEY, Anna Stamper 44
DANLEY, Leroy C. 44
DANRYMPLE, Danl. 68
DAOUGHERTY, Minnie 122
DARIS, Col. F. R. 28
DARIS, Elizth. 7
DARIS, Nancy 14
DARIS, Nancy 15
DARNALL, ----- 65
DARNALL, Cornelia 76
DARNALL, H. J. 74
DARNALL, H. T. 16
DARNALL, Jastena 26
DARNALL, John W. 81
DARNALL, Justine 44
DARNALL, Lizzie 99
DARNALL, Luellen 73
DARNALL, Martha 7
DARNALL, Sarah 109
DARNALL, Sarah A. 5
DARNALL, Sophia 84
DARNALL, Wm. H. 49
DARNATT, Patsy 1
DARNELL, Gilbert 127
DARNELL, Isaac 3
DARNELL, Martha 1
DARNELL, Sallie 125

DEANING, Jas. T. 4
DEANING, Juelda James 4
DEANING, Wm. E. 11
DEARING, Alice 109
DEARING, Burgess 8
DEARING, James T. 46
DEARING, Jas. T. 19
DEARING, Jas. Thos. 18
DEARING, Lucinda F. 8
DEARING, Lydia Mae 34
DEARING, Lyia 68
DEARING, Margaret 18
DEARING, Simpson 23
DEATLEY, Rebecca 130
DEBELL, Alfred 54
DEBELL, Hessie 131
DEBELL, Joel 27
DEBELL, Joel 43
DEBELL, Joel 54
DEBELL, Johua H. 94
DEBELL, Kittie 81
DEBELL, Kitty 51
DEBELL, Lillie 131
DEBELL, Nancy 11
DEBELL, William 79
DEBELL, William H. 25
DEBELL, William J. 25
DEBELL, Wm. 113
DEBELT, William 54
DEBILL, Chas. G. 94
DEERING, Bittie C. 83
DEERING, Elizabeth Edna 43
DEERING, James T. 83
DEERING, John 119
DEERING, William 119
DELBA, David 21
DEMOSS, Lewis 22
DEMOSS, Sarah E. 22
DENT, Lucy 123
DENT, Mary D. 68
DENT, Mary D. 84
DENT, Mary D. 97
DENT, Mary D. 104
DENT, Wm. R. 75
DENTON, Abram 16
DENTON, Abram 20
DENTON, Abram 64
DENTON, Ed 109
DENTON, Ed 119
DENTON, Eliza 89
DENTON, F. G. 14

DENTON, Frances 40
DENTON, James 6
DENTON, James 20
DENTON, John W. 129
DENTON, Jonathan 40
DENTON, Lydia B. 119
DENTON, M. A. 116
DENTON, Mary Alice 6
DENTON, Mary B. 22
DENTON, Melvena 16
DENTON, O. B. 116
DENTON, Sara 77
DENTON, Sarah 42
DENTON, Sarah 62
DENTON, Sarah 63
DENTON, Simpson 20
DENTON, Thomas 129
DENTON, William Ann 14
DENTON, William R. 69
DENTON, Wm. 62
DENTON, Wm. P. 68
DICKEY, Ann E. 47
DICKEY, E. J. 109
DICKEY, Eliza 56
DICKEY, Eliza 73
DICKEY, James I. 109
DICKEY, Sarah 79
DICKSON, Elizabeth 49
DICKSON, James 49
DICKSON, James W. 75
DICKSON, John 75
DICKSON, William F. 80
DIERING, Burgess 43
DILLEN, Ellen 82
DILLEN, James P.A. 84
DILLIN, Britton 84
DILLON, Alice T. 89
DILLON, Britain 60
DILLON, California 122
DILLON, Elizabeth 7
DILLON, Elizabeth 51
DILLON, Elizabeth 72
DILLON, Emma 111
DILLON, Ira 73
DILLON, Isaiah 24
DILLON, Joanna 35
DILLON, Joanne 49
DILLON, L. 64
DILLON, Latitia 21
DILLON, Luticia 40
DILLON, Luticia 69

DILLON, M. C. 109
DILLON, Maggie 107
DILLON, Margaret 43
DILLON, Maria 37
DILLON, Mary 61
DILLON, Mary A. 74
DILLON, Mary Ann 26
DILLON, Mary E. 24
DILLON, Mary E. 117
DILLON, Rebecca J. 128
DILLON, Robert A. 128
DILLON, T. J. 89
DILLON, Thomas J. 59
DILLON, William 117
DINT, Mary V. 75
DISCON, James A. 82
DISCON, Manda E. 82
DITTON, Isaiah 61
DIXON, Alice 114
DIXON, Henry 58
DIXON, Joseph 64
DIXON, Mary J. 124
DLARY, Eliza A. 94
DOBYNO, Sarah J. 72
DOBYNS, ----- 39
DOBYNS, Charles H. 34
DOBYNS, Henry 39
DOBYNS, Henry B. 98
DOBYNS, Henry E. 98
DOBYNS, Sarah J. 42
DODDS, James 27
DODDS, James E. 51
DODGE, John 127
DODGE, John J. 106
DODGE, Lucy J. 127
DODGE, M. C. 106
DODGE, Van 55
DOGGET, Frankey 62
DOLLY, Mary 3
DOLYNS, Henry 34
DONALDSON, Isabella 105
DOODS, Charles 27
DORAIN, Patrick 99
DORSEY, Albin 110
DORSEY, E. J. 110
DORSEY, Julia 51
DORSEY, Juliet E. 66
DORSEY, Juliett 38
DOTRON, ----- 66
DOTSON, C. E. 114
DOTSON, J. W. 114

DOTSON, John W. 124
DOUGHERTY, Barney 84
DOUGHERTY, Catharine 98
DOUGHERTY, J. M. 88
DOUGHERTY, James C. 48
DOUGHERTY, Lewellyn 25
DOUGHERTY, Lewellyn 54
DOUGHERTY, Louellen 79
DOUGHERTY, Louisa L. 88
DOUGHERTY, Mary S. 84
DOUGHERTY, Minerva 10
DOUGHERTY, Minerva 52
DOUGHERTY, Patrick 67
DOUGHERTY, Thos. 37
DOUGHERTY, Thos. 73
DOUGHERTY, Wm. T. 37
DOUGLAS, Emily 103
DOWN, Edward 29
DOWNEY, Charles M. 105
DOWNEY, Emily 77
DOWNEY, Henry C. 105
DOWNEY, James 77
DOWNEY, Jas. C. 133
DOWNEY, M. S. 115
DOWNEY, Mary J. 11
DOWNEY, Richard 115
DOWNIE, Joanna 23
DOWNS, Clementine 70
DOWNS, Clementine 79
DOWNS, Edward 29
DOWNS, Mary J. 29
DOYL, John 32
DOYL, Miles 32
DOYL, Milky 25
DOYLE, Elizabeth 10
DOYLE, Elizabeth 114
DOYLE, Henry F. Belt 42
DOYLE, Jas. F. 94
DOYLE, John 100
DOYLE, John D. 15
DOYLE, John W. 15
DOYLE, John W. 51
DOYLE, John W. 71
DOYLE, Joseph F. 51
DOYLE, Joseph F. 71
DOYLE, Lucinda 71
DOYLE, Maggie B. 120
DOYLE, Malva 25
DOYLE, Maranda 118
DOYLE, Martha 121
DOYLE, Martha J. 53

DOYLE, Martha J. 69
DOYLE, Mary 8
DOYLE, Mary 51
DOYLE, Mary 71
DOYLE, Miles 114
DOYLE, Milky 63
DOYLE, Patrick H. 100
DOYLE, Priscilla 76
DOYLE, Thomas 120
DOYLE, William 10
DOYLE, William 10
DOYLE, William 42
DOYLE, William 69
DREHAN, Georgie 128
DRENNAN, Jas. 109
DRENNAN, Ory 109
DRUMAN, Thomas 79
DRYDEN, Robt. L. 94
DUALEY, John B. 77
DUDLEY(?), Keen R. 77
DUDLEY, ----- 56
DUDLEY, Alice B. 100
DUDLEY, Elizabeth 59
DUDLEY, Elizabeth 73
DUDLEY, Elizabeth 122
DUDLEY, Ella B. 120
DUDLEY, F. A. 84
DUDLEY, Frances 5
DUDLEY, Harriet 93
DUDLEY, James 4
DUDLEY, James B. 110
DUDLEY, Lilie 51
DUDLEY, Lucy 90
DUDLEY, Lucy P. 64
DUDLEY, Martha J. 77
DUDLEY, Robert 110
DUDLEY, W. T. 36
DUDLEY, W. T. 51
DUDLEY, William 122
DUDLEY, William T. 68
DUDLEY, William T. 81
DUETT, Catharine 21
DUFFEY, Lettie 86
DUFFEY, Wm. 86
DULEY, Caroline 117
DULEY, M. J. 116
DULEY, W. N. 60
DULEY, William 23
DULIN, John W. 68
DUNBAR, J. S. 64
DUNCAN, Armilda 46

DUNCAN, Armilda 68
DUNCAN, C. K.B. 59
DUNCAN, Mary 56.
DUNCAN, William H. 78
DUNKINS, America 13
DUNN, Britton 82
DUNN, James A. 82
DUNN, John 82
DUNN, John 117
DUNN, Mary C. 117
DUPERY, Virginia 43
DURANT, J. 112
DURKE, Juliet 44
DURRETT, Ben W. 77
DUVALL, Martha 36
DUVALL, Mosen 36
DYE, Laura B. 124
DYE, Laura D. 86
DYE, Sarah F. 100
DYRE, July Ann 69

EARLES, A. J. 91
EARLES, A. M. 113
EARLES, Nannie 91
EARLES, Rees 113
EARLY, Elias 57
EARLY, John 36
EARLY, Mary 39
EATON, Albert 81
EATON, Mary Ann 81
EATON, William 81
ECKLES, James 51
ECKLES, Mary 26
ECKLES, Mary E. 53
ECKMAN, D. J. 5
ECKMAN, Danl. 75
ECKMAN, James T. 75
EDEN, Louisa 102
EDEN, M. A. 116
EDEN, Rachel 49
EDEN, Wm. 68
EDON, Maggie 120
EDWARDS, Albert James 66
EDWARDS, G. W. 66
EDWARDS, Harvy D. 22
EDWARDS, James A. 130
EDWARDS, John C. 101
EDWARDS, John C. 101
EDWARDS, Martin 130
EDWARDS, S. F. 91
EDWARDS, William 22
ELIOTT, Martha 10

ELIOTT, Martha 42
ELLIOTT, ----- 34
ELLIOTT, Alberta 121
ELLIOTT, Amanda 41
ELLIOTT, Caroline 121
ELLIOTT, G. W. 29
ELLIOTT, George 29
ELLIOTT, George 69
ELLIOTT, James 34
ELLIOTT, James 41
ELLIOTT, Mary J. 120
ELSTON, Edward 24
ELSTON, Edward 41
ELSTON, Edward 77
ELSTON, Louisa C. 24
ELSTON, Mary 42
ELSTON, Mary 72
ELSTON, Nancy B. 100
ELSTON, Nancy Bell 41
ELSTON, Nannie B. 120
EMBRY, B. M. 67
EMBRY, Suan 130
EMMANS, Lou Ellen 81
EMMETT, Michael 119
EMMONS, ----- 97
EMMONS, Amanda 43
EMMONS, Elizabeth 104
EMMONS, Ellen C. 85
EMMONS, Eveline 17
EMMONS, Fenton 122
EMMONS, Geneva 122
EMMONS, Henry P. 74
EMMONS, J. B. 64
EMMONS, J. E. 105
EMMONS, Joseph Belt 39
EMMONS, Lida M. 96
EMMONS, Louisa 11
EMMONS, Louisa 23
EMMONS, Louisa 39
EMMONS, Louisa 52
EMMONS, Louissa 70
EMMONS, Lucinda 11
EMMONS, Mahala 39
EMMONS, Mahala 111
EMMONS, Malissa 118
EMMONS, Mary 122
EMMONS, Mary J. 50
EMMONS, Minnie 122
EMMONS, Patsey Jane 39
EMMONS, Paul Avory 16
EMMONS, Rufus 12

EMMONS, Rufus 62
EMMONS, Rufus 74
EMMONS, Samuel 33
EMMONS, T. A. 105
EMMONS, Virginia 109
EMMONS, W. W. 105
EMMONS, Willaim 33
EMMONS, William 16
EMMONS, William 40
EMMONS, William S.F. 39
EMMONS, William S.T. 69
EMMONS, Wm. 53
EMMONS, Wm. St. Clair 12
EMONS(?), St. Clair 68
ENGLISH, Francis A. 81
ENGLISH, James M. 75
ENGLISH, John E.H.P. 75
ENGLISH, John M. 81
ENILRY, Allen H. 45
ENILRY, R. M. 45
ENIX, Julia Ann 80
EPILE, Elizabeth 24
ERSKIN, Victoria 131
ESTILL, Harriet 52
ESTILL, Harriett 31
ESTILL, James M. 9
ESTILL, Lucinda 63
ESTILL, Lucinda 77
ESTILL, Messa 11
ESTILL, Mollie 125
ESTILL, Nancy 77
ESTILL, S. M. 89
ESTILL, Samuel 22
ESTILL, Sarah M. 22
ESTILL, Sarah M. 130
ESTILL, Silvester 9
ESTILL, Sylvester 63
ESTILL, Sylvester 80
ESTILL, Teressa 41
ESTILL, Teressa 80
ESTILL, Terresa 9
EUBANKS, C. D. 107
EUBANKS, Charles 107
EUBANKS, Charles 127
EUBANKS, Charles M. 123
EUBANKS, Louvina 127
EUBANKS, Milly 91
EUBANKS, William 123
EUISE, Hanna 17
EUNNORS, Amanda 8
EVANS, Allen M. 132

143

EVANS, Amanda 34
EVANS, Annie 132
EVANS, E. E. 115
EVANS, Eli 39
EVANS, Eliza Jane 11
EVANS, Ella 98
EVANS, F. S. 116
EVANS, Franklin 97
EVANS, Franklin 115
EVANS, Harriet 27
EVANS, J. B. 52
EVANS, J. M. 115
EVANS, J. S. 116
EVANS, James 108
EVANS, James B. 34
EVANS, James T. 87
EVANS, Jno. 87
EVANS, John T. 75
EVANS, Josephine B. 11
EVANS, Louisa 95
EVANS, Magners 11
EVANS, Margaret 49
EVANS, Margaret 72
EVANS, Margaret 82
EVANS, Marion 115
EVANS, Martha L. 96
EVANS, Mary 27
EVANS, Mary 66
EVANS, Mary 98
EVANS, Mary E. 51
EVANS, Mattie S. 97
EVANS, Morris 115
EVANS, Nancy 14
EVANS, Nancy 129
EVANS, O. V. 75
EVANS, Robert 42
EVANS, Robt. T. 11
EVANS, S. H. 110
EVANS, St. Clair 96
EVANS, Susan 6
EVANS, Susan 6
EVANS, Susan 34
EVANS, Susan 75
EVANS, Susan E. 37
EVANS, Virginia 7
EVANS, Virginia 54
EVANS, William B. 42
EVANS, William B. 72
EVANS, Wm. B. 34
EVANS, Zacheus 64
EVERETT, Alice 64

EVERETT, Alice H. 53
EVERETT, Jackson 64
EWBANKS, Malinda 54
EWING, ----- 38
EWING, G. W. 108
EWING, George M. 108
EWING, Jane 44
EWING, Wm. 66

FALKNER, George 76
FALKNER, Thomas G. 76
FANOW, John J. 4
FANOW, Thomas Fleming 4
FANT, Martha 35
FANT, Nelson 45
FANT, Nelson 68
FANT, William 84
FAQUA, Letitia 45
FARIS, Amanda 3
FARIS, Ambrose 17
FARIS, C. H. 25
FARIS, Eliza E. 83
FARIS, Ira 108
FARIS, James 127
FARIS, John 2
FARIS, John 19
FARIS, Jos. H. 90
FARIS, Joseph H. 61
FARIS, Joseph H. 87
FARIS, Joseph T. 89
FARIS, Kirk 126
FARIS, Len P. 2
FARIS, Loda 87
FARIS, Lucinda 73
FARIS, Lydia H. 127
FARIS, Mary 36
FARIS, Mary J. 25
FARIS, Mary J. 68
FARIS, Mathilda 81
FARIS, Ollie 126
FARIS, Samuel 83
FARIS, Watson 126
FARIS, Wm. E. 108
FARONS, William 30
FARRAR, Landen D. 54
FARREN, ----- 65
FARRIN, Julie 49
FARRIS, ----- 66
FARRIS, Almeda 17
FARRIS, Haroz 65
FARRIS, Harvey 25
FARRIS, Harvey M. 71

FARRIS, James T. 45
FARRIS, Samuel 66
FARRIS, Virginia M. 25
FARRNER, Louisa 25
FARROW, ----- 35
FARROW, ----- 65
FARROW, Caroline 98
FARROW, Elizabeth 53
FARROW, Elizabeth 54
FARROW, James H. 27
FARROW, John A. 65
FARROW, John William 42
FARROW, Joseph 27
FARROW, Joseph D. 15
FARROW, Joseph D. 43
FARROW, Kenas M. 42
FARROW, Kenas M. 98
FARROW, Mary E. 27
FARROW, Nancy H. 42
FARROW, Nimrod 35
FARROW, Susan 35
FARROW, T. S. 56
FARROW, T. S. 66
FARROW, Thornton S. 81
FARROW, William 81
FAUCETT, Franklin B. 93
FAUCETT, Saml. 93
FAUN, Sarah J. 41
FAWNS, Alfred 115
FAWNS, Eliza 52
FAWNS, Emily 41
FAWNS, John 22
FAWNS, Martha 13
FAWNS, Mary Ann 22
FEE, John 121
FELHOME(?), Thos. 57
FENTON, Rachel 42
FENTON, Rachel 42
FENTON, Rachel 72
FENTON, Rachel 80
FENTON, Rebecca 33
FERGUSON, Elizabeth E. 128
FERGUSON, Elizth. E. 90
FERGUSON, Elizth. E. 90
FERGUSON, L. E. 107
FERGUSON, Nancy 12
FERRIN, Benjm. 8
FERRIN, Mary 8
FICKLEN, Airey 36
FICKLIN, Achsah 5
FICKLIN, Achsah 5

FICKLIN, Ary 58
FICKLIN, Mary 84
FIELD, Jane 35
FIELDS, ----- 55
FIELDS, Artimesa 91
FIELDS, J. T. 108
FIELDS, John 35
FIELDS, Joseph 128
FIELDS, Sarah 103
FIELDS, Saran E. 128
FIELDS, Susan L. 128
FIELDS, Thomas 128
FIELDS, Wm. 108
FIFE, Harry 85
FIFE, Thos. 85
FILSON, Amanda C.C. 43
FILSON, Amanda E. 10
FILSON, Ethania 20
FILSON, George Maxwell 40
FILSON, Lewis D. 40
FILSON, Mystilla C.A. 10
FINDRY, Daniel 89
FINDRY, John H. 89
FINLEY, Ann J. 83
FINLEY, Elizabeth 74
FINLEY, James 37
FINLEY, Jane 45
FINLEY, John S. 37
FINLEY, Martha A. 68
FINLEY, Mary 56
FINLEY, Mary J. 74
FINLEY, Mary J. 99
FINLEY, Robt. T. 89
FINLY, Ann J. 67
FINSLEY, Harrison Dudly 39
FINSLEY, Samuel 39
FISCHER, John G. 29
FISCHER, John G. 72
FISCHER, Theodore 29
FISCHER, Victor 29
FISHER, Clary B. 124
FISHER, Lewis 124
FITCH, David 93
FITCH, David Wall 93
FITCH, Delia B. 54
FITCH, John F. 79
FITCH, Levina J. 54
FITCH, Lulie 120
FITCH, S. E. 111
FITCH, S. T. 54
FITCH, Salathiel 120

FITCH, Sarah A. 43
FITCH, W. D. 111
FITCHGERLD, Jno. 57
FITZGERAL, ----- 66
FITZGERALD, Nancy 50
FIZER, Chas. 94
FIZER, James H. 71
FIZER, James H. 76
FIZER, Ollie D. 131
FIZER, S. B. 52
FIZER, William 131
FIZER, William W. 79
FIZER, Wm. 52
FIZER, Wm. W. 94
FLAHERTY, Sarah 83
FLARITY, Sarah 66
FLAUGLEN, Francis M. 100
FLAUGLEN, Winstow 100
FLEMING, Chas. M. 11
FLEMING, Eliza M. 94
FLEMING, George S. 76
FLEMING, Jno. T. 51
FLEMING, Lewis 125
FLEMING, Mary T. 66
FLEMING, Sally Ann 51
FLEMING, Susan L. 125
FLEMING, Walter Scott 9
FLEMING, William 9
FLEMING, William 11
FLEMING, Wm. 74
FLEMING, Wm. P. 11
FLERAIN, Charlotte 82
FLETCHER, Aaron E. 120
FLETCHER, Ada 120
FLETCHER, Juliet 93
FLETCHER, Thomas 120
FLETCHER, dusey 93
FLEURING, Frank 97
FLINN, Lydia 121
FLOOD, Mary Ann 31
FLORA, Ida 124
FLORA, James 128
FLORA, John 124
FLORA, Josephine 123
FLORA, Matison 48
FLORA, Minnie C. 128
FLORA, Rebecca 92
FLORA, Rebecca 108
FLORA, Sarah 124
FOANG, Eliza 115
FOGG, William H. 99

FOLLAND, Catharine 27
FONDRAY, George W. 122
FONDRAY, William R. 122
FONS, John 40
FONS, Louisa 40
FORD, Hannah 35
FORROW, Kenis M. 79
FORROW, L. D. 79
FOSTER, Amanda 111
FOSTER, Margaret 100
FOUCH, Mary L. 67
FOUCHE, Malissa 30
FOUCHE, Sophia 30
FOUDERY, Adison M. 39
FOUDERY, Alfred Davis 39
FOUDRAY, Elizabeth 52
FOUDRAY, J. L. 54
FOUDRY, J. W. 28
FOUDRY, Jeff 36
FOUNDRAY, C. W. 70
FOUNTAIN, Andrew 11
FOUNTAIN, Andrew 65
FOUNTAIN, Robt. 11
FOURRAY, Elizth. Ann 6
FOX, Daniel 127
FOX, John A. 127
FOXWORTHY, Alex 18
FOXWORTHY, Alexander 42
FOXWORTHY, B. C. 37
FOXWORTHY, Boyd C. 130
FOXWORTHY, Clarissa 42
FOXWORTHY, Clarissa 70
FOXWORTHY, Eveline 70
FOXWORTHY, George W. 131
FOXWORTHY, Jane 42
FOXWORTHY, John 42
FOXWORTHY, John W. 131
FOXWORTHY, M. J. 42
FOXWORTHY, Mary 64
FOXWORTHY, Melvy J. 71
FOXWORTHY, Nancy Ann 24
FOXWORTHY, Nancy M. 53
FOXWORTHY, Nancy N. 94
FOXWORTHY, Squire 130
FOXWORTHY, Teletha 78
FOXWORTHY, Tolitha M. 3
FOXWORTHY, W. M. 53
FOXWORTHY, William M. 64
FRANCE, Elisha 44
FRANCE, John T. 26
FRANCE, Jonas 26

FRANCE, Jonas 44
FRANK, Carol A. 109
FRANK, Elanor 35
FRANK, Henry 75
FRANK, Joseph 125
FRANK, Joseph C. 109
FRANK, Lewis 75
FRANK, Lida 125
FRANKLIN, Addie E. 88
FRAZIER, Margt. A. 86
FREDRICK, J. H. 110
FREDRICK, John 110
FREDRICK, Lydia 123
FREDRICK, N. F. 110
FREDRICK, Sarah E. 124
FREELAN, Martha A. 74
FREELAN, Martha M. 67
FREEMAN, Amanda 59
FREEMAN, Amanda 82
FREEMAN, Amelia 54
FREEMAN, Amelia 79
FREEMAN, Gamaliel 28
FREEMAN, Gamaliel 77
FREEMAN, Louesa 13
FREEMAN, William 132
FREEMAN, William B. 132
FRENCH, Frances Jane 43
FRENCH, Jane 64
FRENCH, John H. 102
FRICKLIN, A. 48
FRIZZELL, Ann 93
FROGGS, Francis 86
FRULEY, Martha E. 28
FULKERSON, J. D. 27
FULKERSON, William T. 27
FULTON, George 22
FULTON, Mary Jane 22
FUQUA, Drucilla 14

GAINES, Alexander 93
GAIREY, ----- 35
GAIREY, Saml. 35
GAIRY, JohN C. 76
GAIRY, Wm. 76
GALLAHAN, Samuel 91
GALLAHER, Elizabeth 48
GALLIGHER, Elizabeth 38
GALLIHER, Elizabeth 83
GALLIHER, John 76
GALLIHER, Sarah E. 76
GALLY, Lewis 16
GANT, Nelson 37

GARDNER, ----- 30
GARDNER, Aaron 13
GARDNER, Aaron 63
GARDNER, Ann Elizabeth 80
GARDNER, B. H. 125
GARDNER, Charlotte 13
GARDNER, Chas. A. 95
GARDNER, Clarissa A. 26
GARDNER, Clarissa A. 45
GARDNER, Clarissa A. 68
GARDNER, France A. 26
GARDNER, Frances A. 60
GARDNER, Francis 82
GARDNER, Harrison 30
GARDNER, Harrison 52
GARDNER, Hiram 7
GARDNER, Lucinda J. 88
GARDNER, Martha A. 80
GARDNER, Parker G. 7
GARDNER, S. D. 61
GARDNER, Sadie B. 125
GARDNER, Sethen D. 67
GARDNER, St. Clair 95
GARDNER, Stephen 82
GARDNER, Thomas 82
GAREY, Anna M. 86
GAREY, Rollen C. 45
GAREY, Wm. 45
GAREY, Wm. 86
GARNER, Frances 36
GARRARD, Sarah 130
GARRISON, Frank 99
GARRISON, Thomas P. 99
GARY, ----- 55
GASKINS, Nannie 125
GAY, John 107
GAY, Samuel 107
GEAZLE, Samuel H. 80
GEOSE, Louisa E. 117
GIDDINGS, James 66
GILKERSON, E. 113
GILKISON, Bell 126
GILL, Malinda 75
GILL, Matilda 50
GILLASPIE, William N. 78
GILLISPIE, Milly 69
GINCOLEN, Abner 66
GIODAN, Elizabeth 31
GIUTY, Edwin 114
GIVENS, Eliza 57
GIVENS, Moses 4

GIVENS, Moses 55
GIVINS, Joshua 4
GLAP(?), Andrew 78
GLASCOCK, Bettie 98
GLASCOCK, D. 110
GLASCOCK, Elizabeth 130
GLASCOCK, Mary 118
GLASCOCK, Mary L. 131
GLASCOCK, Thos. 113
GLASS, Andrew 7
GLASS, Andrew 43
GLASS, Andrew 64
GLASS, Andrew 78
GLASS, Joann 43
GLASS, M. E. 7
GLASSCOCK, Jessie 130
GLASSCOCK, Joseph 64
GLASSCOCK, Joseph R. 54
GLASSCOCK, Malinda 29
GLASSCOCK, Malinda 79
GLASSCOCK, Malinda A. 54
GLASSCOCK, N. D. 71
GLASSCOCK, Newman 79
GLASSCOCK, Thomas 130
GLENN, ----- 66
GLORKY, B. 66
GLOVER, Emily 70
GOADING, Celia 12
GODDARD, Charles E. 78
GODDARD, Sarah 18
GODDARD, Sarah 42
GOGSWELL, Elizabeth E. 30
GOLDEN, Elizabeth 82
GOLDEN, Elizabeth P. 49
GOLLAHER, ----- 65
GOODAN, E. D. 30
GOODING, A. J. 116
GOODING, Abram 17
GOODING, Abram 24
GOODING, Abram 72
GOODING, Abram 77
GOODING, Andrew 31
GOODING, Andrew 118
GOODING, Celia 54
GOODING, Celia 78
GOODING, Cyntha Ann 17
GOODING, Elizabeth 119
GOODING, Elizth. R. 95
GOODING, Hardin 80
GOODING, J. D. 114
GOODING, James 31

GOODING, James R. 40
GOODING, Jessie 118
GOODING, John D. 14
GOODING, Lenox 14
GOODING, Margaret 65
GOODING, Nelson 114
GOODING, Oscar 95
GOODING, Phebe Thomas 40
GOODING, Robert 72
GOODING, Robert A. 55
GOODING, Wesley 95
GOODING, Wesley 116
GOODMAN, Elizabeth 79
GOODMAN, Fielding 42
GOODMAN, Fielding 54
GOODMAN, Fill. 79
GOODMAN, Nancy 98
GOODPASTURE, Sarah Jane 39
GOODPASTURE, Tennett 39
GOODPLASTONE, A. J. 65
GOODWIN, Ira 81
GOODWIN, John B. 130
GOODWIN, Juda 88
GOODWIN, Mary 93
GOODWIN, Mary 110
GOODWIN, Reuben S. 101
GOODWIN, Samuel 130
GOODWIN, William 81
GOODWIN, Wm. H. 88
GORDEN, Ella 94
GORDEN, Perry 94
GORDEN, Polly Ann 63
GORDON, John 131
GORDON, John W. 131
GORMAN, Archibald 122
GORMAN, David 95
GORMAN, Eliza 122
GORMAN, Eliza B. 122
GOURBY, E. D. 41
GOURLEY, E. D. 32
GOURLEY, E. D. 78
GOURLEY, Susan 32
GOUSBY, Elbert 41
GRAHAM, A. F. 25
GRAHAM, Ambrose 83
GRAHAM, Elizabeth 88
GRAHAM, Elizabeth 109
GRAHAM, Elizabeth 119
GRAHAM, Florence 104
GRAHAM, Jane 16
GRAHAM, Lemuel T. 25

GRAHAM, Lydia A. 83
GRAHAM, Mary 74
GRAHAM, Mary Catharine 34
GRAHAM, Mary F. 129
GRAHAM, O. K. 111
GRAHAM, Paulina 23
GRAHAM, Paulina 111
GRAHAM, R. B. 111
GRAHAM, Robt. 15
GRAHAM, Robt. 23
GRAHAM, Robt. 74
GRAHAM, W. S. T. 68
GRAHAM, William S.T. 34
GRANNIS, Harvey 126
GRANNIS, James H. 47
GRANNIS, Wiliam R. 126
GRANNIS, William 47
GRANNIS, William Rueben 17
GRANNIS, Wm. 17
GRANNIS, Wm. 74
GRANVILLE, ----- 36
GRAVES, Carrie W. 124
GRAVES, Charles A. 1
GRAVES, Elizabeth 128
GRAVES, Joseph A. 124
GRAVES, M. 36
GRAVES, Margaret C. 1
GRAVES, Nancy 128
GRAVES, Rebecca 81
GRAVES, W. C. 124
GRAVES, W. H. 55
GRAVES, William H. 124
GRAVES, Wm. 68
GRAY, ----- 55
GRAY, Adam C. 68
GRAY, America 112
GRAY, Celia A. 88
GRAY, Charles 107
GRAY, Elizabeth 70
GRAY, Ellie 126
GRAY, Fielding 132
GRAY, Fielding 132
GRAY, Fielding W. 55
GRAY, Fred 132
GRAY, George W. 22
GRAY, Harriet A. 40
GRAY, Harriett E. 77
GRAY, James 107
GRAY, James M. 12
GRAY, James Wm. 12
GRAY, Jeri 85

GRAY, John 6
GRAY, John 62
GRAY, John E. 88
GRAY, John M. 22
GRAY, John M. 80
GRAY, Leuis 85
GRAY, Lucinda 104
GRAY, Lucinda F. 41
GRAY, M. J. 107
GRAY, Mariah 132
GRAY, Mariah 132
GRAY, Martha J. 132
GRAY, Moses 86
GRAY, Nancy J. 68
GRAY, Nancy J. 81
GRAY, Olivia 10
GRAY, Olivia 28
GRAY, Rebecca 35
GRAY, Ruth M. 86
GRAY, Saml. 55
GRAY, Sarah A. 12
GRAY, Stanford 126
GRAY, Walter 132
GREEN SEN., Fielding 21
GREEN SR., Fielding 7
GREEN, Fielding 16
GREEN, Lucy H. 99
GREEN, Martha H. 21
GREEN, Mary 43
GREEN, Mary C. 99
GREEN, Neuton 91
GREEN, Peter 121
GREEN, Sampson 21
GREEN, Thos. 21
GREGOR, Anfield 53
GREGOR, Edward T. 32
GREGORY, Anfield 33
GREGORY, Jeff P. 82
GREGORY, Nathanel 32
GREGORY, Natheen 82
GRIFFIN, Willoughby 66
GRIFFISH, Sarah J. 13
GRIFFITH, Amy 122
GRIFFITH, Evan 81
GRIFFITH, Louisa 82
GRIFFITH, Martha J. 96
GRIFFITH, Mary 125
GRIFFITH, Mary E. 44
GRIFFITH, S. B. 111
GRIFFITH, W. 111
GRIFFITH, William 82

GRIFFITH, Willoughby 44
GRIFFITH, Willoughby 81
GRIFFITH, Willoughby 99
GRIMES, James C. 123
GRIMES, Jerry 98
GRIMES, Jerry 123
GRIMES, Mary A. 108
GRIMES, Robert C. 98
GRIMSLEY, William 80
GROSE, Almanza M. 25
GROSE, Andrew 90
GROSE, Braceton 25
GROSE, Caroline M. 126
GROSE, P. M. 68
GROSS, Aluretta H. 86
GROVES, Addy B. 84
GROVES, James H. 83
GROVES, Lucinda M. 84
GROVES, Polly A. 76
GROVES, Samuel J. 104
GROVES, William 23
GROVES, William 77
GROVES, William H. 84
GUITY, Charles 114
GULBY, Eliza Jane 41
GULBY, George 41
GULICH, Mary 42
GULICK, John H. 70
GULICK, John H. 79
GULICK, Mary W. 16
GULLEY, John 116
GULLEY, W. J. 116
GULLY, George 64
GULLY, John Robt. 16
GULLY, Lewis 60

HACKER, R.G. J.F. 72
HACKLEY, Fanny 19
HACKLEY, Fanny 23
HAFLIN, Tim 69
HALL, ----- 132
HALL, Adaline 89
HALL, Archabaldd 59
HALL, Charles Robert 43
HALL, E. F. 43
HALL, E. T. 23
HALL, Earnest 122
HALL, Eliza 102
HALL, Fanny M. 43
HALL, Fanny N. 64
HALL, Henel 120
HALL, Jerry 17

HALL, Jerry 26
HALL, Jerry 78
HALL, Julia 99
HALL, Julia Ann 81
HALL, Julian 44
HALL, Julian 66
HALL, Mary 43
HALL, Mary C. 64
HALL, Nancy 132
HALL, Thomas R. 122
HAM(?), Elizabeth 41
HAM(?), Martha A. 121
HAM, Alexander 51
HAM, Alexander 76
HAM, Amazel J. 41
HAM, America J. 18
HAM, Anola C. 131
HAM, Asa 64
HAM, Ashal 80
HAM, Barba S. 118
HAM, Benj. 63
HAM, Birdie F. 122
HAM, Chris 92
HAM, Christopher 9
HAM, Dunitt 44
HAM, Elijah 72
HAM, Elijah 77
HAM, Elizabeth 44
HAM, Elizabeth 54
HAM, Elizabeth 77
HAM, F. R. 131
HAM, Fautley R. 94
HAM, Fielding 18
HAM, Franz 43
HAM, Harriet 42
HAM, J. H. 116
HAM, J. M. 113
HAM, James 116
HAM, James M. 77
HAM, James P. 78
HAM, Jeremiah 9
HAM, Jeremiah 94
HAM, Jno. A. 94
HAM, Joseph 122
HAM, Lucy Ellen 94
HAM, M. M. 116
HAM, Mary 73
HAM, Mary E. 130
HAM, Nancy 132
HAM, P. A. 88
HAM, Sally Jane 42

HAM, Sally Jane 44
HAM, Sally Summers 41
HAM, Samuel D. 25
HAM, Silas C.W. 44
HAM, Smith 44
HAM, Smith P. 42
HAM, Susanah 32
HAM, Thomas 41
HAM, Thos. Wm. 11
HAM, Tilas Keath 42
HAM, Watt A. 94
HAM, Wesley 116
HAM, William M. 41
HAM, William T. 25
HAM, Wm. A. 94
HAM, Wm. B. 11
HAMBRICK, Lucinda 82
HAMILTON, Danl. 13
HAMILTON, David 53
HAMILTON, James W. 13
HAMILTON, Louisa 100
HAMILTON, Rebecca 15
HAMILTON, Rebecca 39
HAMILTON, Rebecca 69
HAMILTON, S. E. 114
HAMILTON, Samuel 51
HAMILTON, William 43
HAMILTON, William Henry 43
HAMILTON, Wm. 6
HAMILTON, Wm. 6
HAMM, D. S. 10
HAMM, Daniel M. 10
HAMM, Robert 9
HAMM, Robt. 10
HAMM, Smith 15
HAMMOND, C. B. 116
HAMMOND, Chas. 93
HAMMOND, J. S. 116
HAMMOND, Matilda 52
HAMMOND, Victoria 108
HAMMONDS, ----- 38
HAMMONDS, A. E. 108
HAMMONDS, C. W. 108
HAMMONDS, Evaline 119
HAMMONDS, John 38
HAMMONDS, Lucinda 34
HAMMONDS, Minnie 89
HAMMONDS, S. J. 54
HAMMONDS, Saml. 89
HAMMONDS, Samuel 119
HAMMONDS, W. W. 34

HAMMONS, Lucinda 49
HAMMONS, Matilda 71
HAMMONS, Sarah 75
HAMMS, Martha 15
HAMNESTID, Nancy 54
HAMRICK, Louisa 122
HAMS(?), Eliza Jane 51
HANEMANS, C. C. 55
HANEY, Lucy 94
HANNAH, Brice 131
HARBESON, James M. 111
HARBESON, Joseph H. 121
HARBESON, W. P. 111
HARBESON, William 121
HARBOR, Elizabeth 21
HARBOR, John 21
HARDIMAN, Samuel 31
HARDIMAN, William 31
HARDY, J. C. 26
HARGATE, Daniel 19
HARGED, Sibby 63
HARGET, Elizabeth Ann 18
HARGET, Elizabeth Ann 53
HARGETT, Elvine 77
HARGETT, Sibby 80
HARGIT, Israel W. 40
HARGIT, Whitfield 40
HARGUS, Whitfield 77
HARMAN, Angeline 48
HARMAN, Eliza J. 73
HARMAN, Evaline 61
HARMAN, John W. 47
HARMAN, July Ann 70
HARMAN, Kesia 18
HARMAN, Mary A. 47
HARMAN, W. M. 51
HARMON, Daniel E. 83
HARMON, Dora A. 95
HARMON, Edward 76
HARMON, Elijah T. 9
HARMON, Elizbh. T. 9
HARMON, Green 60
HARMON, Hanna 17
HARMON, Harriett 81
HARMON, J. W. 112
HARMON, John W. 66
HARMON, Joseph 83
HARMON, Kejiah 62
HARMON, Levina 2
HARMON, Lucinda 82
HARMON, M. E. 112

HARMON, Martha 83
HARMON, Mary Agnes 7
HARMON, Nancy E. 76
HARMON, S. J. 111
HARMON, Sarah J. 87
HARMON, W. M. 72
HARMON, Wesley H. 61
HARMON, Wesley H. 67
HARMON, William 7
HARMON, Wm. T. 95
HARN, Elizabeth 41
HARN, Louisa 9
HARN, Martha A. 121
HARPER, Cordelia F. 48
HARPER, Elizabeth 38
HARPER, Robert 74
HARPER, Wm. W. 48
HARRIS, F. B. 111
HARRIS, Julia 121
HARRIS, N. 37
HARRISON, California 105
HARRISON, Daniel 105
HARRISON, Eliza 97
HARRISON, Elizabeth 120
HARRISON, Emaline 121
HARRISON, Henry 78
HARRISON, Julia 101
HARRISON, Julia 102
HARRISON, Martha 20
HARRISON, Martin S. 97
HARRISON, W. C.R. 71
HARRISON, William 121
HARRISON, William H. 97
HARRISON, Wm. C.R. 53
HARSK, Martha 78
HART, ----- 66
HART, Alex 66
HART, Alexander 43
HART, Alexander 74
HART, Alexander 75
HART, Alexander 81
HART, Elijah 15
HART, Elijah 43
HART, Elijah 75
HART, Henry 29
HART, Henry 50
HART, Henry 55
HART, Henry 74
HART, Mary 29
HART, Mary Catharine 43
HART, Theadore 68

HART, Theodore 67
HART, Theodore 74
HARTLEY, Elizabeth 69
HARTLEY, Elizabeth 119
HARTLEY, George 77
HARTLEY, John 30
HARTLEY, Jos. A. 95
HARTLEY, Louisa 64
HARTLEY, Miam 96
HARTLEY, Reuben 95
HARTLEY, Ruben 63
HARTLEY, Sary 76
HARTLEY, Simpson 96
HARTLEY, Sophia D. 95
HARTLEYM, Sophia 30
HARTLY, George 54
HARTLY, Louisa 80
HARTLY, Rueben 79
HARTLY, Sarah 51
HARVY, James 7
HATTONE, John 75
HAVENS, ----- 28
HAVENS, Alfred L. 54
HAVENS, Angeline 32
HAVENS, Ann 2
HAVENS, Emily 116
HAVENS, Louisa 132
HAVENS, Lydda R. 80
HAVENS, Lydia R. 54
HAVENS, M. A. 111
HAVENS, Mary A. 68
HAVENS, Nancy D. 39
HAVENS, Oleah 75
HAVERE, Mary Ann 8
HAVERES, Alfred 8
HAVERES, Emily 8
HAW(?), Barbara 96
HAW, Susan A. 96
HAWES, Edward E. 95
HAWES, Jno. F. 95
HAWES, Monroe 95
HAWES, Wm. T. 95
HAWIN, John 124
HAWIN, Reuben 124
HAWKINS, A. A. 112
HAWKINS, Benjamin 99
HAWKINS, Francis E. 118
HAWKINS, Henry 91
HAWKINS, Henry S. 7
HAWKINS, Jas. A. 7
HAWKINS, Jennie 99

HAWKINS, John 21
HAWKINS, John H. 99
HAWKINS, John M. 12
HAWKINS, Joholen B. 102
HAWKINS, Margaret 17
HAWKINS, Margaret J. 40
HAWKINS, Margaret J. 80
HAWKINS, Richard 112
HAWKINS, Richd. 12
HAWKINS, Sarah 92
HAWKINS, Sarah F. 21
HAWKINS, T. W.T. 108
HAWKINS, W. T. 108
HAWKINS, thos. 92
HAWS, Eliza J. 71
HAWS, Eliza Jane 51
HAWS, Elizabeth 71
HAWS, John F. 71
HAWTHER, Sarah E. 90
HAYDEN, Nancy 117
HAYDEN, Queen A. 53
HAYDEN, Robert 63
HAYDEN, Robert W. 53
HAYDEN, Robert W. 80
HAYDEN, Sarah 70
HAYDEN, Winifred 35
HAYNES, Gertrude 91
HAYNIE, Catharine 54
HAYS, Melvina 38
HAYTER, Eliza A. 69
HEDDLESTON, C. R. 112
HEDDLESTON, R. 112
HEDGE, George 92
HEDGEL, Louisa 80
HEDGER, James A. 129
HEDGER, John 14
HEDGER, William 129
HEDGES, Addison 70
HEDGES, J. 31
HEDGES, Lavina 20
HEDGES, Wm. W. 14
HEDRICK, Columbus R. 18
HEDRICK, Drura 102
HEDRICK, Elizabeth 31
HEDRICK, Holman 88
HEDRICK, Louisa F. 88
HEDRICK, M. B. 109
HEDRICK, Mary E. 88
HEDRICK, Michael 31
HEDRICK, Roland 18
HEDRICK, W. B. 109

HEEPHEUSTINS, Rebecca 10
HEFFERN, Hannah 101
HEFFLIN, Everest L. 87
HEFFLIN, James M. 87
HEFFLIN, Mary 95
HEFLIN, James 108
HEFLIN, John 122
HEFLIN, Lewis Cap 8
HEFLIN, Maggie M. 108
HEFLIN, Martha 42
HEFLIN, Martha 44
HEFLIN, Mary 9
HEFLIN, Paul 122
HEFLIN, Susan 40
HEFLIN, William 8
HEFLIN, Wm. 13
HEFLIN, Wm. A. 13
HEITHLY, John 54
HEKOE, Michael 58
HELM, Lizzie Barber 66
HELPENSTINE, Rebecca 69
HELPHENSTINE, A. P. 53
HELPHENSTINE, A. P. 69
HELPHENSTINE, Henry 70
HELPHENSTINE, Phillip 76
HELPHENTINE, Nancy L. 89
HELPHINSTINE, Jennie B. 103
HELPHINSTINE, Joseph 25
HELPHINSTINE, Samuel C. 103
HELPHINSTINE, W. P. 25
HELPONSTINE, Wm. P. 63
HELVENSTINE, Rebecca 42
HELVESTINE, Rebecca 119
HEMAN, Michael 37
HEMING, Martha J. 69
HENDERSON, Delila 54
HENDERSON, George W. 2
HENDERSON, Jackson G. 96
HENDERSON, Jas. M. 96
HENDERSON, Wm. 2
HENDRIA, Louisa 12
HENDRIA, Wm. H. 15
HENDRICK, Amanda J. 81
HENDRICK, James P. 84
HENDRICK, James P. 84
HENDRICK, Lizzie D. 84
HENDRICK, Lucinda 87
HENDRICK, William 41
HENDRICK, William H. 78
HENDRICKS, Fanny S. 26
HENDRICKS, William 26

148

HENDRIK, Amanda 82
HENDRIX, Amanda 75
HENDRIX, Louisa 62
HENDRIX, Louisa 74
HENDRIX, Martha 14
HENDRIX, Martha 110
HENDRIX, Oliver 87
HENDRIX, Sue 97
HENDRIX, W. F. 87
HENDRIX, W. H. 55
HENDRIX, Walter P. 87
HENRICK, William H. 72
HERRIN, E. L. 107
HERRIN, Mary E. 86
HERRIN, Thomas 107
HERRIN, Thos. 86
HERRON, James T. 126
HERRON, Thomas 126
HEWITT, Henry 16
HEWITT, Henry 16
HICKERSON, Elizabeth 118
HICKERSON, Garnet 55
HICKERSON, James 7
HICKERSON, James 41
HICKERSON, James 54
HICKERSON, Jane 31
HICKERSON, Jededia Foster 41
HICKERSON, Leroy M. 102
HICKERSON, Maggie 114
HICKERSON, Marshall 32
HICKERSON, Marshall 53
HICKERSON, Marshall 71
HICKERSON, Sarah 102
HICKERSON, William 71
HICKERSON, Winefield 32
HICKISON, James 7
HICKMAN, Elias 49
HICKMAN, Leroy 49
HICKS, Leri T. 2
HICKS, Martha 34
HICKS, Martha J. 48
HICKS, Sarah 36
HICKSERSON, Harriet 69
HIETT, William T. 80
HIGBEE, Judy 133
HILDRETH, Aquilla 75
HILDRETH, Henrietta W. 124
HILDRETH, Robert 124
HILDRETH, Samuel 75
HILEY, John Wally 40
HILEY, William 40

HILL, R. W. 1
HILL, Elizabeth 80
HILL, Harriet 126
HILL, Lucy 85
HILL, Mary E. 45
HILLIGORS, Maggie 126
HILLIGOSS, Thos. 65
HILLIS, Ceplias 106
HILLIS, Earnest 106
HIMES, Lucinda 55
HINER, Elizabeth A. 12
HINER, Saml. 12
HINES, Alice 101
HINES, Margaret 11
HINES, Michael 14
HINES, Michael 119
HINTON(?), Ella 97
HINTON, Amelia 55
HINTON, Amelia C. 118
HINTON, America 108
HINTON, America 122
HINTON, Andrew J. 85
HINTON, Brice 32
HINTON, David 31
HINTON, Drucila 42
HINTON, Ebanor V. 22
HINTON, Edward L. 43
HINTON, Emeline 71
HINTON, H. W. 63
HINTON, Hester 80
HINTON, James 22
HINTON, John 43
HINTON, John D. 85
HINTON, Lucinda 31
HINTON, M. E. 115
HINTON, Martha 32
HINTON, Martha 89
HINTON, Martha 119
HINTON, Mary E. 63
HINTON, Minnie C. 118
HINTON, Nancy 22
HINTON, Nancy J. 7
HINTON, Nancy J. 64
HINTON, R. G. 88
HINTON, Rachel 11
HINTON, Rachel 33
HINTON, Rasana 38
HINTON, Resa 46
HINTON, Russella 79
HINTON, Sarah A. 55
HINTON, Squire 118

HINTON, William 108
HINTON, William H. 71
HINTON, William H. 78
HINTON, Wm. 108
HITT, Catharine C. 35
HITT, Cathn. 37
HITT, Mary L. 87
HITT, Mary L. 108
HITT, W. W. 1
HITT, Wilson 37
HITT, Wilson W. 35
HIVER, Samuel 113
HIX, L. T. 47
HODGES, Bettie W. 77
HOENIG, Mary 29
HOGOT, Elizabeth A. 69
HOLLAND, ------ 65
HOLLAND, America 8
HOLLAND, America 53
HOLLAND, Benson 3
HOLLAND, Celia 15
HOLLAND, Celia 52
HOLLAND, Cely 72
HOLLAND, Fleming E. 3
HOLLAND, John Thomas 101
HOLLAND, Mary J. 82
HOLLAND, Newton 101
HOMBECK, Mary 81
HOOD, Rosanna Ann 27
HOOPER, Alice B. 125
HOOPER, Chas 91
HOPKINS, Eddie E. 105
HOPKINS, Eliza H. 105
HOPKINS, Emily 47
HOPKINS, Emily J. 7
HOPKINS, Emily J. 25
HOPKINS, Herod 7
HOPKINS, Herod 25
HOPKINS, Herod 47
HOPKINS, J. W. 105
HOPKINS, J. W. 105
HOPKINS, John D. 73
HOPKINS, Louisa E. 5
HOPKINS, Louisa E. 27
HOPKINS, Louisa E. 47
HOPKINS, Mary E.J. 25
HOPKINS, Mary L. 47
HOPKINS, Rebecca 127
HOPKINS, Thomas 117
HOPKINS, Thomas H. 117
HOPKINS, Verriller 7

HOPKINS, William B. 120
HOPKINS, Wm. 73
HOPPER, Elizabeth 72
HOPPER, Elizabeth J. 42
HOPPER, Elizabeth J. 80
HOPPER, Francis 97
HOPPER, Mary E. 120
HOPPER, S. 112
HORD, Adison P. 96
HORD, Louisa 96
HORGET, Sarah 52
HORGETH, Sibby 63
HORGOT, Queen America 69
HORNBACK, Polly 68
HORNBOCK, Polly 37
HORTON, Geo. W. 3
HORTON, George W. 3
HORTON, George W. 78
HOUIE, Mrs. Amanda 8
HOUSE, Elizabeth 15
HOUST, Wm. 6
HOWARD, Frank 97
HOWARD, Matilda 128
HOWARD, W. R. 108
HOWE, ------ 36
HOWE, A. 36
HOWE, America 38
HOWE, Andrew 15
HOWE, Betty T. 46
HOWE, Charlotte J. 51
HOWE, David 65
HOWE, David 66
HOWE, David D. 51
HOWE, David L. 37
HOWE, David L. 76
HOWE, David W. 81
HOWE, Dunlap 93
HOWE, Dunlap 112
HOWE, E. M. 109
HOWE, Eli 37
HOWE, Elizabeth 26
HOWE, Elizabeth 41
HOWE, Elizabeth 78
HOWE, James M. 127
HOWE, Jno. M. 90
HOWE, John M. 85
HOWE, John M. 127
HOWE, John W. 100
HOWE, Lucian MC. D. 93
HOWE, Lyda M. 127
HOWE, M. 113

HOWE, M. A. 85
HOWE, M. M. 112
HOWE, M. T. 4
HOWE, Maggie M. 127
HOWE, Margret 70
HOWE, Martha A. 90
HOWE, Mary 118
HOWE, Nancy 46
HOWE, S. 113
HOWE, Sallie 130
HOWE, Sally 36
HOWE, W. J. 36
HOWE, W. S. 46
HOWE, W. T. 36
HOWE, W. T. 62
HOWE, William D. 100
HOWE, Wm. T. 83
HOWSE, Abigail E. 15
HOWSE, Samuel 15
HUBANKS, Eliza 64
HUCLE, William 72
HUDSON, George 42
HUDSON, George W. 77
HUDSON, Mary Isabel 42
HUFF, Charlotte Mary 1
HUFF, Wm. 1
HUFF, Wm. 66
HUGHBANKS, Hannan 123
HUGHBANKS, Malinda 79
HUGHBANKS, Sarah 103
HUGHES, Ardilla F. 33
HUGHES, Arilla J. 80
HUGHES, Charles M. 102
HUGHES, Jane 92
HUGHES, Jasper 108
HUGHES, John 99
HUGHES, Julian 36
HUGHES, Laura 124
HUGHES, Nancy 31
HUGHES, Nancy 54
HUGHES, Thomas W. 70
HUGHES, Wm. 90
HUKLE, Elizabeth 26
HUKLE, Wm. 26
HULE, Susan 75
HULL, Albert Thomas 2
HULL, Archibald 68
HULL, Ida B. 106
HULL, J. A. 111
HULL, James A. 106
HULL, Lucy 82

HULL, Mariam 61
HULL, Marshall 37
HULL, Marshall 46
HULL, Mary E. 67
HULL, Maureen 67
HULL, Miram 82
HULL, Moses 37
HULL, Moses 46
HULL, Moses 83
HULL, Nancy 36
HULL, Nancy J. 83
HULL, Sarah 82
HULL, Sarah 117
HULL, Susan 117
HULL, Wm. R. 2
HULLOON, Penelope 80
HUMPHEYS, Corilla J. 96
HUMPHEYS, Francis M. 96
HUMPHEYS, Louisa 95
HUMPHEYS, Marshall K. 96
HUMPHEYS, Mary A. 96
HUMPHEYS, Wm. H. 96
HUMPHREY, Alice 63
HUMPHREYS, Alfred 42
HUMPHREYS, Alfred 64
HUMPHREYS, Chas. 133
HUMPHREYS, Daniel 43
HUMPHREYS, E. 114
HUMPHREYS, E. A. 115
HUMPHREYS, E. D. 113
HUMPHREYS, Edna F. 132
HUMPHREYS, Eliza 41
HUMPHREYS, James Edin 40
HUMPHREYS, Leuilda Jane 41
HUMPHREYS, Maria J. 55
HUMPHREYS, Mariah 42
HUMPHREYS, Marshall 132
HUMPHREYS, Mary 106
HUMPHREYS, Matilda 115
HUMPHREYS, Minnie H. 133
HUMPHREYS, Rebecca 41
HUMPHREYS, Rebecca 64
HUMPHREYS, Richard 40
HUMPHREYS, Robert P. 43
HUMPHREYS, S. S. 115
HUMPHREYS, Sally J. 52
HUMPHREYS, Samuel 52
HUMPHREYS, Samuel 72
HUMPHREYS, Sarah 106
HUMPHREYS, Sarah 119
HUMPHREYS, Taylor 113

HUMPHREYS, Virginia 132
HUMPHRIES, ----- 34
HUMPHRIES, Alex 6
HUMPHRIES, Alfred 9
HUMPHRIES, Alfred 80
HUMPHRIES, Azrilla 31
HUMPHRIES, Daniel 31
HUMPHRIES, Danl. 6
HUMPHRIES, Elias D. 9
HUMPHRIES, Elizabeth E. 80
HUMPHRIES, Henry M. 10
HUMPHRIES, Mariah J. 69
HUMPHRIES, Milton H. 6
HUMPHRIES, Nelly 5
HUMPHRIES, Rebecca 9
HUMPHRIES, Rebecca 80
HUMPHRIES, Robt. 12
HUMPHRIES, Saml. 10
HUMPHRIES, Virginia 6
HUMPHRIES, William 6
HUMPHRIES, Wm. 34
HUMPHRIES, Wm. M. 12
HUMPHRYS, Rebecca 42
HUNPHRIES, Eliza A. 76
HUNT, Cal 6
HUNT, Jeremiah S. 46
HUNT, John 46
HUNT, John 67
HUNT, Martha 20
HUNT, Mary A. 60
HUNT, Mary Ellen 6
HUNT, Samuel 62
HUNT, Sarah Jane 40
HUNT, Susan 58
HUNTER, Amanda 123
HUNTER, Mary 108
HURST, ----- 19
HURST, Alfred 11
HURST, Alfred 52
HURST, Alice G. 100
HURST, Allen P. 132
HURST, Amanda 70
HURST, America 53
HURST, America J. 80
HURST, Annie M. 118
HURST, Archimides P. 11
HURST, B. H. 100
HURST, Charlotte 31
HURST, Charlotte 96
HURST, Charlotte 96
HURST, Claybourne 8

HURST, Cynthia Y. 119
HURST, Daniel W. 118
HURST, Dicey 41
HURST, Dicy 8
HURST, Elias 15
HURST, Eliza A. 80
HURST, Elizabeth 13
HURST, F. H. 111
HURST, Florence B. 131
HURST, H. E. 114
HURST, J. W. 111
HURST, James 58
HURST, James 119
HURST, Jesse 109
HURST, Jessie 131
HURST, John 114
HURST, Joseph 119
HURST, Laudon 15
HURST, Lewis 82
HURST, Lucinda 51
HURST, Lucy Ann Frances 15
HURST, M. S. 109
HURST, Margt. J. 101
HURST, Marion F. 132
HURST, Marshal 62
HURST, Martha 15
HURST, Miles 8
HURST, Miles 51
HURST, Miles 65
HURST, Miles 71
HURST, Moses 19
HURST, Moses 82
HURST, Narcissa 74
HURST, Narcississ 47
HURST, Nelson 15
HURST, Nelson 51
HURST, Nelson 119
HURST, Nelson H. 78
HURST, Norcissa 17
HURST, Phebe 31
HURST, Phebe 40
HURST, Tho. 37
HURST, Walter W. 51
HURST, Walter W. 71
HURST, Warrick 10
HURST, Wm. 37
HURST, Jr. Miles 31
HURTON, Ella 97
HUSSAY, Thomas 120
HUSSEY, William 120
HUSSTON, Jane 93

HUSTON, F. T. 88
HUTCHINSON, Lottie A. 105
HUTCHINSON, Robert T. 105
HUTCHISON, M. 113
HUTCHISON, Margaret 63
HUTCHISON, T. N. 10
HUTSON, Margaret 28
HUTTON, Bettie A. 79
HUTTON, George 128
HUTTON, Thomas 128
HYATT, Sarah 21
HYATT, William 20
HYNES, Thos. 14
HYSONG, Dally 67
HYSONG, Dolly 46
HYSONG, Dolly 62
HYSONG, J. C. 66
HYSONG, John 5
HYSONG, Martha 5
HYSONG, Nancy 23
HYSONG, dally 67
HZSONG, Dolly 2
INGRAHAM, Aridale 39
INGRAHAM, Jean 39
INGRAHAM, W. H. 54
INGRAIN, Wm. H. 7
INGRAM, F. A. 81
INGRAM, Henry 97
INGRAM, J. 116
INGRAM, Jeses 81
INGRAM, Jesse 97
INGRAM, Jessey 73
INGRAM, John A. 81
INGRAM, John A. 81
INGRAM, M. T. 116
INGRAM, Robt. Simeon 7
INGRHAM, Jesse 67
INLOW, Mary A. 125
INLOW, Mary E. 101
IRISH, Mary 36
IRVIN, S. W. 68
ISHMAEL, Ida B. 123
ISHMAEL, John T. 117
ISHMAEL, John W. 117
ISHMAEL, Samuel 123
ISHMALL, John 60
ISHMALL, Nancy 67
ISHMEAL, Nancy 83
JACKSON, ----- 118
JACKSON, Annie M. 103
JACKSON, Eliza 99

JACKSON, Geo. B. 110
JACKSON, Hannah 93
JACKSON, James 73
JACKSON, James 83
JACKSON, James A. 48
JACKSON, John O. 80
JACKSON, Joseph 1
JACKSON, Joseph 56
JACKSON, Lydia 35
JACKSON, Malinda 72
JACKSON, Martin M. 73
JACKSON, Mary C. 106
JACKSON, Rebecca 26
JACKSON, Susan 101
JACOBS, Alfred 53
JACOBS, Edward 98
JACOBS, Elizabeth 122
JACOBS, Sarah 24
JAESON, James A. 48
JAMES(?)< Rice 106
JAMES, A. 55
JAMES, Elaner 67
JAMES, Elanor 38
JAMES, Elizabeth F. 61
JAMES, John 65
JAMISON, Liddie 104
JAMISON, Mary D. 70
JAMISON, Michael 69
JAMISON, Rosana 26
JANDERS, Amilda 60
JANUS, Catharine 87
JAPP, Elizabeth 46
JIMISON, Mary A. 59
JIMISON, Mary R. 28
JINKINS, Elizabeth 54
JINKINS, Elizabeth 55
JOCKEY, Annie 110
JOCKEY, Jacob 110
JOHNSON, ----- 30
JOHNSON, Adgedent 22
JOHNSON, Adjutant 9
JOHNSON, Alice 9
JOHNSON, Allen G. 111
JOHNSON, Annie 110
JOHNSON, Anniel 123
JOHNSON, Atha J. 28
JOHNSON, Benj. 73
JOHNSON, Benjamin 84
JOHNSON, Benjamin F. 33
JOHNSON, Benjm. 16
JOHNSON, Betsy 28

JOHNSON, Clarinda 70
JOHNSON, Clauda A. 123
JOHNSON, Daniel 55
JOHNSON, Devinda 15
JOHNSON, Elizabeth 3
JOHNSON, Emma 123
JOHNSON, Francis D. 9
JOHNSON, J. S. 110
JOHNSON, J.W. R. 31
JOHNSON, James 123
JOHNSON, Jas. T. 1
JOHNSON, Jeffeson 30
JOHNSON, Jeremiah F. 33
JOHNSON, Jno. N. 58
JOHNSON, John 1
JOHNSON, John 65
JOHNSON, John 123
JOHNSON, John 124
JOHNSON, John B. 3
JOHNSON, John H. 28
JOHNSON, John R. 8
JOHNSON, John R. 8
JOHNSON, Joseph 125
JOHNSON, Louisa 40
JOHNSON, Louisa 94
JOHNSON, Louisa 115
JOHNSON, Lucy 108
JOHNSON, Lucy 114
JOHNSON, Lydia A. 123
JOHNSON, M. B. 110
JOHNSON, M. E. 112
JOHNSON, Martha 125
JOHNSON, Martha A. 4
JOHNSON, Martha J. 79
JOHNSON, Mary 41
JOHNSON, Mary E. 16
JOHNSON, Mary R. 85
JOHNSON, Mattie 108
JOHNSON, Mattie 114
JOHNSON, Nellie B. 125
JOHNSON, Nelly Ann 31
JOHNSON, Noble W.B. 16
JOHNSON, Oscar W. 124
JOHNSON, Polly Amanda 40
JOHNSON, Polly Ann 30
JOHNSON, Rebecca E. 123
JOHNSON, Reda 45
JOHNSON, Samuel P. 33
JOHNSON, Sarah 19
JOHNSON, Sarah 29
JOHNSON, Sarah 39

JOHNSON, Sarah A. 69
JOHNSON, Sarah E. 22
JOHNSON, Selener 10
JOHNSON, Selucius G. 22
JOHNSON, Serene Henry 40
JOHNSON, Thomas J. 16
JOHNSON, Thomas J. 40
JOHNSON, Thos. J. 80
JOHNSON, Vian 29
JOHNSON, Viana 39
JOHNSON, Vianna 69
JOHNSON, Victoria 33
JOHNSON, William 22
JOHNSON, William 100
JOHNSON, William 103
JOHNSON, William 103
JOHNSON, Z. 33
JOHNSON, Z. P. 33
JOHNSON, Z. R. 9
JOHNSON, Zachariah R. 40
JOICE, John 73
JOICE, Mary 27
JOICE, Patrick 73
JOLLEY, Oscar 127
JOLLEY, Thomas 127
JOLLY, Amanda 48
JOLLY, Armstead 127
JOLLY, David 65
JOLLY, Eliza 128
JOLLY, Mary 58
JOLLY, Rachel M. 4
JONES, ----- 23
JONES, ----- 93
JONES, A. C. 30
JONES, Alfred 76
JONES, Alfred C. 12
JONES, Amanda 71
JONES, Amanda 72
JONES, Amanda 78
JONES, America J. 43
JONES, Anderson 99
JONES, Anna T. 95
JONES, Annie E. 99
JONES, Catherine 118
JONES, Charles M. 3
JONES, Charles M. 82
JONES, Chas Newton 11
JONES, Chas. S. 96
JONES, D. A. 106
JONES, E. A. 110
JONES, E. B. 116

JONES, Eleanor F. 3
JONES, Eliza 73
JONES, Eliza 78
JONES, Eliza 87
JONES, Eliza 105
JONES, Ella F. 101
JONES, Emerine 20
JONES, Emily 99
JONES, Emily F. 41
JONES, Evaline 64
JONES, F. 110
JONES, Fielding 53
JONES, Fielding 64
JONES, Harriet 24
JONES, Hiram 120
JONES, Hiram P. 80
JONES, J. J. 113
JONES, James 77
JONES, James 83
JONES, James 119
JONES, James H. 96
JONES, James V. 98
JONES, Jane 84
JONES, Jas. M. 3
JONES, John 79
JONES, John C. 25
JONES, Joseph 118
JONES, Joseph A. 17
JONES, Joseph M. 87
JONES, Joseph T. 17
JONES, Josephine 73
JONES, Julia 89
JONES, Julia A. 86
JONES, Julia A. 86
JONES, K. P. 54
JONES, Logan O. 30
JONES, Maggie G. 119
JONES, Mahala 8
JONES, Malinda 22
JONES, Malinda 62
JONES, Malinda 68
JONES, Maranda 83
JONES, Marcinda 12
JONES, Margaret 118
JONES, Mary 95
JONES, Mary F. 99
JONES, Mathew G. 64
JONES, Matilda 121
JONES, Minerva 39
JONES, Minerva 63
JONES, Perry 123

JONES, Priscilla 53
JONES, Priscilla D. 113
JONES, Prissilla D. 12
JONES, Rachael 33
JONES, Rachael 118
JONES, Rebecca 69
JONES, Richard 14
JONES, Rufus H. 95
JONES, S. 113
JONES, S. S. 113
JONES, Saml. B.H. 13
JONES, Samuel 53
JONES, Samuel B.H. 41
JONES, Samuel B.H. 72
JONES, Sarah 90
JONES, Sarah C. 106
JONES, Stanfield 61
JONES, T. J. 116
JONES, T. S. 110
JONES, Thomas 118
JONES, Thomas 129
JONES, Thomas J. 54
JONES, Thos. J. 79
JONES, W. B. 113
JONES, William B. 119
JONES, William F. 33
JONES, Wm. 61
JONES, Wm. 73
JONES, Wm. B. 13
JONES, Wm. B. 82
JONES, Wm. E. 14
JONES, Wm. E. 93
JONES, Wm. F. 11
JONSON, Roda 67
JORDAN, Alfred 63
JORDAN, Bell 121
JORDAN, Charlotte 18
JORDAN, Charlotte 42
JORDAN, Cyntha J. 77
JORDAN, Dudley 71
JORDAN, Dudley 98
JORDAN, Elizabeth 63
JORDAN, Elizabeth 71
JORDAN, Elizabeth 78
JORDAN, Emily 77
JORDAN, Greenup 10
JORDAN, Greenup 52
JORDAN, Mahala 13
JORDAN, Mary C. 79
JORDAN, Polly A. 5
JORDAN, Polly A. 71

JORDAN, William 77
JORDAN, William F. 71
JORDAN, William S. 72
JORDEN, Elizabeth 64
JORDEN, Emily 51
JORDEN, James 65
JORDEN, Mahala 52
JORDEN, Mahala 64
JORDEN, Mary C. 65
JORDEN, Nancy 52
JORDEN, Polly Ann 52
JORDEN, Priscilla 53
JORDEN, W. F. 52
JORDON, James 71
JORDON, Polly Ann 40
JORICE, Michael 27
JOSKEY, Jacob 93
JOSKEY, Mary 93
JOUDAN, Priscilla 32
JOURDAN, Eliza 17
JOURDAN, Evaline 32
JOURDAN, Harriet A. 32
JOURDAN, Matilda 10
JOURDAN, Polly Ann 33
JOURDAN, William Dudley 10
JOURDAN, William S. 32
JOYCE, Ann 84
JOYCE, Peter 66
JUCSON, Rebecca 44
JUSTIS, Minerva 119

KACKLER, Christine 92
KACKLER, Frederick H. 124
KACKLER, John 115
KACKLER, John 124
KACKLER, John T. 115
KANE, Jno. G. 37
KANE, Mary Catharine 43
KANE, Silas W. 37
KANE, Silas W. 43
KANE, Silas W. 72
KAZOR(?), Jinnetta 40
KEARANS, Ellen A. 86
KEARNS, Atha C. 29
KEARNS, Nancy A. 61
KEARNS, Sarah 47
KEARNS, Thomas 29
KECHLEY, Cephas 76
KECHLEY, Sary G. 76
KEDRICK, John 84
KEEL, Elizabeth 3
KEEL, Leander C. 125

KEEL, Leslie B. 125
KEENINS, Lucinda 76
KEENY, Mary 25
KEERANS, Alice A. 129
KEERANS, Blair 129
KEERANS, John B. 129
KEERANS, Mahilda G. 39
KEERANS, Patrick 102
KEERANS, Thomas 39
KEEREY, Michael C. 25
KEERNS, Sarah 66
KEESANS, Thomas 69
KEITH, James 83
KEITH, Jas. A. 67
KEITH, Lilas T. 55
KEITH, Silas T. 69
KELLEY, George 131
KELLEY, Sarah C. 130
KELLY, J. W. 111
KELLY, John W. 99
KELLY, Johnston B. 99
KELLY, Mary 111
KEMRICK, Louisa 85
KENDAL, Harrison 44
KENDALL, Adeline 44
KENDALL, Amanda 67
KENDALL, Amanda 74
KENDALL, D. A. 43
KENDALL, Florence Jane 41
KENDALL, H. O. 12
KENDALL, H. O. 45
KENDALL, Harvey 12
KENDALL, Henry 44
KENDALL, Jessie 126
KENDALL, Jolson 81
KENDALL, Martha 101
KENDALL, O'banion 74
KENDALL, O. A. 23
KENDALL, O. A. 26
KENDALL, Opal 126
KENDALL, Raleigh 81
KENDALL, Ralleigh 68
KENDALL, Rufus 126
KENDALL, William A. 41
KENDRICK, Jno. B. 55
KENDRICK, William H. 41
KENMAN, James M. 29
KENNAN, James 45
KENNER, Caroline 38
KENNER, Leroy 55
KENNER, Leroy W. 71

KENNON, James 84
KERNS, Ellen 126
KERNS, John A.L. 126
KERNS, John W. 126
KERNS, Nancy A. 73
KERRANS, E. A. 107
KERRINGBRICK(?), Mary 80
KEWTALL, O. A. 65
KEYHOE, Michael 83
KIDESCO(?), Emily 94
KIDMELL, Emily 11
KIDMELL, M. 11
KIDWELL, James 55
KIDWELL, James 71
KIDWELL, Mary 76
KIMBERLEY, Flora 88
KIMBERLEY, Norah 88
KIMBERLY, Clarance 119
KIMBERLY, G. S. 88
KIMBERLY, Geo. S. 112
KIMBERLY, George 119
KIMBERLY, George P. 132
KIMBERLY, M. M. 111
KIMBERLY, William 132
KIMBERLY, Wm. C. 111
KINBRO, M. R. 117
KINCADE, Jno. Thomas 1
KINCADE, Wm. 1
KINCART, Sarah E. 73
KINCURT, Sarah E. 61
KINDER, Eliza 30
KINDER, William 41
KINDER, William G. 30
KING, Ann 115
KING, Enoch. 37
KING, Irvin J. 98
KING, J. W. 115
KING, John 60
KING, Luan 37
KING, Noah S. 98
KING, Richard 63
KIPACK, Jackson 53
KIRK, ----- 38
KIRK, Ann E. 109
KIRK, Eliza 10
KIRK, Elizabeth M. 64
KIRK, George F. 132
KIRK, Jackson 52
KIRK, Jerome 104
KIRK, Jerry(?) P. 86
KIRK, John B. 80

KIRK, Lewis 132
KIRK, Malvina 119
KIRK, Mary F. 86
KIRK, Milton 89
KIRK, N. A. 47
KIRK, Nathaniel 94
KIRK, R. T. 46
KIRK, Rearon 65
KIRK, Reasen S. 38
KIRK, Rosetta 95
KIRK, Shelby T. 95
KIRK, Wm. M. 86
KIRK, Wm. T. 94
KIRTH, Harry 24
KIRTH, James A. 24
KIRTLAND, Enoch 29
KISSICK, Almira 22
KISSICK, Eliza 12
KISSICK, Eliza J. 30
KISSICK, Henry 69
KISSICK, Isaac 95
KISSICK, Jackson 80
KISSICK, John 63
KISSICK, John W. 95
KISSICK, Martha 5
KISSICK, Mary T. 6
KISSICK, Sarah 22
KISSICK, Sarah 40
KISSICK, Sarah 116
KISSICK, William 22
KISSICK, William 26
KISSICK, William 69
KNAPP, Susan 52
KOENIG, Mary C. 72
KOGERS, George W. 73
KONUTZ, Lucinda J. 103
KURST, Eliza Ann 53

LAMAR, Edward W. 11
LAMAR, Elijah 128
LAMAR, William H. 128
LAMAR, Wm. 11
LAMARR, Fredrick 80
LANAGAN, J. S. 55
LANCASTER, Clara 122
LANDER, Catharine A. 84

LANDER, E. H. 89
LANDER, Henry 93
LANDER, John F. 70
LANDER, Joseph 84
LANDER, Mary F. 89
LANDER, Mary Frances 93
LANDERS, Presley 73
LANDSOWN, Sarah J. 69
LANE, Craven 50
LANE, Craven 75
LANE, Margaret M. 50
LANE, Richard F. 92
LANE, Thomas 75
LANSDOWN, J. W. 52
LANSDOWN, Sarah 52
LAPELEY, Carlotte 37
LAPP(?), N. C. 106
LAPP, George A. 106
LAPP, John 106
LAPP, N. E. 106
LAPP, R. T. 106
LAPSLEY, Jas. T. 37
LARWSON, John 36
LATHAM, Samuel C. 128
LATHAM, clarence A. 128
LATHRUM, Charity 14
LAUDER, Olivia 91
LAUSON, James 87
LAUSON, Minerva 85
LAWFTON, Amanda 121
LAWSON, ----- 36
LAWSON, Andrew W. 117
LAWSON, Florence 109
LAWSON, Jacob 14
LAWSON, James 109
LAWSON, James 117
LAWSON, Nancy 36
LAWVILE, Susan 85
LEAFORD, Hester Ann 23
LEARNEY, John 74
LEARNEY, Pat 74
LEDFORD, Esther Ann 13
LEDFORD, Sarah 68
LEE, ----- 30
LEE, A. T. 45
LEE, Alex H. 21
LEE, Ann 58
LEE, Ann Eliza Stone 40
LEE, Cassmara A. 19
LEE, E. A. 60
LEE, Elizabeth F. 98
LEE, Elizabeth J. 61

LEE, Granville 42
LEE, Henry W. 82
LEE, Hiram 19
LEE, Hiram 30
LEE, Hiram 40
LEE, J. H. 47
LEE, J. H. 56
LEE, Jackson 12
LEE, Jacob C. 78
LEE, James 36
LEE, John H. 36
LEE, John William 42
LEE, Joicy A. 17
LEE, Laura 101
LEE, Lawson T. 101
LEE, Louisa 14
LEE, Lucinda 70
LEE, Lucy C. 55
LEE, Mary 56
LEE, Mary A. 74
LEE, Mary J. 60
LEE, Mathias 80
LEE, Matthias 17
LEE, Miranda A. 48
LEE, N. 113
LEE, Nancy 31
LEE, Sallie 112
LEE, Susan 63
LEE, Susan 77
LEE, Susan H. 52
LEE, W. P. 21
LEE, W. R. 45
LEE, W. R. 82
LEE, Wesley W. 12
LEEK, L. 57
LEET(?), Louisa 123
LEET, William 103
LEET, William H. 123
LEFORGE, Lewis 13
LEFORGE, Lewis 23
LEFORGE, Sarah A. 23
LEFORGE, William 23
LEFORGEE, Henry P. 97
LEFORGEE, James C. 97
LEFORGEE, Mary J. 82
LEFORGES, Mary E. 13
LENAGHEN, Alice 83
LENAGHEN, Catharine 83
LENAGHEN, James 83

LEUIS, R. G. 18
LEWIS, A. G. 70
LEWIS, Alice 9
LEWIS, Alice E. 65
LEWIS, Amanda 131
LEWIS, J. A. 112
LEWIS, J. J. 112
LEWIS, John 125
LEWIS, John P. 125
LEWIS, John T. 86
LEWIS, John T. 90
LEWIS, Louisa 22
LEWIS, Lucinda 25
LEWIS, Lucinda 53
LEWIS, Martha 131
LEWIS, Mary A. 12
LEWIS, R. G. 18
LEWIS, Robt. M. 86
LEWIS, William F. 72
LEWMAN, Delily 65
LEWMAN, Elimigh 69
LEWMAN, Ellen 69
LEWMAN, Emily 64
LEWMAN, James P. 64
LEWMAN, Jaretta C. 79
LEWMAN, Joel T. 79
LEWMAN, Johns T. 9
LEWMAN, Jonathan 72
LEWMAN, M. S. 9
LEWMAN, Malinda 32
LEWMAN, Malinda 71
LEWMAN, Matild 65
LEWMAN, Matilda 80
LEWMAN, Polly 7
LEWMAN, Priscille E. 64
LEWMAN, Sophia 11
LEWMAN, Sophia 69
LIGHTFOOD, Marget J. 72
LIGHTFOOT, John S, 121
LIGHTFOOT, John W. 79
LIGHTFOOT, Margaret J. 77
LIGHTFOOT, Mary 82
LIGHTFOOT, R. A. 68
LIGHTFOOT, R. A. 82
LIGHTFOOT, Robert A. 121
LIKES, James F. 54
LIKES, Josephine 14

LIKES, Mary 9
LIKES, Mary 41
LIKES, Thos. M. 14
LIKING, Eli 81
LINDSAY, Henry P. 93
LINDSAY, William E. 93
LINDSEY, Sarah 73
LINEHER, Sally 43
LITEN, Joseph D. 85
LITER, Sarah C. 47
LITON, Lucy E. 85
LITTLEPOHN, Mary 4
LITTLETON, Alma 115
LITTLETON, D. S. 115
LITTLETON, Geo. W. 2
LITTLETON, Henry Thomas 2
LITTLETON, J. F. 115
LITTLETON, Minerva L. 30
LLOYD, Maria 8
LOCKRIDGE(?), Ebanor K. 38
LOGAN, Cornelia 68
LOGAN, Diana 31
LOGAN, Dr. E. 28
LOGAN, E. 6
LOGAN, E. 43
LOGAN, E. 81
LOGAN, Eliza J. 94
LOGAN, Elizabeth 19
LOGAN, Ethbert 55
LOGAN, Frances L. 33
LOGAN, Henry 41
LOGAN, Jesse 81
LOGAN, Lucy Ann 6
LOGAN, Lucy Ann 22
LOGAN, Lucy Ann 40
LOGAN, Susan 7
LOGAN, Thompkins 31
LOGAN, Tobias 40
LOGAN, William 41
LOGAN, William W. 31
LONG, Nancy 66
LONGBOTTOM, Thomas 128
LONLEY, Samuel T. 79
LOOMAN, Farris M. 41
LOOMAN, James P. 41
LOOMAN, Jennette 42
LOOMAN, Jonathan R. 42
LOOMAN, Mary 54

LOOMAN, Matilda 53
LOOMAN, Sophia 52
LOOMAN, Surtilda 53
LOORMAN, Polly 41
LORMAN, Emily 42
LOUREY, Geo. G. 35
LOURY, G. D. 73
LOURY, Geo. D. 73
LOURY, Geo. H.B. 35
LOVEL, Harlents 75
LOVEL, Joshua 75
LOVEL, Joushua 62
LOWERY, Charles 128
LOWERY, Dalia 128
LOWERY, G. G. 65
LOWRY, Nancy 73
LOYD, Emily T. 45
LOYD, Sarah 54
LUCAS, Benjamin 118
LUCAS, G. B. 118
LUCAS, George W. 23
LUCAS, William W. 23
LUKINS, Amanda 79
LUKINS, Annie L. 131
LUKINS, Fannie 110
LUKINS, Joseph P. 131
LUMAN, Lucinda 95
LYMAN, James 67
LYNUM, Charles 54
LYNUM, Chas. 17
LYONS, Bruce T. 18
LYONS, Daniel T. 43
LYONS, Daniel W. 98
LYONS, Druzilla 114
LYONS, J. W. 114
LYONS, John 23
LYONS, Margaret 122
LYONS, Mary 27
LYONS, Mary 43
LYONS, Mary 98
LYONS, Mary A. 80
LYONS, Mary Ann 41
LYONS, Mary E. 76
LYONS, Michael 122
LYONS, S. B. 18
LYONS, S. B. 68
LYONS, Samuel B. 43
LYONS, Samuel B. 82
LYONS, Tandy 89
LYTLE, Edgar L. 88
LYTLE, Louisa H. 88

LYTLE, Parthenia 89
LYTLE, Samuel 21
LYTLE, Samuel 74
LYTLE, Wm. P. 88
LYTTE, Harriet 22
LYTTE, Saml. 12
LYTTE, Saml. R. 61
LYTTE, Sarah E. 12

MACK, Jennie 99
MACKEY, Annie 122
MADDEN, Eddie 120
MADDEN, Squire 120
MADDEX, William 64
MADISON, Nancy 123
MAEUCHY, Rebecca 10
MAGOWAN, Harrison 79
MAGOWEN, Lydia 4
MAHER, Mary A. 74
MAHER, Wm. 74
MAHEW, Isabella P. 28
MAHEW, William 28
MAILEY, John 100
MAISES, Luann 72
MALERY, Chas. 90
MALERY, Henry C. 90
MALLORY, ----- 38
MALLORY, Richard E. 126
MALLORY, Stewart 126
MALLORY, Wilford 38
MAMSON, Maggie M. 99
MANCHESTER, Abel B. 41
MANCHESTER, George 129
MANCHESTER, Hiram 19
MANCHESTER, James D. 41
MANCHESTER, Samuel 129
MANLEY, Nancy 40
MANN, Bridget O. 98
MANN, Rachl. 92
MANSFIELD, Mariah 101
MARCY, Elizabeth C. 53
MARGETT, Mary J. 77
MARIZEY, O. Ann 2
MARK, Clark B. 54
MARK, Clark B. 79
MARK, Elizabeth C. 42
MARK, M. J. 112
MARK, Maria J. 88
MARK, Mariah J. 61
MARK, Samuel G. 72
MARK, Silas 41
MARK, Silas 72

MARK, Simon Peter Jonas 41
MARK, Titus 42
MARK, Titus 79
MARKMELL, Jane 7
MARKWELL, ----- 23
MARKWELL, Abel 63
MARKWELL, Abel 69
MARKWELL, Alfred 25
MARKWELL, Alfred 70
MARKWELL, Alfred 80
MARKWELL, America C. 31
MARKWELL, E. W. 89
MARKWELL, Elias W. 16
MARKWELL, Eliza G. 63
MARKWELL, Eliza J. 21
MARKWELL, Eliza J. 25
MARKWELL, Eliza J. 76
MARKWELL, Eliza Jane 43
MARKWELL, Evaline 28
MARKWELL, Evaline 63
MARKWELL, F. M. 17
MARKWELL, F. M. 81
MARKWELL, Florinda 21
MARKWELL, George W. 52
MARKWELL, Henry 63
MARKWELL, J. S. 111
MARKWELL, Jane 40
MARKWELL, Jerusha 51
MARKWELL, Jesse 103
MARKWELL, Joel 16
MARKWELL, Joel 40
MARKWELL, John L. 16
MARKWELL, Landa. 31
MARKWELL, Lewis 23
MARKWELL, Lewis 112
MARKWELL, Lidia 132
MARKWELL, Lidia 132
MARKWELL, Luther 40
MARKWELL, Malinda J. 53
MARKWELL, Marshall 40
MARKWELL, Martha L. 17
MARKWELL, Mary H. 16
MARKWELL, Mary H. 89
MARKWELL, Mollie 111
MARKWELL, Nancy 6
MARKWELL, Nancy 28
MARKWELL, Nancy 59
MARKWELL, Nancy 81
MARKWELL, Sally Ann 40
MARKWELL, Sarah 1
MARKWELL, Thomas 81

MARKWELL, Thos. P. 13
MARKWELL, Wm. J. 13
MARPLE, Sarah 59
MARS, Minervy 45
MARSH, Martha 37
MARSHALL, A. K. 1
MARSHALL, A. K. 71
MARSHALL, C. H. 115
MARSHALL, Charles 29
MARSHALL, Emily M. 11
MARSHALL, Henry C. 80
MARSHALL, J. W. 115
MARSHALL, Joshua 19
MARSHALL, Juliett 40
MARSHALL, Martin L. 15
MARSHALL, Martin P. 5
MARSHALL, Martin P. 14
MARSHALL, Mary 74
MARSHALL, Mortimer 101
MARTIN, Avina 51
MARTIN, Mary 118
MARTIN, Mary E. 129
MARTIN, Mary F. 94
MARTIN, Perry F. 13
MARTIN, Robt. 13
MARTIN, Wm. G. 94
MASCEY, Henry L. 83
MASCEY, Mary A. 83
MASCEY, Prudence 83
MASE, Elizabeth 32
MASTON, ----- 38
MASTON, Thomas 38
MATCHEL, Elizabeth P. 63
MATCHET, Elizabeth 69
MATINGLY, Andrew 79
MATTHEW, Caroline 23
MATTHEWS, Hennetts 50
MATTHEWS, Henrietta 76
MATTINGLEY, Francis B. 94
MATTINGLY, Amos K. 97
MATTINGLY, Andrew 54
MATTINGLY, Elizabeth 97
MATTINGLY, Henry 97
MATTINGLY, Henry 130
MATTINGLY, Jno. T. 94
MATTINGLY, Nancy 64
MATTINGLY, Sarah 9
MATTINGLY, William 97
MATTINLEY, Chas. P. 94
MAUZEY, Elizabeth 61
MAUZY, Elizabeth 67

MAWZY, Elizabeth 75
MAXEY, E. C. 22
MAXEY, Oliver P. 129
MAXEY, Thomas 55
MAXEY, William 129
MAXWELL, James 5
MAXWELL, Jennet 5
MAY, David P. 16
MAY, James M. 119
MAY, John 16
MAY, John 58
MAY, John H. 119
MAY, John L. 65
MAYERS, Polly Ann 17
MAYHEW, William 53
MAYHUGH, William T. 71
MCADAMS, John 80
MCCABE(?), Elizabeth 68
MCCABE, David 45
MCCABE, Elizabeth 82
MCCALF, Elizabeth 29
MCCALL, Amelia 117
MCCALL, Jackson 2
MCCALL, Jackson 62
MCCALL, Jackson 67
MCCALL, Jackson 67
MCCALL, Jacson 46
MCCALL, James E. 46
MCCALL, Margaret J.A. 2
MCCALL, Mary Ann 2
MCCAMACK, Wm. 92
MCCAN, Elizabeth 45
MCCAN, James W. 61
MCCAN, Sarelda 52
MCCAN, Serrilda 41
MCCANN, ----- 36
MCCANN, Elizabeth A. 32
MCCANN, Elizth. 12
MCCANN, James 82
MCCANN, Jane 74
MCCANN, Marshall 36
MCCARTNEY, Catherine E. 84
MCCARTNEY, John 68
MCCARTNEY, John 84
MCCARTY, A. J. 111
MCCARTY, Alexander 114
MCCARTY, Ann 35
MCCARTY, Clainda A. 96
MCCARTY, David 1
MCCARTY, E. M. 108
MCCARTY, Edmance P. 76

MCCARTY, Emarine 86
MCCARTY, Emerine 124
MCCARTY, Felix 104
MCCARTY, Foster 114
MCCARTY, Francis 128
MCCARTY, Frank 35
MCCARTY, Frank H. 104
MCCARTY, Gabriel 81
MCCARTY, Ger. H. 34
MCCARTY, J. 57
MCCARTY, James 108
MCCARTY, John 34
MCCARTY, John 104
MCCARTY, John 111
MCCARTY, John E. 76
MCCARTY, John R. 34
MCCARTY, Lloyd A. 128
MCCARTY, Malinda 34
MCCARTY, Martha E.J. 1
MCCARTY, Mary 103
MCCARTY, Mary 105
MCCARTY, Mary 124
MCCARTY, Mary J. 50
MCCARTY, Santford 128
MCCARTY, Sarah E. 103
MCCARTY, W. V.E. 81
MCCLAIN, J. W. 26
MCCLAIN, Jno. L. 47
MCCLAIN, Joseph 47
MCCLAIN, Mary 26
MCCLANAHAN, M. J. 111
MCCLANE, Caroline 117
MCCLARY, Mary 112
MCCLAUSE, Cynthia 124
MCCLEING, Sally 64
MCCLERG, Amanda Enise 17
MCCLERG, Joseph 17
MCCLERG, Minerva 119
MCCLERG, Sanford 14
MCCLING, John 14
MCCLINTOCK, Alexander 76
MCCLINTOCK, Wm. 76
MCCLURE, Mary Ann 132
MCCLURE, Sarah E. 131
MCCORD, Alfd. 65
MCCORD, Alfred 49
MCCORD, Becca B. 101
MCCORD, Claudy 101
MCCORD, David 36
MCCORD, David 66
MCCORD, David 101

MCCORD, David 128
MCCORD, E. M. 49
MCCORD, Earnest V. 127
MCCORD, Edward 92
MCCORD, Etta May 92
MCCORD, George 104
MCCORD, James 105
MCCORD, James 124
MCCORD, Jane 35
MCCORD, Jas. A. 96
MCCORD, John A. 92
MCCORD, John E. 92
MCCORD, John W. 100
MCCORD, Margaret 56
MCCORD, Margaret 67
MCCORD, Martha 36
MCCORD, Martha A. 92
MCCORD, Mary C. 49
MCCORD, Rosannah 91
MCCORD, Sarah 100
MCCORD, Sarah A. 86
MCCORD, Silas 128
MCCORD, Sterling P. 96
MCCORD, W. S. 101
MCCORD, William 103
MCCORD, William 127
MCCORD, Wm. S. 92
MCCORD, Yancy E. 124
MCCORMICK, A. B. 106
MCCORMICK, George 102
MCCORMICK, Harrison 103
MCCORMICK, Miles B. 123
MCCORMICK, W. F. 106
MCCORMICK, William F. 123
MCCOWAN, Sarah J. 75
MCCOY, Mary 95
MCCOY, Nancy 119
MCCRACKEN, Mary A. 70
MCCRACKEN, Theodoria 103
MCCRACKEN, William C. 103
MCCRACKEN, Wm. B. 62
MCCRARY, John 75
MCCRARY, Wm. 75
MCCUNACK, Saml. 92
MCDANALL, William H. 101
MCDANIEL, Elizabeth 100
MCDANIEL, Isiah 101
MCDARELL, Adaline C. 93
MCDONALD, Barbary 32
MCDONALD, D. W. 114
MCDONALD, George W. 117

MCDONALD, J. E. 114
MCDONALD, James M. 83
MCDONALD, James W. 117
MCDONALD, Jennie 98
MCDONALD, Margaret 51
MCDONALD, Martin 86
MCDONALD, Richard L. 83
MCDONALD, Robert 51
MCDONALD, Sarah F. 59
MCDONALD, Sarah F. 83
MCDOWELL, A. C. 112
MCDUAVID, H. 114
MCGATH, John 82
MCGATH, Mark 82
MCGINNIS, Pauline J. 127
MCGLOTHIN, Hiram 21
MCGLOTHIN, Hiram 21
MCGOWAN, Abram 27
MCGOWAN, Lydia 42
MCGOWAN, Sary J. 81
MCGREGOR, Alex 25
MCGREGOR, Alex 63
MCGREGOR, Alexander 52
MCGREGOR, Barnesford 63
MCGREGOR, Basford 77
MCGREGOR, Brasferd 42
MCGREGOR, Harriet A. 25
MCGREGOR, James 69
MCGREGOR, James M. 79
MCGREGOR, Jas. 11
MCGREGOR, Jas. Frederick 11
MCGREGOR, R. L. 70
MCGREGOR, Robert A. 42
MCGREGOR, Robert L. 77
MCILHANY, Elizabeth 41
MCILVAIN, Elizabeth 109
MCILVAIN, James 82
MCILVAIN, John W. 82
MCILVAIN, Lizzie 131
MCILVAINE, Nancy 36
MCINTIRE, Dorinda 56
MCINTIRE, Eliza Ann 2
MCINTIRE, Eliza Susan 2
MCINTIRE, James B. 56
MCINTIRE, Jas. B. 2
MCINTIRE, Jos. P. 75
MCINTIRE, T. B. 56
MCINTIRE, Thos. B. 78
MCINTYRE, ----- 65
MCINTYRE, ----- 66
MCINTYRE, B. T. 37

MCINTYRE, Barnett 37
MCINTYRE, Bertha E. 119
MCINTYRE, Charles J. 100
MCINTYRE, Charles S. 119
MCINTYRE, David 119
MCINTYRE, E. S. 113
MCINTYRE, Eliza Ann 37
MCINTYRE, Francis M. 75
MCINTYRE, Geo. 35
MCINTYRE, Jn. H. 65
MCINTYRE, Joseph 126
MCINTYRE, Lucy M. 126
MCINTYRE, Mary 35
MCINTYRE, Mary 35
MCINTYRE, Mary E. 101
MCINTYRE, Mary J. 86
MCINTYRE, Melvina 131
MCINTYRE, Oliver T. 126
MCINTYRE, Sallie E. 100
MCINTYRE, Samuel 119
MCINTYRE, Thomas B. 66
MCINTYRE, William J. 100
MCINTYRE, William J. 126
MCJLACRIM, James 25
MCJLRAIN(?), Sarah C. 25
MCJLVAIN, Rosanna 27
MCJLVAIN, William 27
MCKEE, A. T. 45
MCKEE, Amanda 116
MCKEE, Andrew 6
MCKEE, Andrew 40
MCKEE, Andrew T. 69
MCKEE, Benjm. T. 8
MCKEE, Elizabeth 63
MCKEE, Ellen 76
MCKEE, Emily 12
MCKEE, Frances M. 42
MCKEE, G. W. 85
MCKEE, Geo. S. 96
MCKEE, George 45
MCKEE, Hiram 68
MCKEE, James 21
MCKEE, James R. 40
MCKEE, Jno. A. 10
MCKEE, John A. 42
MCKEE, John A. 80
MCKEE, Joseph 33
MCKEE, Joseph 42
MCKEE, Joseph D. 72
MCKEE, Joseph D. 80
MCKEE, Levi F. 12

MCKEE, Levi F. 96
MCKEE, Louisa 8
MCKEE, Maggie 132
MCKEE, Maggie H. 85
MCKEE, Mary J. 80
MCKEE, Mary Owings 10
MCKEE, Robt. 89
MCKEE, S. T. 109
MCKEE, Simon Dudley 42
MCKEE, Thomas C. 21
MCKEE, William 42
MCKEE, William Edward 42
MCKEE, Wm. 12
MCKEE, Wm. 64
MCKEE, Wm. 109
MCKINNEY, Elizabeth 9
MCKINNEY, Elizabeth 80
MCKINNEY, W. D. 112
MCLAIN, John 69
MCLAIN, Lucy E. 105
MCLAIN, Nancy 105
MCLANE, Elizabeth S. 74
MCLANE, Jos. 74
MCLANE, M. E. 107
MCLEAVE, Maggie E. 91
MCMAHON, Mollie 124
MCMANN, Mary 115
MCMULLIN, G. 102
MCNELLY, Maggie 97
MCNELLY, Maggie 121
MCNESBY, John 18
MCREE, George Ann 33
MCROBERTS, Asa 102
MCROBERTS, Asa 125
MCROBERTS, Ashael M. 32
MCROBERTS, Davis R.E. 13
MCROBERTS, James 109
MCROBERTS, James 125
MCROBERTS, Lewis 12
MCROBERTS, Lizzie 118
MCROBERTS, N. R. 109
MCROBERTS, Rebecca 44
MCROBERTS, Saml. 13
MCROBERTS, Sarah J. 107
MCROBERTS, Trumbo 32
MCROBERTS, Weeks 118
MCROBERTS, Wilford 24
MCROBERTS, William 77
MCROBERTS, Wm. S. 12
MCVESBIT, Evaline 40
MCVESBIT, John 40

MEADOWS, James E. 125
MEADOWS, Rawleigh 125
MEARS, ----- 65
MEARS, Margaret 2
MEARS, Samuel R. 65
MEEKS, Wiliam 129
MEEKS, Zella G. 129
MELFORST, Margt. 95
MENICK, Thos. 79
MEOP, Ann 1
MEREDITH, Ruth 54
MERIDETH, Rutha 79
MERS, ----- 58
MERS, John 84
MERS, Manerva 67
MERS, Mary 76
MERS, Mary M. 84
MERS, Samuel 76
METCALF, ----- 24
METCALF, Elizabeth 43
METCALF, Sabina 58
MEYERS, Martha Ann 1
MEYERS, Wm. 1
MILLBURN, Elizabeth 16
MILLER, A. D. 67
MILLER, Alfred D. 74
MILLER, Clarissa 27
MILLER, Clarra H. 74
MILLER, Elizabeth H. 81
MILLER, Elizabeth H. 82
MILLER, Henry 27
MILLER, Joseph 81
MILLER, Joseph 82
MILLER, Joseph A. 60
MILLER, Margaret J. 73
MILLER, Milly Jane 8
MILLIKEN, James 92
MILLION, Barbara 96
MILLION, George C. 131
MILLION, Isaac 131
MILLION, Squire 44
MILLS, Elizabeth J. 70
MILLS, J. A. 110
MILLS, James 17
MILLS, John 110
MILLS, Lizzie 91
MILLS, Mary 37
MILLS, Mary 52
MILLS, Mary 78
MILLS, Mary D. 12
MILLS, Rosa 98

MIRDER, Mary 18
MITCHEL, Alfred 3
MITCHEL, James 4
MITCHEL, Minerva Ellen 4
MITCHELL, Alvin 105
MITCHELL, Alvin 126
MITCHELL, Alvin R. 102
MITCHELL, David B. 102
MITCHELL, Elizth. 87
MITCHELL, H. E. 107
MITCHELL, Wm. 107
MITCHIE(?), James A. 3
MOGOWAN, Abram 69
MOMSON, Charles B. 99
MONROE, Chas. 95
MONROE, Cora 95
MONTGOMERY, Alex 18
MONTGOMERY, Alexander 51
MONTGOMERY, Wm. S. 18
MONTIMEE, Alice 131
MOODY, E. S. 115
MOODY, J. W. 115
MOONEY, George F. 53
MOORE, ----- 65
MOORE, ----- 65
MOORE, Abigail 33
MOORE, Ann 13
MOORE, Artimena 41
MOORE, Artimeso 63
MOORE, Bridget 99
MOORE, Catharine 53
MOORE, Catharine 64
MOORE, Charles L. 107
MOORE, Elisha 117
MOORE, Elizabeth S. 13
MOORE, Emily 121
MOORE, Emma 102
MOORE, George 128
MOORE, George W. 107
MOORE, Harrison 103
MOORE, Hiram 65
MOORE, Hiram 66
MOORE, James W. 127
MOORE, John 76
MOORE, John 119
MOORE, John P. 104
MOORE, Lavena 46
MOORE, Levi C. 56
MOORE, Levina 38
MOORE, Lucy B. 127
MOORE, Mary A. 128

MOORE, O. S. 88
MOORE, Penelope 54
MOORE, Robert 117
MOORE, Robert B. 119
MOORE, Rosa A. 57
MOORE, Rutha 16
MOORE, Susan R. 85
MOORE, Wesley 121
MOORE, William 13
MORAN, Ann 66
MORAN, Catherine 117
MORAN, John 105
MORAN, John 117
MORAN, Jon 70
MORAN, Joseph P. 117
MORAN, Lucinda 122
MORE, Thomas T. 75
MOREHEAD, A. D. 1
MOREHEAD, A. D. 1
MOREHEAD, Alfred 54
MOREHEAD, Alfred 79
MOREHEAD, Nelson 38
MOREHEAD, Nelson 64
MORELAND, Ludie V. 119
MOREN Jno. 67
MOREN, Angeline 67
MOREN, Angeline 82
MOREN, Ann 74
MOREN, Catherine 105
MOREN, Charles H. 105
MOREN, Daniel B. 122
MOREN, Edward 73
MOREN, James 82
MOREN, James M. 122
MOREN, John 87
MOREN, John E. 82
MOREN, Malinda D. 87
MOREN, Wm. T. 87
MORGAN, ----- 10
MORGAN, ----- 39
MORGAN, ----- 58
MORGAN, Bettie 92
MORGAN, Daniel 71
MORGAN, Delia B. 88
MORGAN, Eliza 29
MORGAN, J. H. 81
MORGAN, John 43
MORGAN, Mary 25
MORGAN, Mary 82
MORGAN, Nancy 43
MORGAN, Raleigh 81

MORGAN, Rawleigh 75
MORGAN, Sarah 62
MORGAN, W. H. 57
MORGAN, William F. 39
MORGAN, Willis 80
MORGAN, Wm. 72
MORGAN, Wm. C. 75
MORGAN, Wm. F. 5
MORGAN, Wm. F. 5
MORGANTHAW, ----- 36
MORGANTHAW, Henry 36
MORMAN, Edward 44
MORRIS, George V. 76
MORRIS, M. M. 85
MORRIS, Wm. 76
MORRISON, Anna 89
MORRISON, David 69
MORRISON, David 115
MORRISON, Helen 54
MORRISON, Helen 78
MORRISON, John B. 4
MORRISON, Joseph Samuel 4
MORRISON, W. H. 115
MORRISON, William A. 70
MORRISON, William A. 78
MORRISON, William H. 76
MOSS(?), Ann 1
MOSS, America 44
MOSS, M. E. 111
MOTHWEN, Jennet 5
MOUEY, E. 96
MOUEY, Richard D. 101
MOXEN, Edward 2
MTOUT, Thomas 104
MUAL, Fomtty R. 63
MUIR, Malinda 90
MULAY, Fanny 57
MULLARKEY, Jas. 90
MULLARKEY, Wm. 90
MULLAY, Fannie T. 78
MULLAY, W. J. 77
MULLIKEN, ----- 104
MULLIKIN, Ruth 123
MURPHY, Jeremiah 70
MURRY, Martha 78
MURS, John 58
MUSE, Addaide 41
MUSE, Amanda V. 132
MUSE, Eliza 115
MUSE, Etkelbert 10
MUSE, Fanny 13

MUSE, Faritty R. 52
MUSE, Geo. S. 89
MUSE, George 10
MUSE, George 63
MUSE, George 78
MUSE, George 89
MUSE, Hiram 42
MUSE, Hiram B. 10
MUSE, J. B. 71
MUSE, James B. 34
MUSE, James B. 52
MUSE, James D. 34
MUSE, Marion 129
MUSE, Martha A. 72
MUSE, Mary E. 129
MUSE, Mary Mahala 42
MUSE, Othela 41
MUSE, Robt. H. 10
MUSE, Sarah A. 96
MUSE, Wm. M. 96
MYER, Lenna 73
MYERS, Catherine A. 42
MYERS, J. H.H. 56
MYERS, Jacob 77
MYERS, John 43
MYERS, John 63
MYERS, John Trumbo 43
MYERS, K. R. 30
MYERS, Lucinda 78
MYERS, Lydia 40
MYERS, M. J.N. 83
MYERS, Nancy 48
MYERS, Nancy 91
MYERS, Owen 92
MYERS, Sally Ann 30
MYERS, Samuel 81
MYERS, Sanford B. 81
MYERS, Sary O. 81
MYRES, ----- 37
MYRES, Cervia 21
MYRES, E. B. 86
MYRES, Jas. 37
MYRES, John 21
MYRES, Louisania 21
MYRES, Mahala 21
MYRES, Sarah 35
MYRES, Wilburn 21

NAILOR, George Ann 54
NAILOR, Margaret 39
NALIS, Charles 20
NALIS, David 20

NALIS, Elizabeth 20
NALIS, James 20
NALIS, Mary Bell 20
NALIS, Robt. G. 20
NALIS, Sally A. 20
NALIS, Sarah 20
NALL(?), Julia Ann 81
NASH, James 35
NASH, Jas. B. 95
NASH, Jas. S. 95
NASH, John 35
NATE, Mary D. 29
NAYLOR, Emily 28
NEAL, Sarah Ann 25
NEALIS, David R. 62
NEALIS, Elizabeth J. 41
NEALIS, John 8
NEALIS, Martha Ann 17
NEALIS, Minerva 103
NEALIS, Rushan 84
NEALIS, Ruth A. 60
NEALIS, S. E. 116
NEALIS, S. M. 111
NEALIS, Sarah A. 62
NEALIS, Thomas 111
NEULAND, Saurin W. 44
NEWDIGATE, William 65
NEWGEN, America 42
NEWMAN, Alex 2
NEWMAN, Alexander 46
NEWMAN, Alexander 73
NEWMAN, Amanda 41
NEWMAN, Amanda 83
NEWMAN, Amanda J. 16
NEWMAN, Fidella 70
NEWMAN, Hamilton S. 17
NEWMAN, James 8
NEWMAN, James M. 46
NEWMAN, James W. 104
NEWMAN, Jane 44
NEWMAN, Jane 68
NEWMAN, Jas. 68
NEWMAN, John 2
NEWMAN, John D. 30
NEWMAN, John S. 30
NEWMAN, Leislie B. 104
NEWMAN, M. 116
NEWMAN, Mahida 2
NEWMAN, Martha E. 129
NEWMAN, Nancy 76
NEWMAN, Nancy J. 89

NEWMAN, Phidilla 55
NEWMAN, Sarah 63
NEWMAN, Sarah 78
NEWMAN, Seran 116
NEWMAN, Simpson R. 116
NEWMAN, Thomas 17
NEWMAN, William Andrew 73
NEWMAN, William C. 8
NICKIE, Mary 65
NICKLE, Elizabeth 32
NICKLE, Greenup 32
NICKLE, Robt. 32
NICKLE, William 32
NOLIN, Effie 124
NOLIN, William W. 124
NORRIS, George M. 6
NORRIS, Harvey Sanders 40
NORRIS, James H. 22
NORRIS, William 22
NORRIS, William 40
NORRIS, Wm. H. 6
NORTHCOTT, Jas. C. 11
NORTHCOTT, Joseph B. 11
NORTHCOTT, Lucretia 23
NORTHCUT, J. B. 70
NORTHCUT, Joseph B. 39
NORTHCUT, Lewellyn 39
NORTHCUTT, Joseph B. 52
NORTHWITT, Joseph B. 23
NORTON, C. A. 110
NORTON, Wm. 110
NORWOOD, Alfred 42
NORWOOD, Eliza G. 42
NOWOOD, Alfred W. 72
NUDGIATE, Robert 133
NUDIGATE, C. H. 116
NUDIGATE, Mary A. 33
NUDIGATE, Minnie J. 133
NUDIGATE, Robert 116
NUDIGATE, William 33
NUTE, Charles 29
NUTE, Charles 54
NUTE, Charles 79
NUTE, Louisa 79
NUTE, Obed P. 79
NUTE, Obed. P. 53
NUTE, Obed. P. 71
NUTE, Wm. G. 37

O'BANNON, W. B. 79
O'GAR, Bell 111

O'GAR, Patrick 71
O'GAR, Patrick 76
O'GAR, Patrick 111
O'MANN, Bridget 98
OAKERSON, John S. 106
OALEY, Lucy Ann 15
OBANION, James T. 42
OBANION, Mary Susan 42
OBANNON, Lucy M. 127
OBERLEY, James W.H. 26
ODOHORTY, P. W. 56
OHARN, B. T. 99
OKERSON, John H. 106
OKERSON, Tabitha J. 106
OLIVER, Mary 129
OLIVER, Mary V. 88
OLIVER, Thomas 44
OLIVER, Thomas 71
ORMSTADT, Geo. 36
ORMSTADT, Sarah 36
OSULLIVAN, John 99
OVERBY, Elizth. 16
OVERBY, Jonathan 26
OVERBY, Lucinda 36
OVERLEY, A. H. 112
OVERLEY, Allie 87
OVERLEY, G. W. 61
OVERLEY, Jane 100
OVERLEY, Jas. H. 94
OVERLEY, Mahala 24
OVERLEY, Mary 120
OVERLEY, Mary L. 109
OVERLEY, Michael 49
OVERLEY, Millie 87
OVERLEY, Nannie D. 94
OVERLEY, S. 112
OVERLEY, Sarah 108
OVERLEY, W. S. 112
OVERLY, ----- 66
OVERLY, Ann 75
OVERLY, Elizabeth 60
OVERLY, George W. 73
OVERLY, Jonathan 36
OVERLY, Jonathan 60
OVERLY, Jonathan 82
OVERLY, Jonathan F. 82
OVERLY, Joseph 59
OVERLY, Mahala 67
OVERLY, Mahala 83
OVERLY, Mary J. 84
OVERLY, Sarah F. 83

OVERLY, Sarah M. 52
OVERLY, Sarah T. 49
OVERTON, Creed 28
OVERTON, Eliza Bell 28
OVERTON, J. G. 70
OVERTON, Sarah 28
OVERTON, Sary 77
OVERTOW, James J. 101
OWENS, A. R. 121
OWENS, Emily 42
OWENS, Jeremiah 80
OWENS, John 109
OWENS, Minerva 121
OWENS, Saml. T. 109

PAINTER, Sylvanus 48
PALMER, Jas. D. 36
PALMER, P. O. 112
PALMER, Penuelia A. 77
PALMER, Philip O. 36
PALMER, R. D. 112
PARDUM, John 83
PARK, ----- 65
PARK, James F. 129
PARK, John 129
PARKER, Amanda 113
PARKER, Frank 123
PARKER, Harriet 11
PARKER, Jemima 126
PARKER, John 102
PARKER, Lauria B. 119
PARKER, Lizzie 120
PARKER, Mary Y. 118
PARKER, R. F. 57
PARKER, Richard 74
PARKER, Richard 75
PARKER, Shelton 119
PARKER, William 118
PARKER, Wm. H. 75
PARKERSON, ----- 31
PARKS, Joannah 4
PARKS, John 108
PARKS, Octavia 108
PARKSTONE, ----- 57
PARSONS, James 48
PARSONS, Mary J. 127
PARSONS, Mollie 107
PARSONS, P. V. 107
PATON, Miranda 130
PATTERN, Margaret V. 86
PATTERSON, James B. 33
PATTERSON, James M. 33

PATTERSON, M. 112
PATTERSON, Margaret V. 127
PATTON, A. M. 5
PATTON, A. M. 38
PATTON, Ann Bell 5
PATTON, Fannie J. 130
PATTON, James 35
PATTON, John 50
PATTON, John 130
PATTON, Mary A. 130
PATTON, Mary E. 50
PATTON, Sarah E. 75
PAUL, Charles 111
PAXTEN, Belle 89
PAXTON, ----- 36
PAXTON, G. T. 60
PAXTON, Rubena 75
PAYNE, ----- 39
PAYNE, ----- 66
PAYNE, Adrian 113
PAYNE, Amanda F. 81
PAYNE, Ann 5
PAYNE, Bruce 109
PAYNE, Eddie D. 123
PAYNE, Edward B. 109
PAYNE, Edwin 88
PAYNE, Edwin 119
PAYNE, Emmett 119
PAYNE, F. J. 81
PAYNE, Frances 36
PAYNE, Henry 117
PAYNE, J. V. 113
PAYNE, James 73
PAYNE, James 123
PAYNE, James V. 59
PAYNE, James V. 82
PAYNE, Jeannett 63
PAYNE, Jenetta 77
PAYNE, Jennett 52
PAYNE, John H. 92
PAYNE, Louisa E. 117
PAYNE, Maranda 73
PAYNE, Maria 75
PAYNE, Mariah 50
PAYNE, Marion 91
PAYNE, Martha 59
PAYNE, Martha 74
PAYNE, Martha J. 8
PAYNE, Mary 73
PAYNE, Nannie 123
PAYNE, Orlando 88

PAYNE, Robert 39
PAYNE, William 123
PEARCE, Annie 117
PEARCE, Charles 26
PEARCE, Charlotte 55
PEARCE, E. B. 15
PEARCE, E. E. 9
PEARCE, E. E. 62
PEARCE, E. L. 50
PEARCE, Edward E. 117
PEARCE, Edwin 50
PEARCE, Eliza J. 81
PEARCE, Eliza Jane 6
PEARCE, Elizabeth 82
PEARCE, Emmy Lucy 44
PEARCE, Isaac E. 87
PEARCE, J. M. 26
PEARCE, James M. 44
PEARCE, Jas. M. 63
PEARCE, Jesse Mason 5
PEARCE, John M. 69
PEARCE, Lucinda 32
PEARCE, Maranda R. 28
PEARCE, Mary 122
PEARCE, R. A. 117
PEARCE, R. H. 111
PEARCE, Rawleigh W. 28
PEARCE, Ruth A. 87
PEARCE, Thos. M. 15
PEARCE, Wineford 62
PEARCE, Wm. 5
PEARCE, Wm. S. 60
PEARSON, Nannie 99
PECK, Elizth. 85
PECK, Elizth. 90
PECK, George 87
PECK, George 106
PECK, George 117
PECK, George D. 82
PECK, George W. 117
PECK, Hattie 106
PECK, Inez B. 82
PECK, John 37
PECK, John 67
PECK, John 82
PECK, Julia 106
PECK, Julia 117
PECK, Nat 58
PECK, Nathaniel 82
PECK, Sallie 87
PECK, Susan 39

PECK, Susan 56
PECK, Susan 75
PEDUE, Angeline 73
PEED, Fleming 10
PEED, W. F. 101
PEEK, Mary E. 37
PEID, Florence J. 94
PEID, Francis D. 94
PENLAND, Sarah A. 33
PEPPER, Isabella 3
PEPPER, Joseph 57
PEPPER, Lucy 102
PEPPER, Lucy B. 57
PEPPER, Lucy E. 125
PEPPER, Nancy 36
PERCELL, Nancy 105
PERDEW, Mary 7
PERDOO, Anjeline 60
PERKINS, G. B. 67
PERKINS, Isaac 116
PERKINS, Louisa 108
PERKINS, Louise 87
PERKINS, M. A. 116
PERKINS, Martha 82
PERRY, ----- 17
PERRY, Amelia A. 95
PERRY, H. J. 78
PERRY, Nancy S. 17
PERVIS, Jane 111
PETTY, Daisey A. 96
PETTY, Elijah 96
PETTY, M. C. 116
PETTY, Mathew M. 116
PHELPS, ----- 34
PHELPS, Aaron J. 102
PHELPS, C. B. 112
PHELPS, J. B. 31
PHELPS, J. B. 69
PHELPS, Johnson 20
PHELPS, Mary A. 105
PHELPS, Mary J. 31
PHELPS, S. R. 115
PHELPS, Samuel R. 34
PHELPS, William J. 5
PHELPS, Z. J. 112
PHELPS, Z. R. 5
PHIELDS, James P. 52
PHILIPS(?), William O. 10
PHILIPS, ----- 36
PHILIPS, Martin 36
PHILLIPS, Ephraim 64

PHILPS, Samuel K. 76
PHISSENHAMMER, Cristina 77
PICKEEL, Lydia 7
PICKERAL, Eliza 69
PICKERALL, Nancy 69
PICKEREL, Ann E. 60
PICKEREL, Emily 59
PICKERT, John 29
PICKERT, Sophia A. 29
PICKETT, Daniel 78
PICKREL, Eliza Ann 44
PICKREL, Matilda 44
PICKRELL, Eliza 79
PICKRELL, Elizabeth 117
PICKRELL, Elizth. 87
PICKRELL, Greenup 18
PICKRELL, Martha 82
PICKRELL, Matilda 73
PICKRELL, Matilda 109
PICKSEL, Matilda 23
PIERCE, Benj. 67
PIERCE, Isaac 50
PIERCE, Mary 18
PIERCE, William 53
PILES, Mary Eliza 83
PILES, Milton 83
PILGRIM, Mary 53
PIOBB, Louisa A. 11
PIPPER, Joseph J. 50
PIPPER, Lucy 50
PIRKINS, Jno. 68
PITTS, Dianah 49
PITTS, Effa 132
PITTS, Elizabeth 132
PITTS, John T. 132
PITTS, M. 110
PITTS, Wm. B. 110
PLANCK, Charles M. 117
PLANCK, Evaline 109
PLANCK, John 26
PLANCK, John H. 74
PLANCK, William 26
PLANCK, William 117
PLANEK, Harriet 37
PLANK, Emily 67
PLANK, Harriet 51
PLANK, Harriet 65
PLANK, Isaac 46
PLANK, John 62
PLANK, John H. 46
PLATER(?), Lucy E. 49

PLAUCK, Harriet 76
PLAUCK, Jacob 122
PLAUCK, Lucy E. 122
PLEAK, Sarah J. 69
PLEAKRUATRLUER, Emily 11
PLUMMER, ----- 32
PLUMMER, Allen S. 97
PLUMMER, Amanda 27
PLUMMER, Amanda 59
PLUMMER, Bell 118
PLUMMER, Benj. A. 97
PLUMMER, Benjamin J. 72
PLUMMER, Cyrus 98
PLUMMER, Dewps 8
PLUMMER, Eliza 32
PLUMMER, Francis 26
PLUMMER, Francis 69
PLUMMER, Franklin P. 17
PLUMMER, George 8
PLUMMER, George 26
PLUMMER, J. S. 115
PLUMMER, James M. 98
PLUMMER, Jeremiah 118
PLUMMER, Joseph 32
PLUMMER, Louisa 133
PLUMMER, M. J. 116
PLUMMER, Malinda 42
PLUMMER, Martha 41
PLUMMER, Martha 72
PLUMMER, Martha M. 13
PLUMMER, Matilda 34
PLUMMER, Matilda 72
PLUMMER, O. L. 115
PLUMMER, Sarah 34
PLUMMER, Sarah M. 118
PLUMMER, Sary 76
PLUMMER, Simpson H. 17
PLUMMOR, Henry 91
PLUMMOR, James 91
PLUMMOR, Jennie Mae 91
PLUMMOR, Nannie 91
PLUNNER, Jno. S. 95
PLUNNER, Martin P. 95
POINTER, Cordelia 115
POINTER, Salvanus 61
POLLAND, Emily 91
POLLETT, A. 113
PORTEN, William 22
PORTER, Andrew 46
PORTER, Andrew 81
PORTER, Andrew M. 106

PORTER, E. M. 18
PORTER, Eliza 44
PORTER, Eliza 67
PORTER, Elizabeth M. 7
PORTER, Esskine 81
PORTER, George M. 7
PORTER, James 61
PORTER, John 46
PORTER, John 67
PORTER, John 73
PORTER, John 82
PORTER, John H. 82
PORTER, Kenten C. 22
PORTER, Lucy 24
PORTER, Lucy 43
PORTER, Lucy 44
PORTER, Margaret 87
PORTER, Margaret 109
PORTER, Mary 115
PORTER, N. M. 114
PORTER, Priscilla Ann 2
PORTER, R. S. 85
PORTER, Rebecca 74
PORTER, Roley S. 36
PORTER, Ruth M. 106
PORTER, Samuel P. 81
PORTER, Thomas 109
PORTER, William 81
PORTER, Wm. S. 109
PORTEY, ----- 32
PORTEY, Edmund 32
PORTEY, George 32
PORTOR, Margt. 90
POTER, Andrew 3
POTMAN, Mary 129
POTTS, Cynthia 85
POTTS, Eliza 36
POTTS, John J. 78
POTTS, M. E. 47
POTTS, Sarah 56
POTTS, Thomas R. 84
POWEL, Ellen B. 74
POWEL, John 74
POWEL, Martha P. 2
POWEL, Rhoda 73
POWEL, Roda 2
POWELL, A. M. 114
POWELL, Abbie 29
POWELL, Absolem 63
POWELL, Absolyn 39
POWELL, Andrew M. 105

POWELL, Charles 105
POWELL, J. W. 114
POWELL, John A. 39
POWELL, Mary 117
POWELL, Ninetta 130
POWELL, Roda 44
POWELL, Thos. J. 130
POWER, Ann 109
POWER, Eliza 9
POWER, James M. 82
POWER, Jerry 82
POWER, John D. 32
POWER, John S. 100
POWER, Julia A. 26
POWER, Louisa Lander 41
POWER, Margaret A. 131
POWER, Martha M.N. 32
POWER, Samuel C. 100
POWER, Sarah V. 101
POWER, Sary 71
POWERS, Ben F. 41
POWERS, Claud 41
POWERS, E. 12
POWERS, Isaac K. 66
POWERS, John D. 41
POWERS, Nancy 3
POWERS, Nancy 70
POWERS, Sally 33
POWERS, Sara R. 78
PRATEMAN, Elastima 51
PRATER, Elizabeth 53
PRATER, Elizabeth 71
PRATER, Louisa 67
PRATER, Lucy 123
PRATHER, Ann 38
PRATHER, Mary 75
PRATHER, Walter 38
PRATHER, Walter 47
PRESTON, Coleman 73
PRESTON, Daniel W. 82
PRESTON, Jef 60
PRESTON, Jefferson 82
PRICE, ----- 39
PRICE, Eliha 39
PRICE, H. 112
PRICE, J. N. 107
PRICE, Mary 76
PRICE, Wm. A. 112
PRICE, Wm. G. 83
PROCTOR, ----- 20
PROCTOR, Emily 36

PROCTOR, Emily 46
PROCTOR, Emily 83
PROCTOR, Ida 88
PROCTOR, J. N. 88
PROCTOR, J. N. 110
PROCTOR, N. 110
PROTER, James 67
PROTER, Mary 50
PUGH, Charles D. 128
PUGH, George 128
PUGH, Mariah 32
PUGH, Millie 98
PUGH, Rebecca S. 32
PUGH, William A. 98
PUMPHREY, Anna 92
PUMPHREY, Howard G. 120
PUMPHREY, Thomas L. 120
PURDUM, John H. 4
PURKINS, America E. 8
PURKINS, Edwing 8
PURKINS, James 81
PURNELL, M. 52
PURNELL, Nancy J. 96
PURNELL, Roxa J. 72
PURVIS, ------ 33
PURVIS, James 33
PURVIS, N. A. 110
PURVIS, Nancy A. 33
PURVIS, William 33
PUTER, Nannie W. 85
PYLES, Clifton 131
PYLES, G. F. 81
PYLES, Milton 81
PYLES, Milton 104
PYLES, Milton 131

QUAINTANCE, Lucy 7
QUAINTANCE, Lucy Grace 1
QUAINTANCE, Wm. 1
QUAINTANCE, Wm. 7
QUALLS, Elizth. 96
QUEEN, Julia 76
QUICKSALL, Aaron 71
QUICKSALL, Aron 53

RAFTERY, Dan 114
RAFTERY, John 114
RAIBURN, Lucinda 30
RAIMEY, John A. 100
RAIMEY, Letitia B. 100
RALLINS, Amanda 58
RALLS, Alber 121
RALSTON, John 100

RALSTON, Robert E. 100
RAMEY, Casey 58
RAMEY, Emily 8
RAMEY, Harrison 8
RANDALL, A. J. 5
RANDALL, Rebecca 5
RANKIN, Eliza 128
RANKIN, Francis 81
RANKIN, J. G. 105
RANKIN, James 62
RANKIN, Matilda 67
RANKIN, Nancy 36
RANKIN, Robert 128
RANKINS, A. D. 111
RANKINS, Alvin 105
RANKINS, D. J. 115
RANKINS, Green F. 18
RANKINS, J. 111
RANKINS, Jackson 105
RANKINS, Martha 105
RANKINS, Nan 105
RANKINS, W. M. 105
RARONS, Matilda S. 30
RASH, Claud 130
RASH, Elizabeth 67
RASH, Elizabeth 82
RASH, Jacob M. 12
RASH, Miranda 37
RASH, Morris 12
RASH, Susan 38
RASH, Tabath 46
RASH, Tabitha 83
RASH, Tobitha 37
RASH, William 37
RASH, William 130
RASNEY, Elizabeth 50
RATCLIFFE, Annie B. 108
RATCLIFFE, Annie B. 114
RATCLIFFE, Simpson 129
RATCLIFFE, William 129
RAUKIN, Barinda 131
RAUKINS, Elizabeth 92
RAUKINS, James 18
RAVES, Sarah S. 22
RAVIK, James O. 52
RAWLINGS, Amanda J. 28
RAWLINGS, Anthony 28
RAWLINGS, Anthony 65
RAWLINGS, Barber A. 64
RAWLINGS, Eliza J. 77
RAWLINGS, Emily 70

RAWLINGS, Emily M. 77
RAWLINGS, Frances 14
RAWLINGS, Frances 40
RAWLINGS, Francis Leonia 9
RAWLINGS, Matilda 37
RAWLINGS, Middleton 14
RAWLINGS, N. B. 109
RAWLINGS, Northcott 65
RAWLINGS, Northroll 9
RAWLINGS, Parthena D. 14
RAWLINGS, Presley 69
RAWLINGS, Richard 109
RAWLINGS, Russel M. 28
RAWLINGS, Sanford 28
RAWLS, S. A. 112
RAWLS, Taylor 112
RAYBORNS, Nancy C. 94
RAZOR, Elizabeth 31
RAZOR, G. W. 21
RAZOR, Jerietta 17
RAZOR, Jinnetta 40
RAZOR, John 122
RAZOR, John H. 112
RAZOR, Mardolete 63
RAZOR, Mersolete 80
RAZOR, W. A. 112
REAL, Saml. J. 67
REDDEN, Elizabeth M. 42
REDDEN, Elizabeth M. 79
REDENOUR, Juliann 5
REDNIK, Isabella 35
REED, Caroline 53
REED, Elizabeth 71
REED, Elizabeth 111
REED, Mary 76
REED, Nancy 133
REED, Rebecca 9
REED, Rebecca 128
REED, Sarah 10
REEDER, Amos A. 130
REEDER, Benjamin 130
REEDER, Jacob 72
REEVE, Nancy 116
REEVES, Amanda 22
REEVES, Amanda 69
REEVES, B. F. 59
REEVES, B. F. 70
REEVES, Benj. J. 28
REEVES, Eliza 119
REEVES, Elizth. 14
REEVES, Geo. 61

REEVES, Geo. E. 67
REEVES, George 32
REEVES, George 64
REEVES, Henrietta 63
REEVES, J. N. 58
REEVES, James 63
REEVES, James 69
REEVES, James Alfred 43
REEVES, James W. 98
REEVES, Jane 53
REEVES, Jane 63
REEVES, Jane 80
REEVES, Jas. C. 17
REEVES, Jesse 93
REEVES, John 31
REEVES, John 54
REEVES, John 98
REEVES, Lucien 93
REEVES, Lucinda 95
REEVES, Malinda S. 28
REEVES, Martha 28
REEVES, Mary 3
REEVES, Mary A. 69
REEVES, Mary C. 119
REEVES, Mary J. 80
REEVES, Mary J. 113
REEVES, Noah 53
REEVES, Noah 69
REEVES, Robt. G. 32
REEVES, Sarah J. 49
REEVES, Sarah J. 74
REEVES, Sarah M. 31
REEVES, Sary J. 81
REEVES, Sebby Ann 69
REEVES, Susan 16
REEVES, Susan 39
REEVES, Susan 69
REEVES, William 28
REEVES, William G. 43
REEVES. Elijah 77
RHODAN, Lettie A. 102
RHODEN, Lucy Ellen 2
RICE, ------ 37
RICE, Cunthia 106
RICE, Ester 40
RICE, Henry 44
RICE, Henry 82
RICE, Henry A. 2
RICE, Henry W. 2
RICE, J. H. 109
RICE, Jackson 37

RICE, Jacson 45	RIGGS, Angeline 71	ROBERTSON, Mary 20	ROSS(?), Polly Ann M. 30
RICE, James S. 87	RIGGS, Caleb 14	ROBERTSON, Rebecca 20	ROSS, ----- 35
RICE, Jefferson 14	RIGGS, E. E. 39	ROBERTSON, Sarah 92	ROSS, ----- 56
RICE, John 3	RIGGS, Malica 124	ROBERTSON, Sarah 104	ROSS, ----- 58
RICE, John 60	RIGGS, Polly 39	ROBERTSON, Sarah A. 67	ROSS, ----- 65
RICE, John H. 87	RILEY, Ellen 74	ROBERTSON, Sarah J. 85	ROSS, A. Duley 54
RICE, John Henry 90	RILEY, Harriet J. 27	ROBERTSON, Sary A. 82	ROSS, Alex P. 95
RICE, John Wm. 3	RILEY, James 66	ROBERTSON, Thos. 13	ROSS, America 13
RICE, Lucinda Jane 44	RILEY, Jas. 74	ROBERTSON, William F. 85	ROSS, Annie F. 101
RICE, Martha 61	RILEY, John S. 27	ROBINSON, Lucinda 33	ROSS, Augusta 55
RICE, Martha E. 45	RILEY, Timothy 74	ROBINSON, Mary 10	ROSS, Ben 15
RICE, Mary 22	RILY, Ellan 60	ROBINSON, Mary J. 7	ROSS, Benjamin 20
RICE, Polly Ann 54	RINGO, Charles E. 131	ROBINSON, Mildred 122	ROSS, Benjamin 52
RICE, Samuel 82	RINGO, Elsie M. 131	ROBINSON, Sarah 37	ROSS, Benjamin 76
RICE, William A. 44	RINGO, Fannie 84	ROBINSON, William P. 33	ROSS, Benjamin H. 72
RICE, Wm. 45	RINGO, J. 48	ROBINSON, Wm. P. 7	ROSS, Berry F. 46
RICE, Wm. 67	RINGO, Jas. D. 11	ROBISON, Lucinda 20	ROSS, Charles 76
RICHARD, Joseph A. 103	RINGO, Jas. D. 67	ROBISON, William R. 20	ROSS, Debby Jane 78
RICHARDS, E. W. 117	RINGO, Mary Catharine 40	ROBNET, Catharine 84	ROSS, Edith 114
RICHARDS, Ettie 127	RINGO, William W. 40	ROBWERTSON, Elizabeth 128	ROSS, Eliza 32
RICHARDS, Joseph 128	RINGOE, Henry C. 74	ROBY, Jas. M. 68	ROSS, Eliza Ann 77
RICHARDS, Lectia 128	RINGOE, Joseph P. 74	ROCK, ----- 38	ROSS, Evaline 73
RICHARDS, Paulina J. 92	ROBB, Louisa 65	ROCK, Charles 38	ROSS, Fannie A. 119
RICHARDS, T. R. 117	ROBBINS, Elizabeth 7	RODEN, Susan 40	ROSS, G. W. 70
RICHARDSON, Maria 110	ROBERSON, Elias 55	RODEN, Thomas 2	ROSS, Geo. S. 95
RICHARDSON, Maria L. 88	ROBERT, W. W. 65	RODGERS, Ann 55	ROSS, Geo. W. 3
RICKETS, Elizabeth 48	ROBERTS, Edward 28	RODGERS, John J. 29	ROSS, George S. 119
RICKETTS, Amanda 37	ROBERTS, Edward 28	RODGERS, Mertill 133	ROSS, Harrison W. 120
RICKETTS, Elizabeth 37	ROBERTS, Edward 39	ROE, Elizabeth 18	ROSS, J. W. 91
RICKETTS, Jane 62	ROBERTS, Newell G. 8	ROE, William 18	ROSS, James 4
RICKETTS, Jno. B. 90	ROBERTS, Rebecca M. 10	ROGERS, Henry P. 87	ROSS, James 15
RICKETTS, John R. 85	ROBERTS, Sarah E.J. 39	ROGERS, James 129	ROSS, James 35
RICKETTS, John R. 90	ROBERTS, Thomas 50	ROGERS, James F. 87	ROSS, James 50
RICKETTS, John S. 85	ROBERTS, William H. 8	ROGERS, John 73	ROSS, James 76
RICKETTS, Juliett 37	ROBERTSON, ----- 65	ROGERS, John J. 4	ROSS, James 120
RICKETTS, Margaret 37	ROBERTSON, A. S. 1	ROGERS, Linnie T. 129	ROSS, Jane 60
RIDDLE, Elenor 129	ROBERTSON, Abigail 48	ROGERS, Mary B. 4	ROSS, Jas. D. 76
RIGDEN, Eli 41	ROBERTSON, Bettie C. 125	ROGERS, Mirtil 89	ROSS, John W. 3
RIGDEN, Eli Sanford 41	ROBERTSON, Calvin 125	ROGERS, Myrtle 115	ROSS, Johnson 78
RIGDEN, Wm. 2	ROBERTSON, Calvin L. 13	ROLLAND, ----- 65	ROSS, Jonson 56
RIGDON, Eli T. 8	ROBERTSON, Cliff 104	ROMEY, Lucy E. 85	ROSS, Jula D. 50
RIGDON, Elizabeth 3	ROBERTSON, E. A. 60	RONEY, Margaret 8	ROSS, Lenora 91
RIGDON, Elizabeth 60	ROBERTSON, F. P. 28	RONEY, Margaret 77	ROSS, MarY C. 105
RIGDON, Elizabeth 113	ROBERTSON, F. P. 68	RONEY, Marget 72	ROSS, Margaret 55
RIGDON, Lewis H. 8	ROBERTSON, Ima 125	ROONEY, John A. 85	ROSS, Margaret C. 1
RIGDON, Mary 79	ROBERTSON, James 125	ROONEY, Margaret 43	ROSS, Mary C. 92
RIGDON, Michael 2	ROBERTSON, James W. 85	ROP(?), Johnson 78	ROSS, Mary J. 49
RIGDON, Tabitha J. 31	ROBERTSON, Lee 104	ROSE, E. S.T. 112	ROSS, Richard 79
RIGGS, Amos 14	ROBERTSON, Martha 75	ROSE, R. R. 112	ROSS, Richd. 10
RIGGS, Angeline 28	ROBERTSON, Martha 75	ROSOR, Margaret 129	ROSS, Samuel 20
RIGGS, Angeline 53	ROBERTSON, Martha A. 28	ROSS(?), Louisa 46	ROSS, Sarah A. 52

ROSS, Sarah Matilda 13
ROSS, Serilda 111
ROSS, Serilda E. 99
ROSS, Silas 13
ROSS, Silas 46
ROSS, Silas 68
ROSS, Susan 56
ROSS, Susan F. 83
ROSS, Susan Levina 10
ROSS, William 13
ROYAL, Hiram W. 63
ROYAS, Hiram T. 63
ROYCE, Aaron 132
ROYCE, Francis M. 132
ROYCE, Polly 77
ROYCE, Polly Ann 8
ROYCE, William 77
ROYS, Isabella 29
ROYS, Samuel H. 29
ROYS, William 30
ROYS, William 40
ROYSE, ----- 30
ROYSE, Abram 40
ROYSE, Anthony 30
ROYSE, Elizabeth 64
ROYSE, Esther 16
ROYSE, George Fleming 41
ROYSE, Hiram T. 41
ROYSE, Hiram W. 80
ROYSE, L. P. 52
ROYSE, Mary C. 13
ROYSE, Nancy Jane 40
ROYSE, Polly Ann 40
ROYSE, Rebecca 13
ROYSE, Rebecca 40
ROYSE, Rebecca E. 29
ROYSE, Samuel 53
ROYSE, Samuel Kenton 40
ROYSE, Sarah Jane 40
ROYSE, William 40
ROYSE, William T. 29
ROYZE, William 13
ROZSE, ----- 19
RUGGLES, Francis A. 131
RUGLESS, Sarah 94
RUNYON, B. P. 115
RUNYON, E. J. 107
RUNYON, Ezekiel F. 85
RUNYON, Geo. C. 85
RUNYON, George C. 92
RUNYON, George C. 104

RUNYON, Jno H. 85
RUNYON, John 115
RUSKINS, Isaac 81
RYAN, Absolem 103
RYAN, Mary 37
RYAN, Tos. 37

SADLER, Eugene 99
SADLER, Thomas 77
SADLER, William C. 77
SADWICK, Sarah M. 106
SAMPP(?), Wm. 106
SAMPSON SR., James 8
SAMPSON, Elmira 55
SAMPSON, Henry J. 16
SAMPSON, James 8
SAMPSON, Jemima 22
SAMPSON, Norris 16
SAMUEL B. F. 91
SAMUEL, Lizzie 91
SAMUEL, Mary E. 88
SAMUELS, R. P. 71
SANDERS, Abigall 43
SANDERS, Amanda A. 33
SANDERS, Amanda Ann 9
SANDERS, Amanda Ann 40
SANDERS, Ann Mariah 13
SANDERS, Elizabeth 14
SANDERS, George A. 2
SANDERS, Harriet 14
SANDERS, Hiram 43
SANDERS, Jas. A. 2
SANDERS, Joel 53
SANDERS, Nancy 31
SANDERS, Rhoda 2
SANDERS, Sarah Ann 7
SANE, Margaret 104
SANLEY, Lanna 85
SAPP(?), Elizabeth 46
SAPP, Eliza A. 48
SAPP, James E. 75
SAPP, Mary E. 48
SAPP, N. C. 106
SAPP, Peter 61
SAPP, Wallace 117
SAPP, William 117
SAPP, Wm. 75
SAPPLEE, Mary 75
SASHBROOK, Laurea 121
SAUDERS, Asa 73
SAUDERS, Harriet 74
SAUDERS, Matilda C. 74

SAUDERS, Nancy N. 69
SAUMDERS, Nancy 20
SAUNDERS, ----- 35
SAUNDERS, A. D. 116
SAUNDERS, Abigail 31
SAUNDERS, Alberta 106
SAUNDERS, Austin 101
SAUNDERS, C. T. 116
SAUNDERS, Chambers E. 45
SAUNDERS, Elizabeth 33
SAUNDERS, Harriet 48
SAUNDERS, Hiram 31
SAUNDERS, Hiram Fleming 43
SAUNDERS, James A. 31
SAUNDERS, James A. .47
SAUNDERS, Joel 65
SAUNDERS, Joel 80
SAUNDERS, L. S. 62
SAUNDERS, M. F. 116
SAUNDERS, Manerva 61
SAUNDERS, Margaret 117
SAUNDERS, Mary 35
SAUNDERS, Mary A. 48
SAUNDERS, Mary E. 129
SAUNDERS, Matilda 48
SAUNDERS, Monroe D. 47
SAUNDERS, Moses 46
SAUNDERS, Moses 63
SAUNDERS, Oliver B. 106
SAUNDERS, Rebeca 68
SAUNDERS, Robert 64
SAUNDERS, Ruth 129
SAUNDERS, Ruth Minerva 48
SAUNDERS, Samuel 2
SAUNDERS, Squire 35
SAUNDERS, Sylvania 45
SAUNDERS, W. E. 116
SAUNDERS, William O. 2
SAYE, A. C. 116
SCARY, Ellen 120
SCOTT, ----- 35
SCOTT, Amelia 105
SCOTT, Daniel N. 105
SCOTT, Danl. N. 76
SCOTT, Ellan J. 61
SCOTT, Ellen J. 67
SCOTT, Jemmia 35
SCOTT, John 37
SCOTT, John P. 35
SCOTT, Lizzie M. 76
SCOTT, Nancy P. 14

SCOTT, Sary M. 70
SCOTT, Wm. 37
SCRUGGS, Emma 123
SCRUGGS, J. 110
SCRUGGS, J. W. 110
SCRUGGS, John 123
SCRUGGS, John 123
SCRUGGS, Samuel P. 123
SEAMONS, Barnet 32
SECREST, Emily 19
SEE, Elizabeth F. 98
SEE, Granville 72
SEE, Lawson T. 101
SEET(?), William 103
SEET, Louisa 123
SEEVER, J. F. 115
SEEVER, Mary 114
SEEVER, Mary 124
SEEVER, O. A. 115
SEEVERS, Casper H. 52
SEGBOLD, Clarissa 71
SEIVERS, Casper K. 131
SEIVERS, James 131
SELBY, James 116
SELBY, M. J. 116
SELBY, Sybvina 105
SERVER, ----- 30
SERVER, Casper H. 30
SETTERS, J. P. 108
SETTERS, J. S. 108
SETTERS, N. J. 108
SEUER, Nancy Ann 17
SHANKLIN, Ann A. 42
SHANKLIN, Ann A. 72
SHANKLIN, Jos. A. 11
SHANKLIN, Mary Bell 11
SHANNON, Ellen 102
SHANNON, Paulina R. 18
SHARPE, Jennie 109
SHAY, Catharien 55
SHEARS, G. A. 88
SHEARWOOD, John 50
SHEARWOOD, Wm. 50
SHEEL, Mary 63
SHELTON, Lizzie 125
SHEPARD, Ben 93
SHEPARD, Joseph 91
SHEPARD, Martha 93
SHEPARD, Mary W. 105
SHEPARD, Robt. 7
SHEPARD, Samuel P. 7

SHEPARD, William H. 105
SHEPARD, Wm. H. 92
SHEPERD, D. B. 47
SHEPHERD, Lucinda 83
SHEPHERD, Millie 121
SHERROD, ----- 66
SHERWOOD, Daniel 83
SHERWOOD, George C. 92
SHERWOOD, John 36
SHERWOOD, John 83
SHERWOOD, John 92
SHERWOOD, John 107
SHERWOOD, L. M. 107
SHERWOOD, Robert M. 124
SHERWOOD, William 124
SHIELD, James M. 20
SHIELDS, A. F. 70
SHIELDS, Alexander 19
SHIELDS, Alexander 70
SHIELDS, David M. 77
SHIELDS, E. G. 20
SHIELDS, Elizabeth 19
SHIELDS, James 77
SHIELDS, James L. 40
SHIELDS, James L. 77
SHIELDS, James William 40
SHIELDS, Mary E. 124
SHIELDS, Mary E. 130
SHIELDS, Mary Ellen 41
SHIELDS, Saml. P. 63
SHIELDS, Samuel 20
SHIELDS, Samuel 41
SHIELDS, Samuel 70
SHIELDS, Samuel F.L. 20
SHOAT, Delila 70
SHOCKEY, Elizabeth 5
SHOCKEY, Harriet 35
SHOCKEY, James M. 55
SHOCKLEY, Ben H. 65
SHOCKLEY, Emily J. 47
SHOCKLEY, H. B. 49
SHOCKLEY, Harriet 49
SHOCKLEY, James M. 65
SHOCKLEY, Martha B. 49
SHOCKLEY, Mary 73
SHOCKLEY, Nancy A. 72
SHOCKLEY, Rasa 55
SHOCKLEY, Sarah A. 76
SHOCKLEY, W. H. 47
SHOCKLEY, William H. 73
SHOCKLEY, Wm. H. 56

SHOCKNEY, ----- 35
SHOCKNEY, William 35
SHOFE, Mary 78
SHOPE, George W. 78
SHOUCH, G. B. 40
SHOUCH, Mary Elizabeth 40
SHOULT, Eliza 30
SHOUPE, Hannah 113
SHROUT, David 69
SHURLOCK, Charles 69
SILLON, Thos. 67
SILLVENA, ----- 66
SILORY, John 19
SILVEY, Elmiretta 17
SILVEY, Harrison 43
SILVEY, Harrison 64
SILVEY, Jerusha 43
SIMMERS, Benjamin T. 2
SIMMERS, Jesse 2
SIMMS, Ally Grace 75
SIMMS, Duncan 75
SIMMS, Jos. 75
SIMON, S. P. 116
SIMONS, Rachael 33
SIMS, Joseph 56
SIMS, Rachel 7
SIMS, Rachel 20
SIMS, Wm. F. 75
SINGLETON, Elizabeth 99
SINGLETON, James W. 99
SISLEBROOK, S. 112
SITER, Mariel W. 120
SITER, William 120
SIUTHERCOM, J. M. 114
SKILLMAN, Joseph 73
SKILLMAN, Joseph 82
SKILLMAN, Mary K. 82
SKINNER, D. N. 70
SLICER, ----- 35
SLICER, A. G. 35
SLICER, Alfd. G. 35
SLICER, Arison W. 101
SLICER, G. 35
SLICER, James W. 101
SMART, S. 108
SMART, Stella M. 124
SMETHERS, Mary 131
SMITH, Albert T. 24
SMITH, Catherine 129
SMITH, Catherine 130
SMITH, Charles 125

SMITH, Cynthia Ann 28
SMITH, E. T. 46
SMITH, E. T. 83
SMITH, Edwin C. 46
SMITH, Edwin T. 15
SMITH, Effa Lilian 75
SMITH, Eliza 125
SMITH, Elizabeth 121
SMITH, Evaline 34
SMITH, Francis 130
SMITH, George W. 47
SMITH, Henry 48
SMITH, Isaac W. 47
SMITH, J. B. 75
SMITH, James 12
SMITH, James 84
SMITH, James 130
SMITH, James E. 24
SMITH, James E. 47
SMITH, James E. 75
SMITH, Lizza D. 73
SMITH, Margaret Jane 40
SMITH, Mary R. 15
SMITH, Matthew W. 47
SMITH, Nancy 46
SMITH, Robert C. 83
SMITH, Robert H. 102
SMITH, Sarah E. 102
SMITH, Thomas B. 73
SMITH, Thomas E. 47
SMITH, Thos. E. 68
SMITH, W. H. 24
SMITH, W. H. 47
SMITH, Warner 125
SMITH, Willie 125
SMITH, Wm. 46
SMITH, Wm. 62
SMITH, Wm. H. 16
SMITH, Wm. H. 24
SMITH, Wm. R. 75
SMOOT, Elizabeth 55
SMOOT, Lander 70
SMOOT, Lucinda 40
SMOOT, Lucinda 77
SMOOT, Margaret T. 63
SMOOT, Mary 6
SMOOT, Nancy 40
SMOOT, Nancy 53
SMOOT, Phidela 64
SMOOT, Salem J. 64
SMOOT, St. Clair 64

SMOST, Cyntha 14
SNOOT, Elizabeth 76
SONGBOTTOM, Henry S. 128
SOPUSLEY, Malinda 93
SOROFF, Isabella 14
SORREL, John H. 30
SORREL, Rachel 30
SORREL, Sarah E. 30
SORRELL, John 40
SORRELL, Melvina 40
SOURNEY, Emily 98
SOUSLEY J. C. 67
SOUSLEY, ----- 38
SOUSLEY, ----- 39
SOUSLEY, ----- 65
SOUSLEY, Belinda 76
SOUSLEY, Catherine 106
SOUSLEY, D. C. 83
SOUSLEY, Elizabeth 126
SOUSLEY, Elizabeth S. 100
SOUSLEY, Ervin J. 44
SOUSLEY, F. P. 56
SOUSLEY, Franklin 39
SOUSLEY, Franklin 75
SOUSLEY, Geo. D. 44
SOUSLEY, Geo. D. 57
SOUSLEY, George D. 126
SOUSLEY, H. C. 49
SOUSLEY, H. C. 56
SOUSLEY, H. C. 66
SOUSLEY, Harrison 74
SOUSLEY, Harrison 84
SOUSLEY, Isabel 76
SOUSLEY, Isabella 35
SOUSLEY, J. H. 105
SOUSLEY, James R. 126
SOUSLEY, James W. 100
SOUSLEY, Jane 124
SOUSLEY, John 75
SOUSLEY, John B. 126
SOUSLEY, John D. 99
SOUSLEY, John D. 105
SOUSLEY, John E. 38
SOUSLEY, John E. 74
SOUSLEY, Late 127
SOUSLEY, Lizzie 121
SOUSLEY, Louisa 90
SOUSLEY, M. E. 110
SOUSLEY, M. Omar 100
SOUSLEY, Mary E. 127
SOUSLEY, Mary F, 93

SOUSLEY, Phenton C. 126
SOUSLEY, Sophia 58
SOUSLEY, W. B. 66
SOWARD, R. 4
SOWARD, Richard 4
SOWARD, Richard 34
SOWARD, Richard 42
SOWARD, Richard 54
SOWAREL, ----- 24
SPENCER, ----- 35
SPENCER, ----- 38
SPENCER, C. H. 109
SPENCER, E. S. 106
SPENCER, Hattie 109
SPENCER, Martha J. 75
SPENCER, Mary 34
SPENCER, Mary A. 83
SPENCER, R. G. 55
SPENCER, R. G. 83
SPENCER, Richard 74
SPENCER, Rosanna 49
SPENCER, Roseta 83
SPENCER, W. H. 49
SPENCER, William 35
SPENCER, Zaddock 38
SPRADLING, Henry 115
SPRADLING, J. F. 115
SPRIGGS, Lamar 92
SPURGEON, M. 113
SPURGEON, T. S. 113
SPURGSON, Moses 95
SPURGSON, Taylor L. 95
ST. CLAIR(?), Emons 68
STABLETON, Joshua 72
STAGGS, Bailey 119
STAGGS, Charles 119
STAGGS, Charles M. 33
STAGGS, Fannie M. 118
STAGGS, Fanny 41
STAGGS, Hiram 64
STAGGS, Hiram 71
STAGGS, Hiram 78
STAGGS, Malinda 51
STAGGS, Marion 40
STAGGS, Mary J. 95
STAGGS, Thomas 33
STAGGS, Thomas 40
STAGGS, Thomas 52
STAGGS, Thomas 71
STAGGS, Thos. 5
STAGGS, Thos. 63

STAGGS, Thos. D. 95
STAGGS, William 9
STAGGS, William 41
STAGGS, William 80
STAGS, John 5
STAHORN, Samuel 20
STAIMFORD, Robt. 57
STAMFIELD, James 3
STAMFIELD, Sally 3
STAMPER, Hiram 116
STAMPER, John W. 92
STAMPER, Martha 17
STAMPER, Richard 17
STAMPER, William 116
STAMPLER, amos S. 92
STANDIFORD, J. T. 72
STANDIFORD, Jarvis 78
STANESFER, Jemima 23
STANFIELD, Elizabeth 126
STANFIELD, Louisa 75
STANFIELD, Pleasant 75
STANFORD, Susan 31
STANFORG, Susannah 6
STANIFORD, Lucinda 75
STANIFORD, Robt. 75
STANIFORD, Susan 43
STEEL, Mary 25
STEETE, Mary 52
STEPHENS, A. J. 59
STEPHENS, Andrew J. 83
STEPHENS, Gusta 83
STEPHENS, Mary 57
STEPHENS, Mary 93
STEPHENS, Pearly J. 124
STEPHENS, Richard 124
STEPHENS, Samuel W. 52
STEPHENSON, Mary 75
STEPHESON, ----- 65
STERRETT, J. 113
STERRETT, John 113
STEVENS, Sarah 132
STEVENS, Wm. B. 102
STEWARD, E. J. 106
STEWARD, J. H. 106
STEWARD, J. T. 106
STEWART, Amelia C. 99
STEWART, Daniel T. 86
STEWART, Elizth. 85
STEWART, John 86
STEWART, John R. 99
STEWART, Lizzie A. 100

STEWART, Mary 51
STEWART, Mary 122
STEWART, V. M. 116
STEWART, William H. 99
STIDMAN, Berta A. 118
STIDMAN, James 118
STILES, Laura B. 91
STILES, Laura B. 104
STILLA, Rica 93
STIRY, Martha 89
STIRY, Sarah L. 89
STITT, Melvina 102
STOAT, Ethral 91
STOAT, Thos. 91
STOCKDALE, Elizabeth 92
STOCKDALE, Elizabeth 101
STOCKDALE, Elizabeth 128
STOCKDALE, Elizabeth E. 127
STOCKDALE, Emma S. 86
STOCKDALE, Grant 103
STOCKDALE, Lucy 104
STOCKDALE, Margaret M. 92
STOCKDALE, S. C. 86
STOCKDALE, Sallie 104
STOCKDALE, Santford 55
STOCKDALE, Susan 124
STOCKDALE, Susan A. 96
STOCKDALE, Thos. 65
STOCKDALE, William H. 84
STOCKTON, L. D. 37
STOCKTON, Phebe 37
STOCKTON, Richard L. 3
STOCKWELL, Louiza 71
STOCKWELL, Sallie E. 68
STOCKWELL, Sarah E. 82
STOCKWELL, Sarah E. 121
STODDARD, Edna A. 88
STOGDALE, Lucy E. 75
STONE, Frances M. 6
STONE, H. Clay 97
STONE, Maranda R. 6
STONE, Mary R. 64
STORY(?), Nancy E. 48
STORY(?), Sarah L. 89
STORY, Alfred 6
STORY, Alfred 81
STORY, Allen 53
STORY, Cyntha 18
STORY, E. 116
STORY, Emma 122
STORY, Geo. S. 59

STORY, Jennie 119
STORY, Jery 62
STORY, John 17
STORY, John 53
STORY, John 63
STORY, John W. 48
STORY, Joseph 16
STORY, L. E. 105
STORY, Lewyllen 6
STORY, Matilda R. 13
STORY, Nelson 16
STORY, Rosannah 16
STORY, Simpson Miner 16
STORY, William 122
STORZ, John 82
STORZ, Miriam 82
STORZ, Nelson 81
STORZ, Oliver 81
STORZ, Rebeca 68
STORZ, Rosanna 81
STOUT, Delila 75
STOUT, Sarah S. 75
STOUT, Shipman P. 103
STOUT, Virginia L. 103
STOVY, Cynthia 32
STOVY, Martha 25
STRABAN, Sarah K. 82
STRAHAM, Eliza J. 23
STRAHAM, Sally Ann 22
STRAHAN, Sally Ann 81
STRATTEN, Johnathan 52
STRATTON, Abraham 97
STRATTON, Jonathan 69
STRICKROD, Elizabeth 1
STRICKTON(?), Franklin 3
STRODE, Ann E. 41
STRODE, Ann Eliza 77
STRODE, Anny E. 24
STRODE, Estella 120
STRODE, Jno. 94
STRODE, Luisa 62
STRODE, Luther 120
STRODE, Luther M. 100
STRODE, Malinda M. 94
STRODE, Nannie 130
STRODE, Penelope 54
STROGDALE, Thomas 75
STUART, Jane 130
STUART, Lizzie 127
STUART, Margaret 4
STUBBLEFIELD, Marshall 53

STUCKROD, Joseph 84
STUSE, Fautty R. 77
SUITHERCOM, W. T. 114
SUKINS(?), Fannie 110
SULLIVAN, ----- 35
SULLIVAN, ----- 35
SULLIVAN, James 49
SULLIVAN, Johnnah 99
SULLIVAN, Margt. 36
SULLIVAN, Mary 35
SULLIVAN, Pat 35
SULLIVAN, Patrick 49
SUMAN, Nancy 113
SUMMERS, Adaline 99
SUMMERS, Ellen 102
SUMMERS, George 3
SUMMERS, George 84
SUMMERS, John 3
SUMMERS, Mary A. 5
SUMMITT, Elizabeth 14
SUMMITT, George 14
SUMMITT, James 50
SUMMITT, Jas. 14
SUMMITT, Odd Biggetoff 14
SUMMONS, J. B. 102
SUNNITT, Lizze L. 88
SUPPLEE, George W. 75
SUPPLEE, Wm. 75
SUTTON, Eliza Ann 7
SUTTON, Eliza Ann 78
SUTTON, Ellen 77
SUTTON, Helan 68
SUTTON, Jane 64
SUTTON, Louisa 12
SUTTON, Mary Ann 44
SUTTON, Matilda 27
SUTTON, Richard 31
SUTTON, Thomas D. 31
SUTTON, Thomas P. 54
SUTTON, Thos. P. 12
SUTTON, Thos. P. 78
SWAIN, Eliza 1
SWAIN, Hulda 40
SWAIN, Mary 56
SWAIN, Mary 84
SWANTZ, Granville H. 91
SWART, Caroline 84
SWART, Caroline 124
SWART, Granville 124
SWART, James S. 104
SWART, Louisa C. 104

SWEENEY, Martin 125
SWEENEY, Thomas 125
SWEET, ----- 98
SWEET, Annie 97
SWEET, Anny 130
SWEET, Ellen 71
SWEET, Louisa 108
SWIM, Arnethia 112
SWIM, Asahel L. 7
SWIM, Biddy Ann 9
SWIM, Eliza J. 41
SWIM, Emma Ann 13
SWIM, H. S. 41
SWIM, James Moses Bailey 41
SWIM, John H. 13
SWIM, John W. 41
SWIM, Marshall P. 7
SWIM, Matilda J. 41
SWIM, Nancy E. 7
SWIM, Susan 52
SWIM, Susannah 11
SWIM, Wm. L. 7
SYBOLD, Sarah 53
SYBOLD, Stephen 14
SYKES, D. F. 115
SYKES, Edgar 115

TABER, James 66
TABER, Louwllan 66
TABER, Victoria 116
TABIS, Henry 53
TAIBBY, Saml. 85
TALLY, William J. 3
TALLY, Wm. Jno. 3
TALRYMPLE, Elizabeth 60
TANNER, Elenor A. 52
TANNER, John 73
TANT, Martha Ann 2
TARBET, Nancy Ann 44
TASSON, Mattie 98
TAYLOR, A. R. 4
TAYLOR, Amelia B. 107
TAYLOR, Amelia B. 126
TAYLOR, Amelia B. 128
TAYLOR, Amelia Botts 35
TAYLOR, Benjamin 121
TAYLOR, Charles 35
TAYLOR, Charles 51
TAYLOR, Charles F. 75
TAYLOR, E. 58
TAYLOR, Ellen 121
TAYLOR, Elvira 5

TAYLOR, Frank 104
TAYLOR, Frank 121
TAYLOR, Geo. A. 36
TAYLOR, Geo. W. 1
TAYLOR, Geo. W. 36
TAYLOR, George A. 75
TAYLOR, James 121
TAYLOR, Jane 37
TAYLOR, Jennie 110
TAYLOR, John 121
TAYLOR, John 126
TAYLOR, Martha Ann 4
TAYLOR, Mary 37
TAYLOR, Mary A. 121
TAYLOR, Mary Ann 38
TAYLOR, Milton 104
TAYLOR, Miranda 36
TAYLOR, Robert 121
TAYLOR, Sharlott 113
TAYLOR, Wilford 23
TEAGAR, Lucy C. 110
TEAGAR, M. M. 93
TEAGLE, Abram 6
TEAGLE, Ann Maria 6
TEARNEY(?), Pat 74
TEARNEY, Patrick 60
TEETIERS, Caroline 102
TEMPLEMAN, Mahala 32
TERHUNE, ----- 36
TERHUNE, Barnett 34
TERHUNE, Barnett 36
TERHUNE, Martha A. 34
TERRY, John 42
TERRY, Mary 70
THACHER, Daniel 42
THACHER, Emily 41
THACKER, Abraham 118
THACKER, Jaley 118
THOMAS, Asa 8
THOMAS, Demida 5
THOMAS, E. 59
THOMAS, E. J. 114
THOMAS, Elizabeth 5
THOMAS, Elizabeth 75
THOMAS, Elizabeth 91
THOMAS, Emily 86
THOMAS, George W. 124
THOMAS, Henry 35
THOMAS, James M. 31
THOMAS, Jas. 96
THOMAS, Joseph 47

THOMAS, Lucy H. 47
THOMAS, Marsh 98
THOMAS, Mary A. 94
THOMAS, Mary A. 131
THOMAS, Mary Alice 26
THOMAS, Mary B. 98
THOMAS, Mary E. 123
THOMAS, Nathanel 8
THOMAS, Nathaniel 53
THOMAS, Perry J. 124
THOMAS, R. M. 53
THOMAS, Sarah E. 130
THOMAS, Susannah 26
THOMAS, T. J. 31
THOMAS, William 35
THOMAS, William 99
THOMPSON, Angeline 24
THOMPSON, Angeline 47
THOMPSON, Angeline J. 12
THOMPSON, Anna 110
THOMPSON, Anna 110
THOMPSON, B. M. 110
THOMPSON, Benjamin 7
THOMPSON, Bethuel M. 127
THOMPSON, Betsy Jane 19
THOMPSON, Elizabeth 83
THOMPSON, Elizabeth Jane 4
THOMPSON, Elizabeth T. 4
THOMPSON, J. H. 114
THOMPSON, J. M. 110
THOMPSON, James 62
THOMPSON, James 114
THOMPSON, James W. 7
THOMPSON, Jno. R. 104
THOMPSON, John 87
THOMPSON, John B. 131
THOMPSON, John W. 131
THOMPSON, Margaret A. 28
THOMPSON, Margaret Ann 39
THOMPSON, Mary Jane 40
THOMPSON, Mary V. 122
THOMPSON, Naraissa 70
THOMPSON, Sarah 70
THOMPSON, Sarah F. 96
THOMPSON, Sarah F. 119
THOMPSON, Sibba 18
THOMPSON, Thomas 122
THOMSON, Anjeline 75
THOMSON, Edgar 87
THOMSON, Narah 111
THORNTON, Charles F. 86

THORNTON, Frank 86
THORNTON, Frank 90
THURMAN, Malinda 41
THURMAN, Malinda 72
TIBBS, Alkaner Y. 14
TIBBS, Amelia B. 41
TIBBS, Francis 121
TIBBS, Mary G. 25
TIBBS, Nina 121
TIBBS, Susan 107
TIBBS, W. T. 41
TIBBS, William T. 25
TIBBS, Willoughby 14
TICKLEN, Mary N. 3
TINBLEY, James S. 22
TINBLEY, Samuel 22
TINCHER, Sarah 79
TINSLEY, Samuel P. 69
TOBE, Ann 111
TODD, A. S. 105
TODD, Elizabeth 21
TODD, Elizabeth 61
TODD, Elizabeth 74
TODD, Elizabeth B. 119
TODD, Elizth. 12
TODD, George 82
TODD, George W. 46
TODD, James 46
TODD, James L. 82
TODD, John G. 104
TODD, John W. 82
TODD, Joseph 87
TODD, Joseph 111
TODD, Lilly A. 82
TODD, Margaret 21
TODD, Margaret 45
TODD, Margaret 82
TODD, Mary A. 61
TODD, Mary A. 61
TODD, Mary Ann 24
TODD, Mary Ann 73
TODD, Mary J. 46
TODD, Minerva 47
TODD, Rebecca 20
TODD, Rebecca 111
TODD, Rebecca B. 87
TODD, Thomas 20
TODD, Thomas 46
TODD, Thomas 68
TODD, Tilden 111
TODD, W. B. 105

TODD, W. W. 104
TODD, William 119
TOLAN, Margaret 2
TOLLER, Elizabeth 131
TOLLER, Joseph 131
TOLLER, Robert B. 131
TONER, Sarah 101
TOOLE, Mary J. 128
TORING, Margaret 7
TOWLER, A. 113
TOWLER, A. S. 114
TOWLER, B. B. 113
TOWLER, C. A. 113
TOWLER, L. S. 113
TOWLER, N. 113
TOWLER, W. S. 114
TOYS, Rebecca 30
TREBBY, Mary 52
TRIBBY, Benj. F. 48
TRIBBY, Charles 105
TRIBBY, Columbus 60
TRIBBY, Columbus 73
TRIBBY, George T. 48
TRIBBY, James W. 45
TRIBBY, Jas. W. 67
TRIBBY, Lucinda 45
TRIBBY, Mary 30
TRIBBY, Mary 37
TRIBBY, Samuel 105
TRIMBLE, Frank 3
TRIMBLE, Harriet 3
TRIMBLE, Lewis 3
TRIPLET, James M. 68
TRIPLETT, Abner 97
TRIPLETT, Andrew M. 109
TRIPLETT, Ann Elizth. 12
TRIPLETT, G. 52
TRIPLETT, Green B. 78
TRIPLETT, Greenbury 12
TRIPLETT, James 47
TRIPLETT, James 48
TRIPLETT, James M. 28
TRIPLETT, Jas. M. 7
TRIPLETT, Jas. M. 9
TRIPLETT, Joshua 23
TRIPLETT, Laurence 25
TRIPLETT, Lawrance 52
TRIPLETT, Lawrence 69
TRIPLETT, Lydia 109
TRIPLETT, Susan M. 68
TRUITT, Andrew J. 131

TRUITT, Minnie 131
TRUMBO, Oliver H. 40
TRUMBO, William 40
TUBBY, Murtle 122
TUBBY, Samuel 122
TUCKER, Caroline 99
TUCKER, Emily 99
TULLY, Angeline 78
TULLY, James 58
TULLY, James A. 50
TUNE, Maranda 120
TURNER, Edgar 49
TURNER, Eliza 4
TURNER, Elizabeth 70
TURNER, Harry 88
TURNER, Jno. H. 1
TURNER, Joel R. 55
TURNER, John 49
TURNER, Lida B. 88
TURNER, Louisa 41
TURNER, Mary 2
TURNER, N.Cary H. 1
TURNER, Nancy M. 42
TURNER, Robert 42
TURNER, Robert C. 4
TURNER, Susan P. 54
TURNEY, Mary 37
TURNEY, W. W. 20
TUTTON, Eliza Ann 43

ULERS, M. A. 106
UMSTADDT, John 103
UMSTADT, ----- 34
UMSTADT, Ann 39
UNDERWOOD, Lavina 94
UTTERBACK, Daird 6
UTTERBAKC, Barbary A. 6

VAILES, Angeline 132
VALE, Eliza 80
VAN CLINE, John 69
VANARSDALE, B. M. 112
VANARSDALE, Isaac 112
VANARSDALE, Mary 121
VANDEN, Motie 129
VANGANT, Aaron H. 6
VANGANT, John 6
VANLANDINGHAM, Acrist 81
VANLANDINGHAM, Harrit Ann 6
VANLANDINGHAM, Wm. 54
VANLANIGHOUR, Sary 69
VANLUNDINGHAM, William 80
VANNATTEN, Angeline 77

VANNATTEN, Jane 54
VANNATTEN, Sarah 39
VANSANETT, G. M. 9
VANSANETT, G. W. 70
VANSANETT, George B. 9
VANSANT, A. B. 51
VANSANT, David M. 121
VANSANT, Eliza 28
VANSANT, G. W. 53
VANSANT, John 101
VANSANT, John K. 28
VANSANT, John K. 59
VANSANT, John K. 81
VANSANT, John T. 28
VANSANT, Lillian H. 101
VANSANT, Virginia 81
VANSAUDT, Isiah 12
VARNARSDALL, Isaac 121
VAUGHN, Mary E. 87
VEACH, Nancy 103
VERNATTIN, Jane 17
VICE, Cynthia 87
VICE, Cynthia 117
VICE, Marion 129
VICE, Mary D. 87
VICE, Mary E. 129
VICE, Sarah 129
VICE, Simpson 55
VICE, Wm. 87
VILLAGE, B. G. 72
VINSANT, George W. 39
VINSANT, James C.M. 39
VIZE, A. F. 97

WACKER, Irena 6
WAGENOR, E. J. 115
WALINGFORD, James 70
WALINGFORD, Maggie E. 127
WALKER, Ada L. 95
WALKER, Addison 130
WALKER, Amelia 120
WALKER, F. V. 114
WALKER, J. T. 49
WALKER, James M. 62
WALKER, John T. 2
WALKER, Johnson S. 31
WALKER, Jonathan W. 31
WALKER, Levin 42
WALKER, Livey Ann 42
WALKER, Mariah L. 12
WALKER, Nancy 34
WALKER, Nancy W. 84
WALKER, Paulina 94
WALKER, R. H. 84

WALKER, Saml. 6
WALKER, Samuel 31
WALKER, Samuel 71
WALKER, Sarah 34
WALKER, Sarah 52
WALKER, Sarepta 130
WALKER, Sary 71
WALKER, W. H. 114
WALKER, W. T. 59
WALKER, William T. 81
WALKER, Wm. 91
WALKER, Wm. M. 3
WALKER, Wm. M. 70
WALL, John T. 59
WALL, John T. 73
WALLINGFORD, Alice 130
WALLINGFORD, Amelia 54
WALLINGFORD, Amelia 79
WALLINGFORD, B. F. 70
WALLINGFORD, Benj. F. 98
WALLINGFORD, Benjamin F. 130
WALLINGFORD, Charles 98
WALLINGFORD, Columbus 127
WALLINGFORD, Edward O. 94
WALLINGFORD, Elizabeth 54
WALLINGFORD, Elizabeth 97
WALLINGFORD, F. M. 111
WALLINGFORD, Fannie M. 120
WALLINGFORD, H. M. 109
WALLINGFORD, Harriet 96
WALLINGFORD, Helen 78
WALLINGFORD, Jas. M. 94
WALLINGFORD, Joseph S. 54
WALLINGFORD, Joseph S. 78
WALLINGFORD, Julia Ann 78
WALLINGFORD, Lulu 130
WALLINGFORD, M. P. 42
WALLINGFORD, M. P. 70
WALLINGFORD, Margaret 42
WALLINGFORD, Margaret 98
WALLINGFORD, Mark 54
WALLINGFORD, Mary F. 54
WALLINGFORD, Mary F. 79
WALLINGFORD, Mary M. 79
WALLINGFORD, Sarah 97
WALLINGFORD, Sarah A. 54
WALLINGFORD, Sarah A. 79
WALLINGFORD, Sarah E. 131
WALLINGFORD, Stella E. 130
WALLINGFORD, T. 113
WALLINGFORD, Valentine B. 120

WALLINGFORD, W. H. 113
WALLINGFORD, Walter 70
WALLINGFORD, William 42
WALLINGFORD, William H. 71
WALLINGFORD, William M. 120
WALLINGSFORD, James 42
WALLINGSFORD, Wm. 4
WALLINGTON, Mary M. 102
WALLLINGFORD, Joseph 130
WALSH, Nanna 72
WALSH, Nanno 43
WALSON, Margaret 82
WALSON, Sarath 60
WALTON, ----- 20
WALTON, Amanda E. 104
WALTON, Cyntha 77
WALTON, Jennie C. 88
WALTON, John 132
WALTON, John 132
WALTON, Julia D. 89
WALTON, Mystillia 40
WALTON, Parker 20
WALTON, Presly 54
WALTON, R. R. 88
WALTON, Saunders 132
WALTON, Suaan 28
WALTON, Susan 65
WALTON, Susan E. 20
WALTON, Thos. H. 88
WANNITTON, Sary 69
WARD, Frederick 129
WARD, Thomas 54
WARD, William 129
WARDER, Celia 98
WARNER, Emily 130
WARREN, Julila B. 122
WARREN, Miriam 114
WARREN, William H. 122
WASHBURN, Maranda 75
WASHBURN, Miranda 36
WATKINS, Elias A. 105
WATKINS, Eliza A. 105
WATKINS, John 87
WATKINS, Maggie 87
WATSON, Charles M. 123
WATSON, Chas. 90
WATSON, David 117
WATSON, Henry 2
WATSON, James M. 123
WATSON, John 13
WATSON, John S. 117
WATSON, Manchester 2
WATSON, Margaret 17

WATSON, Nancy J. 106
WATSON, Saml. 90
WATSON, Sulbria 6
WATTON, Elbert 2
WATTON, James M. 76
WATTON, Lear M. 75
WATTON, Rawleigh 76
WATTS, Claudie C. 94
WATTS, Hester Ann 24
WATTS, Jno. A. 94
WATTS, John A. 24
WATTS, John A. 53
WATTS, Leannor 85
WAUGH, Annie 106
WAUGH, George W. 106
WCMILLEN, Sarah 100
WEARE, Evaline 1
WEAVER, David 57
WEAVER, David 84
WEAVER, Reuben S. 84
WEBSTER, Edward 32
WEBSTER, James 26
WEBSTER, James 26
WEBSTER, James D. 45
WEBSTER, Jas. D. 68
WEBSTER, John A. 11
WEBSTER, John A. 32
WEBSTER, John E. 11
WEBSTER, Joseph W. 80

WEBSTER, W. H. 68
WEEKS, Sarah 94
WEING, William 38
WEIR, Dorcas K. 95
WEIR, Julian 4
WEIR, Margaret 99
WEIR, Mellisia 94
WEIR, N. H. 4
WEIR, Wm. 95
WELCH, Quille(?) 100
WELLS, ----- 36
WELLS, John H. 35
WELLS, John H. 74
WELLS, John H. 84
WELLS, Lucy 110
WELLS, Lucy 124
WELLS, Martha 81
WELLS, Martha J. 103
WELLS, Mary 35
WELLS, Mary 120
WELLS, Mat. 36
WELLS, Thos. 78
WEST, James 15

WEST, James Henry 15
WEST, Jas. H. 69
WEST, John H. 39
WEST, Joseph Franklin 39
WHALEY, Eliza 110
WHEELER, Mary 125
WHESLEY, Nancy 22
WHITE, Atta B. 120
WHITE, Car. B. 71
WHITE, Crissia 75
WHITE, Dehla 33
WHITE, Deliba 21
WHITE, Eliza 92
WHITE, Eliza 120
WHITE, Hester 116
WHITE, Hester 118
WHITE, James 120
WHITE, John D. 41
WHITE, John T. 133
WHITE, Lilla Bell 41
WHITE, Martha 125
WHITE, Mattie 86
WHITE, Nancy J. 33
WHITE, Nathan F. 12
WHITE, Nathanel 12
WHITE, Polly 72
WHITE, R. 115
WHITE, Robert 30
WHITE, Robert 133
WHITE, Susanna 45
WHITE, Susannah 9
WHITE, W. O. 115
WHITE, William 127
WHITE, William C. 127
WHITECRAFT, DR. Jno. E. 10
WHITECRAFT, Dr. John E. 20
WHITECRAFT, George 10
WHITECRAFT, Jane 20
WHITNEY, Mary R. 46
WHITNEY, Mary R. 82
WHITNEY, Sarah A. 89
WHITNEY, Sarah Ann 16
WHITTE, Eliza Ann 30
WIBBY, ----- 84
WIBBY, Rhoda A. 82
WIBBY, Samuel 82
WIBBY, Sarah 82
WIGGINS, Thos. 35
WIGHTMAN, Jno. E. 103
WIGINS, Lawson 35
WIGLETMAN, John Herbert 103

WILES, Emma 84
WILES, Peter B. 84
WILKERSON, A. 113
WILKERSON, Ida B. 113
WILLEROY, J. W. 89
WILLEROY, John W. 130
WILLEROY, Mary L. 89
WILLEROY, William C. 130
WILLETT, Benjamin H. 130
WILLETT, John M. 130
WILLETT, Mary 109
WILLETT, Mary 127
WILLETT, Sarah 37
WILLETT, Walker 37
WILLIAM, ----- 65
WILLIAM, J. S. 113
WILLIAM, O. S. 113
WILLIAMS Henry W. 3
WILLIAMS, ----- 65
WILLIAMS, Aaron 48
WILLIAMS, Abner C. 90
WILLIAMS, Adaline 76
WILLIAMS, Adeline 81
WILLIAMS, Alfred 2
WILLIAMS, Alfred 61
WILLIAMS, Alfred 67
WILLIAMS, Alfred 75
WILLIAMS, Amanda 112

WILLIAMS, Amanda 129
WILLIAMS, B. L. 65
WILLIAMS, Cynthia 8
WILLIAMS, Dorca 126
WILLIAMS, Eliza 56
WILLIAMS, Elizabeth 6
WILLIAMS, Elizabeth 61
WILLIAMS, Elizabeth 67
WILLIAMS, Elizabeth 126
WILLIAMS, Elizabeth M. 84
WILLIAMS, Evaline 20
WILLIAMS, Hannah 126
WILLIAMS, Harrison 5
WILLIAMS, Harrison 30
WILLIAMS, Henry B. 10
WILLIAMS, Hilda A. 62
WILLIAMS, Isabell J. 74
WILLIAMS, J. N. 116
WILLIAMS, J. P. 109
WILLIAMS, J. W. 85
WILLIAMS, James 43

WILLIAMS, James 48
WILLIAMS, James 74
WILLIAMS, James G. 85
WILLIAMS, Jas. 14
WILLIAMS, Jno. W. 38
WILLIAMS, Jno. W. 61
WILLIAMS, John 120
WILLIAMS, John D. 5
WILLIAMS, John W. 3
WILLIAMS, John W. 67
WILLIAMS, John W. 110
WILLIAMS, Joseph J. 46
WILLIAMS, Joshua W. 43
WILLIAMS, L. B. 58
WILLIAMS, Lawrence 85
WILLIAMS, Levi O. 90
WILLIAMS, Lida M. 95
WILLIAMS, Lucinda 2
WILLIAMS, Lucy Bell 45
WILLIAMS, Lucy H. 83
WILLIAMS, M. D. 110
WILLIAMS, Marcus 5
WILLIAMS, Marget 78
WILLIAMS, Martha 109
WILLIAMS, Martha F. 67
WILLIAMS, Mary 35
WILLIAMS, Mary E. 5
WILLIAMS, Mary E. 83
WILLIAMS, Mary E. 85
WILLIAMS, Mattie 120
WILLIAMS, Maud 133
WILLIAMS, Miles 116
WILLIAMS, Miles 133
WILLIAMS, Nancy J. 30
WILLIAMS, Nannie 119
WILLIAMS, Permelice 78
WILLIAMS, Peter 45
WILLIAMS, Peter F. 46
WILLIAMS, Phebe 85
WILLIAMS, Phoebe 105
WILLIAMS, Phoebe 114
WILLIAMS, Poington 14
WILLIAMS, Rachel 35
WILLIAMS, Ranny T. 90
WILLIAMS, Richard 104
WILLIAMS, Sally 35
WILLIAMS, Samuel 71
WILLIAMS, Sarah 45
WILLIAMS, Sarah A. 75
WILLIAMS, Sarah I. 2
WILLIAMS, Sarah J. 46
WILLIAMS, Sarah Jane 73
WILLIAMS, Thos. J. 78
WILLIAMS, Virginia 76

WILLIAMS, W. H.H. 56
WILLIAMS, Wiley(?) E. 85
WILLIAMS, William 10
WILLIAMS, William H. 84
WILLIAMS, William K. 84
WILLIAMS, Wm. 75
WILLIAMS, Wm. A. 75
WILLIAMS, Wm. F. 109
WILLIAMS, Wm. Franklin 38
WILLIAMSON, Osa Lewellyn 42
WILLIAMSON, Thomas 42
WILLIS, Columbus 117
WILLIS, Elizabeth M. 117
WILLIS, Jetty 100
WILLLIAMS, James O. 120
WILLS(?), James 17
WILLS, Caroline 102
WILLS, Elizabeth 67
WILLS, Mary 59
WILLSON, George T. 44
WILLSON, Lavinia 82
WILLSON, Mary E. 88
WILLSON, Mary H. 81
WILSON(?), Sarath 60
WILSON, ----- 38
WILSON, ----- 65
WILSON, Amanda T. 59
WILSON, Annie E. 102
WILSON, Annie E. 102
WILSON, Catharine 47
WILSON, Catherine 68
WILSON, Daniel 2
WILSON, Eleanor 1
WILSON, Eli 2
WILSON, Eli 44
WILSON, Eliz(?) 3
WILSON, Enfield R. 73
WILSON, H. S. 45
WILSON, Harvey T. 74
WILSON, Hester Jane 2
WILSON, James 36
WILSON, Jas. A. 73
WILSON, Jesiah 44
WILSON, John 59
WILSON, John W. 45
WILSON, Johnathan 73
WILSON, Josiah W. 67
WILSON, Lavena 73
WILSON, Martha 46
WILSON, Martha A. 3
WILSON, Mary 5

WILSON, Mary 35
WILSON, Mary 36
WILSON, Mary J. 67
WILSON, Michael 38
WILSON, Nancy 37
WILSON, Rachel 66
WILSON, Rebecca 19
WILSON, Rebecca 33
WILSON, Rebecca 40
WILSON, Sarah T. 67
WILSON, W. S. 45
WINDER, Mary 64
WIRELKELD, Amelia 1
WIRELKELD, James 1
WISE, ----- 58
WISE, Mary 108
WISE, Mary 128
WISE, Mary E. 75
WISE, Nancy 56
WISE, Nancy 104
WITE, Robert 89
WITTY, Mary A. 79
WOOD, A. T. 44
WOOD, Andrew T. 23
WOOD, Andrew T. 73
WOOD, Cydrova(?) C. 32
WOOD, James H. 23

WOOD, John 44
WOOD, John 60
WOOD, John 82
WOOD, Laben M. 82
WOOD, Matilda 23
WOOD, Matilda 60
WOOD, William T. 44
WOODARD, J. W. 25
WOODARD, Samuel M. 25
WOODFORD, Buckner 126
WOODFORD, John W. 67
WOODFORD, Samuel 126
WOODS, Abigal 68
WORICK, Jane 62
WORKMAN, Martha 100
WORRICK, Hurst 39
WORRICK, John 79
WORRICK, Susan 39
WORY, Matilda R. 8
WREN, Ollie 121
WREN, Samuel 121
WRENCHY, Rebecca 75
WRIGHT, Cami 93
WRIGHT, Hannah 13
WRIGHT, Harriet 41
WRIGHT, Jackson 9

WRIGHT, James M. 9
WRIGHT, Joseph M. 41
WRIGHT, Margaret 63
WRIGHT, T. M. 41
WYATT, Almedia 43
WYATT, Ann E. 79

YANTIS, R. H. 113
YANTIS, Robert 118
YASEL, Hiram 34
YASEL, Joseph 34
YAZEL, E. A. 116
YAZELL, Joseph 69
YAZLE, Abram 52
YAZLE, Daniel 63
YAZLE, Joseph 52
YAZLE, Rachel 53
YEAZLE, Manerva 8
YORK, Armilda 128
YOST, Caroline 35
YOUNG, E. H. 114
YOUNG, Louisa 49
YOUNG, Margaret 32

ZIMMERMAN, Ella 88
ZIMMERMAN, Eva 88
ZIMMERMAN, Henry Augustine 17

www.ingramcontent.com/pod-product-compliance
Lightning Source LLC
Chambersburg PA
CBHW080240270326
41926CB00020B/4317

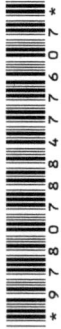